EN TRAVESTI

John Michael Cooper
Bloomington, Illinois
11 May 1996

WOMEN,

GENDER SUBVERSION,

OPERA

29 April 96

To Dr. Michael Cooper:

Thank You for inspiring and encouraging me. Teachers who care so much are very rare. You will be missed. This is in remembrance of an independent study that brought forth many intellectual (well at least humorous) debates. These articles may be useful in demonstrating the blur between gender & sex that causes so many problems. I will be in touch....

Gina Pellegrino

Between Men ~ Between Women

Lesbian and Gay Studies

Lillian Faderman and Larry Gross, Editors

Claudia Card, *Lesbian Choices*

Joseph Carrier, *De Los Otros: Intimacy and Homosexuality Among Mexican Men*

John Clum, *Acting Gay: Male Homosexuality in Modern Drama*

Gary David Comstock, *Violence Against Lesbians and Gay Men*

Laura Doan, editor, *The Lesbian Postmodern*

Allen Ellenzweig, *The Homoerotic Photograph: Male Images from Durieu/Delacroix to Mapplethorpe*

Lillian Faderman, *Odd Girls and Twilight Lovers: A History of Lesbian Life in Twentieth-Century America*

Linda D. Garnets and Douglas C. Kimmel, editors, *Psychological Perspectives on Lesbian and Gay Male Experiences*

Richard D. Mohr, *Gays/Justice: A Study of Ethics, Society, and Law*

Sally Munt, editor, *New Lesbian Criticism: Literary and Cultural Readings*

Timothy F. Murphy and Suzanne Poirier, editors, *Writing AIDS: Gay Literature, Language, and Analysis*

Noreen O'Connor and Joanna Ryan, *Wild Desires and Mistaken Identities: Lesbianism and Psychoanalysis*

Judith Roof, *A Lure of Knowledge: Lesbian Sexuality and Theory*

Alan Sinfield, *The Wilde Century: Effeminacy, Oscar Wilde, and the Queer Moment*

Kath Weston, *Families We Choose: Lesbians, Gays, Kinship*

Carter Wilson, *Hidden in the Blood*

EN TRAVESTI

• ❧ •

WOMEN,

GENDER SUBVERSION,

OPERA

EDITED BY

CORINNE E. BLACKMER AND PATRICIA JULIANA SMITH

Columbia University Press

New York

Columbia University Press
New York Chichester, West Sussex

Library of Congress Cataloging-in-Publication Data
En travesti: women, gender subversion, opera/edited by Corinne E. Blackmer and Patricia Juliana Smith.
p. cm.—(Between men—between women)
Includes bibliographical references and index.
ISBN 0-231-10268-2 (cloth).—ISBN 0-231-10269-0 (pbk.)
1. Women in opera. 2. Lesbianism in opera. I. Blackmer, Corinne E. II. Smith, Patricia Juliana. III. Series.
ML2100.E6 1995
782.1'08'6643—dc20 95-19594
CIP
MN

Casebound editions of Columbia University Press books are printed on permanent and durable acid-free paper.

Printed in the United States of America

c 10 9 8 7 6 5 4 3 2 1

Contents

Between Men ~ Between Women
Lesbian and Gay Studies

Between Men ~ Between Women is a forum for current lesbian and gay scholarship in the humanities and social sciences. The series includes both books that rest within specific traditional disciplines and are substantially about gay men, bisexuals, or lesbians and books that are interdisciplinary in ways that reveal new insights into gay, bisexual, or lesbian experience, transform traditional disciplinary methods in consequence of the perspectives that experience provides, or begin to establish lesbian and gay studies as a free-standing inquiry. Established to contribute to an increased understanding of lesbians, bisexuals, and gay men, the series also aims to provide through that understanding a wider comprehension of culture in general.

EN TRAVESTI

• ❧ •

WOMEN,

GENDER SUBVERSION,

OPERA

Introduction

Corinne E. Blackmer and Patricia Juliana Smith

I'm either the girl who doesn't get the guy, or I *am* the guy, and that's fine with me.

—Marilyn Horne, explaining the function of the mezzo-soprano

1. *Semiramide*, or, the Paradoxes of Opera

Convinced that opera is about the pleasures of artifice and, as our contributor Margaret Reynolds expresses it succinctly, "sex," we launch this collection of essays on women, gender subversion, and opera on a note that might seem, at first glance, paradoxical, but whose sense, we trust, will become evident. We begin, that is to say, with the authority of personal testimony, with a true story told to us on condition of anonymity by a lesbian literary critic. But while this narrative, like a number of essays in this volume, begins in the confessional mode, it returns, with the irresistible logic peculiar to opera, to sexuality, and to artifice.

As an undergraduate during the mid-1970s, our source became weary of the male domination and closely prescribed gender roles of rock-and-roll culture and sought identification with an art form that might be more liberating for one such as she. While engaging one evening in the activity that has since come to be known as channel surfing, she happened, quite by accident, on a public television broadcast of a recital by two divas. She knew nothing about opera other than what she had been told, namely, that it was an overblown, histrionic form of entertainment relished by "the Establishment." Hence she felt conflicted about her attraction to the erotic luxury of this conjunction of female voices. But despite ideological resistance to this symbol of "privilege," our heroine found herself "accidentally" tuning in to opera on television and radio, reading about divas, and, at last, being unable to throw away a day-old newspaper because it contained a particularly striking photograph of Leontyne Price. She began to justify this unlikely behavior by reminding herself that the great fin-de-siècle artistic salons included lesbians *and* female opera singers, that the lesbian novelist Willa Cather wrote a novel about a Wagnerian diva, and that Gertrude Stein wrote two opera librettos. *Maybe* there was some connection? More than simply being a closeted lesbian at the time, our protagonist was well on the way to becoming a closeted opera fan. Indeed, which of the eventual comings out would prove more difficult in her milieu would be difficult to predict, a situation our contributor Terry Castle ponders, from her position as a lesbian opera fan, in her paean to the German mezzo-soprano Brigitte Fassbaender.

As is usually the case in coming out stories, the self-acknowledgment and public manifestations of irrepressible desire gradually come to pass. One day our friend decided that the time had come, at last, to buy an opera record, and she drove to a neighboring town that had a sizable record store. Getting past rows of thousands of rock recordings in an environment blaring with songs about feeling "really real," she found her way to the back of the store and, declining all help from sales personnel who thought she must be lost back there, faced the *real* dilemma. She had *no* idea of what any of these operas *sounded* like, no notion of composers, librettos, or plots, no knowledge of French or Italian, and only rudimentary German. Although there could have been no more than a dozen opera records in stock, she was overwhelmed by the variety; nevertheless, she was determined to fulfill her *secret* desire. Deciding against recordings whose covers featured photographs of frighteningly feminine women with big hair and unpronounceable names—women who did not, as a matter of course, appear routinely on PBS—she made the unlikely choice of Gioacchino Antonio Rossini's *Semiramide* (1823). She had no way of knowing that relatively few people would have chosen this somewhat obscure bel canto opera as an introduction to the genre; rather, she selected it because it featured not one but *two* women singers, Joan Sutherland and Marilyn Horne, both of whom she had seen on television. But in what configuration *Semiramide*—an opera whose plot defies even the most ingenious Freudian analysis—featured two "women" was, at that moment, beyond her experience and imaginings.

Arriving home with her purchase, our heroine did what any serious student of literature would do. She delayed the pleasure of consummation, feeling she could not play the record until she had made a careful study of the booklet enclosed in the package. First, she familiarized herself with the major characters: Semiramide, the Queen of Babylon; Arsace, the Commander of the Assyrian Army; Assur, a Prince; Azema, a Princess; and the Ghost of King Nino, Semiramide's late husband. Then, she read the synopsis of the dizzyingly convoluted plot: Semiramide, with help from Prince Assur, has murdered King Nino. Assur, quite logically, now expects Semiramide to marry him and make him king. But Semiramide is in love with the handsome young Arsace, who, unknown to her, is her long-lost son. As the opera unfolds all assemble at the tomb of Nino, whose ghost announces that Arsace, not Assur, shall be his successor, a revelation that should cheer Semiramide but instead gives her a clue to her paramour's true identity. Nino's ghost promises to reveal the identities of his murderers if Arsace will return to the tomb at midnight. Arsace keeps the appointment, followed by Assur, who is understandably upset, and Semiramide, who has come to warn her son against Assur. Nino tells all, Arsace attempts to stab Assur, and Semiramide throws herself between the two men. Thus the queen is slain by the son with whom she was in love and Arsace becomes king and lives happily ever after with Princess Azema, who has, until this moment, been thoroughly insignificant.[1]

That Joan Sutherland would sing the role of Semiramide was evident: she appeared on the album cover in high-kitsch Babylonian queenly regalia, garbed in an elaborate gold lamé gown with a serpent motif. As there was only one other woman in the opera, it seemed a puzzle and a pity that Marilyn Horne, a major opera star who had second billing on the cover, would be relegated to the tiny role of Princess Azema. But our heroine's moment to consummate her desire had arrived. With English and Italian libretto in hand, she put the needle to the vinyl and sat back to let the sound of these women's voices envelop her. But . . . something was *wrong*. When Arsace made *his* entrance, she could hear the unmistakably plangent, resonant, dark-hued voice of Marilyn Horne. What? Azema is not in this scene. Wait. Marilyn Horne is singing the words, the Italian words, marked "Arsace" in the libretto. There must be a misprint. Let me check the cast. Semiramide: Joan Sutherland. Arsace: . . . Marilyn Horne! Perhaps they mean Azema—no! There is a third woman in this cast—but Marilyn Horne is not a . . . man! Can she do *that?* Can she *get away* with that?

Our friend's amazed reaction to the homoerotic vocal dynamics of what our contributor Elizabeth Wood has elsewhere called "Sapphonics" (27–66), and, later, to the spectacle of female operatic cross-dressing, should give some indication of the depth of her naïveté, at this juncture, with opera. But let us recall the cultural context that formed her frame of reference and, once again, the manifold paradoxes of opera. For, as Catherine Clément has observed in *Opera, or the Undoing of Women*, the prima donnas of the nineteenth- and early twentieth-century romantic operas, such as *Carmen*, *Otello*, *Aida*, *Il Trovatore*, *Lucia di Lammermoor*, *Rigoletto*, *Norma*, *La Traviata*, *Der Ring des Nibelungen*, *La Bohème*, *Pelléas et Mélisande*, *Tosca*, *Madama Butterfly*, and *Turandot*, that still form the standard repertoire may be the indispensable jewels of these works but they "perpetually sing their eternal undoing" (5). Nevertheless, as Ralph P. Locke points out in his essay in this volume, Clément in her analysis overlooks not only comic operas such as *Il Barbiere di Siviglia*, *Don Pasquale*, *Gianni Schicci*, *La Périchole*, and

• **Fig. 1.1. Mother and child reunion: Semiramide, the queen of Babylon (Dame Joan Sutherland) falls in love with Arsace (Marilyn Horne), who, unknown to her, is her long-lost son, in Rossini's *Semiramide*. Lyric Opera of Chicago, 1971.** *Courtesy of David Fishman.*

Le Nozze di Figaro, in which women express considerable ingenuity and free will and regularly triumph, but also "mixed" or more "problematic" operas such as *L'Incoronazione di Poppea*, *Alceste*, *Eugene Onegin*, *La Fanciulla del West*, *Bluebeard's Castle*, *Ariadne auf Naxos*, *Euryanthe*, and *I Puritani* in which women characters evade or, ultimately, successfully resist, in Clément's words, "being undone." Yet Locke, with several of our contributors, notes that operas of considerable artistic merit featuring strong women characters, such as Tchaikovsky's *The Maid of Orleans* or Verdi's *Atilla*, are seldom performed, thus showing that opera audiences have needed women characters to enact for them an emotional catharsis.

The works that Clément discusses in her invaluable study are not the whole story of opera, for the art form that seems the frivolous and misogynistic plaything of conservative elites also permits an unparalleled range of opportunities for women to subvert and, often, overturn traditional gender roles. As our contributors Wendy Bashant, Terry Castle, Hélène Cixous, and Margaret Reynolds note in their analyses of trouser roles, what other art form permits women to make love to each other in a public place and *get away* with it? Herein lies another paradox of opera. Because the voice, in opera, transcends both sex and gender, the woman *en travesti*, literally "in travesty" or "male drag," sings as and looks like, in theory at least, a man, but sounds like—and, we all know, *is*—a woman. Hence, the eloquent interplay of erotically charged identification and difference that informs Hélène Cixous's meditation on Rossini's *Tancredi* (1813), a work based on such traditional if not patriarchal sources as Torquato Tasso's *Jerusalem Delivered* and Voltaire's *Tancrède*. In this opera the title role is sung by a female contralto *en travesti*. The knight Tancredi, in love with the soprano, Amenaide, rescues her from an unwanted marriage to the tyrant Orbazzano. But the jealous villain intercepts a letter Amenaide has written to her lover, pretends that the missive was addressed to the leader of the Saracens, and falsely accuses her of consorting with the enemy, imprisoning her under a sentence of death unless a champion should come forward to defend her honor. Although Tancredi believes Amenaide to be untrue, love overcomes political considerations and "he" slays her accuser in a duel. The truth is finally revealed, and the lovers are happily reunited. In Cixous's lyrical reading *Tancredi* becomes an allegory of feminist struggle and transcendent love between women, in which the hero[ine], "a-man-who-loves-a-woman-as-if-he-were-a-woman," puts on the attributes usually constructed as masculine in order to rescue the beloved.

Thus Cixous effectively delineates what our anonymous heroine intuitively recognized but could not articulate those many years ago. Only in opera—that seemingly forbidding and improbable realm of artifice—could a woman, through the power of her voice, transcend her gender and, more than love, rescue her own sex. This transcendence, though, is not restricted to those operatic roles that are literally en travesti. The essays in this volume not only address such transvestite characters, those androgynous women who exist onstage in an almost angelic condition of being not-men, not-women, but also the women in opera—whether characters, performers, librettists, or composers—who figuratively "put on the trousers": women who challenge and transgress the limits that normally define female identity on the lyric stage, who break what the feminist musicologist Susan McClary calls the "house rules" of music's metaphorical Bluebeard's Castle, "enter[ing] resolutely into the forbidden chamber with its dark, hidden codes and . . . transform[ing] it into a carnival—a playground of signifiers—for their own pleasure" (34). Thus, we sketch the outlines of a *queer* history of opera, whose "oddness" resides in this volume's insistence on reconnecting opera with contemporary feminist and queer interpretations of the arts and, in this fashion, with opera's rich if still undersung traditions of subverting categories of sexuality and proscribed gender roles.

2. A Short Queer History of Opera

Our queer history, like that of opera at large, begins with a woman: Hildegard von Bingen, the twelfth-century German mystic nun who composed, for the dedication of the cloister church of her Benedictine convent in Rupertsberg, the musical drama *Ordo Virtutum*, or *Play of the Virtues* (1158). In a recent study of problems associated with traditional medieval musicology, Robert Cogan argues that Hildegard's musical innovations of plainchant are so striking that she should be regarded as the "earliest appearance in the history of European music" of the "composer as star, *auteur*, quasi-mythical being" (2). Bruce Wood Holsinger describes the context of Hildegard's music as follows:

> A group of nuns, led by Hildegard, living in intimate proximity, raising their voices together in song, allowing music itself—the actual music produced by and resonating between the bodies of the nuns as well as the music that emerges from the bodies of the Virgin and the feminized Church on Earth—to create and enliven the social, devotional, and erotic bonds both between one another and between themselves and God (108).

In other words, Hildegard is not only the first musical celebrity but also the now recognized foremother of opera, who composed this work and others as specifically female homoerotic, homosocial religious devotions.

As Corinne E. Blackmer notes in her essay on queer literature and opera inspired by the works of St. Teresa of Ávila, the sixteenth-century foundress of the Discalced Carmelite order, *Ordo Virtutum* and *Four Saints in Three Acts* (1927) have in common not only a central focus of female mystical devotion but also the presence of the creators of these works as characters in the drama. In *Four Saints* the composer Virgil Thomson and librettist Gertrude Stein appear as the commère and compère, just as Hildegard appears in her own person at the opening of her musical drama to announce her "vision . . . [of] greatest radiance, in which was formed a voice from heaven" (31). Hildegard explains, much as St. Teresa does in her *Life*, how autobiographical experience inevitably both authenticates and inspires her artistic works (indeed, this pattern is repeated in many of the essays in this volume, in which the autobiographical openly rather than implicitly informs a given critic's response to and understanding of a particular opera). Subsequently, the allegorical figures of the Virtues, played by women, enter singing praise songs. The protagonist of this drama is the Human Soul, who, as *Anima*, is represented as female. Her seducer, the Devil, is the only role played by a man, who, significantly, *speaks* (in what can best be described as loud, screeching *Sprechstimme*) but is not allowed the rapture and beauty Hildegard associated with music. The Virtues lament the temporary victory of the Devil over the Human Soul, but the Soul, embittered and weakened by her experience with the World, calls upon her sisters the Virtues, who lift her up and from whom she accepts the white robes of immortality. The Devil makes one last desperate appeal, in harshly guttural tones, to waylay the Soul, but *Victoria* swoops down and enchains him, and *Ordo Virtutum* ends on a triumphant note of utopian female homosocial solidarity that deliberately invokes Eden: "In the beginning all creation was verdant" (59).

Ordo Virtutum, which represents temptation in the form of seductive, worldly heterosexuality, offers a striking contrast to later romantic operas in which soprano *prime donne* are the sacrificial victims at the crossroads of heterosexual romance and nationalistic rivalries. But yet other, distinctly more urbane and sexual operatic representations of homoeroticism developed in seventeenth-century Italy. While it would be anachronistic to term individual members of the Venetian Accademia degli Incogniti (i.e., academy of the anonymous) who worked behind the scenes to promote this new genre *homosexual*, they were staunchly opposed to the interference and intellectual dogmatism of churchmen and devoted to Greco-Roman culture and vigorous social debate that encompassed a multiplicity of viewpoints.[2] The earliest Venetian operas, including Claudio Monteverdi's *Orfeo* (1607) and *L'Incoronazione di Poppea* (1642), have what might be termed "flexible central casting," which allows roles such as Orfeo in the former and, in the latter, Poppea's former lover Ottone, her nurse Arnalta, and her new husband Nero to be played *either* by men or women, with accompanying innovations and complications regarding vocal register. Similar observations may be made of other early operas, such as Francesco Cavalli's *La Callisto* (1651), Giacomo Castoreo's *Pericle Effeminato* (1653), and Aurelio Aureli's *Alcibiade* (1680). Representing same-sex desire between men and between women through the medium of classical mythology and cross-gendered casting—and often through the barely convincing guise of moral didacticism—all met with the vitriol of the enemies of the accademia, who denounced the works as "decadent."

One of the most significant of the early "queer" innovations in opera was that of employing castrati singers, a practice justified within the Catholic Church on the basis of St. Paul's injunction (I Cor. 14:34)—certainly ignored by Hildegard—that women should remain silent in church. In her essay Margaret Reynolds delineates the history whereby young boys with beautiful voices were surgically castrated to retain their high tessitura, since high voices, as Michel

Poizat points out, held enormous appeal for Western culture in their transcendent, angelic, and, indeed, transsexual purity (116). While the original purpose of this extreme artifice was to deny the female voice its place, the decline of this practice in the late eighteenth century, ironically, created new operatic opportunities for women, for as the castrati grew fewer in number, their roles were taken over by female contraltos en travesti.

What, then, is the overall picture of the highly popular public entertainment called *dramma per musica* from Claudio Monteverdi to George Frideric Handel? Castrated men with high voices are heroes who rescue cities and defeat foreign enemies; powerful pagan sorceresses and witches seduce virtuous Christian knights; ambitious female courtesans employ their sexual charms and the figures of classical rhetoric to gain their worldly ends; female mezzo-sopranos and contraltos play Greek demigods, shepherds, oracles, foreign princes, Roman emperors, and the aforementioned virtuous Christian knights; sopranos appear as everything from femme romantic leads to angelic young boys; the "natural" or "logical" sex of various family members is regularly and, one is forced to conclude, *deliberately* subverted; tenors are, for the most part, insignificant secondary characters; and baritones and basses sing minor if indispensable parts as various gods, military figures, and old men. In other words, opera is, at this stage, a very evidently *queer* art form.

The nineteenth- and early-twentieth-century operas that form the basis of Clément's discussion of the "undoing" of prima donnas have, until very recent times, so completely tyrannized over popular conceptions, audience expectations, and academic discussions of what opera is, or, perhaps, should be, that our contributor Judith A. Peraino feels like an outsider in her admiration for and identification with Henry Purcell's *Dido and Aeneas* (1689). Contemporary musicologists, approaching opera through a priori assumptions about the inherent superiority of nineteenth-century German music, have labeled *Dido* a queerly flawed anomaly because it "failed," perhaps like an impotent parent, to "engender" an English national opera, is somehow too "short" to be considered a "real" opera, and, as Peraino suspects, commits the "sin" of having a plot that revolves around the actions of women, who also hold all the musical interest. Given the unabashed queerness of so much of the actual historical canon of opera, it becomes rather difficult not to conclude, as Peraino suggests, that the supposed "objective aesthetic criteria" of academic musicology not only disguises biases against women and homosexuals but also preferences for tragedy over comedy, seriousness over *sprezzatura*, and the dramatization of implacable differences of gender, race, sexuality, class, religion, and nationality over the comic suspension, dissolution, or intermixture of such Kantian "categorical imperatives."

Indeed, what would a critic trained to regard Beethoven and his earnest moral seriousness as the pinnacle of Western musical culture make of Handel—that queerest of opera composers—and his *Serse* (1738), which must be regarded not only as one of the finest examples of baroque style but also one of the most ambitious elaborations of queerly protolesbian opera?[3] Although critics have regularly attempted to "explain away" the queerness of baroque opera, it is nonetheless somewhat far-fetched to argue that Handel (whose *Serse* is merely one of his many gender-bending operas), in addition to his culturally conditioned *musical* preference for high voices, did not self-consciously exhibit his queer *sexual* preferences as well, perhaps not so much in casting the tyrant King Serse as a castrato but, more evidently, in assigning the role of Serse's brother Arsamenes to a female mezzo-soprano, Maria Antonia Marchesini in the original London production. As in many queer operas, *Serse* delights in the convolutions of an immensely complicated plot, filled with secret intrigues and an elaborate series of star-crossed and cross-dressed loves. Yet such plots are the bearers of central intellectual and philosophical tenets, the vehicles for the dramatization of witty ingenuity and mental agility through which characters, such as the cross-dressed Cherubino in Mozart's later *Le Nozze di Figaro* (1786), defeat the pretensions and arrogant worldly power of political tyrants. The symbol for this triumph of intelligence over the forces of implacable "destiny" that will tyrannize over so many later operatic characters is Eros, a mischievous boy who delights, through the vehicle of cross-dressing, in subjecting the emotions of lovers to as much confusion and flux as the categories of gender and sexuality.

In brief, *Serse* employs the cultural preference for high voices in a political allegory of ingenious confusions of gender and sex through which the arrogant designs of King Serse are defeated. King Serse (originally castrato but more recently female mezzo or countertenor) and "his" brother Arsamenes (female mezzo) are both in love with Romilda (female soprano), the daughter of the bumbling and gullible commander of the army, Ariodate (bass), whose comic misrecognitions provide, serendipitously, the felicitous denouement. The protolesbian love interests are developed not only through Romilda's rejection of Serse and love for Arsamenes but also through the equally determined love of her conniving sister Atalanta (female soprano) for the apparently irresistible Arsamenes. Confused yet? But wait: Handel has not finished sharpening our inner wits by confusing our commonplace modes of outward perception. Amastris (female mezzo), a foreign princess betrothed to Serse, decides to don military disguise, in a move that foreshadows Rossini's later armor roles for female mezzos, in order to gain access to and rewin the love of the king, apparently convinced that Serse will find her more charming as young man. Moreover, Arsamenes' perpetually grumbling servant Elviro (baritone) disguises himself as a flower seller in order to deliver a letter that, inevitably, falls into the wrong hands and almost results in disaster until Ariodate, who comprehends nothing of what is happening around him, "accidentally" arranges for the wedding of Arsamenes and Romilda, forcing Serse to marry Amastris. Thus, with the marriages, respectively, of mezzo to soprano and mezzo (or, in the original cast, castrato) to mezzo, *Serse* ends with what is surely among the most curious couplings in opera.

Although Wolfgang Amadeus Mozart created typically heroic roles for castrati in such classically themed operas as *Idomeneo* (1781) and *La Clemenza di Tito* (1791), by the late eighteenth century the castrato was in decline, both in number and in popularity; thus many of the roles originally written for this voice became the province of the female mezzo-soprano. Simultaneously roles intended by their composers for women en travesti became a commonplace. Following Beaumarchais's stage directions for *Le Mariage de Figaro* that Cherubino "can only be played . . . by a young and very pretty woman" (Beaumarchais 222), Mozart cast the part in his own *Le Nozze di Figaro* for soprano or high mezzo. The visual and vocal presence in this comic opera of a clearly female singer performing the part of the highly libidinous and ostensibly male page provides, as a matter of course, considerable titillation, much of it intentional. The gender confusion already at play is compounded when Cherubino is interrupted by the importunate Count Almaviva as he is being dressed *as* Susanna *by*

Fig. 1.2. Intentional gender confusion: Cherubino (Frederica von Stade) in Mozart's *Le Nozze di Figaro*. *Courtesy of Winnie Klotz, Metropolitan Opera.*

Susanna and the countess (in order to trap the count in a presumed assignation with Susanna) in the countess's chambers. The spectacle of this woman-dressed-as-man-dressed-as-woman—which Richard Strauss repeats more than a century later with Octavian in *Der Rosenkavalier*—leads to a number of questions, which many have contemplated but few have cared (or dared) to answer. Is dressing Cherubino as a woman merely another layer of disguise, or is it the revelation of what we have *really* known all along? If this planned assignation with this ostensible boy *were* to come about (as it nearly does it Strauss's opera), what would the count—or, for that matter, Cherubino—*do?* And what is the bigger threat to the count, a male Cherubino in his wife's dressing room or a female Cherubino?

Rossini, as we have seen, gave the armor roles to women in possession of vocal cords agile and heroic enough to negotiate what Marilyn Horne has judged "the most difficult music ever written for the human voice" (Kellow 10). Gaetano Donizetti and Vincenzo Bellini carried on Rossini's bel canto tradition of highly ornamental singing and travesti roles. One of the most interesting gender reversals of this period occurs in *I Capuleti ed I Montecchi* (1830), Bellini's reworking of *Romeo and Juliet*, in which the role of Romeo is sung by a mezzo-soprano.[4] Notable for its duel duet between mezzo-soprano and tenor (Romeo and Tebaldo), the opera also features an extended passionate love duet for two female voices (i.e., Romeo and Juliet), which musically foreshadows the far more famous scene between female romantic friends in Bellini's *Norma* (1831). In the later opera the Druid high priestess Norma has violated both her sacred vows and national loyalty by sleeping with the enemy, namely, the Roman leader Pollione, whom she has secretly borne two children. But Pollione has lost interest in Norma and now desires her acolyte, the virgin Adalgisa. When Norma discovers this misalliance she threatens to kill herself and her children, but she is dissuaded by Adalgisa, who forsakes Pollione ("I used to love him. Now my heart feels only friendship for him") and vows her eternal affection for Norma ("I swear by heaven and men to stay concealed with you forever"). Thereupon the two women declare their own undying bond in some of the most rapturous music written for two female voices: "With you I shall set my face firmly against the shame which fate may bring, as long as I feel your heart beating on mine." Norma eventually goes to the pyre for her sexual dalliances with Pollione; it should come as little surprise that in some recent stagings of the opera Adalgisa, while not actually *singing* in the last act, joins her there.

But as the nineteenth century progressed, and opera increasingly centered on nationalism and the "undoing of women," the heroine was less likely to experience anything resembling friendship, much less love, for another woman. More typical was the isolated woman among men, like Giuseppe Verdi's Violetta

Fig. 1.3. Love duet for two female voices: Romeo (Tatiana Troyanos) and Juliet (Cecilia Gasdia) in Bellini's *I Capuleti ed I Montecchi*. Lyric Opera of Chicago. *Courtesy of Tony Romano.*

Fig. 1.4. Romantic friendship: Adalgisa (Elena Obraztsova) and Norma (Shirley Verrett) swear eternal loyalty in Bellini's *Norma*. *Courtesy of Winnie Klotz, Metropolitan Opera.*

or Giacomo Puccini's Manon, "sola, perduta, abbandonata" (alone, lost, and abandoned), or the woman engaged in a jealous rivalry with another woman for the love of the hero, by now almost exclusively a male tenor. The dynamics behind this shift are delineated in a trio of essays on mid-nineteenth-century opera in this volume. In tracing the [illegible] of the British novelist George Eliot, Wendy Bashant demonstrates how the dictates of the then emerging "science" of medical sexology influenced not only Eliot's own literary representations of intimate relationships between women but, by extension, the roles of the diva as well. The profuse displays of affection once considered acceptable among women came to be considered perverted and even civilization-destroying manifestations of the new category of sexual identity, lesbianism (or "inversion"), a concern that subsequently forms the subtext and the history, as Patricia Juliana Smith observes, of Puccini's *Turandot* (1926). Consequently, when an operatic scenario featured more than one woman, the *secunda donna*, if not merely the maid or the slave of her more prominent counterpart, functioned primarily as the antagonist in a romantic triangle.[5]

This growing fear of female homoeroticism in opera did not, ironically, give the diva permission to disport herself as an explicit or unashamed heterosexual woman either. As Mary Ann Smart chronicles in her essay on the French singer Rosine Stoltz, the overtly sexual diva, who conducted a number of affairs with prominent men, found her talent discredited, her portrayal of roles (particularly that of Leonore, the royal mistress in Donizetti's *La Favorite*) perceived as reflections of her private life, and her actions attributed to be the cause of the destruction of the men around her. In response to such fantasy projections of her life in the press and the public imagination, Stoltz re-created herself, through her own writings and personal adventures, into a living fiction, yet throughout the course of her long life this "fallen woman" was never able to recuperate her early acclaim and popularity. Indeed, the public required, as Lowell Gallagher reveals in his essay on Jenny Lind, that the prima donna who enacted the part of the long-suffering female victim be nothing less than, quite literally, a *casta diva*, a chaste, even disembodied, goddess able to transcend the dross of earthly existence. In her mid-nineteenth-century American tour, her audience looked to Lind to provide them with a quasi-religious experience that would, through the magical power of her desexualized body and voice, heal the social divisions of the nation. In the case of Lind, who made every attempt to fulfill her devotees' expectations, the playful perversity of opera's gender-bent past gives way to a fetishistic mode of diva-worship. Thus the respective careers and public images of Rosine Stoltz and Jenny Lind could not offer a greater contrast, nor could they offer a more telling illustration of the very *strangeness* of the nonqueer gender roles imposed upon the female operatic figure.

The fin-de-siècle aesthetic movement commonly referred to as decadence, closely associated with the emergence of a distinct and visible gay and lesbian subculture, allowed the sporadic representation of a wide variety of "sex variant" women now openly at odds with the social and religious norms of patriarchal culture. In his then shocking and sensationalistic operas *Salome* (1905) and *Elektra* (1909), Richard Strauss employed the bodies and voices of semimasculinized women to undermine the foundations and reveal the violence at the heart of the heterosexual "family romance."[6] In *Der Rosenkavalier* (1911) and *Ariadne auf Naxos* (1916), however, Strauss combined both baroque and modernist motifs in his female travesti roles, as they oscillate between signifying male and female and are represented more distinctly as lesbian. *Der Rosenkavalier* opens with an erotic bedroom scene (enacted with increasing explicitness in recent years) between the Marschallin and the cross-dressed Octavian and *Ariadne auf Naxos* takes the even more subversive step of assigning the role of the Composer to a cross-dressed mezzo-soprano. As Carolyn Abbate points out, "Strauss's homage to this re-sexing of our archetypal Opera Composer . . . that begins with Monteverdi's *Orfeo* and continues through Strauss's Composer might

Fig. 1.5. In the boudoir: the Marschallin (Dame Gwyneth Jones) and Octavian (Tatiana Troyanos) in Strauss's *Der Rosenkavalier*. *Courtesy of Winnie Klotz, Metropolitan Opera.*

Fig. 1.6 Resexing the archetype: the Composer (Tatiana Troyanos) in Richard Strauss's *Ariadne auf Naxos*. *Courtesy of Winnie Klotz, Metropolitan Opera.*

indeed be seen as a secret narrative, a history that traces symbolically opera's capacity to disrupt male authority" (258).

The creation of early-twentieth-century opera is strongly influenced by this very "re-sexing" of the composer, not only in terms of male and female and gay and lesbian collaborative efforts that disregard traditional heterosexual romance plots but also in the actual presence of the lesbian in the opera, both as character and composer. Just as the conjoined talents of Maurice Ravel and Colette create in *L'Enfant et les Sortilèges* (1925) a whimsical yet serious meditation on the progression from childish narcissism to adult responsibility, so Virgil Thomson and Gertrude Stein, as Corinne E. Blackmer demonstrates, present tableaux of the life of St. Teresa (and her host of historical and invented saintly companions) on her "way of perfection" in *Four Saints in Three Acts* (1933). Similarly, the British lesbian composer Ethel Smyth, whose operas Elizabeth Wood examines in light of their "secret narratives," might be seen as the realization of Strauss's allegorical character. Through settings of highly unconventional libretti and the use of melody fraught with personal association, Smyth disrupted the male authority of which Abbate speaks and encoded her lesbian desires. While Smyth covertly interwove female homoeroticism into the compositional process, obliquely lesbian characters, such as Puccini's *principessa di morte*, made their presence felt on the operatic stage. Significantly, only after *Turandot* brings the long tradition of grand opera to a close does an *overtly* lesbian character make her debut on the opera stage. Although Countess Martha Geschwitz has been traditionally perceived as a type of the pathetic invert, Mitchell Morris offers an admiring queer analysis of her character. He sees her, he argues, as Alban Berg did—a heroic, grandly tragic figure who, unlike the others in the opera, rises far above the banal hatred and petty self-interest that inform *Lulu*'s general ethos.

Given her long and illustrious history in opera, perhaps the relative lack of attention accorded the female character en travesti testifies, ironically, to the very naturalness and ubiquitousness of her presence. Opera would be severely impoverished and possibly inconceivable without her. When on stages throughout the world opera celebrates its festive rites with New Year's Day gala performances of Johann Strauss's *Die Fledermaus* (1876), we are ushered into the villa of the champagne-loving, humorously world-weary, cross-dressed Prince Orlofsky (female mezzo), who plays our master-/mistress-of-ceremonies in the musical and theatrical entertainments that follow. We cannot imagine a more fitting description for the passionate eclecticism of the essays in this volume or a more appropriate emblem for the spirit of courageous independence by women characters who discard the rules than that summed up in Orlofsky's famously offhanded line, "Chacun à son goût."

Fig. 1.7. Overt lesbianism: Lulu (Catherine Malfitano) flirts with the Countess Geschwitz (Brigitte Fassbaender) in Alban Berg's *Lulu*. *Courtesy of Foto Studio Sabine Toepffer.*

Fig. 1.8. "Chacun à son goût": Prince Orlovsky (Anne Sofie von Otter) in Johann Strauss's *Die Fledermaus.*
Courtesy of Winnie Klotz, Metropolitan Opera.

Notes

1. The recording in question, however, features Rossini's alternative "happy" ending. Semiramide in this case has an attack of good conscience and abets Arsace in destroying Assur. She does not die; she is merely superannuated by her son's new queen.

2. For an exhaustive study of seventeenth-century Venetian opera, see Rosand, *Opera in Seventeenth-Century Venice*.

3. For an intensive and thoughtful examination of the historical evidence of Handel's sexuality (and the tradition of musicological attempts to deny or distort this body of evidence), see Thomas, "'Was George Frideric Handel Gay?'"

4. Since the 1960s attempts have been made to "heterosexualize" *I Capuleti ed I Montecchi* by revising the role of Romeo for a tenor, since many audiences (and opera directors) have clearly found the female homoeroticism Bellini portrays too overt and discomfiting. According to Herbert Weinstock, this "distortion of Bellini's intentions" has "inaugurated an unhappy train of events," inasmuch as this revision, by Claudio Abbado, threatened to become the standard mode of performing this work. See Weinstock, *Vincenzo Bellini*, p. 251. Recent years, however, have marked an auspicious return to Bellini's original vocal and gender assignments. See also Lanfranco Rasponi, *The Last Prima Donnas*, p. 597.

5. We must not, however, take the "straightness" of such scenarios for granted. As Eve Sedgwick (*Between Men*, pp. 21–27) has demonstrated and Terry Castle (*The Apparitional Lesbian,* pp. 67–74, 250–52n) has elaborated, the structures of romantic triangulation function as a means to conceal yet perpetuate homosocial bonding (if not homoerotic desire) through the medium of the "shared" person of the opposite sex. We might ponder, for example, the extent to which the actions of Amneris in Giuseppe Verdi's *Aida* stem from her desire to control and possess the Ethiopian princess as her slave as much

as they do from her heterosocial desire to marry Radames. Similarly, in what must surely be the most elaborate case of confused motivations in the operatic repertory, the masochistic heroine of Amilcare Ponchielli's *La Gioconda* spends most of her time performing extraordinary feats in order to rescue, protect, and advance the cause of Laura, her rival for the love of Enzo Grimaldo. (This is one of the few instances, pace Marilyn Horne, in which the mezzo "gets the guy.") Ostensibly, Gioconda is compelled to these extremes out of obligation to Laura for saving the life of La Cieca, Gioconda's mother, when the elderly woman was accused of witchcraft, but even so this incredible sacrifice of heterosexual possibilities (which ends with both Gioconda and La Cieca dead and Laura and Enzo living happily ever after) evokes numerous (and problematic) psychological theories of the homoerotics of the mother-daughter bond.

6. Indeed, there has been an increasing inclination in recent years to portray Elektra as a lesbian gripped by the Freudian Elektra complex, identifying with her father against her mother and engaging in an incestuous relationship with her sister Chrysothemis (thus conjoining Western culture's two principal taboos). For soprano Leonie Rysanek's ironic (and hilarious) comments on the queering of Elektra in Götz Friedrich's 1981 film of the opera, see Philip Kennicott, "Song of the Wild," p. 36.

Works Cited

Abbate, Carolyn. "Opera; or, the Envoicing of Women." In Ruth A. Solie, ed., *Musicology and Difference: Gender and Sexuality in Music Scholarship,* pp. 225–58. Berkeley: University of California Press, 1993.

Beaumarchais, Pierre-Augustin Caron de. *The Barber of Seville and The Marriage of Figaro.* Trans. John Wood. Harmondsworth: Penguin, 1964.

Bellini, Vincenzo. *Norma.* Libretto by Felice Romani. Trans. Kenneth Chalmers. With Joan Sutherland, Marilyn Horne, John Alexander, and Richard Cross. Cond. Richard Bonynge. London Symphony Orchestra. London 425 488–2, 1965.

Castle, Terry. *The Apparitional Lesbian: Female Homosexuality and Modern Culture.* New York: Columbia University Press, 1993.

Clément, Catherine. *Opera, or the Undoing of Women.* Trans. Betsy Wing. Minneapolis: University of Minnesota Press, 1988.

Cogan, Robert. "Hildegard's Fractal Antiphon." *Sonus* (1990), 11(1):1–19.

Handel, George Frideric. *Serse.* With Deborah Cole, Phoebe Atkinson, Anna Teal, Anita Terzian, Sarah Schumann-Halley, Norman Andersson, and Ryan Allen. Cond. Agnieska Duczmal. Amadeus Orchestra. Koch Schwann CD SC 100 300, 1990.

Hildegard von Bingen. *Ordo Virtutum.* Libretto trans. Ingeborg Neumann and Viviane Jesbois. With Sequentia. Cond. and arr. Barbara Thornton. Deutsche Harmonia Mundi 77051–2-RG, 1982.

Holsinger, Bruce Wood. "The Flesh of the Voice: Embodiment and the Homoerotics of Devotion in the Music of Hildegard of Bingen (1098–1179)." *Signs* (1993), 19(1):-92–125.

Kellow, Brian. "Notebook." *Opera News.* September 1994, p. 10.

Kennicott, Philip. "Song of the Wild: Leonie Rysanek on the Women of Atreus." *Opera News*. April 11, 1992, pp. 34+.

McClary, Susan. *Feminine Endings: Music, Gender, and Sexuality*. Minneapolis: University of Minnesota Press, 1991.

Poizat, Michel. *The Angel's Cry: Beyond the Pleasure Principle in Opera*. Trans. Arthur Denner. Ithaca: Cornell University Press, 1992.

Rasponi, Lanfranco. *The Last Prima Donnas*. New York: Limelight, 1990.

Rosand, Ellen. *Opera in Seventeenth-Century Venice: The Creation of a Genre*. Berkeley: University of California Press, 1991.

Rossini, Gioacchino. *Semiramide*. With Joan Sutherland, Marilyn Horne, and Joseph Rouleau. Cond. Richard Bonynge. London Symphony Orchestra. Decca 425 481–2, 1966.

——— *Tancredi*. With Marilyn Horne, Lelia Cuberli, Ernesto Palacio, and Nicola Zaccaria. Cond. Ralf Weikert. Teatro La Fenice Orchestra. CBS M3K–39073.

Sedgwick, Eve Kosofsky. *Between Men: English Literature and Male Homosocial Desire*. New York: Columbia University Press, 1985.

Thomas, Gary C. "'Was George Frideric Handel Gay?': On Closet Questions and Cultural Politics." In Philip Brett, Elizabeth Wood, and Gary C. Thomas, eds., *Queering the Pitch: The New Gay and Lesbian Musicology*, pp. 155–203. New York: Routledge, 1994.

Weinstock, Herbert. *Vincenzo Bellini: His Life and Operas*. New York: Knopf, 1971.

Wood, Elizabeth. "Sapphonics." In Philip Brett, Elizabeth Wood, and Gary C. Thomas, eds., *Queering the Pitch: The New Gay and Lesbian Musicology*, pp. 27–66. New York: Routledge, 1994.

In Praise of Brigitte Fassbaender: Reflections on Diva-Worship

Terry Castle

To "come out" as the fan of a great diva is always an embarrassing proposition—as difficult in its own way, perhaps, as coming out as a homosexual. For what can be more undignified than confessing one's susceptibility to a thrilling female voice? As Brigid Brophy has observed in *Mozart the Dramatist*, the "listening" role is by its very nature regressive: the audience at an opera must "renounce the power of speech" and can only signify pleasure "by the infantile methods of inarticulate cries and hand-clapping."[1] Even after the performance, though one's powers of utterance may return, the baby-mood often continues, resulting in effusions of a typically absurd and cloying sort. Witness, for example, the painfully empurpled prose of James Huneker, music critic for the *New York Times*, commenting on a performance by the famous Scottish-American diva Mary Garden in 1926:

> Nuance, which alone makes art or life endurable, becomes an evocation with Miss Garden. I lament that she is not in a more intimate setting, as the misted fire and rhythmic modulations of her opaline art and personality are lost in such a huge auditorium as the Lexington Theatre. I saw her, a slip of a girl, at Paris, early in this century, and framed by the Opéra Comique, of whose traditions she is now the most distinguished exponent. She was then something precious: a line of Pater's prose, the glance of one of Da Vinci's strange ladies; a chord by Debussy, honey, tiger's blood, and absinthe; or like the enigmatic pallor we see in Renaissance portraits; cruel, voluptuous, and suggesting the

> ennui of Watteau's L'Indifférent. . . . One can't praise the art of Mary Garden without loving the woman![2]

At best, the diva-worshiper is a kind of parody adult, a maker of silly sounds and fatuous conceits—a sort of gurgling, burbling semi-idiot.

How much more embarrassing, then, to have to come out as a *female* diva-worshiper. For if Brophy once again is correct, the female fan is not only abject but perverse. The great diva's appeal is intrinsically erotic in nature, Brophy argues; through prodigies of breath control and muscular exertion—virtuoso feats easily reinterpreted as "metaphors of virtuoso performance in bed"—she stimulates repressed sexual memories in her listeners. Declares Brophy, deliciously embellishing on Freud: "[The prima donna's virtuosity] is of a kind precisely calculated to figure to the unconscious as a metaphor of sexual virtuosity, since the fluctuation of lovers' breathing is the indication of sexual intercourse which children most commonly contrive to eavesdrop."[3] In particular, by evoking a sound-memory of one's mother having sex, the diva reawakens the infantile fantasy of having sex *with* the mother. For female fans, the implication is obvious: to enthuse over the voice is, if only subliminally, to fancy plumping down in bed with its owner.

None of which makes any easier my principal task in this essay—to bear witness, without seeming too hopelessly fixated, to the peculiar power that one opera singer in particular (the superlative German mezzo Brigitte Fassbaender) has for some time exerted over my own imagination. I am conscious that in coming out in this way, as a female fan, as a victim of *Schwärmerei*, I risk giving too much away—and that the "coming out" will appear just that, a coming out. Perhaps one of the reasons that the most vocal diva admirers of the past two hundred years have tended to be homosexual men is that it is the least embarrassing for them—of all the modern sexual subgroupings—to enthuse in public over the female singing voice: the libidinal element inspiring the enthusiasm is there, by happy circumstance, most artfully disguised and displaced.[4]

Given the risks of self-revelation, it is comforting to discover that unlike Stephen Gordon in *The Well of Loneliness* one is not the only one ("like Cain . . . marked and blemished!") and that even in the realm of perversity one can find compatriots and companions-at-arms. Though seldom advertised as such, there is in fact a long tradition of "sapphic" diva-worship in the world of opera: a history of female-to-female "fan" attachments as intense, fantastical, and sentimental as any ever enacted on the fabled isle of Lesbos. From Catalani, Malibran, Melba, and Mary Garden to Sutherland, Baker, Horne, and Von Stade, the greatest divas have always excited ardor in their female as well as male fans—and an ardor often implicitly tinged, if not openly charged, with homoeroticism. The otherwise sober-minded feminist film critic who recently admitted in the pages of the *Village Voice* to a stupefying crush on Jessye Norman (with whom she had once shared an elevator) was—though perhaps without realizing it—reviving a tradition of awe, delight, and comic self-abasement as old as the opera itself.[5]

That such a tradition should exist makes sense, of course, especially when we turn back the clock. Particularly for women of ninety or a hundred years ago, when the expression of passionate interest in one's own sex was inhibited by a host of cultural taboos, it must have been curiously exhilarating to enter an alternate universe—the opera house—in which many of the more restrictive norms governing ordinary female-female experience were temporarily suspended. Where else but in the plush darkness of Covent Garden, the Met, or the Opéra Comique, say, might a respectable woman of the nineteenth century have spent two or three hours staring raptly at another through binoculars? Before very recent times, the opera house (along with the theater) was one of only a few public spaces in which a woman could openly admire another woman's body, resonate to the penetrating tones of her voice, and even imagine (from a distance) the blood-warmth of her flesh—all in an atmosphere of heightened emotion and powerful sensual arousal. It is no wonder that for women whose erotic interest in other women was strong—the young Willa Cather, for example—the opera house should become almost a holy site, a kind of Temple of Love, or Venusberg of the homoerotic.[6]

Not every woman—admittedly—automatically fell under the spell: Virginia Woolf's jaundiced comment to a friend after attending a performance at Bayreuth ("Imagine a heroine in a nightgown, with a pigtail on each shoulder, and watery eyes, ogling heaven") suggests a certain intellectual resistance—at the very least—to the opera's peculiar pansexual magic.[7] Yet Woolf may be the (wary) exception proving the rule. What has always attracted women to opera, or so the unsung history of female diva-worship would appear to suggest, is precisely its homosexual dimension—the space that it allows for "loving" another woman, if only from afar. Before turning to my own perhaps too-transparent infatuation with *die Fassbaender*, I would like to offer a brief history of this tradition—not so much to exculpate myself, but as a way of diluting, as it were, some of the inevitable mortifications of self-exposure.

1

One could do worse than to begin with Queen Victoria—the ranking female diva lover of the nineteenth century. Victoria's adolescent passion for the Italian soprano Giulia Grisi is well-documented: after first hearing Grisi at the King's Theatre in 1834 in the role of Donizetti's Anna Bolena, the fourteen-year-old princess (who was a singer herself and already something of a connoisseur of

Fig. 2.1. Drawing of Giulia Grisi in *I Puritani* by the young Victoria, 1834. From George Rowell, *Queen Victoria Goes to the Theatre* (London, 1978). *Courtesy of Stanford University Libraries.*

voices) began filling her diaries and letters with effusive paeans to her new idol. "She is a most beautiful singer and actress and is likewise very young and pretty," she wrote after Grisi's debut; "she sang *beautifully* throughout but particularly in the last scene when she is mad, which she *acted* likewise *beautifully*."[8] Hearing her as Desdemona a week later, the enraptured princess wrote that "she *sang* and *acted* quite beautifully! and looked lovely."[9] And again, the following week: "Desdemona, Mdlle. Grisi, who looked BEAUTIFUL and sung MOST EXQUISITELY and acted BEAUTIFULLY. She personates the meek and ill-treated Desdemona in a most *perfect* and *touching* manner."[10] Not even the charismatic, ill-fated Maria Malibran could dislodge the Italian prima donna from her place in the young princess's affections: when both divas sang at Kensington Palace for Victoria's sixteenth birthday celebration, she wrote (somewhat heartlessly) afterward that Malibran was "shorter than Grisi and *not nearly so pretty* . . . her low notes are *beautiful*, but her high notes are thick and not clear. *I* like *Grisi by far better* than her."[11]

After her accession and marriage Victoria directed her attention toward other celebrated female singers—Pauline Viardot-Garcia, Emma Albani, and, most famously, the so-called Swedish Nightingale, Jenny Lind, who became the object of extensive royal patronage in the 1840s and 1850s. At Lind's London debut in Meyerbeer's *Robert le Diable* in 1847, or so her biographers recount, "an incident occurred . . . illustrating in a remarkable manner the effect produced in the Royal box by Jenny Lind's transcendent talent":

> When the fair *cantatrice* was summoned before the curtain, Her Majesty cast a superb bouquet, which lay before her in the Royal box, at the feet of the *debutante*. The incident—certainly unparalleled on any former occasion in this country—was unobserved by the great majority of the audience; but the gracious act of condescension did not escape the fair songstress, and a profound curtsey acknowledged the Royal recognition of her success.[12]

In the succeeding months Lind was invited several times to sing at Buckingham Palace, "where the purity, the sweetness and softness of her voice were much dwelt upon by the Queen, as well as the charming and unpretending grace of her manners."[13] Included among the tokens of favor the queen subsequently bestowed on her were a finely worked jewel bracelet and a Pekingese dog from the royal kennels.

Later in life, despite retiring from public operagoing after the death of Prince Albert, Victoria was still giving way to these regal diva enthusiasms. In her autobiography from 1922 the French singer Emma Calvé (the creator of Massenet's Sapho) describes being approached by the queen's sculptor cousin, the Countess Theodora de Gleiken, who had been commissioned by Victoria to make a portrait bust of Calvé as Santuzza in *Cavalleria Rusticana*. The bust was subsequently installed in the queen's private suite at Windsor Castle. After Victoria's death, when Calvé asked Princess Beatrice, the queen's daughter, what had become of it—assuming that it had been relegated to some attic storeroom—the princess assured her she was mistaken: "We have gathered together all our mother's favourite possessions, portraits, statues, mementos of all kinds, and placed them in a room known as the Victoria Room. There they will remain as long as the castle stands."[14]

Yet for all her sentimental connoisseurship, Victoria cannot be considered the typical diva-worshiper. Her high status gave her unusual powers (such as the right to command private performances) while her celebrated devotion to husband and children effectively disguised whatever element of latent homoeroticism may have been present in her obsessions with certain singers. More typical of the phenomenon of "sapphic" diva-worship—especially in the later nineteenth and early twentieth century—were those young, usually anonymous female fans who pursued their idols from opera house to opera house, much in the manner of modern groupies chasing after a rock star. The so-called Gerry-flappers who waited every night at the stage door of the Met for Geraldine Farrar in the teens and twenties, casting flowers and love notes in her direction when she emerged, exemplify this more humble yet fanatical kind of fan devotion; so too those impassioned "student girls" who signed on as supers

Fig. 2.2. The Gerry-flappers: Geraldine Farrar's female fans, 1920s.
Courtesy of Stanford University Libraries.

for a performance of *Dinorah* with the Italian soprano Galli-Curci in 1918, so that they might steal glimpses of their heroine at close range from behind the scenery.[15]

It is true, of course, that not every diva attachment carries with it exclusively romantic-erotic meanings: many of the most fervent diva-worshipers of the past have been budding divas themselves, for the simple reason that young singers often find in older singers technical and personal attributes worth emulating. It is a standard feature of "diva autobiography," for example, for the singer-author to eulogize a prima donna from her youth who functioned as a model and inspiration. Thus Frida Leider, the great Wagnerian soprano, on her girlhood devotion to Geraldine Farrar: "She seemed to me the most elegant and bewitching creature, and I used to colour all the sepia postcards which showed her in a long evening gown, a little diadem of pearls in her gently waved hair, with long white kid gloves, her head gracefully rested on one hand."[16] Farrar herself described being bowled over as a child by "the fascinating Calvé" ("the supreme and daring French woman never to be forgotten once heard!"), while Galli-Curci remembered spending hours in her teens dwelling reverently on the fact that her own name—Amelita Galli—contained the same number of letters as Adelina Patti's.[17] In one of the most ludicrous of such anecdotes, the sublime

Rosa Ponselle, an admirer in her adolescence of Tetrazzini, Calvé, and Melba, claimed to have quarreled with the priest at her confirmation when he refused to let her take *Melba* as her saint's name.[18]

Yet it hardly seems a coincidence that so many of the distinguished women of the past who have recorded obsessions with opera singers have been bisexual or lesbian in emotional inclination. Some, like George Sand, who adored Maria Malibran and found the inspiration for her romantic novel *Consuelo* in the singing of Malibran's sister, Pauline Viardot-Garcia, are well known; others, such as Anne Lister, a Yorkshire woman of the early nineteenth century who kept a coded diary both of her concertgoing and of her numerous lesbian love affairs (she heard Catalani in York in 1823), are, if obscure, no less interesting.[19] Indeed, one could almost speak of diva-worship as an "objective correlative" of female homoeroticism in the nineteenth and early twentieth century—so obviously and so often, especially among women of a certain class and educational background, were its rhapsodies and exaltations the token of a deeper emotional and physical yearning after the feminine.

Witness Sand, for example, writing to her husband in 1831 after abandoning him in order to take up a bohemian life in Paris: "I saw Madame Malibran in *Otello*. She made me weep, shudder, and suffer as though I had been watching a scene from real life. This woman is the foremost genius of Europe, as lovely as a Raphael madonna, simple, energetic, naive, she's the foremost singer and foremost tragedian. I'm mad about her."[20] The "madness" for Malibran was in part responsible for Sand's notorious adoption of male dress at this time: she first assumed her sleek top-hatted costume, she later maintained, precisely in order to procure cheap standing-room tickets (available only to men) at the Théâtre des Italiens where Malibran was performing.[21] Malibran inspired one of Sand's first short stories—*La Prima Donna*—as well as her subsequent love affair with the actress Marie Dorval, who bore a striking resemblance to the Spanish singer. Writes Sand's biographer, "like Maria Malibran, Marie Dorval was anything but handsome, being too small and frail to have a commanding stage presence. . . . But what she lacked in natural attributes was more than matched by a passionate intensity and a lack of theatrical artificiality which had made her the darling of the Romantics."[22] In Sand's infatuation with her "dear loved one" ("Never did Erinna reply to Sappho in a more caressing voice") there is more than a little hint that she wished to recreate in the flesh the idealized passion for Malibran.[23]

A bit later, across the Channel, the lesbian composer and conductor Ethel Smyth was another flagrant diva-worshiper. In *Impressions That Remained*, her engaging autobiography from 1919, Smyth (whose later infatuations would include the elusive Virginia Woolf) described holding a love-struck vigil while a teenager, her "heart beating furiously," outside Jenny Lind's house in London in the early 1870s. "From allusions to her triumphs in old volumes of *Punch*, and my mother's descriptions of her supreme art, she had long been one of my heroines, and if anyone had told me that one day I should become fairly intimate with this striking and terrifying personality I should have gone off my head on the spot."[24] Later, while studying composition in Leipzig, Smyth conceived a passion for the celebrated operetta singer Marie Geistinger, who came to epitomize for her "all the heroines I loved and pitied . . . Maria Stuart, Adrienne, Phèdre, Hermione (in *Winter's Tale*), and others." Indeed, Smyth recollected, "I was quite mad about the Geistinger, and after the performances used to stand for long half hours in snow or slush to see her muffled form shoot out of the stage door into her fly."[25] When "the Geistinger" responded with an invitation to visit her at home, the "shock of seeing Maria Stuart at close quarters, in a tight-fitting dark blue satin bodice covered with spangles, rouged up to the eyes, and wearing a fluffy light wig," Smyth wrote, "produced a commotion in my breast as when the tide turns against a strong wind."[26] Though the relationship soon petered out—Geistinger being absorbed in her needlework and dogs and accompanied by a skulking husband—Smyth subsequently named her next musical composition, a somewhat turgid Brahmsian pastiche, the "Geistinger Sonata."[27]

Certain famous turn-of-the-century divas seem to have inspired such homoerotic emotion as a matter of course. Nellie Melba's numerous female admirers included both Vita Sackville-West and Violet Trefusis: when forced by her hypocritical family to marry—precisely in order to cover up the scandal of her affair with Sackville-West—the unregenerate Trefusis demanded that Melba sing at the wedding.[28] Janet Flanner, the Paris correspondent for the *New Yorker* and a prominent figure in Parisian lesbian circles in the 1920s and 1930s, was an ardent Mary Garden fan: in a letter to a lover in 1961 she recalled how during her college years in Chicago she braved the freezing winds coming off Lake Michigan just to hear her idol sing in Prokofiev's *The Love of the Three Oranges.*[29] And in *My Thirty Years' War* (1930), Margaret Anderson, the founder of the avant-garde *Little Review*, described how she and Jane Heap, her first lover, once wangled a meeting with Garden by writing a series of adulatory articles about her. "The air was charged with an animal magnetism that one rarely has the pleasure of feeling," wrote Anderson, recollecting the event; "the challenge of Mary Garden's presence is one of the most thrilling human experiences I remember."[30]

Garden, who cultivated an air of sexual ambiguity quite brazenly—she created the lesbian role of Chrysis in Erlanger's *Aphrodite* in 1906 and sang the *tenor* part of the Jongleur in Massenet's *Le Jongleur de Notre-Dame* in 1908—inevitably provoked strong feminine reactions. In 1913, following a Garden performance in Philadelphia, a hysterical young woman named Helen Newby killed herself

Fig. 2.3. Mary Garden (1874–1967). "The challenge of Mary Garden's presence," said Margaret Anderson, "is one of the most thrilling human experiences I remember."
Courtesy of the Bettmann Archive.

after being refused admittance to Garden's hotel room. Newby, reported the *New York Times*, had "fallen in love" with Garden after seeing her photograph two years earlier, and suffering from a delusion that the singer was Queen Cleopatra and she herself her slave, worshipped her "as a heathen worships his idol." Newby was found dead clutching Garden's picture to her breast.[31] (Garden, although shaken, managed to sing Thaïs at the Met the following evening.) And in James Huneker's *Painted Veils*, a scandalous roman à clef about the opera world published in 1920, the Mary Garden character is shown pursuing and being pursued by a wealthy lesbian admirer in men's clothes ("a crazy-cat but a jolly girl") who later pays her way to Europe. In her pioneering bibliography *Sex Variant Women in Literature*, Jeannette Foster hints that the admirer may have had her counterpart in real life.[32]

Even more enthralling to female fans than Garden, however, was the great Swedish-American soprano, Olive Fremstad, who sang Isolde, Kundry, Brünnhilde, and other leading Wagnerian roles at the Met between 1903 and 1914. Given the sheer number and distinction of her women admirers—not to mention the Garbo-like eccentricities of her personal life—Fremstad might be considered the sapphic "cult" diva par excellence. Fremstad's most famous devo-

Fig. 2.4. Mary Garden as Salomé, 1908. *Courtesy of Stanford University Libraries.*

tee was the novelist Willa Cather: Cather befriended the diva in 1913 after interviewing her for *McClure's* and later used her as the model for Thea Kronberg, the austere yet curiously compelling heroine of *The Song of the Lark*, the novel Cather published in 1915 about the coming of age of a celebrated singer. When Fred Ottenburg, Thea's would-be suitor in that novel, tries to describe the special quality of her vocalism, it is not difficult to read into his sensual, almost libertine appreciation something of Cather's own powerfully eroticized feeling for Fremstad:

> "The people who chatter about her being a great actress don't seem to get the notion of where *she* gets the notion. It all goes back to her original endowment, her tremendous musical talent. Instead of inventing a lot of business

> and expedients to suggest character, she knows the thing at the root, and lets the musical pattern take care of her. The score pours her into all those lovely postures, makes the light and shadow go over her face, lifts her and drops her. She lies on it, the way she used to lie on the Rhine music."[33]

"With Mme. Fremstad," wrote Cather elsewhere, "one feels that the idea is always more living than the emotion; perhaps it would be nearer the truth to say that the idea is so intensely experienced that it becomes emotion."[34]

Less familiar, however, may be the case of Mary Watkins Cushing, who began by worshipping Fremstad from afar and ended up living with her for a number of years as a sort of private secretary-companion. In her amusing though also somewhat reticent 1954 memoir, *The Rainbow Bridge*, Cushing described becoming infatuated at nineteen with Fremstad after hearing her debut as Brünnhilde at the Met. The performance had been an unusual one: tortured in the past by the traditional "steel bodices of Bayreuth," Fremstad had chosen to wear for the occasion "a mere bandeau slung to her shoulders with leather straps," an Amazonian cloak and kirtle, and sandals with leather thongs—a boyish and athletic costume in which her youthful admirer, gazing through binoculars, unabashedly delighted. Desperate to meet the "goddess" who had so entranced her, the enterprising Cushing (who was an art student) drew a sketch of Fremstad in her new costume and sent her a letter describing it. Fremstad responded with an invitation to tea—an event for which Cushing, "speechless with joy," prepared herself by taking a perfumed bath and shampooing herself "to a high degree of elegance." "I felt like a medieval esquire in vigil on the eve of knighthood. I was a foolish and star-struck girl, but I had a vague and disturbing sense of fate in operation, and wished to meet it in a state of grace."[35]

Fate was indeed operating, because Fremstad—besides being enchanted by the sketch—was taken enough with her new fan to ask her, not long after, to accompany her on a European tour. With her parents' grudging permission (they were clearly cowed by the impetuous diva) Cushing did so, and for the next eight years lived with Fremstad in the capacity of lady companion and self-described "buffer" against the world.[36] The relationship lasted until 1918, when Cushing, in a fit of patriotism, joined a women's ambulance corps going out to France. (It was seeing a pickled human head, cut in half lengthwise, which Fremstad used to demonstrate the physiology of the vocal organs to her singing students, that convinced Cushing, she said later, she had the psychological stamina to cope with the horrors of war.) The two women remained close, however, and Cushing was with Fremstad at the singer's death in 1951.[37]

Whether Cushing's relationship with Fremstad should be characterized as a homosexual one is questionable: there is no evidence to suggest that the two

Fig. 2.5. Sketch of Olive Fremstad as Brünnhilde, 1903, by Mary Watkins Cushing. From *The Rainbow Bridge* (New York, 1954). ***Courtesy of Stanford University Libraries.***

women were ever actually lovers. Among sophisticated contemporaries, however, it is clear that their intimacy aroused gossip and speculation. In Marcia Davenport's *Of Lena Geyer* (1936)—the mock-biography of a fictitious Wagnerian diva modeled largely, like Cather's Thea Kronberg, on Fremstad—the relationship between the singer, Lena Geyer, and her companion Elsie deHaven closely parallels that between Fremstad and Cushing, though with its homoerotic element rather more plainly spelled out. (Davenport, daughter of the soprano Alma Gluck and an opera commentator for the National Broadcasting Company in the 1940s, was herself no stranger to the intoxications of diva-worship.)[38] "Miss deHaven" first appears in Davenport's novel as a mysterious black-clad young heiress of "strange" and "morbid" disposition who follows Geyer across Europe from opera house to opera house, always sitting alone in the same seat in the sixth row. When she begins sending Geyer gigantic flower bouquets, the singer's jealous French lover, the Duc de Chartres, tries to shield her from deHaven's "unnatural" obsession. "I felt as if a cold hand, nay, the fin of a cold-blooded creature of

Fig. 2.6. Olive Fremstad as Isolde, early 1900s. *Courtesy of Stanford University Libraries.*

the sea, had swept over my heart," he says after being introduced to her; "her worship of my darling Lena could be construed only in the most horrible light; and I boiled with fiery determination never to allow the two to meet."[39]

The duc's efforts notwithstanding, Geyer becomes secretly fascinated with her new admirer, and after a performance of *Le Nozze di Figaro* (a change from her usual Wagnerian fare) invites deHaven backstage. There, "goggle-eyed with wonder," the smitten heiress is allowed to watch while the singer proceeds to divest herself somewhat provocatively of the heavily brocaded gown she has worn as Mozart's Countess. "Madame Geyer stood up and shook herself," deHaven recollects later:

> The whole thing slipped off around her feet, leaving her in a high-busted corset and a pair of lacy cambric drawers. I must have shown the question in my mind—how could she sing in such stays? She answered by remarking that she was about ready to throw them all into the fire and start a vogue for nat-

> ural lines on the stage. The sequel is that she did. Dora unlaced her, and removed the harness. As she did so, Madame Geyer groaned and stretched delightedly, then slipped a dressing gown over her shoulders and sat down again while Dora took off her white wig.[40]

Reclothing herself in a glamorous silk-lined cloak and "velvet carriage boots," Geyer then sweeps the younger woman off to her hotel room for an intimate late-night supper of "favorite Mozart dishes," including eggballs and a *Himmeltorte*. When the love-struck deHaven, trembling, like a sort of Cherubino-in-training, confesses her infatuation, Geyer enfolds her in a voluptuous embrace. "I was so unnerved by the emotions of the past twenty-four hours," deHaven says later, "I could not regain control of myself. For the first time in my life I was freely and utterly giving way to deep feeling. Lena Geyer pressed my head against her shoulder and murmured to me in German, tender broken phrases that one would use to a child. I felt as if I should die for love of her."[41] Geyer, it is now revealed, has tired of the duc, and finding all other men "brutish," longs for a faithful female companion with whom to share her life. Over the next few weeks the duc—to his mortification—is phased out, and the adoring deHaven (who asks nothing more of life "than the privilege of living with Lena Geyer and of acting as companion, secretary, housekeeper, amanuensis, and confidante") joyfully takes her place as the singer's unofficial consort. "I cannot imagine what Lena saw in me," she remarks later, after Geyer's death; "we will have to let it go as the same sort of mystery that holds a forceful, handsome, desirable man to a homely little shadow of a wife."[42]

Davenport's novel might be said to encapsulate the most narcissistic, and even absurd, of sapphic fan fantasies—that of being "taken up" (recognized, petted, and adored in turn) by the one whose voice enthralls. Yet as Davenport's barely disguised reworking of the Fremstad-Cushing story suggests, it was a fantasy that could on occasion come true. More than one fan in the annals of female diva-worship has, like Mary Watkins Cushing or the fictional Elsie deHaven, ended up "marrying" her favorite singer. The most famous of English lesbian novelists, Radclyffe Hall, lived for nine years with Mabel Batten, a well-known lieder singer and concert performer of the Edwardian era; they met in Homburg in 1907 and were lovers until Batten's death in 1916.[43] And Margaret Anderson—the same Margaret Anderson who enthused in her youth over Mary Garden—lived for twenty-one years with the celebrated French opera singer Georgette Leblanc, the first Mélisande and widow of Maeterlinck. Anderson and Leblanc shared their ménage (a romantic lighthouse in Normandy) with a Belgian woman named Monique Serrure, who had herself given up a career as a schoolteacher many years earlier after hearing Leblanc sing Thaïs at the Opéra de la Monnaie in Brussels. Merely listening to Leblanc's voice, Serrure said, had made her want to serve her—which she did, as cook and housekeeper, for the next forty years.[44]

It would be easy enough, I imagine, to find examples of similar fan devotion in more recent times; for despite the incursion of new and more up-to-date forms of mass entertainment, both operagoing and its colorful corollary, "sapphic" diva-worship, continue to flourish. Indeed, thanks to the proliferation of cheap recordings and videotapes and what one might call the "privatization" of the operatic experience, more of such worship may in fact be going on—behind closed doors—than ever before. Unless I am utterly mistaken, numerous postwar divas (and Kathleen Ferrier, Joan Sutherland, Jessye Norman, Janet Baker, Frederica Von Stade, and Tatiana Troyanos are among those who come immediately to mind) retain same-sex followings at least as large—if not always as comically conspicuous—as those inspired in an earlier age by Lind and Fremstad and Garden. Although hysterical fan "hunting packs" of the sort that carried Geraldine Farrar aloft down Broadway after her farewell performance at the Met may no longer exist (except perhaps in Japan, where same-sex performer worship continues to take unusual and extravagant forms), the rituals of adoration, to judge by ticket sales and fan club subscriptions, still entice the susceptible.[45]

At the same time, with the gradual change in social attitudes toward homosexuality, it has become possible—or nearly possible—to acknowledge the libidinal element in such veneration. As early as 1956, Brigid Brophy—in her novel *The King of a Rainy Country*—depicted a tender lesbian scene between diva and female fan.[46] The homoerotic impulse animating much diva-worship of the past has been, as it were, desublimated: to the point that certain singers have become popular icons within a newly enfranchised female homosexual subculture. (Ferrier was perhaps the first major modern singer to inspire a visibly lesbian following; Norman, Von Stade, Brigitte Fassbaender, Ann Sophie von Otter, and Hildegard Behrens are among the more recent sapphic cult divas.) Nowadays it is hard to attend an opera in a city like San Francisco, for instance, with its large and vocal lesbian population, without becoming aware—however subtly—of the various female claques attracted by certain charismatic divas.[47]

Rather than trace out any of these fan networks in more detail, however, I would like to turn instead to my own case—to explore the question of diva-worship, as it were, from within. The purely sociological approach can, perhaps, only take us so far. My hope is that by disclosing as fully and shamelessly as possible the extent of my own partisanship for the aforementioned Fassbaender, I can illuminate some of the more subjective aspects of the phenomenon. I confess to some lingering apprehension—the thought of being lampooned as a "Briggy-flapper" gives pause—but in the interests of scholarship, I proceed.

2

We "Octavians" get some very peculiar fan mail.
—*Brigitte Fassbaender, 1991*[48]

The obvious question, perhaps, though also a perplexing one, is why Brigitte Fassbaender? There are singers whose voices—as instruments—I find more beautiful; there are singers, even among the rather inglorious cohort currently active, who possess a demonstrably superior technique. (Marilyn Horne would certainly be among the latter: though she and Fassbaender are both dramatic mezzos with fairly heavy, rich voices, Horne's strength and agility—bordering at times on the superhuman—are considerably greater.) There are, moreover, *singers I have actually heard*. The most paradoxical aspect of my fixation is its curious ineffability. It is not just that I have never once cast a bouquet of roses in Fassbaender's direction or waited patiently in the slush by a stage door in order to watch her getting into a taxi cab; despite nearly twenty years of opera- and recital-going, I have never—strangely enough—seen and heard her sing in the flesh. Fassbaender remains for me a singing simulacrum: a creation of digital and analog and video tape, a sort of auditory hallucination or disembodied (though always musical) electronic emanation.

The way that my attachment evolved will perhaps account for this peculiar state of affairs. I first became aware of Fassbaender almost ten years ago as a result of reading a squalidly entertaining Anne Rice novel, *Cry to Heaven* (1982), about the life and loves of a sex-crazed castrato in eighteenth-century Italy. There, in an afterword, Rice confessed that she had written one of the novel's many bizarre love scenes "to music"—namely, to a 1964 Deutsche Grammophon recording of Alessandro Scarlatti's chamber cantata *Il Giardino d'Amore*, featuring Brigitte Fassbaender as Venus and the American soprano Catherine Gayer as Adonis.[49] Intrigued by this odd admission—the central relationship in Rice's novel is a curious affair between the bisexual castrato and a depraved old cardinal—I acquired the same recording myself a short time later.

Though impressed by Fassbaender's strange androgynous timbre and the precocious skill with which she and Gayer wove their seductive vocal lines (Fassbaender was only twenty-four at the time), I can't say I was immediately struck by un coup de foudre. Indeed, for the next seven or eight years, though I continued to collect the odd Fassbaender disc here and there (a *Così* highlights album, some Schubert masses), my attention was drawn to more flamboyant divas such as Callas and Horne, and then to a succession of historical singers, including Lehmann, Flagstad, Ponselle, Elisabeth Schumann, and the glorious, all-too-short-lived Conchita Supervia. Nor did I become aware of Fassbaender's achievements on stage: despite going to the opera as often as possible—first on a graduate student's, then on an assistant professor's salary—I never happened to see her "by accident," as it were, though I was fairly often in places in which she had sung: San Francisco, London, and New York.

A couple of years ago two events snapped me out of my semistupor. The first was the reissue of the Scarlatti cantata on compact disc; the second was an interview with Fassbaender in the music magazine *Gramophone*. To hear Fassbaender's Venus in the new "silver" format, with the sound immeasurably cleaned up and the voice projected with a presence so direct and intimate as to be startling, was a revelation. Here, I realized—listening to her lilting, dignified, yet amorous traversal of Venus's "Care selve, amati orrori"—were portamenti to be reckoned with. This miniature epiphany (as I now think of it) was loosely akin to those moments in Iris Murdoch novels when two characters who have known one another for years—without feeling the slightest emotional attraction—suddenly fall wildly and improbably in love. Apathy gave way to emotion; cool diffidence to a sudden aching, acute attentiveness.

But the interview, devoted to Fassbaender's then just-released recording of Schubert's *Winterreise* (1990), was in its own way equally galvanizing. Long considered the most profound and difficult of Schubert song cycles, the *Winterreise* has traditionally been "off limits" to women singers on account of its (seemingly) intractable heterosexual premise: the speaker—inevitably presumed to be a man—wanders despairingly through a bleak winter landscape, lamenting the loss of a female beloved. To have a woman perform the songs, or so it has usually been felt, is to complicate—rather uncomfortably—an otherwise familiar (if gloomy) romantic scenario. So intense and potent are the sexual yearnings expressed in Schubert's settings, so *neurotic* the dramatic situation, the use of a female singer inevitably "perverts" the desired aesthetic effect—precisely (it is implied) by raising the problematic specter of lesbianism.[50]

The handful of female singers brazen enough to sing the cycle in the past, such as Elena Gerhardt and Lotte Lehmann, have typically defended themselves against charges of unnaturalness and impudence by stressing the "universality" of the cycle. "This most beautiful cycle of songs," wrote a pious Gerhardt in her autobiography,

> can well be interpreted by a woman. It expresses unhappy love, despair and a complete resignation to the fact that life may not hold anything more worth living for. Why should a woman, who is capable of understanding these emotions, not be able to perform it? For me, the psychology of this cycle is that of unhappy love in general, and does not depend on a particular masculine or feminine approach.[51]

Yet Fassbaender, I was intrigued to see, avoided any such diplomatic cant.

Indeed, responding to her interviewer's (to my mind) subtly loaded question—"Had she always wanted to sing the *Winterreise*?"—she seemed instead to accentuate, albeit obliquely, the subversiveness of the endeavor. Yes, she replied, though she hadn't "dared" to until she had spent three months working on it with an accompanist in New York. Then, she said, she had premiered it in a little church somewhere outside the city. "The old ladies in the church all sat there eating their cake and sipping coffee, then slowly they began to stop and listen, and they listened more and more! That was, as it were, the performance in secret. Then I brought it to Europe and sang it at Hohenems."[52] In the comical image of a cohort of elderly females, mesmerized, cake in hand, by this mysterious "secret" performance, Fassbaender seemed—to me at least—to acknowledge the sexual politics involved in her choice of repertoire and the covert (if eccentric) homoeroticism with which it might be associated. The "old ladies," or so I fondly imagined, had put their authorizing seal on the performance—had in fact, despite coffee and crumbs, called it forth into sensuous life. I quickly sought out the Schubert disc and, like them, was at once transfixed by its uncanny, transsexual beauty.

Struck now with a sense not only of a magnificent voice but also with Fassbaender's idiosyncratic, even daredevil musical personality, I immediately embarked on a search for other Fassbaenderiana. Within a month I had acquired a 1986 collection of Mahler and Berg songs, a Loewe recital, a recording (with

Fig. 2.7. Brigitte Fassbaender. "There is no more vibrantly characterful Lieder-singer today, man or woman" (Ivan March).

Courtesy of Werner Neumeister.

Giulini) of *Das Lied von der Erde*, and a second Schubert disc, complete with a cover photograph of the sloe-eyed singer sitting moodily in a graveyard. Yet with each new purchase the compulsion to hear *more* became greater. And soon enough, I am embarrassed to say, I found myself haunting local record stores, shuffling through CD racks, and perusing *Opus* catalogues with the eager tremulousness of the addict.

My new habit was hardly an inexpensive one. Not only was Fassbaender's discography from the 1970s and 1980s large, she had been involved from the start of her career in some rather plush projects. (She has held long-term contracts with EMI, Deutsche Grammophon, London, and Philips.) In one frightening two-week period, soon after starting in on her operatic recordings, I greedily bought up whole boxed sets of Mozart's *La Clemenza di Tito* and *La Finta Giardiniera*, Strauss's *Die Fledermaus*, Berg's *Lulu*, and Schoenberg's *Gurrelieder*, all simply in order to sample my idol's contributions. Fate seemed to be working obscurely to intensify my fixation: the Loewe disc, for example, which quickly became a special favorite, I uncovered by accident while twiddling—as if impelled by invisible forces—through a remainder bin at Tower Records.

Had I known at the peak of my obsession where to see Fassbaender "live"—whether Bayreuth or Tokyo, Buenos Aires or Sydney—I would probably, madly, have tried to get there. (I was unaware then, in late 1991, that she had already retired several of her most famous roles.)[53] In a belated attempt to catch up with her stage career, I did the next best thing and began raiding the opera video racks. The fact that I didn't own a VCR didn't deter me: I immediately got one. I first "saw" Fassbaender, somewhat anticlimactically, in one of her goofier trouser roles—as a pop-eyed Hänsel, complete with baggy lederhosen, in Humperdinck's *Hänsel and Gretel*. But before long, I had taken her in in an array of more sophisticated parts: as a farouche, tuxedo-clad Orlovsky in *Fledermaus*, as a sensuous yet implacable Charlotte in Massenet's *Werther*, and, most fearsomely, as a lurching, makeup-encrusted, get-your-ya-ya's-out Klytemnestra in Strauss's *Elektra*. This scopophilic compulsion finally came to a head one day when I found a Laserdisc version of *Der Rosenkavalier* with Fassbaender as Octavian—her most celebrated part—and spent most of an afternoon exulting over it like a voyeur in a soundproof concrete cubicle at the Stanford University audiovisual center. Seldom has the Presentation of the Rose taken place in less salubrious quarters.

Still one may ask:, why this riot of fondness over one particular singer? The answer that comes first to mind is a simple one: low notes. I confess to being what Marilyn Horne has termed a "chest nut" (as in "chest notes for chest nuts") and invariably thrill to Fassbaender's voluptuous command of the reverberant mezzo/contralto register. I share this predilection for the low voice, I find, with numerous female diva-worshipers of the past. Willa Cather cherished Fremstad for her swooping low notes; Ethel Smyth describes Marie Geistinger's voice as "deep and thrilling."[54] And in Marcia Davenport's *Of Lena Geyer*, we discover the following:

> [Geyer] had almost a contralto range; its quality, all in her chest, was thrilling beyond description. In some ways her low voice was more thrilling than her fiery middle and high one, and in later days the critics used to go wild looking for terms in which to describe it. It was pure earth, female, sex if you want to call it that. You might say that where her high tones were enchanting to the imagination, her low ones warmed the body like an embrace.[55]

Even among diva-worshipers who go in for sopranos rather than mezzos, it's the bottom notes, one finds, that count: in *Così fan tutte*, writes Brigid Brophy, it is the "astonishing low notes" sung by Fiordiligi that suffuse her arias with their almost unbearable emotional plangency.[56] In Fassbaender's case, the velvety richness of the lower register—what her admirers refer to as her "smoky" or "dark" or "chocolate" tone—comes across especially well in recordings, creating unparalleled effects of shading, depth, and sensuality. (Witness, for example, the vertiginous downward plunges in "Gefrorne Tränen" in the *Winterreise*, or the ravishing gravitas with which she imbues the Wood Dove's bottom notes in Schoenberg's *Gurrelieder*.)

Yet just as compelling, if not more so, is the style in which the notes are produced. Fassbaender's manner is typically noble, extroverted, even virile. She is not a recessive or shyly self-effacing mezzo, content to lurk in the background, murmuring little bits of advice to the soprano. On the contrary there is a boldness and edge, almost a "butchness" to her singing—even in lieder, where her interpretations are often highly unorthodox. This "butch" element (if one may call it so) may have something to do with the fact that she was trained exclusively by her father, Willi Domgraf-Fassbaender, a prominent Mozart baritone of the 1930s and 1940s. Music journalists have made much of this interesting Oedipal connection. A 1981 *Opera* profile devoted to Fassbaender began, in fact, with the following:

> An unidentified author of sleevenotes for an Acanta album of Willi Domgraf-Fassbaender concludes his description of the baritone in the incomparable Glyndebourne recordings of *Così fan tutte* and *Le Nozze di Figaro* as follows: "The greatness of this artist lay in his ability to use singing as a means of expressing tangible human emotions. His character portrayals were natural and convincing; his diction precise even in the most lyrical of phrases and his intelligent approach to the dramatic action gave all that he did a penetrating

> intensity. Seldom have words and music, language and song, been in such agreement." It is no coincidence that these same words, put into the present tense and substituting "her" and "she" for "his" and "he" could be the perfect description of Brigitte Fassbaender, mezzo soprano: she happens to be his daughter, and her only vocal studies were with him; from her Nuremberg Conservatory days (1958–1961), until his death in February 1978 she went over her roles and Lieder with him.[57]

One hesitates to say that Fassbaender "sings like a man" (though the reviewer here comes close), yet there's an element of truth to the observation: the sound produced is often a curiously unfeminine one. Fassbaender's attack is typically forthright, almost guttural—and not only when she is singing in German. In Don Ramiro's "jealousy" aria in act 3 of *La Finta Giardiniera*, for example, every "t" cuts and every "p" explodes. (She makes the same exaggerated "t" sound at the end of words too, as in the brutal "Ewigkeit" at the end of the Countess Geschwitz's Adagio in *Lulu*.) The breath control is that of the proverbial athlete. Like many mezzos, Fassbaender takes very audible breaths, yet never to distracting effect: she somehow manages to make the intake of breath an integral part of the emotional statement. At times, as in some of the more savage *Winterreise* songs—"Rückblick" or "Die Krähe"—she seems almost to gnaw on, or bite into, the air as she sings, gulping it down, like one craving for sustenance, yet also capturing perfectly the engulfing desperation of Schubert's mad wanderer. But Fassbaender's timbre itself can often sound oddly masculine—to the point that critics have on occasion been confounded by what they hear. Assessing a recent recording of *Die Fledermaus* in which Fassbaender appears as Prince Orlovsky, a writer for *Classic CD*, while marveling at her performance, questioned whether it could really be she delivering Orlovsky's "astonishingly deep" spoken dialogue.[58]

Yet the spell that Fassbaender casts cannot simply be reduced to a matter of sound or technique. Maria Callas, after all, had low notes, power, awesome virtuosity—and even, one might argue, a similar "masculine" forwardness to her singing. Yet while I admire Callas—fiercely—I do not adore her. It's a matter of role-playing: with Callas, the unambiguously heterosexual persona gets in the way—the sense she projected, both onstage and off, of being in thrall to, and exclusively concerned with, a world of men. Dynamic though she is, one seldom has a sense of Callas singing "to" or "for" another woman: the implied auditor is almost always a man. Her most famous parts—Norma, Tosca—merely reinforce what might be called the heterovocalism of her singing: it is an address to a male beloved.

In Fassbaender's case, the address—what one might term the directionality of the vocal appeal—is completely different. Fassbaender seems by contrast acutely aware of female listeners, and to include precisely where Callas seems to exclude. The distinctive virility of Fassbaender's singing may be less a matter of vocal technique, in other words, than a matter of theatricality, of a certain attitude toward her audience. Indeed, she often gives the illusion of singing "for" women and women alone—of conceiving her roles, and projecting them outward, in a manner carefully designed to appeal to an attending, if invisible, corps of female fans. Where Callas is heterovocal, Fassbaender is homovocal.[59]

And yet, the cynic will object, might not such an effect simply be attributed to the fact that Fassbaender—as a mezzo—has had out of necessity to sing a particularly large number of trouser roles? Given that so many of the standard mezzo parts nowadays—from Sesto in *La Clemenza da Tito* and Arsace in *Semiramide* to Orlovsky in *Fledermaus* and Octavian in *Rosenkavalier*—require the singer literally to sing in drag (and often very passionately) to another woman, is it really so surprising that Fassbaender's onstage persona should seem more homosexually inflected than Callas's? Had Fassbaender had to make a career out of Violettas or Butterflys, matters might be very different.

Indisputably, the present-day mezzo repertoire has a lot to do with what I am calling the "homovocality" of Fassbaender's stage presence. At this point in operatic history it is indeed the mezzo or contralto who is most likely to become a homoerotic icon—precisely because so many of her roles will be travesty parts. This was not always the case. At the turn of the century, apart from Mozart's Cherubino, very few of the standard roles for the mid-to-low female voice were in fact transvestite roles. And as a consequence the divas with the largest female followings tended not to be mezzos at all but heavy dramatic sopranos, like Olive Fremstad, whose speciality was Brünnhilde. (Brünnhilde was in its own day of course the most boldly androgynous of the soprano parts.) Only with the mid-twentieth-century revival of opera seria and bel canto, in which low-lying travesty roles proliferate, have the majority of sapphic "cult" divas tended to come from the mezzo or contralto ranks. Ferrier was luminous in the trouser part of Orfeo, and Horne, Troyanos, Von Stade, Baker, and Fassbaender have all carried on the distinguished "mezzo-in-drag" tradition.

What separates Fassbaender, however, even from some of her most gifted peers, is the almost shocking intensity with which the transvestite illusion—in all of its giddying psychological complexity—is brought off. Fassbaender is not afraid to identify with the male role, and to identify completely. One critic, describing her controversial *Winterreise*, put the matter this way:

> Any woman who sets out to perform *Winterreise* must decide whether she is going to *be* the young man singing the songs or merely a reciter of his words,

• **Fig. 2.8a. Kathleen Ferrier in *Orfeo,* Covent Garden, 1953.**
Courtesy of the Houston Rogers Collection, Theatre Museum, London.

> and then she must somehow make her point of view clear to her audience. Ludwig [i.e., the German mezzo Christa Ludwig, who recorded the cycle in the 1960s] seems to take the more aloof, empathic approach. Her readings are almost maternally consoling. She feels the sentiments deeply, but at second-hand. Fassbaender goes beyond empathy to identify completely with the boy himself, stepping into his boots with such peremptory conviction that we forget a woman is singing. . . . This is Schubert's forlorn wanderer standing in the flesh before us, sounding a little younger than usual and all the more pitiable because of it.[60]

Yet even this may be an oversimplification. If the writer here (who is male) errs in any point, it is in his assertion that Fassbaender en travesti makes us "forget a woman is singing." For the very opposite, I think, is in fact the case. It is true, as he implies, that Fassbaender often seems driven from within, possessed by a kind of dramaturgical daemon—to the point that she can sometimes appear to merge, eerily, with her roles, as in the case of Schubert's unhappy wanderer or Strauss's Octavian. But the male persona is only that: a persona, a narrative fiction. Brilliant though "he" is, no one I think ever seriously confuses Fassbaender's Octavian, for example, with a seventeen-year-old boy. What we see before us—in the intoxicating boudoir scene at the start of *Rosenkavalier*—is Fassbaen-

Fig. 2.8(a–b). Kathleen Ferrier in *Orfeo,* Covent Garden, 1953. *Courtesy of the Houston Rogers Collection, Theatre Museum, London.*

der, the diva, draped langorously across another, making passionate love to her. No matter how artfully "true to life" the boyish gestures, Fassbaender-in-drag fools no one: the fact that the body is female, that the voice is a woman's voice, remains inescapable.

The effect (on this listener at least) is both stirring and paradoxical—like something out of a dream. Precisely to the degree that Fassbaender seems to enter "into" her male roles, precisely as I watch her approach (though without ever reaching) a kind of "zero degree masculinity," I find myself becoming more and more acutely aware of, and aroused by, her femininity. The very butchness with which she tackles, say, a role like Octavian—the sheer, absolutist bravado of the impersonation—infuses it with a dizzying homosexual charge. The more dashingly Fassbaender pretends, the more completely she fails—with the result that a new stage illusion takes shape: that of a woman robustly in love with another woman. When Fassbaender-as-Octavian, singing of her passion for the Marschallin, takes her fellow diva in her arms, I find it difficult not to take *her* literally—to read "past" the narrative fiction toward what I am actually seeing: a woman embracing a lover, even as she pantomimes the part of an impetuous boy. The very deftness of the pantomime prompts a kind of lesbian chauvinism: this is a woman (we are invited to imagine) who is as good as, if not better than, any man.[61]

What exactly is Fassbaender conveying at such moments? Fassbaender's great theme—the emotion she communicates onstage better, I think, than any other living diva—is gynophilia: exaltation in the presence of the feminine. She is unsurpassed at conveying adoration: of female voices, bodies, and dreams. This is true whether she is herself playing a woman or a man, a tragic or a comic part. Her female roles are as strongly homovocal in conception as her male roles. When asked in a recent interview, for example, about her favorite Wagnerian part—Brangaene, Isolde's lady-in-waiting in *Tristan und Isolde*—Fassbaender said that what she found most "riveting" about it psychologically was precisely the ardent tenderness that Brangaene displays toward Isolde: "Brangaene is the intermediary, the mother substitute who, out of love for Isolde, substitutes the death for a love potion. In doing that she assumes a crucial part in the unfolding of events and her maternal love and anxiety find full expression in the finale."[62] She is—after a fashion—as fixated as Tristan. And indeed to listen to the singer's rapturous, no-holds-barred traversal of "O Süsse! Traute! Teure! Holde! / Goldne Herrin! Lieb' Isolde!" (O sweetest, dearest, fairest, / golden lady! Beloved Isolde!) is to sense more powerfully than ever a note of wild, almost idolatrous devotion in Brangaene's love for her doomed mistress.

In the case of the Countess Geschwitz in Berg's *Lulu*, the gynophilia is explicitly weighted, of course, with homosexual feeling. Yet here too Fassbaender is unafraid to get at the passionate core of the character. At the beginning of that opera's second act, for example, when Geschwitz expresses her delight that the prostitute Lulu, with whom she is besotted, has agreed to attend a lesbian ball that she is hosting, Fassbaender catches both the character's awkward, misplaced chivalry and the urgent sexual longing behind it. In turn, when Geschwitz, gazing raptly at a portrait of Lulu as Pierrot, murmurs, as if in a dream, "Hier sind Sie wie ein Märchen" (Here you are like a fairy tale), Fassbaender's voice seems almost to bend around the words, caressing each syllable with voluptuous precision. And in the famous Adagio in act 3, after Lulu has been murdered offstage by Jack the Ripper, and Geschwitz herself is bleeding to death from the stab wound he has dealt her, the singer's wrenching delivery of Geschwitz's death cry, the voice veering crazily upward on the word *einmal*, then plunging down again—"Lulu! Mein Engel! Lass dich noch einmal sehn!" (Lulu! My angel! Appear once more to me!)—achieves an effect of erotic pathos no less striking for its brevity and compression.[63]

Yet it is in the trouser roles, and the comic ones especially, that Fassbaender's skill at enacting such exaltation is most vividly apparent. She has been described, rightly, as the greatest of modern-day Orlovskys, and part of what makes her so outstanding in this difficult role—as the film version of the 1987 Munich *Fledermaus* makes clear—is the panache with which she enters into "his" somewhat bibulous brand of *galanterie*. In the celebrated ball scene in act 2, for example, when the vodka-loving prince first meets the buxom chambermaid Adele (who has sneaked in disguised as an "artiste"), Fassbaender's slyly inflected delivery of his line, "Ich liebe Künstlerinnen" (I *love* artistes), conveys perfectly Orlovsky's droll, well-mannered, somewhat alcoholic sexual appreciation.

Later on, when Adele boasts in song about her "Grecian profile" and attractive figure, Fassbaender's mouth droops open salaciously, even as she continues to appraise, with politely vulpine connoisseurship, the particular features in question. Yet even more telling, a few moments later, are her scene-stealing antics when Rosalinde, the opera's heroine, arrives at the ball disguised as a Hungarian countess and proceeds to sing a wild romantic "Csárdás" about the beauties of her supposed homeland. While Rosalinde (sung here by Pamela Coburn) undulates seductively at center stage, Fassbaender-as-Orlovsky—seated on an overstuffed sofa behind her and clearly smitten with the new arrival—mimes a kind of half-tipsy sexual ecstasy: writhing in suppressed pleasure, swaying back and forth to the music, gesturing feebly in awe and wonderment. At one point during the song, which grows slowly more and more frenzied, Fassbaender actually picks up a feather boa Coburn has discarded and buries her face in it, only to slump weakly backwards after inhaling its (apparently) intoxicating scent. Seldom, one might say, has diva-worship, hetero or homo, been given a more direct—or suggestive— onstage representation.

Fassbaender's most ravishing study in gynophilic rapture undoubtedly remains, however, her Octavian—the part with which she has always been most closely identified and her undisputed masterpiece of cross-sexual characterization. Which isn't to say (as videotapes of her performances again reveal) that she underplays any of the humor in Strauss's often farcical confection. In the scenes with Baron Ochs, when Octavian is forced by his lover, the Marschallin, to masquerade as her servingmaid "Mariandel" and then has to fight off the baron's crudely pawing embraces, Fassbaender excels in the somewhat mind-boggling physical comedy involved. Commenting on the role, she has remarked that much of the pleasure she derives from it has to do precisely with these uncanny moments of double drag—when she is "a woman singer playing a man who in turn must impersonate a woman."[64] Tromping ludicrously across stage in Mariandel's bonnet and petticoats, or attempting to wriggle brusquely away from the baron, Fassbaender manages through body language alone to convey every giddying twist in Octavian's sexual charade.

In the opera's great love scenes, however—the opening dialogue with the

Marschallin, the ethereal Presentation of the Rose, the ecstatic trio and duet in act 3—Fassbaender becomes by turns tender, noble, fervent, even sublime. She has said that after performing Octavian so many times onstage—she debuted the part in 1967—she gradually reached a point "of feeling completely under his skin." [65] Certainly to judge by the noted 1979 production under Carlos Kleiber, with Gwyneth Jones as the Marschallin and Lucia Popp as Sophie, the metaphor is appropriate. In the opening scene in the Marschallin's bedroom, when Fassbaender as Octavian, disheveled from his night of passion, reaches over to kiss his still-beautiful older mistress, marveling softly how "das Ich vergeht in dem Du" (this I is lost in this you), Fassbaender's mode is passionate and uninhibited—her very body moulding itself to Jones's as they first embrace, then kiss. (Kiri Te Kanawa has described the first five minutes of this scene as "the most awkward to perform in any opera.")[66] There is none of that fleeting physical embarrassment that mars Sena Jurinac's otherwise perceptive performance in the 1962 Karajan *Rosenkavalier*: Fassbaender lets her body itself exemplify delight, even as she invests Octavian's melting *Sprechgesang* with its full measure of boyish charm and provocation.

Fig. 2.9. Fassbaender at the Metropolitan Opera as Octavian in Strauss's *Der Rosenkavalier,* 1980s. *Courtesy of Winnie Klotz, Metropolitan Opera.*

During the Presentation of the Rose at Faninal's house, where Octavian first meets and falls in love with Sophie, Fassbaender (clad in breathtaking silver-white coat and pantaloons) catches with unerring delicacy the exact moment of his transformation: as he watches Sophie breathe in the heavenly "drop of attar" in the silver rose and gives way to love-struck adoration. (While Popp's voice soars upward at the line "Wie himmlische, nicht irdische, wie Rosen" [Like roses of heaven, not of earth], Fassbaender closes her eyes, blissfully, like one overcome by some mystical vision.) In turn, when Octavian himself, lost in joyful bafflement, begins singing softly, "Wo war ich schon einmal und war so selig?" (Where and when have I been so happy?), Fassbaender leans in, as it were, to the emotion—conveying by look and gesture, as well as by her liquid, delving vocal tone, Octavian's rapture at his newfound passion.

And finally, in the concluding moments of the opera, when Octavian realizes that the Marschallin has already forgiven him for his unfaithfulness and that she wishes him well with his new love, Fassbaender captures to the fullest his astonished gratitude—modulating swiftly into tender reverence—at her goodness and generosity of spirit. Here Fassbaender is inspired: imbuing the famous line "Marie Theres, wie gut Sie ist" (Marie Theres, how good you are) with all of its turbulent layers of emotion, even as she turns toward the audience—hand softly clenched to heart—to join in on the famous trio. When, at the last, after the Marschallin has made her departure and Octavian enfolds Sophie in an embrace, Fassbaender sustains the mood of exaltation by giving Popp a ravishing soul kiss at the end of their final duet: full on the mouth, dignified yet sensual. Nor is the mood broken at the curtain call: here, as if still half in character, Fassbaender can be seen glancing over at one point at Gwyneth Jones, fixing her with a look of piercing admiration, even as she squeezes her hand in quiet triumph.

Is it wrong to celebrate such artistry? There will always be those, I suppose, who find the frank display of female-to-female adoration freakish—even when presented, as in *Der Rosenkavalier*, under the legitimating rubric of the dramaturgical. For some, the fact that Fassbaender is playing a young man in Strauss's drama will be no excuse: to see someone carry on in such a way, even in the most stylized or refined fashion, is still embarrassing and unsettling. (An elderly psychoanalyst—heterosexual—once told me, with some contempt, that she found *Der Rosenkavalier* the most infantile opera ever written.) Yet this is exactly what for me is so moving: Fassbaender's ability to give voice to her pleasure, to reveal herself onstage, without shame or self-censoring, as a *fan* of other women.

What Fassbaender provides is a sensual reminder that the love of woman for woman is not only possible but cherishable—and not only for the recipient.

Some perceptive remarks by Willa Cather spring to mind here. Writing, in 1913, in *McClure's* about the great American soprano Geraldine Farrar, Cather spoke insightfully about the crucial importance in the singer's career of her youthful "capacity to admire."

> The best thing that ever happened to Miss Farrar—and insofar as luck goes, she has been the very darling of the gods—was that her parents had courage enough to borrow money and take her abroad to study *early*, before her self-confidence became too confident. Once she got to Paris, the finest thing in her, her capacity to admire, was aroused. Her photographs, taken after a year in Paris, look like another girl. Not that she was humbled. The peculiar note of her personality is that she has never been humbled, but quickened.[67]

It was precisely Farrar's wish to pay tribute to the woman she had come to idolize (her teacher Lilli Lehmann) that made her, according to Cather, what she was: a singer of brilliance, with "an impulsive and tender sympathy with human life." Admiration, Cather affirms, is necessary for growth.[68]

Intellectuals, on the whole, are not used to thinking of the "capacity to admire" as a valuable human quality; indeed, so profound are our modern prejudices against anything smacking of enthusiasm or emotional excess, we are more likely to take such receptivity to others as a sign of moral and intellectual weakness. As I suggested at the outset, coming out as a "fan" can be an embarrassing business, especially if one wants to continue to be regarded by friends and associates as a normally functioning member of society. Being grown-up, maintaining a properly critical and self-conscious attitude toward the world—or so the ideologues teach us—requires self-control: the rooting out, the rationalization, the analyzing away of all exaggerated feeling. To "worship" someone (and especially someone as frivolous as a diva) is to be a victim of illusion and false consciousness.

Nor is it only among gloomy leftover Marxists and dour Freudians that such views hold sway: one of the enduring negative stereotypes in tabloid journalism since the late nineteenth century has been that of the "deranged fan"—the person so demented by his love for someone famous he commits an outrage either against himself or the person he reveres. Hero-worship, we are admonished, leads to mania—to violence or its threat.[69]

But it may also be possible—indeed worthwhile—to try to rehabilitate such emotion. Not that I mean to redeem fans like Mary Garden's suicidal admirer Helen Newby: as long as we live in a culture in which certain individuals are marketed as celebrities and surrounded with an aura of confounding wealth, prestige, and power, there will always be those maddened—sometimes horrifyingly—by their adoration. Yet for every diva-worshiper like Newby, one could find, I am convinced, hundreds of thousands of others, "quickened" (as Cather puts it) by their infatuations: enriched and nourished, made more happy and alive, made more conscious of who they are.

The nourishing power of admiration lies precisely in its connection with the imagination. Since the eighteenth century, opera and diva-worship—that soaring, numinous love of the woman who sings—have been inextricably linked with the gynophilic imagination. It is no accident that the burgeoning of opera in eighteenth-century Europe coincided with the rise of modern feminism—as Brigid Brophy has pointed out, both opera and feminism reflect the new Enlightenment respect for and fascination with the female voice.[70] But in the rush toward generalities, we should not ignore the powerful and inspiriting role that diva-worship has played in the lives of actual women. From Malibran to Fremstad, from Fremstad to Fassbaender, the diva has always offered special consolation to women who love and cherish their own sex. For lesbian opera fans in particular, the diva's passion is a mirror: a fluid, silvery form in which desire itself can at times be recognized. By the liberating way that *she* desires—by the bold ardor of her own "homovocal" exaltation—a singer like Fremstad or Fassbaender becomes a collective emblem: a poignant, often thrilling token of homoerotic possibility.

In relating the history of my own infatuation I have adopted, I find, a somewhat facetious tone, mainly in hopes of avoiding that "purple" quality which so often creeps into the literature of sapphic diva-worship. (To those who, nonetheless, still find my expressions of devotion tasteless, I can only say that I have tried to be as *tastefully* tasteless as possible.) And yet such defensiveness, I also realize, is perhaps misplaced. In the same way that in a perfect world no shame would ever attach itself to the desire of woman for woman, no shame attaches—or should attach itself—to the adoration inspired by a passionate female voice. If I have, however crudely, inspired a desire to hear, or hear again, the singing of Brigitte Fassbaender, I am glad: in the presence of such brave and tender artistry, there is nothing in the end to fear, and much—oh so very much—to love.

Notes

1. Brophy, *Mozart the Dramatist*, p. 40.

2. Huneker, *Bedouins*, pp. 18, 22. In *Interpreters*, invoking the "subtle fragrance" of Garden's name, Carl Van Vechten offered a similarly rhapsodic meditation: "Since Nell Gwynn no such scented cognomen, redolent of cuckoo's boots, London pride, blood-red poppies, purple fox-gloves, lemon stocks, and vermillion zinnias, has blown its delicate odour across our scene. . . . Delightful and adorable Mary Garden, the fragile Thaïs, pathetic Jean . . . unforgettable Mélisande" (92–93).

3. Brophy, *Mozart the Dramatist*, pp. 38, 43.

4. On some of the complex aesthetic, psychological, and political meanings that opera and diva-worship hold in contemporary European and American gay male culture, see Michael Bronski, *Culture Clash*; and Andrew Ross, *No Respect*. Both Bronski and Ross emphasize the culturally enfranchising power of opera: in the act of becoming fans, both argue, gay men gain access to a social world of prestige, power, and glamour. For a more diffident, and in many ways more enlightening, view, see Wayne Koestenbaum's "The Queen's Throat."

5. See Rich, "A Queer Sensation," p. 42.

6. On the youthful Cather's use of music (especially opera) to emblematize powerful feelings for her own sex, see O'Brien, *Willa Cather*, pp. 170–73. In emphasizing opera's enlivening and arousing effect on female spectators, I implicitly take issue with the rather more gloomy view espoused by Catherine Clément in her influential *L'Opéra, ou la défaite des femmes*, published in English as *Opera, or the Undoing of Women*. Far from seeing opera (as Clément does) simply as an institution devoted to the ritualized "undoing" and debasement of the feminine, I consider it a much more complex and subversive cultural phenomenon, precisely because of its power to evoke homoerotic *jouissance* in its female fans.

7. Virginia Woolf, letter to Vanessa Bell (August 16, 1909), in *The Letters of Virginia Woolf*, 1:407. Not all of Woolf's comments on opera, it must be said, are so disdainful. Though unimpressed by what she saw at Bayreuth in 1909, she became a frequent, even avid operagoer in the 1930s. Gluck and Mozart were particular favorites; Gluck's *Orfeo*, she wrote in 1933, was "the loveliest opera ever written." On June 12, 1935, she attended a Glyndebourne performance of Mozart's *The Magic Flute* in which the part of Papageno was sung by none other than Willi Domgraf-Fassbaender, the father of Brigitte Fassbaender. See *The Letters of Virginia Woolf*, 5:259, 400.

8. Esher, *The Girlhood of Victoria*, 1:93.

9. Esher, *The Girlhood of Victoria*, 1:94.

10. Esher, *The Girlhood of Victoria*, 1:111.

11. Esher, *The Girlhood of Victoria*, 1:115.

12. Holland and Rockstro, *Memoir of Jenny Lind*, 2:73.

13. Holland and Rockstro, *Memoir of Jenny Lind*, 2:153.

14. Calvé, *My Life*, pp. 95–96.

15. On the notorious "Gerry-flappers" see Sheean, *First and Last Love*, pp. 61–62; Christiansen, *Prima Donna*, pp. 192–93; and Farrar's own autobiography, *Such Sweet Compulsion*, pp. 133 and 216. Though she complains at one point about an especially "ardent" Gerry-flapper who infected her with the measles on the eve of a performance, Farrar seems to have taken on the whole a remarkably good-humored attitude toward her female fans, and often kept in touch with them for many years. On Galli-Curci and her devotees, see Le Massena, *Galli-Curci's Life of Song*, pp. 132–33.

16. Cited in Christiansen, *Prima Donna*, p. 192.

17. See Farrar, *Such Sweet Compulsion*, p. 24; and Le Massena, *Galli-Curci's Life of Song*, p. 19.

18. Christiansen, *Prima Donna*, p. 198.

19. On Lister's veneration for Catalani and her fellow Handelian, Mrs. Salmon, see *I Know My Own Heart*, pp. 300–3. After meeting Catalani at a supper party and engaging her successfully in conversation, Lister noted with satisfaction that the singer was "certainly a very handsome, elegantly mannered & fascinating woman. I stammered on in French very tolerably" (303).

20. Sand, *Correspondance de George Sand*, 1:789–90.

21. Cate, *George Sand*, p. 177.

22. Cate, *George Sand*, p. 221.

23. Cate, *George Sand*, p. 227.

24. Smyth, *Impressions That Remained*, p. 80.

25. Smyth, *Impressions That Remained*, pp. 154–55.

26. Smyth, *Impressions That Remained*, p. 156.

27. Smyth, *Impressions That Remained*, p. 197.

28. See Trefusis, *Violet to Vita*, p. 110. Like Henry James's Olive Chancellor, who in *The Bostonians* takes Verena Tarrant to *Lohengrin* in the hope that the shared experience of listening to Wagner's music will strengthen the younger woman's love for her, Trefusis used opera, like a kind of magic talisman, to keep the moody Sackville-West under her spell. In a love letter to "Dmitri" (her nickname for Vita) from 1918, one finds the following:

> My sister is playing Prince Igor—the part that is so like my Dmitri . . .
>
> I shall take you to hear "Khouantchine" which is of all music the most sensuous, the most "bariolé," the most abandoned, and the most desolate. . . . One day I shall write a book on the baleful influence music has had on my life. (78)

Elsewhere she opines to Vita, "Oh my sweet, how I miss you. How I *longed* for you at the opera" (125). Though we know a good deal about opera's aphrodisiac role in heterosexual culture (especially in literature: think of the opera scenes in Flaubert, Stendhal, Tolstoy, or Edith Wharton), a study has yet to be written on the interesting part opera plays in the mediation of homosexual and especially lesbian relations.

29. Flanner, *Darlinghissima*, p. 302.

30. On this same occasion, the ever-provocative Garden, noticing her two fans' interest in an "enormous" photograph of Oscar Wilde on her piano, told them that "if I had only been where I am to-day, I would have gone to the prison when he came out, taken him with me, re-established him before the world." There was "nothing enveloped, nothing enveloping about Mary Garden's charm," wrote Anderson; "It was tangible, unadorned, compelling." See *My Thirty Years' War*, p. 138.

31. The hapless Newby, a Bryn Mawr student and daughter of a wealthy Pennsylvania businessman, was found in the woods near her home on February 17, 1913, having shot herself in the head. Garden, who mentions the incident briefly in the autobiography she coauthored with Louis Biancolli, *Mary Garden's Story*, subsequently maintained she hadn't known about Newby's desire to meet her but would have agreed to see her had she known the state of her distress. (She nonetheless hinted to friends that she

believed Newby had wanted to kill her too, in a kind of murder-suicide.) The Newby story appears on the front page of the *New York Times* for February 18, 1913. Other accounts of the incident—some more colorful than others—can be found in the *New York Herald*, *New York Tribune*, *Chicago Daily Tribune*, *Philadelphia Inquirer*, *Philadelphia Record*, and *Harrisburg Patriot* for the same date.

32. Thus Huneker's description of Allie Wentworth, who pursues the heroine, Easter, after meeting her at her singing teacher's house:

> Allie Wentworth was a masculine creature, who affected a mannish cut of clothes. She wore her hair closely cut and sported a hooked walking stick. Her stride and bearing intrigued Easter, who had never seen that sort before. All of Wentworth's friends were of the sporting order. All smoked, and, a shocking deviation from the conventionality of that time, they drove their own motor-cars. Easter thought them rather free in their speech, and too familiar. Allie was always hugging her when alone. She drank liqueurs with her coffee and wasn't ashamed to avow the habit. She invited Easter to visit her and Madame Frida gave her consent. They are immensely wealthy, she confided to her pupil and may be of use to you some day. Allie is a crazy cat but a jolly girl.

Huneker is fairly explicit regarding the lesbian aspects of the relationship: when Easter returns from Europe with Allie, where she has become a singing sensation, she taunts a jealous male admirer with her newfound love of Gautier and Zola: "That girl helped me over some rough places in Europe. I shall never give her up, never. . . . I love sumptuous characters. That's why I love to read *Mlle. Maupin*. Also about that perverse puss Satin in *Nana*. She reminds me of Allie and her pranks—simply adorable, I tell you! Toujours fidèle." See *Painted Veils*, pp. 67 and 257. For Foster's remarks on the novel see *Sex Variant Women in Literature*, pp. 265–66 and 316.

33. Cather, *The Song of the Lark*, pp. 325–26.

34. Cather, "Three American Singers," p. 46. On the influence of Fremstad on Cather's own artistic development, see O'Brien, *Cather: The Emerging Voice*, pp. 167, 237, and 447, and Lee, *Willa Cather: Double Lives*, pp. 120–22.

35. Cushing, *The Rainbow Bridge*, pp. 13–17.

36. Cushing, *The Rainbow Bridge*, p. 4.

37. Cushing, *The Rainbow Bridge*, pp. 314–15.

38. Davenport's numerous works include biographies of Mozart and Toscanini, several novels, and a book of musical and personal reminiscences, *Too Strong for Fantasy*. Lena Geyer, Davenport maintained in the latter, was a composite figure based on real prototypes: "Anybody who knows the history of opera can name the prototypes" (216).

39. Davenport, *Of Lena Geyer*, p. 193.

40. Davenport, *Of Lena Geyer*, p. 205.

41. Davenport, *Of Lena Geyer*, p. 208.

42. Davenport, *Of Lena Geyer*, p. 237.

43. See Baker, *Our Three Selves*, pp. 33–38. "Ladye" (as Batten was known to her friends) studied music in Dresden and Bruges and had a "beautifully produced" mezzo voice. John Singer Sargent's 1897 portrait of her, in full vocal flight, is reproduced in Baker's biography.

44. See Anderson, *The Fiery Fountains*, especially pp. 3–14. In a letter to a friend after Monique Serrure's death at the age of ninety-one, Janet Flanner described Serrure's lifelong attachment to Leblanc, begun at the opera, as "a true stage love." See Flanner, *Darlinghissima*, p. 312.

45. An interesting counterpart to Western-style "sapphic" diva-worship can be found in contemporary Japanese society, in the often hysterical adulation bestowed on the actresses of the Takarazuka Revue—an all-female transvestite theater founded in 1914 in Tokyo—by their young female fans. The actresses who play exclusively male roles—the *otokoyaku*—are particularly popular and have huge fan followings. The revue since its founding has frequently come under attack from moralists and social reformers for promoting "abnormal sensations" in its mostly female audience. See Robertson, "Gender-Bending in Paradise" and "Theatrical Resistance, Theatres of Restraint."

46. The scene in question occurs near the end of the novel, when the heroine and the singer, Helena Buchan, stay overnight in the small Italian village of Strà on the mainland near Venice. See Brophy, *The King of a Rainy Country*, pp. 256–58. In its subtle exploration of the emotional ramifications of diva-worship, Brophy's brilliant and cultivated novel remains unmatched.

47. A fascinating study might be written on the role that diva-worship has played in the evolution of contemporary lesbian identity. As it is, small pieces of this history have begun to emerge. In Van Kooten Niekerk and Wijmer's *Verkeerde Vriendschap*, for example, there is a telling interview with "Tina B." (born 1912), who reminisces about the cult status of Kathleen Ferrier among Dutch lesbians in the 1940s and her own admiration for the singer:

> The first time I heard Kathleen Ferrier sing—now that we can tell all, literally all—*that* was erotic. This woman had something that sent me into ecstasy. It was not only that magnificent voice, that unique voice, but her whole being, her very essence, and the interpretation you took from her tone. I would sit there in tears, it was so absolutely pure that you felt yourself becoming warm inside. It was all there—eroticism, sexuality, charm, and admirability. (128–29)

(I am grateful here to Patricia Juliana Smith both for the original reference to Van Kooten Niekerk and Wijmer's book and for the translation from the Dutch.) Exactly why Ferrier became such a powerful lesbian icon is a subject yet to be taken up, it's worth noting, by any of the singer's mainstream biographers. Works such as Cardus's *Kathleen Ferrier* are hagiographical to the point of obfuscation, and frustratingly silent on the subject of Ferrier's own sexuality.

48. Interview with Brigitte Fassbaender, in Matheopoulos, *Diva*, p. 273.

49. Rice, "Afterword," p. 534.

50. Nowhere is the implication more flagrant, perhaps, than in Gurewitsch's lengthy denunciation of Fassbaender's *Winterreise* in the *New York Times*—"Can a Woman Do a Man's Job in Schubert's 'Winterreise?'" The answer, according to Gurewitsch, is no. So "irreducibly confessional" is the Schubert cycle, it remains intractably "unsuitable" material for a woman singer. His elaboration is at once coy and knowing:

> Oh, sure, a chanteuse in a cabaret can purr "Lili Marlene" to the soldiers. But in the usual course of things, men don't sing "Bill" or "My Man," and women pass up "Maria" and "Man of La Mancha" and "Just Like a Woman." No one needs to tell you why. . . . Except for purposes of travesty, where the lyrics call for a man rather than a woman or the other way around, what the lyrics say goes. The sexes are equal but separate, and *vive la différence*.

Along with displaying numerous vocal flaws ("savage timbres, wild wobbles, sobs fetched—heaved—from the chest") Fassbaender's version is one in which "nothing works," says Gurewitsch—not least because the singer herself fails to grasp that "'Winterreise' belongs uniquely to men, for reasons that lie not in principles but in the nature of the work."

51. Gerhardt, *Recital*; cited by Alan Blyth, in liner notes to *Winterreise*, Brigitte Fassbaender, mezzo-soprano (EMI CDC-7–49846–2).

52. Jolly, "A Timeless Journey," p. 176. In other interviews, it must be said, Fassbaender sometimes reverts to the "universalist" line, as in her comment to Barbara Hammond in "Music Makes Me Free": "I don't feel any difficulty [singing *Winterreise*]. There is loneliness, and lost love, and longing for death, and that emotional world is lived by women too. As long as a woman has the strength to sing it, then why not?" But even so one often detects an ironic note. In an interview with Ingrid and Herbert Haffner in *Opernwelt*, Fassbaender says at one point: "No doubt that a woman—at least I—can identify entirely with the *Winterreise*'s walk on the edge. Of course, I am familiar with Fischer-Dieskau's incomparable recordings; yet I am fascinated by the idea that a totally new dimension is added if the cycle is sung by a woman." What this "totally new" dimension is she doesn't specify, yet it seems unlikely that she is referring to purely vocal matters.

53. She retired Octavian, for example, in 1988. "One day," she confessed in a 1990 interview, "you wake up and find that you have had enough of those pant roles, with one diet after another in order to fit into your trousers. I want to have my spaghettis now whenever I want them." See Hammond, "Music Makes Me Free," p. 61.

54. Smyth, *Impressions That Remained*, p. 193.

55. Davenport, *Of Lena Geyer*, p. 55.

56. Brophy, *Mozart the Dramatist*, p. 37. The peculiar erotic charge associated with low female voices has often been noted, especially by opera buffs (like Brophy) of psychoanalytic bent. In a brilliantly suggestive recent book, *The Angel's Cry*, the French Lacanian psychoanalyst Michel Poizat notes that "the voices considered most erotic,

those that hold the greatest fascination for the listener, whether male or female, are voices that may be called trans-sexual—the deep voice of a woman (think of Kathleen Ferrier, or Marlene Dietrich, the 'blue angel'), the high voice in a man (the castrato, the tenor)" (105). The phenomenon can be attributed, in Poizat's view, to the complicated manner in which the voice is "inserted"—in infancy—into the network of unconscious sexual drives.

57. Gould, "Brigitte Fassbaender," p. 789.

58. Hughes, Review of *Die Fledermaus*, p. 52.

59. Which is not to say that Callas has ever lacked for lesbian admirers. Witness Janet Flanner's exuberant paean to the diva in the *New Yorker* (March 10, 1965) after hearing her sing Tosca in Paris in 1965:

> Her tragic top notes, sung *mi-voix*, as if to herself, are loudly covered by the orchestra, but the middle and lower registers are unique in their physical loveliness and in their ministrations to her genius for emotive acting—for magnificently incarnating the musical melodrama in which Sardou and Puccini perfectly met on the same desperate, passionate human level. In her duality as actress and singer, Callas has seemed doubly unrivalled. In the opening act, in the church, when, thin and agitated, she enters in full voice and in full love, one does not know which complete concentration of the senses to offer her—whether of the ears or of the eyes—so prodigious is her performance. (*Paris Journal*, 2:23)

It is my impression, however, that Callas does not function *specifically* as a lesbian icon. Her most fervent admirers have usually been men—and homosexual men in particular.

60. Lucano, Review of Schubert, *Winterreise*.

61. Part of Fassbaender's success in the role of Octavian has undoubtedly had to do with her affection for his youthful and somewhat volatile personality: she claims never to have found him "boring" (Matheopoulos, *Diva*, p. 273). By contrast, Christa Ludwig, who sang him often in the 1950s, always disliked him "because he is vapid and always uttering the stupidities of a seventeen-year-old, while all the interesting things are said by the Marschallin" (Matheopoulos, *Diva*, p. 283). Not surprisingly, Ludwig's characterization of Octavian—preserved in a famous Karajan recording from 1956—though beautifully sung, lacks almost entirely that element of enthusiastic homovocality so prominent in Fassbaender's.

62. Matheopoulos, *Diva*, p. 276.

63. Fassbaender has confessed to disliking the role of Geschwitz—but not, interestingly, out of any emotional discomfort with the part:

> Only a couple of her phrases amount to real singing. She had a bit more to do in the three-act version, but I'm not sure the "Paris" scene is worth sitting through to get to the completed "London" scene. All those characters talking endlessly about stocks and shares—interestingly it is also the only boring scene in the original Wedekind play. I'm sure Berg would have cut it drastically. You tire your

voice in the role without deriving any satisfaction from having contributed something.

See Matheopoulos, *Diva*, p. 278.

64. Matheopoulos, *Diva*, p. 273. Because of its blatantly erotic gender-bending and heady "girl games" atmosphere, *Der Rosenkavalier* has always been something of an icon in lesbian culture. In "Der Rosenkavalier," a poem in her *Collected Poems*, the lesbian poet and novelist Maureen Duffy writes of "learning" how to love an older woman by watching Octavian—

No pride shall spur me
Out of sight. I will not leave that room:
The casket cannot hold my petalled heart.
I am too old to play she loves me not.

—while in a poem of the same name, in Nestle's *The Persistent Desire*, Pam A. Parker uses the opera and its metaphors to calibrate the pleasures of a "butch" sexuality and sensibility ("embrace her, take hold the way / a woman who fucks women does"). Rather more comically, in a recent issue of the *Los Angeles Reader* (May 12, 1992), the lesbian conceptual artist Linda Montana confessed that a new performance piece—in which she sat for three days and nights on a sawhorse next to some campus horse statues at the University of Texas—was inspired by a childhood fantasy of "running away to Texas and riding a horse while listening to Richard Strauss's *Der Rosenkavalier*."

65. Matheopoulos, *Diva*, p. 273.

66. Says Te Kanawa, bluntly, on singing the Marschallin: "Once you get past these first few minutes when you are in bed with another woman, you can get on with the role." See Matheopoulos, *Diva*, p. 215.

67. Cather, "Three American Singers," p. 36.

68. Elizabeth Bowen makes a similar point in her discreetly lesbian-themed novel *The Hotel* (1928). "One has had it so ground into one," complains Bowen's young heroine, Sydney, "that admiration, any exercise of the spirit, is only valuable to its *object*, to drive her, his, somebody's mill." The fact that Sydney loves and will later be betrayed by the very person she is speaking to here, the amoral Mrs. Kerr, adds a certain ironic resonance to her remark, but the novelist's own sympathies are clearly with her. See Bowen, *The Hotel*, p. 77.

69. Not entirely without reason, of course. Even in the relatively sedate world of opera there has always been a lunatic fringe. During the balcony scene in a Chicago performance of Gounod's *Roméo et Juliette* in 1894, for example, a psychotic fan clambered onstage and aimed a pistol at the Roméo, Jean De Reszke, but was disarmed before he could fire, while Nellie Melba, the Juliet, hid behind the shutters on the balcony, screaming "Ring down the curtain! My voice is gone!" De Reszke, who never flinched, continued singing a moment later as though nothing had happened—to the cheers of the astonished crowd. See Melba, *Melodies and Memories*, p. 144; and Garden and Biancolli, *Mary Garden's Story*, pp. 20–21.

70. Brophy, *Mozart the Dramatist*, p. 37.

Works Cited

Anderson, Margaret. *The Fiery Fountains.* New York: Hermitage House, 1951.

——— *My Thirty Years' War.* New York: Covici, Friede, 1930.

Baker, Michael. *Our Three Selves: The Life of Radclyffe Hall.* New York: William Morrow, 1985.

Bowen, Elizabeth. *The Hotel.* New York: Avon, 1980.

Bronksi, Michael. *Culture Clash: The Making of Gay Male Sensibility.* Boston: South End, 1984.

Brophy, Brigid. *The King of a Rainy Country.* [1956.] London: Virago, 1990.

——— *Mozart the Dramatist.* New York: Da Capo, 1988.

Calvé, Emma. *My Life.* Trans. Rosamond Gilder. New York: D. Appleton, 1922.

Cardus, Neville, ed. *Kathleen Ferrier: A Memoir.* [1954.] London: Hamish Hamilton, 1969.

Cate, Curtis. *George Sand: A Biography.* Boston: Houghton Mifflin, 1975.

Cather, Willa. *The Song of the Lark.* New York: Bantam, 1991.

——— "Three American Singers: Louise Homer, Geraldine Farrar, Olive Fremstad." *McClure's Magazine* (December 1913), 42:33–48.

Clément, Catherine. *L'Opéra, ou la défaite des femmes.* Paris: Bernard Grasset, 1979.

Clément, Catherine. *Opera, or the Undoing of Women.* Trans. Betsy Wing. Foreword by Susan McClary. Minneapolis: University of Minnesota Press, 1988.

Christiansen, Rupert. *Prima Donna: A History.* Harmondsworth: Penguin, 1984.

Cushing, Mary Watkins. *The Rainbow Bridge.* New York: Putnam's, 1954.

Davenport, Marcia. *Of Lena Geyer.* New York: Grosset and Dunlap, 1936.

——— *Too Strong for Fantasy.* New York: Scribner's, 1962.

Duffy, Maureen. *Collected Poems: 1949–1984.* London: Hamish Hamilton, 1985.

Esher, Viscount, ed. *The Girlhood of Queen Victoria: A Selection from Her Majesty's Diaries Between the Years 1832 and 1840.* London: John Murray, 1912.

Farrar, Geraldine. *Such Sweet Compulsion.* New York: Greystone, 1938.

Flanner, Janet. *Darlinghissima: Letters to a Friend.* Ed. Natalia Danesi Murray. New York: Random House, 1985.

——— *Paris Journal: 1965–1971.* Ed. William Shawn. 2 vols. New York: Harcourt Brace Jovanovich, 1971.

Foster, Jeannette. *Sex Variant Women in Literature.* [1956.] Baltimore: Diana, 1975.

Garden, Mary, and Louis Biancolli. *Mary Garden's Story.* London: Michael Joseph, 1952.

Gerhardt, Elena. *Recital.* London: Methuen, 1953.

Gould, Susan. "Brigitte Fassbaender." *Opera* (August 1981), pp. 789–95.

Gurewitsch, Matthew. "Can a Woman Do a Man's Job in Schubert's 'Winterreise'?" *New York Times,* October 28, 1990, 2:31.

Haffner, Ingrid and Herbert. "'Man könnte Oper viel billiger machen': Gespräch mit Brigitte Fassbaender." *Opernwelt* (June 1991), 32:14–16.

Hammond, Barbara. "Music Makes Me Free: A Profile of Brigitte Fassbaender." *Classic CD* (November 1990), pp. 60–63.

Holland, Henry Scott, and W. S. Rockstro. *Memoir of Madame Jenny Lind-Goldschmidt: Her Early Art-Life and Dramatic Career, 1820–1851.* London: John Murray, 1891.

Hughes, Gwen. Review of *Die Fledermaus,* cond. André Previn (Philips 432 157–2). *Classic CD* (March 1992), p. 52.

Huneker, James. *Bedouins.* New York: Scribner's, 1926.

——— *Painted Veils.* New York: Boni and Liveright, 1920.

Jolly, James. "A Timeless Journey: James Jolly Talks to Brigitte Fassbaender About Recording 'Winterreise.'" *Gramophone* (July 1990), p. 176.

Koestenbaum, Wayne. "The Queen's Throat: (Homo)sexuality and the Art of Singing." In Diana Fuss, ed., *Inside/Out: Lesbian Theories, Gay Theories,* pp. 205–34. New York: Routledge, 1991.

Lee, Hermione. *Willa Cather: Double Lives.* New York: Pantheon, 1989.

Le Massena, C. E. *Galli-Curci's Life of Song.* New York: Paebar, 1945.

Lister, Anne. *I Know My Own Heart: The Diaries of Anne Lister (1791–1840).* Ed. Helena Whitbread. London: Virago, 1988.

Lucano, Ralph V. Review of Schubert, *Winterreise,* Brigitte Fassbaender, mezzo-soprano (EMI Angel CDC 7 49846). *Fanfare* (September-October 1990), 14:378.

Matheopoulos, Helena. *Diva: Great Sopranos and Mezzos Discuss Their Art.* London: Victor Gollancz, 1991.

Melba, Nellie. *Melodies and Memories.* London: Thornton Butterworth, 1925.

Nestle, Joan, ed. *The Persistent Desire: A Femme-Butch Reader.* Boston: Alyson, 1992.

O'Brien, Sharon. *Willa Cather: The Emerging Voice*, pp. 170–73. New York: Oxford University Press, 1987.

Poizat, Michel. *The Angel's Cry: Beyond the Pleasure Principle in Opera.* Ithaca: Cornell University Press, 1992.

Rice, Anne. "Afterword." In *Cry to Heaven.* New York: Knopf, 1982.

Rich, B. Ruby. "A Queer Sensation," *Village Voice,* p. 42. March 24, 1992.

Robertson, Jennifer. "Gender-Bending in Paradise: Doing 'Female' and 'Male' in Japan." *Genders* (July 1989), 5:50–69.

——— "Theatrical Resistance, Theatres of Restraint: The Takarazuka Revue and the 'State Theatre' Movement in Japan." *Anthropological Quarterly* (October 1991), 64:165–78.

Ross, Andrew. *No Respect: Intellectuals and Popular Culture.* New York: Routledge, 1989.

Sand, George. *Correspondance de George Sand.* Ed. Georges Lubin. 25 vols. Paris: Garnier, 1964–73.

Sheean, Vincent. *First and Last Love.* New York: Random House, 1956.

Smyth, Ethel. *Impressions That Remained.* [1919.] New York: Knopf, 1946.

Trefusis, Violet. *Violet to Vita: The Letters of Violet Trefusis to Vita Sackville-West.* Ed. Mitchell A. Leaska and John Phillips. London: Methuen, 1989.

Van Kooten Niekerk, Anja, and Sacha Wijmer. *Verkeerde Vriendschap: Lesbisch leven in de jaren 1920–1960.* Amsterdam: Feministische Uitgeverij Sara, 1985.

Van Vechten, Carl. *Interpreters.* New York: Knopf, 1920.

Woolf, Virginia. *The Letters of Virginia Woolf.* Ed. Nigel Nicolson and Joanne Trautmann. 6 vols. New York: Harcourt Brace Jovanovich, 1980.

What Are These Women Doing in Opera?

Ralph P. Locke

What are these women characters doing on the operatic stage? By this rude-sounding question I do not mean, "What right do *they* have to be there?" That right is unquestioned. Opera, from its very beginnings, has brought women characters front and center, usually played by women. (The most notable exception to this rule was the practice, in seventeenth-century Rome, of having female roles sung by castrati.) I want rather to stress the verb and the indirect object that it implies: What were those characters put there to *do* by librettist and composer? What are they made to *do* by astute interpreters of the roles, on their own or in joint effort with producers, stage directors, conductors, other singers? And what do they *do to us*—the audience—today, as we watch in the theater or on video or listen to radio or recordings?

Wide-ranging questions profit from some initial setting of limits. Women characters in opera are too diverse to permit easy generalizations. To be sure, they are, in absolute terms, by no means as numerous as men characters, since in plenty of operas the heroine is set in a predominantly male world. For example, Lucia (in *Lucia di Lammermoor*) and Elvira (in *Ernani*) are berated, consoled, and argued over by no fewer than three men of various ages and social stations. Isabella (in *L'Italiana in Algeri*), Marina (in *Boris Godunov*), Kundry (in *Parsifal*), Manon, Minnie (in *La Fanciulla del West*), Lulu, and Katrina (in *Lady Macbeth of the Mtsensk District*) are even more drastically outnumbered.

But, of the characters many of us care about and feel an emotional bond to,

I would venture that easily half, and perhaps many more than that, are female. The roles that draw devoted fans—female and male alike—back into the opera house, the ones we want to hear again and again in recordings, are, I'd guess, more often than not those of women: Ottavia and Poppea in Monteverdi's *L'Incoronazione di Poppea*, Purcell's and Berlioz's Dido, the astonishing Queen of the Night, the heartbreaking Violetta, Rossini's Rosina (and her more mature self, Mozart's Countess), Brünnhilde, Dalila, Tatiana, Mélisande, Mimì, Salome, the Marschallin.

Of course there are plenty of fascinating male characters, and what makes *them* fascinating—what, in heaven's name, *they* are doing on stage, with their spears and stentorian high Cs, their unctuous paternal solicitude (genuine or feigned), and, yes, their moments of touching vulnerability—is a question to which I'll briefly return later. But I'd like to focus this discussion primarily on opera's women characters and what they are telling us.

Victims in/of Opera

They are telling us, argues French critic Catherine Clément, that women are "undone" by society and by society's mirror, opera: "If I am touched by [the standard operas in the repertory], it is because they speak of women and their misfortune. . . . Dead women, suffering women, women who are torn. . . . These women preyed on by their womanhood, adored and hated . . . simulate a society that is all too real" (8–9).

Clément then launches a catalogue of plots, an unbroken litany of women punished for daring to desire and to act. If you're a woman in opera, she notes, it matters little whether you're costumed in a Parisian ball gown or Japanese kimono, whether you're princess, prostitute, or pure-minded peasant. You will drag your tuberculosis-wracked body around the stage till you collapse like a rag doll, or you'll go mad, or get crushed to death by the king's guards, or be strangled, or—if you can manage a little act of defiance—leap from the top of a Roman prison or stride into the immolating blaze. Even Carmen is revealed as a clear victim—a stabbing case—in this revised account, which reduces to an aside her frankly self-serving manipulation of Don José (11, 48–53).

Clément's book touches a nerve already raw. Carmen, as many viewers have probably felt at the moment of her murder, pays the ultimate penalty for having done . . . what? She enticed—yet never forced—a weak-willed man into giving up his military career for a life of crime: should the punishment for that be death in the sand? Or is "should" not the right question? Are operas like *Carmen* reflecting not what should be but what *is*? "A woman who refuses masculine yokes must pay for it with her life." (Clément states things pretty categorically, but the fact is that many men resort to physical violence, including rape and murder, when dealing with women who have rejected them, or bucked their authority, or—in the case of total strangers—have simply risked taking an evening stroll alone.)[1] Bizet, Puccini, and the rest "show a destiny and a politics" that are—at least under existing social conditions—inexorable and "inseparable" (48, 20).

Such a discouraging view of opera rests on strong evidence. Most female characters in serious opera are based—if not in every detail—on one of a small number of stereotypes of womanly behavior (some of these are evoked in figure 3.1). There is the passive innocent who, through her devoted love, either gets her man (Agathe) or dies (Liù). The woman who dares to love against the rules and ends up losing her lover, her sanity, her own life, or several of the above (Lucia, Gilda, Cio-Cio San, Aida, Senta, Isolde, Rusalka, Mélisande, Marie in *Wozzeck*). The possessive mother (Fidès, Azucena, Kostelnička in Janáček's *Jenufa*). The coquette or femme fatale (Manon, Dalila, Salome, Lulu).[2] To be sure, some complex and interesting characters in opera blend traits of several different stereotypes. Violetta, for example, is simultaneously coquette, devoted innocent, and someone who has risked loving across the boundaries of social class.[3]

Fig. 3.1. Women's roles in opera. Illustration by Jeffrey Fisher for *Opera News* magazine, "Women in Opera" issue, July 1992. *Courtesy of the Metropolitan Opera Guild and Riley Illustration.*

And Carmen, of course, is an unusually rich and internally contradictory character (in her mix of independence and fatalism), making her seem more specific, more "real," than most. Yet even she, perhaps she most vividly of all, remains an elaborated version of one primary stereotype: the dangerous woman who holds no allegiances and thus disturbs the placid world of good bourgeois wives and husbands.[4] Or should we say that she "embodies" or "reinforces" that stereotype? The metaphor, invoked earlier, of opera as "mirror" is inadequate: as Clément and others rightly stress, cultural products are also cultural practices, not merely reflecting but also shaping and intensifying the images we carry in our heads, and into our lives, of gender-appropriate behavior and the like.

The defender of opera will quickly point out, as reviewers of Clément's book did, that such a cataloging of noxious female stereotypes (or, to be kinder, archetypes) consistently neglects comic operas. Not that comic operas present a plain and simple alternative view. After all, even though the women characters in these operas don't die, or even do much lamenting, they do end up being safely redomesticated at the end, thereby (Clément might argue) celebrating society's main plot for women, the "successful marriage" plot. Still, we can't help but notice that these heroines often take matters into their own capable hands and manage to end up with a husband whom they have freely chosen rather than with one assigned to them by lord or guardian. This is indeed the primary action in *Il Barbiere di Siviglia* and *Don Pasquale*, and a similar expression of female (and, to a degree, male) resistance to patriarchal custom (i.e., le droit du seigneur) drives *Le Nozze di Figaro*.

Even in a comic opera generated by some other problem-situation, such as *La Périchole* or *Gianni Schicchi*, the female "lead" tends to be spunky, wily, sometimes outright exploitive. I should note that such adjectives, especially when applied to females, often carry a charge of disapproval or condescension. But anything less colorful—e.g., "an alert tactician"—misses the resonance of, say, an Offenbach heroine, a born survivor who also makes it fun along the way for herself, her pals, and the happily complicit audience.

The female lead in comic opera may even use her supposedly feminine traits—and men's weakness for them—to her own ends, as if taking a critical distance from the behaviors that society encourages in women. This sometimes becomes quite explicit, as for instance in *Die Fledermaus*. When both Rosalinde and her maid Adele go secretly to the ball at the Prince Orlovsky's mansion, they not only don disguises and new names (Adele borrows clothes from Rosalinde) but at crucial moments mobilize their attractiveness to men. Their aim, and it is well achieved, is to tease and reprimand, each in turn, the man who in daily life lords it over both of them—Rosalinde's husband Eisenstein—and also to gain a brief respite from the dull, confining routine that both of them suffer, in different ways, in domestic life. The masked Rosalinde, claiming to be a Hungarian countess, plays along with and then inverts to her own advantage the sexual advances of Eisenstein: in their duet, he feels the beating of her heart and counts the beats with a high-tech pocket watch of which he is inanely proud, then she seizes the watch—and the melodic advantage—and repeats his chest-touching game on him, to his growing agitation. She finally pockets the pocket watch (or, in many productions, slips it deep into the bosom of her gown); in the opera's final act she will unmask herself and return it pointedly to her embarrassed though perhaps never fully chastened husband.

Earlier in the ball scene Adele, in her waltz-rhythm aria "Mein Herr Marquis," pretends to be insulted that Eisenstein has mistaken her for his wife's maid. In the process she drives home the real point that maid and lady are indeed distinguished more by their clothes and their assigned status and duties than by any "essential" differences (as we would say today). Furthermore, Adele, like the lady she serves, makes her points both bodily—pointing out her own trim waist and elegant foot—and musically: she revels in an enticing, dismissive laugh, constructed pleasurably for the onlookers at the party (who happily join her refrain reproving the baffled Eisenstein)—and of course for the audience—as rippling coloratura and staccato high notes.

This subversive potential of comic opera goes easily unremarked, so delightful and carefree does the music sound. But maybe the messages get through in the theater all the more powerfully because our guard is down. Much the same may be said of American musical comedies: a work such as *My Fair Lady*, based on George Bernard Shaw's *Pygmalion*, today seems protofeminist for much of its length, or at the very least antimisogynist, and this despite the Broadway team's decision to depart from Shaw and bring Eliza back at the end of the show to—it is implied—become Henry Higgins's at least somewhat obedient wife. Of course, regarding comic operas and musicals generally, the reverse can equally be argued: the apparently subversive moments, since they are treated comically and since, as noted above, they are often undone in the work's final minutes, may finally serve to reinstate social norms. To some extent, it comes down to how much one wishes to let the outcome of a plot determine the reading of everything that came before.[5]

Less ambiguous is a second category of works sometimes cited in defense of opera's treatment of women: *serious* works whose heroines strive rather than wilt. Such a list might well begin with sorceress operas (most but not all from the seventeenth and eighteenth centuries), such as Handel's *Alcina* or the Armida-and-Rinaldo operas of Lully, Handel, and Gluck.[6] Things really get rolling, though, with works reflecting the turbulence of the French Revolution, notably Beethoven's *Fidelio* and the Cherubini works (notably *Lodoïska* and

Médée) that helped inspire it.[7] And examples are found thereafter in a variety of national traditions: the Joan of Arc operas of Verdi and Tchaikovsky (as well as certain other Verdi operas),[8] the *Ring* with its Valkyries, *Tosca*, Strauss's *Elektra*, and Dukas's *Ariane et Barbe-bleue*, in which the remarkable heroine liberates Bluebeard's wives (or tries, but they choose not to walk out of the castle to freedom). One might also mention operas in which women interact primarily with women and thus take an astonishing variety of dramatic and musical roles, such as Poulenc's *Les Dialogues des Carmélites*. Does it say something about what visions of woman our society tends to promote that several of the operas listed in this paragraph are performed less often than their musical and dramatic merits would suggest?[9]

Outdated(?) Tragedy, Powerful(?) Song

But an attempt to argue for the merits of comic opera and of "strong-woman" operas does not speak to the real problems many people have with the Romantic tragedies that still form perhaps the best-loved chunk of the operatic repertory. (I here extend this category back to include *Don Giovanni*, one of the earliest operas of at least partly tragic nature—though, of course, it is also in many ways an opera buffa—to have remained in the repertoire without break.) Gregory Sandow has argued that opera singers nowadays tend to give performances that are "colorless" and "blankly sung," not just because of the endemic lack of rehearsal time, or the alienating effect of singing in a foreign language, but because a work like *Lucia di Lammermoor* is too imprinted with outdated ideals and social values to engage their sympathetic involvement. The singers simply "can't figure out . . . why they should care" about "the behavior in *Lucia*" and other works "from historical periods with a way of life vastly different from our own," works shaped by "the emotional life of another age," when "people asked if they'd ever be free to love," whereas we "think we *are* free, [and] wonder what to do with our freedom" (78).[10] This, I think, underestimates the ability of performers—and, by extension, audiences—to knowingly enter the consciousness of an earlier era in order to enjoy exploring the ways that it differs from that of today.

Differs and also *resembles*. Lucia, to take Sandow's own example, is manipulated and driven crazy by the men in her life. The primary culprits, we are led to believe, are her brother and at least one male coconspirator, who prevent her letters from reaching her beloved Edgardo (because he represents the opposing political party) and his from reaching her. In addition, I would argue, some blame attaches to Edgardo himself, who has pursued Lucia from the beginning and plighted his troth to her, knowing full well the treacherous gulf that separates them and that yawns even more inexorably for a woman in Lucia's position than for a man in Edgardo's. He, after all, has the support of his family and party and is even sent on an important political mission to France.[11] Lucia has few rights, except the right to say no; she can't even control her incoming and outgoing mail, which is what leads her to say yes, in despair, to the man her brother has, for purely political and financial reasons, chosen for her. To watch men working out their various private and public agendas across the body and mind of an unempowered woman may not be pleasant, nor, to be sure, can it serve as a model of equitable gender relations. But is it so unfamiliar as to seem quaint?[12]

The agendas, I said, are being worked out across a woman's body, but that body is figured as voice. Indeed, arguments about whether operas are outdated often ignore the precise element that makes operas so strikingly different from spoken plays and novels: their music, and, more particularly, their focus on the power and impulse of the human singing voice. Beauty and flexibility of voice in opera are, I would suggest, roughly equivalent to physical beauty in literature and art. Tenor Stanford Olsen understands this: "If you have [a silken, caressing tone], suddenly Ottavio may actually be a handsome and interesting guy" (Guinther 38). True opera lovers—as opposed to habitual scoffers—don't much care if a singer conforms to some conventional standard of physical beauty or even if she or he matches a character's physical "type." *La Bohème* becomes ludicrous not if the consumptive Mimì is rotund but if she is *vocally* and *interpretively* overnourished (or, worse, undernourished).

To be sure, vocal beauty is often made the object of fetishistic worship. Lucia's coloratura-laden "Mad Scene" and the "Bell Song" from Delibes's *Lakmé* surely have much in common with the erotic European novels and canvases of their day: the audience is placed in the position of gazing admiringly, sometimes judgingly, at a woman displaying her attributes—though some operagoers fall into that mindset rather more willingly than do others.[13]

There is nevertheless something irresistibly admirable and troubling about woman's voice in opera, something that commands our attention and our deeper involvement, almost in spite of ourselves. Even—perhaps especially—in their coloratura flights, these women characters, as Paul Robinson puts it, "are rarely experienced as victims. Rather they seem subversive presences in a patriarchal culture, since they so manifestly contain the promise—or rather the threat—of women's full equality." Their "vocal assertiveness"—their ability to match and in many ways outsing men—places them on an "absolutely equal footing" in many love duets and "give[s] the lie to the notion that women are inferior creatures, destined by physiology to a lesser existence" ("It's Not Over" 3).[14] Robinson's attempt to write a narrative of resistance-to-plot-through-song is valiant, but it risks turning the female voice into a disembodied instrument (and thereby turning an opera into a string of little vocal concertos). Or worse, the female voice becomes the primary musical device by which an abhorrent tale is made more seductive and compelling. After all, audiences do not willingly ignore or take ironic distance from the words that are being sung and the actions taking place before their eyes.

Noticing the Music (and the Libretto)

To find the way out of this impasse, I feel, we need to take two steps. One is that we come to see, in these Romantic tragedies, poetic visions of human drives and qualities (whether universal or as currently constituted) and the various tensions to which they give rise, rather than trying to read them as realistic reportage (or attempts at historical veracity), much less as treatises on how human life ought to be led. (I will discuss this interpretive "step" in more detail later.)

The other step, which I would like to linger on for the next while, involves paying closer attention to the full "text" of a given opera, especially in the case of a work rich enough to have outlived the era that created it. This means noticing the music as well as crucial clues in the sung text and in the stage directions. (The last named are too often ignored or flatly contradicted by stage directors and by critics.)

One of the things we notice, when we look at the rather complex text of the standard repertoire operas, is that some of the heroines are not as spineless as we have been led to believe. Take, for example, Donna Anna in Mozart's *Don Giovanni*. Ever since E. T. A. Hoffmann, writers have speculated about how much Anna was attracted to Giovanni and may even have welcomed his advances. Hoffmann explicitly fantasized that she was roused by him to an "erotic madness": his "superhuman sensuality . . . made her powerless to resist" (32–33).[15] Peter Sellars, in the teasingly updated plot summary that he published with his video version of the opera, states (though the libretto gives no basis for it) that Anna is stricken with "strange pangs of conscience" in her first duet with her fiancé Ottavio: her father, Sellars asserts, would not have been murdered if she had not been "seeing another man," namely Giovanni. Regarding Anna's later, fuller report of the encounter to Ottavio, Sellars states unequivocally that she "airbrushes out several crucial details. . . . As her passion and rage and guilt erupt uncontrollably he senses that she has been two-timing him" (3). The conflicting passions described here by Sellars are, of course, given visible expression in the on-screen performance: this Giovanni, for one thing, does not—as Anna will later report to Ottavio (and us)—have his face hidden from her in a big (hooded?) cloak, nor is the night a dark one; we are thus given to understand that Anna knows perfectly well who her seducer/attacker is.[16]

A careful reading of Da Ponte's libretto reveals a story very different from this supposed love triangle. When we first see the Anna and Giovanni emerging from the house, she has broken loose from him and he is trying to flee before she can identify him, but she is "holding him strongly by the arm"; he continues to threaten her with physical violence ("Be quiet, and fear my wrath"), she continues to shout for help and declares herself an avenging "Fury" (example 3.1). This is, as Joseph Kerman puts it, "a woman of formidable courage, pride, purpose, and, by the way, physical strength" (113).

Mozart's music firmly seconds Da Ponte's scenario here, giving the distinct impression of a woman whose private space has been violated and who, at risk to her own life, fights off the intruder and even seeks to apprehend him ("per fermarlo," as she later puts it: to hold him fast). How far the intended rape had progressed before the two come running out of the house is left unstated and, as Wye Jamison Allanbrook notes, "it hardly . . . matters" (229). In other words, the moral issue, at least in 1787, was quite clear-cut. Da Ponte and Mozart give no hint that Anna invited or in any way responded encouragingly to Giovanni's attention, and they make indelibly clear that she did not even know who he was.

Example 3.1.

• Mozart, *Don Giovanni*, act 1, no. 1 (Introduzione). Donna Anna calls for help ("Servants!") and tries to prevent the rapist who attacked her from fleeing, until she can determine his identity. Don Giovanni hides his features, threatens her ("Be silent, and fear my wrath"), and seeks to flee from her grasp. She cries out, "Like a desperate Fury shall I pursue you." (The third character here, Giovanni's servant Leporello, voices his fear that his master's latest risky business has gone too far.)

(Allanbrook, one of the most scrupulous of modern-day "readers" of Mozart and Da Ponte, finds no evidence of any "involvement" of Anna with Giovanni, even in the scene in which Anna later gives more details about the attack to Ottavio.)[17] One wonders why stage directors and commentators in a supposedly more enlightened age continue to harp on this theme and give it ever new embellishments.[18] Is an unsolicited attack and a woman who fights back considered not interesting enough, not believable enough? By whom? Or, put another way, whose interests—in the audience and the larger society—are served by this supposed enrichment or deepening of Anna's characterization, by which she becomes possibly complicit in her own attempted rape? Indeed, one wonders why critics find it to so hard to see that rape is the issue when Leporello, risking his master's displeasure, can frankly berate him for having now twice stooped to violence: "Bravo, two brave deeds! Assault the daughter [*sforzar la figlia*] and murder the father!"

Donizetti's Lucia di Lammermoor is an even clearer case of a character whose courage and forthrightness are underappreciated. Richard Bonynge, in an influential essay, emphasizes that from the moment the curtain goes up Lucia is presented as "a pallid, frail creature, with the highly overactive imagination that so easily topples into delirium," and that Donizetti and his librettist Salvatore Cammarano were faithfully copying the Lucy of their source, *The Bride of Lammermoor*. "The whole tragedy [of Sir Walter Scott's novel] stems from the passivity of Lucy herself—not once did she exert her will to stay the impending catastrophe and inevitable doom" (Bonynge 8).[19] In fact, though, the heroine (in the opera, at least) does not yield quickly and passively to the bullying arguments and conniving protests of sympathy proffered by her brother Enrico. Quite the contrary, she puts up strong resistance, in a multisectional duet that is significantly more elaborate than the one she sang with her beloved Edgardo before they parted at the end of the previous act.[20] Indeed, *she* launches the duet, with verbally and musically forceful accusations (see example 3.2).

Lucia's part here and elsewhere demands a soprano of real heft and dramatic insight, despite posterity's attempts to transform the role into a canary turn by adding inauthentic high-lying passages in a number of scenes. After Enrico shows Lucia a forged letter "proving" that Edgardo is faithless, she is crushed by the news, yet not even then is she entirely reconciled to Enrico's plan for her to marry another. Only when browbeaten by Raimondo (the man of God who is also her brother's unwitting tool), in a crucial duet that is still sometimes omitted, does she give up the fight and accept Arturo's hand (though not without giving vent to her distress—see figure 3.2).[21]

By cutting the scene between Raimondo and Lucia and jumping right to the wedding, live performances (and numerous recordings, such as three otherwise

Fig. 3.2. Lucia (Joan Sutherland) venting her distress at marrying against her will. *Courtesy of Winnie Klotz, Metropolitan Opera.*

splendid ones featuring Maria Callas) truncate a process of emotional brutalization delineated by the librettist and composer. Whether it is *well* delineated is less clear. Raimondo's music (the duet is mostly an aria for him with some added "reaction" lines for Lucia) is, most opera lovers would agree, a little smug, even undistinguished, but how shall we "read" this? Might we be seeing here a conscious act of characterization on Donizetti's part: the chaplain as sententious blowhard? Or were the librettist and composer perhaps unable to fully imagine a character who is at once a decent principled man and a reprehensible bully sure that God is on his side? (In their defense, it should be noted that the scene was not originally part of the opera: they wrote it under great time pressure, shortly before the premiere, at the insistence of the basso singing Raimondo. But, from early on, it has been included in published scores—except the stripped-down French version—and cannot on genetic grounds alone be considered otiose.) Either way, this chunk of the opera is worth experiencing and thinking about, not least in that it gives the woman playing Lucia a chance to complete, before our pained eyes, the curve of her character's submission to patriarchal will.[22]

At something like the other end of the woman character spectrum is Carmen. She, too, is a victim, but one whose survival instinct, perceptiveness, humor, and

Example 3.2.

• Donizetti, *Lucia di Lammermoor*, act 2 duet. Lucia accuses her brother Enrico of causing her grief: "The deathly, horrid pallor that covers my face reproaches you silently for my suffering, my sorrow."

ability to think fast under pressure—all artfully constructed through Bizet's music—remain vivid in our memories after the opera and its violent death scene are done. In this regard one scene in particular has been inadequately appreciated by commentators: the Seguidilla duet near the end of act 1 (see figure 3.3). A traditional reading, repeated by Lesley A. Wright, holds that Carmen, whom Don José is leading to prison, "promises" him that she will be his lover if he will only let her go free (26).[23] Susan McClary has recently offered an exactly opposed reading, in which Carmen simply witholds assent: "He tries to force promises

from her while acquiescing in her escape. . . . She finally responds by singing once more the refrain of her song, which is as much answer as José is granted" (*Georges Bizet: Carmen* 89). I would propose instead that to Don José's insistent badgering ("Carmen, tu m'aimeras!") Carmen, a virtuoso manipulator, at once does and does not respond. She does sing "Oui," a point not noted by McClary, but the restless continuity of her stepwise melodic line over a dominant pedal (the "Oui" is voiced not on the dominant but on a chromatic passing tone away from it), combined with the reappearance of her dance music in the orchestra, makes "Oui" the first word in an extended, dreamy thought completed with her following words: "Oui. . . . Nous danserons la Séguedille": Yes, we will dance the Seguidilla (at the tavern tonight). This last is, it is true, a promise that she hadn't quite made before, but it is not the promise that José was trying to elicit.[24] José, though, seems to want to understand her "Oui" as at least possibly implying, "Yes,

Example 3.3.

• Bizet, *Carmen*, act 1, "Séguedille" duet. When Carmen lets José think she will be his lover, he unties her hands: "Carmen, will you love me?" "Yes . . . we will dance the seguidilla and drink manzanilla." "At Lillas Pastia's . . . Carmen, you promise . . . you promise!"

Fig. 3.3. Carmen (Alicia Nafé) thinking intently about how to persuade Don José (Gary Lakes) to let her out of her latest bind.
Courtesy of Winnie Klotz, Metropolitan Opera.

I will love you in return," for immediately after that "Oui" he does Carmen's bidding and unties the rope around her wrists.[25]

This spot, I hasten to add, seems to have been perfectly well understood by performers. (Despite my remarks on *Don Giovanni* and *Lucia*, I do not want to give the impression that performance traditions uniformly weaken or deform.)[26] Perhaps because Bizet has done his work so effectively, there is not, to my knowledge, a single recording of this scene (among the dozens that have been made) on which the effects that I have just described are botched. Of the many distinctive exponents of the role of Carmen, including Solange Michel, Victoria de los Angeles, Leontyne Price, Maria Callas, Julia Migenes, and (singing in German) Christa Ludwig, each grasps Bizet's strategically ambiguous reading of that "Oui . . ." and projects it to our ear, or at least plays it neutrally enough for it to make its effect on its own. Certainly none makes Carmen seem to be doing what Wright implies, namely directing that "Oui" *to* Don José. (This is clear also in several video versions that are, or were once, available commercially: Karajan's old Salzburg film with Grace Bumbry, the Francesco Rosi film with Migenes, and videos of two very different stage productions with Maria Ewing.) Each Carmen simply allows José to overhear her crucial (non-)answer. After all, as she has already twice warned him a minute or two earlier, "Je chante pour moi-même" (I am singing to myself).[27]

Not Women at All

I would go further and argue that these women characters, even in their moments of greatest "feminine" helplessness and despair, are not really women at all. Rather, they are, like their male counterparts, provisional, socially conditioned visions or models—negative or positive—of gender-appropriate behavior, models that a given member of the audience may accept at face value or selectively reinterpret.[28] Can we not then appreciate in opera's "women" a whole range of concerns that are more broadly *human* ones but that a given society could not comfortably express through (or attribute to) "men"?

My phrasing here is admittedly problematic. What we think of as universally *human* concerns are every bit as culture-bound as our categories of feminine or masculine behavior. But surely there are feelings that women and men can all experience, even if, to varying degrees, influenced by gender and other cultural factors. Lawrence Lipking lists the "strong" or "shameful" emotions that a character like Mozart's Donna Elvira traverses, including "self-loathing, infatuation, fury," and "longing." "Most of us," he points out, "know something about feeling lost and lonely. Donna Elvira speaks for those private feelings" (40, 44).

She had to, in other words, because no male character would have been permitted to. Sensitivity, vulnerability, guilt (especially about sex), "hysterical" rage, fear, affection, warmth, and personal devotion to and even dependence on another person—these are all emotional experiences and states of being that tend to be considered signs of weakness generally and, in men, are regarded as dangerous, suspicious, possibly leading to traitorous behavior, as in the cases of Radames and Samson. Hence, I posit, audiences—and the (male) composers themselves—use women characters in opera partly as a means of searching for a way to restore emotional wholeness, to find or construct the "missing pieces," that is to say, the pieces that men, especially, tend to be missing or rather cannot acknowledge having.[29] That this kind of cross-gender identification can be particularly intense or treasurable for gay men, as some recent writings suggest,[30] should not lead us to think that it is inaccessible to or even particularly unusual among other operagoers, whether female or male. As Charles Rosen reminds us in his otherwise appreciative review of Wayne Koestenbaum's *The Queen's Throat: Opera, Homosexuality, and the Mystery of Desire*, "The erotic power of music, which achieves its most obvious effects in opera . . . presents the listeners [of whatever sexual orientation] with both a momentary release from anxiety and a transient sense of ecstasy" (15).[31]

In arguing that operagoers of either sex do identify with the suffering heroines of Romantic opera, I do not mean to deny that Violetta is a woman (or at least a "woman"). Rather I wish to stress that she is not only a woman but, no less crucially for the plot and for our feelings toward her, a victim of class prejudice who is pummeled by the condescending reasoning of an individual of wealth and standing (Germont *père*), as many woman *and men* daily are. Mimì is a woman but also a *person* who has known brief happiness (in the midst of a life of hardship) and sees it vanishing before her eyes. And Carmen was thrilling to nineteenth-century audiences, surely not just because she declared herself free from social constraints on women, but because she was a free spirit in a bourgeois world where men and women were *all* warped and confined, to different degrees and in different ways, by narrow definitions of personhood, social decorum, and "healthy" expressions of sexuality. That men tended to profit from these arrangements more than women should not lead us to neglect the ways that many of them suffered or were in some way lamed by social expectations. Some men, for example, were judged "inadequate," their yearnings (sexual, aesthetic, intellectual, spiritual) considered in some way "unmanly"; other, supposedly "successful" men went through life intent on conquering or on achieving status but never developed a rich and stabilizing affective existence. The continuing popularity of Bizet's opera—seen also in the willingness of film directors to try out new versions of her story and her song—suggests that we are many of us still in need of our Carmen (McClary, *Georges Bizet: Carmen* 130–46; Tambling 25–29).

Once we accept this possibility of momentarily ignoring—though not denying—a character's gender, we may listen to Pamina pouring out her grief at losing Tamino's love and yet not need to think of her at every moment of her aria primarily as a despairing *woman*.[32] Similarly, nothing obliges us to hear Manrico's impetuous and (with the belted high Cs that tradition has added) vocally violent "Di quella pira" as a quintessentially *male* sentiment rendered in music, rather than as, say, an empowering emblem of heroism in the face of risk that men *or women* can appropriate today—and perhaps always could, at least in fantasy.[33] Local operatic conventions, often drenched in gender ideology, dictated rather thoroughly who would get assigned the songs of courage and principled determination (men, preferably a *tenore di forza*), the songs of sweet relief (women, with Nemorino's "Una furtiva lagrima" a welcome and much-loved exception), the cries of "vendetta" against an enemy family or nation (men, which is part of what makes Lady Macbeth so extraordinary), the songs of sadness and grief, the scenes of mental dislocation, the power to invoke supernatural forces, and so on.[34]

Further, it should be stressed, portrayals that may strike us today as misogynistic in their emphasis on woman's fragility or even self-destructiveness—Violetta gradually assenting to Germont's cruel common sense, Senta rapturously merging her fate with the Dutchman's, the water sprite Rusalka willingly giving up her voice in exchange for loving an earth-walking male—may have been figured as visions of personal (not just female) devotion and of a form of courage no less admirable than that of Manrico or Siegfried. Conceivably, if approached sympathetically and metaphorically (by performers and audience alike), such portrayals can be so felt even today, rather like the courageous resignation and self-abnegation that we see, sometimes only in brief flashes, in various, mostly elderly, male opera characters (King Philip, Hans Sachs, the remorseful Onegin of act 3, or Pagano, the murderer-turned-hermit in *I lombardi*).[35]

Reclaiming the Repertory (and Replacing It)

Times have changed. They no doubt need changing still. The operas in the repertory, particularly through their women characters, remind us of where we were in the old days of gender relations, and, to an extent, still are. Resistance is dramatized, through music, and so is acquiescence; both profound piety and rank cynicism are memorably reenacted, as are many other human qualities. All in all, these operas give us rich materials to rethink, oppose, creatively reclaim.

Of course, as we think about these operas, we may find ourselves longing to see onstage some more current images of women, some newly composed operas that might reflect and thus help shape our own emerging values of what it means to be a woman—or man. "Shape," I say, because (as hinted earlier) operas are not pale copies of "real" social attitudes: they are active units of cultural discourse, contributing materially to the ways we understand and respond to issues of gender, race, and social class, constructing images for us of what the individual owes to the larger community (and vice versa), and so on. Despite my lingering affection for Lucia, Carmen, and their ilk, and my increasing admiration for certain of the repertory operas as I look at them more closely, I can also see that bringing in more new works would be a welcome and much-needed shift. Opera is an expensive art, constantly on the brink of financial insolvency and dependent on the continuing passion and support of its audiences and patrons. Critical engagement with the past *and* active participation in the present may together help build a solid future for opera.[36]

In the meantime, though, we often find ourselves stuck with this wonderful if limited opera house repertoire. We might as well let ourselves have some fun with it. If we can't replace it overnight—and don't necessarily want ever to part from part of it—we can play with it by giving the canonical works various new contexts.

One relatively standard way of assigning a new context to an opera these days is literally to re-"place" it, to change its sets and costumes to those of a very different period and national or ethnic locale. We know by now that some works stand up well to such changes and even reveal aspects previously unnoted. The Peter Sellars productions of Mozart operas, set in today's South Bronx and Trump Tower, bring home the vector of social class that we can too easily ignore in traditional performances, where squires and ladies, maids and servants easily seem a matched set of Dresden china figurines, charming but decorative, distant from our own concerns.[37]

Once we admit that ethnicity and historical setting may not be absolutely fixed elements in opera, why not gender? Through the centuries, opera, in its very distance from conventional realism, has repeatedly made use of one or another version of cross-dressing. Sometimes we are asked to suspend disbelief and accept the gender signal of the clothing, as with those seventeenth-century castrati playing women or the many trouser roles for mezzos or for sopranos relatively free of warm, "womanly" vibrato—roles such as Cherubino, Isolier, Siébel, Oscar, Nicklausse, Orlovsky, Hänsel, Octavian, the Composer in Richard Strauss's *Ariadne auf Naxos*, and, in our own day, Omar in John Adams's *The Death of Klinghoffer* and Max in Oliver Knussen's *Where the Wild Things Are*.[38] Sometimes we are meant to keep both the biological and clothed gender in mind at once, as when cross-dressing is enacted before us, usually as a way of propelling the plot or adding humor: numerous characters don clothes of the opposite gender, including three of the young men just mentioned—Cherubino, Isolier, and Octavian—but also the boyfriend in Stravinsky's *Mavra*, and—two cases of females in male garb, playing not at all for laughs—the Leonoras of Beethoven's *Fidelio* and of Verdi's *Forza del Destino*.[39] With all these varieties of operatic transvestitism in our collective memories, some further unauthorized gender-bending may not be as hard for audiences—and performers—to swallow as one might at first think.[40]

After all, what we might call unauthorized gender reversals have proved very revealing in the spoken theater. In opera, oddly, it has hardly been given a try (except in performances of castrato male roles, often taken by mezzos today, or the occasional male Witch in *Hänsel und Gretel*). To some extent we are used to serious gender switching in German lieder: women sing *Dichterliebe*, for example (adjusting the keys to suit their particular range, as singers generally do when singing lieder written for other voice ranges). But women almost never sing men's arias, or men women's, even in recital.[41] Of course, in a real opera production, where voices have to blend and support—and contend with—each other and the orchestra, changing the voice types and ranges would sometimes create havoc.

But I'm not going to worry about that for the moment. Right now I'm too busy imagining myself the all-powerful director of the biggest opera house in the galaxy.

Opera House Fun (for a While)

At my opera funhouse I choose each work, cast the singers, hear and see the results, write the review, and can even move the video camera in on a particularly touching or thrilling scene. At my behest, Birgit Nilsson yanks the sword out of the tree, grabs her twin brother—his eyes twinkling with admiration—and runs off in the spring moonlight, safe from his brutish, violent wife. (I'm referring to Nilsson singing in her prime. In my world of opera great singers never age or retire.) I see Dietrich Fischer-Dieskau as a male version of the Marschallin, gazing wistfully in the mirror and bemoaning his fading charms. And, striking a blow for men's right to express emotional desolation, I give Pavarotti, as Lucio di Lammermoor, his long-denied chance to wig out (with flute obbligato), believing himself jilted by his Edgarda, Joan Sutherland.

Such switching of gender might be easiest, might seem less of a stunt, in characters that are already complex or deeply conflicted: Leontyne Price or Janet Baker as a commanding yet thoughtful Dogess of Genoa in *Simonetta Boccanegra* or Jon Vickers as a male Turandot, *principe di morte*, full of repressed anger and distorted desire.[42] Something of a trial run has already been carried out on the dance stage: in choreographer Mark Morris's *Dido and Aeneas*, danced to the music of the Purcell opera (with the singers in the pit or to the side of the stage), Dido is played by a man (Morris himself), by all reports quite movingly.[43]

But perhaps more revealing, more troubling, are my reversed versions of more sharply gender-polarized works. Teresa Stratas (Alfreda di Germont) throws her roulette winnings at Plácido Domingo's (Violetto Valéry's) feet and is chastised by the crowd (and by Germont *mère*, Marilyn Horne, in the doorway) for treating a helpless male so unkindly; the poor tenor ends up alone in his bed, coughing, sighing over a faded letter in his trembling hand, and sweetly expiring. "How about that?" I beam.

"Er, yes, how about that? . . . " I myself begin to wonder. Is the fun already beginning to fade, as when one stands just a bit too long before the distorting mirror in the more usual (amusement park) funhouse?

I persist one more time. How about a *Rigoletta* in which Alfredo Kraus, son of a court jesterwoman, lets himself get stabbed (for love of the seductive but faithless Duchess of Mantua) and stuffed into a sack that is then yanked about by his overprotective mother?

Over this *Rigoletta* I truly pause: would anybody, including myself, really want to see it?[44]

Deadly (Directorial) Sins?

"Well, what does it matter? . . ." you may begin to think with relief. "These gender benders will never happen anyway." And maybe, as I think on it more, I realize that I don't really want to see them put onstage quite as literally as I have suggested here.

Indeed, my fantasies have, I learn, recently been put to the test of reality. Excitement and dread contend in my breast as I skim one favorable newspaper review after another of a 1990 performance in Cologne of Weill's *Die Sieben Todsünden* (*Seven Deadly Sins*, 1933), in which the role of Anna I—originally written for the soprano voice of the young Lotte Lenya—was taken by a man (see figure 3.4) singing, we must assume, in some combination of falsetto and a high tenor

• Fig. 3.4. Photo, reproduced in numerous German newspapers at the time, from the 1990 production of Weill and Brecht's *Die sieben Todsünden* at Schauspiel Köln: Lucky (Ludwig) Boettger (Anna I) applies makeup, controllingly, to a passive, mannequin-stiff Katja Bellinghausen (Anna II). *Courtesy of Klaus Lefebvre, Miserony.*

(and dressed sometimes as a woman, sometimes as a man).[45] This assumption that falsetto was employed is based on reports that the singer, Lucky [Ludwig] Boettger, used the low-key version (which conductor Wilhelm Brückner-Rüggeberg made in the 1950s, after Weill's death, to suit the deepened voice of the middle-aged Lenya) and that he sang it at pitch rather than down an octave.[46] Boettger's vocal technique, as we will at least glimpse later, has some bearing on the questions of gender we have been addressing. But for present purposes I prefer to focus attention primarily on the simple fact of his gender (which was apparent, in part *through* his manner of vocal production) and to explore how such a fact—the reversal of gender in the primary singing role—might alter the way that audience members and critics "receive" the ideological message and the poetry of this accessible yet complex work and how it might either reinforce or challenge conventional conceptions of femaleness and maleness.

Brecht and Weill's basic musicodramatic conceit consists of splitting the main character, Anna, into two sisters: Anna I (played by a singer) and Anna II (played by a nonsinging dancer). Anna I is the quicker to compromise with the demands of male-dominated society, and she leads Anna II—which is to say herself—to commit one sin after another (or, more accurately, to overcome inverted sinful tendencies, e.g., "idleness in the committing of evil" and "pride in being a good person"), in order to earn money to send back to their (her) family in Louisiana. The exploitive bourgeois family, by the way, is represented in Weill's score by a rigidly patriarchal male vocal quartet (Anna's mother is played by the basso profundo). The four male voices complain that the sums the two half-Annas are sending back are meager and "nothing one can build a house with."[47] I would guess that, if Anna I is played by a man in live performances, this powerful conceit of the "Pharisaic" family (as one critic has termed it) is not extended but rather somewhat neutralized.[48] (The four family members were kept male at Cologne but—consistent with the current trend toward visually "busy" productions—were assigned additional, silent dramatic functions, such as digging graves for the two Annas at the work's conclusion. Oh, yes, the Annas died, exhausted, in the Cologne production, which, again, seems to miss the point: most of us live, not die, by our compromises.)

To be sure, casting a man in the singing role of a sometimes subjugated woman might be considered by some a welcome assault on machismo. I would be more convinced of this if Anna II were also played by a man, thus raising the question of how men as well as women sell themselves, how they, too, cooperate in their own abasement and corruption. But even this imagined, all-male version—let's call the characters Andy I and Andy II—raises a troubling question: Is a man taking from a woman one of the few paying jobs (or two: namely, singer of a female role and dancer of same) that are uniquely hers?[49]

Besides, this opera-ballet (*ballet chanté*) is in certain respects one of the few frankly feminist statements in the active repertoire. (I'm willing to admit that it is also one of the most frankly misogynistic: the Brecht-Weill irony here cuts several ways at once.) Is it not perhaps something of a backlash move—under the guise, perhaps, of a feminist reinterpretation—to cast Anna I as a man? Newspaper accounts welcomed the novelty, arguing that a man appropriately filled the role of the "dominant" or "crude" sister (Oehlen). "Lucky Boettger (Anna I) was a cadaverous Mephisto in tuxedo: the dark, evil, and, by the way, masculine side of the complete Anna [*Gesamt-Anna*]."[50] But Brecht and Weill, in their text and music, were boldly claiming for their female protagonist—the *Gesamt-Anna*, taking the two sisters together—the right to be as dominant, crude, and greedy as many men. Now stage director Torsten Fischer steps in and (to much acclaim in the press, reinforced by several striking production photos) makes Anna I a male pimp armed with a whip; this neatly restores a conventional binarism of gender roles—male victimizer and female victim—and thus blunts the subversive thrust of Brecht and Weill's arrangement.[51] The authors' subversiveness is, of course, also tied up with their anticapitalist message, which seems to have been by turns downplayed and cheapened in the Cologne production.[52]

In fairness, the (male) singer of the role of Anna I is said to have found facets in the role that resisted the imposed gender polarity, including "tender traces of 'respectability' ": he even "turns away with disgust" when, in this staging, men who are carrying money appear and lean over Anna II.[53] Such are the advantages of the gender switching that I have been proposing: the same tender traces, if a woman were singing, might not have seemed so notable, since they are more expected of a woman, and the fact that Boettger sang the role in his upper register (or indeed in falsetto) may have further contributed to the impression of some delicacy of feeling. But the disadvantages already noted, in a real production before real audiences, need also to be reckoned.

The Theater of the Imagination

Fortunately, though, opera lovers can choose not to let our attention focus on the practical ramifications of the real-world opera stage. We do not need to feel limited or distracted by whatever happens to be appearing before us, whether the casting and staging are steeped in traditional routine or have been self-consciously "rethought." We need not even, at any given moment, compel our attention to focus on the biological sex of the bodies acting out the drama, any more than on waistlines or bustlines, on innocent blond curls or prideful false mustaches (no matter who is wearing them), on the supposed ethnic and racial identity of a given character ("blacked up" skin, "slanted" eyes), or even on the gender implications of the voice ranges and types prescribed by the composer and, in most cases, responsibly carried out by opera house impresario and staff.

For, regardless of how little or how much of what I have proposed in my fun-house opera scenarios ever gets carried out on opera house stages, we can—in our heads, at least—restage operas any way we like, or in any number of changing ways. Even—and maybe especially—*as* we're watching and listening to a real, perhaps somewhat disappointing performance. And maybe that's what lots of us, perhaps without realizing it, have been doing all along.

Notes

I first aired some of the ideas in this article in a little piece (bearing the same title) in Opera News, *August 1992, pp. 34–36. The cover illustration of that issue, taking off from various phrases in that little piece, amusingly (depressingly?) catalogued some of the archetypal women's roles in opera (see figure 3.1 above). The present article was greatly strengthened by suggestions, in the intervening two years, from Philip Brett, Susan C. Cook, Robert Fink, Anselm Gerhard, Wendy Heller, Kim H. Kowalke, Susan McClary, Mario R. Mercado, James Parakilas, Richard Pearlman, Mary Ann Smart, Jürgen Thym, Gretchen Wheelock, Janet Wolff, and the editors of the present volume.*

1. "In the U.S., almost four million women are beaten by male partners every year" (Jensen, "Day in Court," p. 48).

2. The literature on these various characters is substantial. Two recent articles on Dalila, for example, are Locke, "Constructing the Oriental 'Other' " and Baruch's rich psychological study, "Forbidden Words—Enchanting Song."

3. See John, *Violetta.* This multilayering is even more true of Puccini's women characters, few of whom are, for instance, stereotypically "pure" as Verdi's women often are: see Weaver, "Puccini's Manon." Still, Rieger is no doubt right to notice that Mimì's music (especially in the act 1 love duet) is in various ways constrained and delicate, making her a *femme fragile* (a "good" women by definition was "passive/weak," Rieger stresses) and setting her in sharp contrast to Rodolfo, whose music is full of self-confidence and driving thrust ("*Und wie ich lebe?*").

4. Yet another stereotype—woman as "muse"—is found often in nineteenth-century visual art and perhaps, once one thinks about it, in certain repertory operas, too (Euridice, Pamina, Senta, Hoffmann's Antonia). See Higgonet's "Images—Appearances, Leisure, and Subsistence" and "Representations of Women" and Hadlock, "Return of the Repressed." On a variant, the "dead beloved as muse," see Bronfen, *Over Her Dead Body*, pp. 360–83.

5. Reading popular genres against the outcomes of their plots is widely accepted outside of musicology, in such fields as the Harlequin romance novel, the "weepie" film, and the Western novel. See, respectively, Radway, *Reading the Romance*, Basinger, *A Woman's View*, and Robinson, *Having It Both Ways*. An insightful review by Karla Jay

pushes Basinger's point about disregarding the usual cautionary plot (and its punitive ending) even further than Basinger herself, stressing that various types of female moviegoers, e.g., lesbians and members of racial and ethnic minorities, might respond very differently to a given film or woman character than does Basinger's somewhat homogenized (white mainstream) female spectator. "Members of minority groups acutely perceive . . . what's been left out" and also perceive, or creatively reinterpret, what is present but not stressed.

6. I stress the sorceress operas rather than "heroine" operas for the eighteenth century, because it has been questioned whether in that period "heroism" is meaningfully understood as a category transcending gender ("einen übergeschlechtlichen Gesamtbegriff"); see Hortschansky's preface ([8–9]) to the collection he edited, *Opernheld und Opernheldin*. Lühning notes that the libretti that Metastasio wrote for the nameday of Emperor Charles VI are political at the core; in contrast, those that he wrote for the Empress and for family celebrations at court often have a historical female figure, such as Semiramis, as their main character, "but she does not determine the plot" ("Metastasio's *Semiramide riconosciuta*," p. 138); rather, the plot tends to be driven by an evil figure, fateful events, or an unsolvable riddle. Even more complex and contradictory is the construction (and sometimes sarcastic undercutting) of female heroism in *seventeenth*-century opera, as Wendy Heller has revealed in several writings. See Heller, "The Queen as King" and "Women Who Lament."

7. On the operas of Cherubini and other composers of the Revolutionary period, see Locke, "Paris," pp. 32–83.

8. See Smart, "Verdi's Amazons."

9. The same is true of two later Armida operas, by Rossini and Dvořák.

10. Sandow goes on to admit that we have not transcended the "old ideas" as completely as we might like to think but doubts that those ideas are "strong enough to bring old operas alive." Perhaps his implication that the life of a young American adult is one of limitless possibilities, held back only by outdated social values (he gives no indication that the old ideas may have had some merit), was still appropriate in 1987; in 1995, as I write, in a society plagued by sexually transmitted disease and by increasing and seemingly random violence against strangers, the life of a young woman or man no longer seems so carefree, and the yearning for an unattainable freedom of affective expression and attachment may again, for better or for worse, seem not such an inexplicable construct.

11. Heilbrun rightly stresses that "Edgardo has already lost" his "property, wealth, power, dominion" before the opera begins (true: Enrico has usurped his title and estates and apparently has brought about the death of Edgardo's father—"Mi tolse il padre, il mio retaggio avito!"). But she goes on to imply that, when Edgardo is "sacrificed" in the end (i.e., when he commits suicide after hearing of Lucia's death), it is his punishment for letting "love interfere with what Othello calls his 'occupation'—his place in the male world" ("Method in Madness," p. 45). In fact, though, neither the librettist nor the composer stresses Edgardo's neglect of duty, and Enrico pointedly mentions in the first scene that, while "the star of my destiny has grown pale," Edgardo has been "raising his audacious head and laughing" at Enrico. This suggests that Edgardo has been publicly

ridiculing Enrico or threatening to kill him and reclaim Ravenswood castle—precisely what a usurped heir would have been expected to do; claiming Lucia may even be part of this revenge, not an avoidance of it.

12. Koestenbaum seems to elaborate on Sandow's point, arguing that *Lucia* is "easy to mock" but that Callas, by taking it seriously, "gave the gay fan a dissonance to match his own" and, more generally, "challenged our belief . . . that there is a difference between past and present, and that modern reality is real" (*The Queen's Throat*, p. 145). Charles Rosen both agrees and disagrees with the last phrase: the "distance between opera and modern life . . . imposes a form of alienation on the spectator," but this alienation "is inseparable from opera since its invention" ("The Ridiculous and Sublime," p. 14).

13. On voice fetishists and other operagoers, see Littlejohn, *The Ultimate Art,* pp. 66–78. On the much discussed ideas of Laura Mulvey regarding the "gaze" of the female filmgoer (how does said gazer identify with a male hero, with an emotionally subjugated female, and so on?), see Klinger, "In Retrospect," pp. 131–36, and Bergstrom and Doane, *Camera Obscura,* pp. 20–21, which is a special issue on the female film spectator. (The latter contains statements by around sixty commentators; Carol Flinn, for example, posits on p. 153 that "portions" of the "critical or interpretive position potentially available to any woman . . . in a male-dominated culture . . . are available to male viewers as well.") For an application of the concept of the male gaze to (instrumental) music, see Kramer, "Liszt." As for the immediate problem of the "gaze" (or whatever the sonic equivalent would be) of the *operagoer*, this has begun to be explored recently by such writers as Michel Poizat (*The Angel's Cry*) and—specifically on the gay "opera queen," who (as Mitchell Morris puts it) interprets works "by assuming 'feminine' subject positions" (Morris, "Reading as an Opera Queen," p. 198)—in a number of writings, including Koestenbaum's *The Queen's Throat* and Robinson's "The Opera Queen."

14. Abbate spins complex variations (primarily in regard to Strauss's *Salome*) on this theme in "Opera; or, the Envoicing of Women." See also her *Unsung Voices.* On women opera singers as models of feminine assertiveness, in the real world and in novels of Willa Cather and others, see Rutherford, "The Voice of Freedom," and Wood, "Sapphonics."

15. Conrad stresses that Hoffmann, "expert at enticing unlawful meanings from texts," was here offering an intentional, romantic misreading of Da Ponte and Mozart's more classically conceived work: "Hoffmann concentrates on Donna Anna who, seditiously reinterpreted, is Don Giovanni's spiritual bride" (Conrad, "The Libertine's Progress," p. 87). See also Rushton, *Mozart: "Don Giovanni,"* pp. 129–31 [Hoffmann's remarks]; pp. 37–38, 58–60, 83–84, 102–08, 114.

16. Furthermore, this Giovanni has slashed or deeply scratched this Anna several times across the upper chest; the fatigue that she displays (even in her attempts to break free from his grasp) may thus be "read" in several ways at once (weakness from the wounding, postcoital flaccidity, and so on), but in any case none of this can be supported by evidence in the libretto or score, both of which emphasize that at this point *she* is holding *him* fast. (Sellars's Anna admittedly does a little of that, too, in this rather confused staging.) Further on Sellars's reworkings, see Littlejohn, *The Ultimate Art,* pp. 130–55.

17. "The seeds of [Hoffmann's] fantasy are contained only in a careful ambiguity" in

Da Ponte's libretto, about "the pain, the horror of the unspeakable attempt [*attentato*]" (Allanbrook, *Rhythmic Gesture in Mozart*, p. 228). The ambiguity arises primarily from Anna's remark that she took Giovanni for Ottavio, whose (late-night) visit she was apparently expecting; so she may have opened the door to him, but that is not the same thing as inviting, much less responding to, the advances of a hooded stranger. (John Mueller notes that Ottavio's nighttime visit, even if it included sexual relations, would have been considered entirely proper, since Anna and Ottavio were betrothed ["Giselle," p. 152].) Kerman suggests that Giovanni's method "traces a sequence from play to pressure to assault" ("Reading *Don Giovanni*," p. 111), which is clearly true in Zerlina's case but surely should not be extrapolated (as Kerman perhaps inadvertently suggests) to Giovanni's masked attack on Anna under cover of night.

18. Warner suggests, in a discussion of the film *Dangerous Liaisons*, that such a simple blaming of the female victim is passé: "No one would now claim, with Ovid, that Valmont's victims were begging for it really" ("Valmont—or the Marquise Unmasked," p. 105). "No one" clearly does not include Sellars, or some of the people who have praised his productions so unstintingly. Moreover, respected and thoughtful commentators, such as Hildesheimer, continue to suspect Anna of having "enjoyed the theft of her innocence" (Hildesheimer, *Mozart,* p. 225). As McClary puts it: "Whether Mozart meant to write it in this way or not, the fact that critics have read the opera so consistently in this light is extremely chilling. For if a society takes an artifact to mean a certain thing, then it does mean just that—or at least it does so as long as that shared understanding holds sway" ("Mozart's Women," p. 3). More questionable—too casually made, and quite anachronistic—is McClary's claim that in this opera, "Giovanni alone knows truly how to manipulate notes, in contrast to the noblewomen . . . [who] are given high, treacherously difficult parts that are riddled with artifice" (ibid., p. 2). Surely Mozart and his contemporaries considered the majestic, athletic leaps (from the tradition of opera seria) in Donna Anna's "Or sai chi l'onore" as a mark of her eloquence and as evidence of the intensity of her feelings, the righteousness of her rage. That the effect can remain potent even today (for at least one outspoken feminist critic) is clear from Wolff's autobiographical essay, "Eddie Cochran, Donna Anna, and the Dark Sister."

19. Bonynge's views were influential through their wide dissemination (this recording is still considered in many ways one of the classic and most satisfying contributions to the bel canto revival); presumably his views also influenced to some degree (and/or were influenced by) Sutherland's reading of the role, which has always—as have many of her roles—emphasized sorrowfulness rather than, say, feistiness. (To be sure, though, her astounding vocal prowess and sturdy carriage often seem to work at cross-purposes to the doleful acting, as now can be seen, sometimes to puzzling effect, on her recently released videos of various operas.)

20. Of the four main sections of the typical early- to mid-nineteenth-century duet, as described by Gossett, "Gioachino Rossini," the duet with Enrico contains all four, whereas that with Edgardo contains only three, collapsing into a single movement the opening two: the tempo d'attacco (with its confrontational opposition of parallel statements for the two characters) and the second movement (the cantabile or, as it later

became known, cavatina movement). Ashbrook ("Lucia di Lammermoor") is one of the few to appreciate the richness of this number. Beverly Sills's 1970 recording—to name just one—reveals more forthright anger than Sutherland's in the tempo d'attacco under discussion, as well as a more touching and believable sense of shock and heartbreak just before the cantabile (at "Ahi! la folgore piombò") and again at the end of the third section (the tempo di mezzo), just before the cabaletta or faster concluding section (at the words "Oh ciel!"). Smart offers a plot summary that, as she expressly notes (and could note of my summary here), "reveals Lucia's [un-Scott-like] flashes of resistance" ("Silencing Lucia," p. 123).

21. Recent feminist readings of the opera have focused on the Mad Scene, later in the opera, and have suggested, with some reason, that Lucia's madness (like Carmen's refusal to run away from the abusive Don José in act 4) is a form of courageous protest. See McClary, *Feminine Endings*, pp. 80–111, and an overview of critical responses to madness in Smart, "Silencing Lucia," pp. 119–22. (Smart's article goes on to explore several ways, including structural, in which madness is figured in Donizetti's music for the Mad Scene.) Heilbrun recently and it seems independently concludes (regarding Lucia and Elektra): "Whatever the restoration of male order that results, these protagonists have, by their very madness, questioned the principles they have been trained to serve . . . [in] a world madder than they" ("Method in Madness," p. 45).

22. Ashbrook agrees: "This episode was traditionally omitted, but its importance in charting Lucia's crumbling resistance is now generally recognized" ("Lucia di Lamermoor," p. 71; "increasingly recognized" might be more accurate). It is admittedly missing (as I have already noted) from the version of the opera that Donizetti prepared for the Théâtre de la Renaissance in 1839, but, though that version incorporates a few improvements, the various extensive cuts (including this number) seem to have been made primarily to accommodate the company's limited forces and funds. For this reason, "*Lucie* cannot be regarded as a satisfactory substitute for the original Italian version" (Ashbrook, *Donizetti and His Operas*, pp. 381–82).

23. Carmen "conquers him by first hinting and then promising to become his lover."

24. She had (as Wright senses) hinted at it: "Vous arrivez au bon moment." Interestingly, though, as James Parakilas has pointed out to me, the "Vous" is still the generic second person of her song, as opposed to the more familiar "tu" of her "dialogue" with José ("Je ne te parle pas!"). This further reinforces the vagueness of the "Oui," which not only is accompanied by a return to her dance music but also by a verbal shift to a vague "nous": the "we" who will dance and drink thus seems not so much "Carmen plus *toi*" but rather "Carmen—or the persona of her song—plus the *vous* of her song." In that sense, no promise is made at all; slippery character, indeed!

25. And even he seems to realize that her answer is not quite an answer, since he keeps saying to her "You promise?" (stuck, as McClary notes, on a single pitch) as he unties the cord.

26. The whole problem of how women performers enact and enrich opera roles written for them by men deserves separate study. Many valuable observations no doubt lie scattered in studies and critical reviews of individual operas and singers (and audio

recordings of operas—see the following note). Video recordings now allow much closer analysis of interpretations than was available earlier. I was thus able to compare two very different Shirley Verrett readings of Dalila in "Constructing the Oriental 'Other'," p. 293. McClary's valuable discussion (*Georges Bizet: Carmen*, pp. 130–46) of theatrical films based, closely or freely, on *Carmen* (e.g., *Carmen Jones*) unfortunately does not discuss the several more or less faithful videos of staged productions from the Met or elsewhere. For a related study concerning the spoken theater, see Cima, *Performing Women*.

27. Whether singers *should* resist the composer's intentions, should feel free to rewrite their roles, much as stage directors in opera regularly reshape plots these days, is a topic worth discussing. Cusick expressly welcomes "resistant readings," alienated performances that distance themselves from (and thus call into question) the outdated gender ideology of a vocal work. But where (as others surely will ask Cusick) does creative interpretation end and irresponsible license begin? See Cusick, "Gender and the Cultural Work."

For an astute overview of the commercial recordings of *Carmen* (unfortunately not up-to-date enough to include Dunn, Baltsa, Norman, Migenes, or Ewing), see Milnes, "Carmen." Some of these more recent recordings are described by Gruber (*The Metropolitan Opera Guide*, pp. 48–59) and Greenfield, Layton, and March (*The Penguin Guide to Opera*, pp. 25–29).

28. I am taking off here from various recent feminist writings, including Heilbrun, Lauretis, Riley, and the female spectator issue of *Camera Obscura* edited by Bergstrom and Doane (see note 13).

29. See Seydoux, *Laisse couler,* passages of which are summarized in Littlejohn, *The Ultimate Art,* pp. 74, 168. Somewhat analogous in attitude is Donington's Jungian *Opera and Its Symbols.* For a related approach to paintings, books, photographs, and films, see Lesser, *His Other Half.*

30. See the two articles by Mitchell Morris (both of which include quotations from Terrence McNally's play *The Lisbon Traviata*), "On Gaily Reading Music" and "Reading as an Opera Queen." See also Koestenbaum, *The Queen's Throat*; an article by Rothstein ("Grand Seductions") reflecting on Koestenbaum's book, on related writings, and on the (comic, all-male) Gran Scena Opera Company; and the reviews of Koestenbaum in the following note. Further on gay responses to music—as well as on whether certain musical works (e.g., Handel's, Schubert's, Britten's) offer countervisions to societal (patriarchal) norms—see various of the articles in Brett, Wood, and Thomas, *Queering the Pitch*.

31. A similar point is developed in reviews by Hadlock ("Peering") and by Mattick. Mattick notes:

> Perhaps operatic song can embody sexuality—as pleasure, danger, social construction—for straights as well as gays. ('Straight' sex is hardly straightforward.) And why shouldn't gays find more than sexual identity in opera? Koestenbaum's Whitman finds his gay self listening to the singer's voice, but . . .

> [Whitman] also found an idea of himself as a poet and as an American of the Civil War era. (p. 508)

Alex Ross is spurred by one of Koestenbaum's rhapsodies to point out that opera's grandness of luxuriant gesture can make a listener—any listener—"want to speak out," but equally can confirm his or her "sense of anonymity" and physical or affective impoverishment ("Grand Seductions," p. 116). (Further reviews of Koestenbaum's book are discussed in Kopelson, "Tawdrily, I Adore Him.")

Adorno spoke to this same point in 1941: popular love songs and romantic movies make listeners "dare to confess to themselves what the whole order of contemporary life ordinarily forbids them to admit, namely, that they actually have no part in [such gloriously unconflicted] happiness" ("On Popular Music," p. 313).

32. This can be the case, even though only a woman could normally be given such an aria and though the aria, paradoxically, may still be particularly effective *because* Pamina is a woman. (Perhaps women will remain the more numerous and effective lamenters on stage so long as women are caused to suffer in society more than men.)

33. This is quite different from Hisama's recent proposal that the ability of "male readers [and listeners] to occupy female subject positions and vice versa" might conceivably allow operagoers (or at least readers of gender studies about opera) to develop "the ability to understand a reality that one has not actually lived" (pp. 223–24). I would argue that Hisama's "avowedly [feminist-]political" extension of Abbate's reading of *Salome* is less novel than she thinks (or else such operas would not have held the affections of women and men alike for so long). More crucially, it also ignores the possibility that—to encapsulate my argument—the experience of Tchaikovsky's Tatiana or Berg's Marie has always overlapped with (been *felt* as overlapping with) the reality of many men in the audience (and of the operas' male creators), even if to acknowledge this openly would have occasioned too much distress. Madame Bovary, in short, *was* Flaubert in some ways (as he insisted, in a famous, anxiety-raising avowal); similarly, the inner monologues of Newland Archer (in *The Age of Innocence*) must to some extent have reflected Edith Wharton's own concerns and impulses, not just (as Hisama might have it) those of certain men she knew. I would argue further that critics of the position that I am taking here should resist any temptation to dismiss it as somehow less than fully feminist, setting it in opposition to what Hisama calls "avowedly political" work, namely, work that is "rooted in the recognition of the inequity of women in relation to men and the desire to improve their status." Studies that stress the fluidity (and occasional symmetries) of reader/listener identification in *art* can, as has been shown in regard to film (see note 13), be perfectly compatible with (and strengthened by) an awareness of asymmetrical gender realities in the surrounding *society*.

34. The problem of women's association with the minor mode—and thus with sadness, madness, and much else—in Mozart operas is subtly explored by Wheelock in "Schwarze Gredel."

35. A recent study (in literature, but the argument is extendable to opera) by Aisenberg (*Ordinary Heroines*) explicitly seeks to remind us of the admirable qualities of

female heroes, distinguishing them from individualistic and elitist male heroes. Related arguments are explored by Heller, regarding Baroque opera heroines and their various types of laments ("Women Who Lament").

Gay-male opera lovers have been particularly explicit about the fluid nature of audience identification with opera characters, notably certain passionate-but-trapped women (Lucia, Violetta, Tosca). In one scene from the film *Philadelphia* (based on a script by gay screenwriter Ron Nyswanger), the central character, a gay man with AIDS, explicates Callas's recording of Maddalena's aria "La mamma morta" from Giordano's *Andrea Chénier* (and dances to it). David Denby notes that this scene, "written, directed, and played with the utmost daring and emotional commitment," helps make clear "exactly what opera means for its most passionate fans and for gays in particular. . . . [Opera] uses voice and music to clarify and heighten emotion—to produce moments of ecstatic being. . . . In this scene, a man who is dying feels rescued from despair (like Maddalena) by the power of love" ("Emotional Rescue," pp. 52–53).

Some critics, I suspect, will be uncomfortable with even a limited recuperation, for whatever purpose, of the suffering or self-denying operatic heroine. Rieger, for one, tries to neutralize any such attempt in advance: "The argument that suffering of the soul enobles and that female characters are thereby among the most nuanced and beautiful on stage is hardly consoling, considering how they are devalued and how limited their options are for living and deciding, in all of which they inevitably [go on to] serve as models for [real-life] women" ("angesichts ihrer Entwertung und der beschnittenen Lebens- und Entscheidungschancen, die Frauen als Vorbild dienen müssen"; "*Und wie ich lebe?*" p. 132). Rieger cites approvingly Sabine Schutte's rather unnuanced overview of women characters in opera: "In ihren Bemühungen gibt es kein Gelingen und kein Glück" (in their strivings there is no achievement, no happiness). Such a summary begs numerous questions, including whether "happiness"—in opera and in "real life"—should always be equated only with "achievement" (e.g., a paying job or direct involvement in politics), as if gratification could not also be found in volunteer, community, and religious work, familial interactions (caregiving, etc.), well-nurtured friendships, and other tasks and life choices traditionally assigned to women (and thus publicly devalued yet nonetheless helpful or, in some cases, essential to a well-functioning society). See Locke and Barr, *Cultivating Music in America* (introduction and chapters 1 and 10).

36. For visions of what antipatriarchal opera might be like, see the novel by Davis, *The Girl Who Trod on a Loaf*.

37. See the highly traditionalist and generally disapproving (though learnedly so) account of recent directorial impositions in Donington, *Opera and Its Symbols*. The poetic and enlivening effect of recontextualised stagings (e.g., by Jean-Pierre Ponnelle, Franco Zeffirelli, Patrice Chéreau, Nicholas Hytner, Jonathan Miller) is more appreciatively viewed in Conrad, *A Song of Love and Death*, and in Carlson's astute review of Donington's book. Miller himself gives a persuasive account of the need for altering the visible surface of an opera in order for a later age to grasp its messages, in his *Subsequent Performances*. Directors interested in doing consciously feminist work in opera might profit

from the recent and wide-ranging book on spoken theater edited by Donkin and Clement, *Upstaging Big Daddy*.

38. One might also mention a special category of reverse-trouser (skirt?) roles: the various "Nurse" characters in Baroque opera, mostly comic and mostly written to be played by men (e.g., Monteverdi's Arnalta, in *L'incoronazione di Poppea*).

39. Trouser roles are discussed in Castle's article in this volume and by Garber (*Vested Interests,* p. 192).

40. Griffiths goes so far as to claim that opera has always been "an art form disposed to trespassings across sexual boundaries" ("The Song of the Sheik"). This too-brief remark has clear merit, but only if taken as *part* of the story of gender in opera, not the whole of it. "Opera," Griffiths insists further, "has consistently found its biggest attractions in creatures—artists or characters—[who are poised] between male and female: the castrato; the dramatic soprano, who takes on masculine qualities in swerving the world to her own course; the tenor, who, alone among the big boys, is allowed, and even encouraged, to cry" (85). I doubt that most characters played by dramatic sopranos can fairly be said to swerve "the world" to their own course. Even such "strivers" as Brünnhilde and Tosca, mentioned earlier, are, in the end, sideswiped by "the world." These characters do succeed in getting audiences (and sometimes other characters) to admire their (often unsuccessful) efforts and to care about their fate, but that's not quite the same thing as getting their way. Griffiths is surely on firmer ground with the *singers* of those roles: clearly Flagstad, Welitsch, Milanov, Tebaldi, Callas, Gencer, Nilsson, Crespin, Price, Caballé, Marton, and Norman hold sway over the denizens of *their* world, the opera fans.

41. A professional guitarist has told me of a male singer who was discomfited by his suggesting that they perform Manuel de Falla's *Seven Popular Songs*, which include, among other things, a lullaby and a song about a beautiful red cloth. It is reported that the omnivorous Dietrich Fischer-Dieskau released a recording of Schumann's *Frauenliebe- und Leben* in the 1970s; if so, it quickly sank from view. More acceptable, because disguised as humor, was comedian Anna Russell's singing of bits from various leading roles of Wagner's *Ring* cycle, in her (well-informed) capsule version (on the Columbia, now Sony, label). Riding the fine line between these two approaches—between emulation or appropriation of the "real thing," on the one hand, and affectionate parody, on the other—is Michael Aspinall's falsetto recording of coloratura soprano arias (*The Surprising Soprano*, out of print but formerly on Decca/London), which gains much of its fascination and a peculiar authority from the singer's rich familiarity with traditional embellishments and other vocal devices peculiar to opera.

42. Some of the complexities of Turandot are briefly explored by Judith Tick, the soprano Rose Marie Freni, and myself in a "round-table" article put together by Marian Jacobson. See Jacobson, "Who Is Turandot?"

43. Acocella reports that "we never forget that this is a man" who is "playing what is unequivocally a woman. . . . The violation of sexual identity depersonalizes the portrait, just as masks presumably did in Attic tragedy. This, and not just Morris's size, is what

gives Dido her grand, marmoreal character" (*Mark Morris*, p. 101). To be accurate, Morris's version does not carry out a strict and total gender inversion. My current opera house fantasy would require Dido to be an unequivocal male role: an abandoned, perhaps balding *rex* rather than a tragic *regina abbandonata* played by a man with long curls and painted fingernails. Aeneas would be a woman too caught up in her work of founding the Roman empire to stay with the man who loved her so. (Morris instead gave the role to a bare-chested male dancer who "looks like a wrestler" [p. 75; see also p. 110]).

44. For that matter, do I really want to see the standard version get enacted any more? And, if I don't want to see either the Verdi/Piave version or my own, is it because I don't want to celebrate, even by inversion, men's war against women and women's sometimes willing submission to it? Or do I simply find scenarios of patriarchal (and even matriarchal, in my *Rigoletta*) victimization too painful to watch, as if not watching such things will somehow make them go away?

45. My knowledge of this production comes from newspaper clippings in the Kurt Weill Foundation archives and from further information kindly made available by the foundation's President, Kim H. Kowalke, and its former director of programs, Mario R. Mercado.

46. Interestingly, a third and even lower-pitched "version" has recently been created: the British pop singer Maryanne Faithfull, at a spring 1995 concert of the Brooklyn Philharmonic under Dennis Russell Davies, is scheduled to take Weill's own soprano version down a full octave. (Brückner-Rüggeberg's authorized "low-voice" version generally lowers things by a mere fourth.) This decision to shove the role deep into lyric-baritone range must almost inevitably lead to a chest-voice-heavy reading of Anna that emphasizes (even more than performances of the Brückner-Rüggeberg version, such as the recording by Gisela May) toughness, cynicism, and forthright sexiness at the expense of, say, hesitancy, tenderness, or vulnerability.

47. "Das geht nicht vorwärts! / Was die da schicken / Das sind keine Summen, mit denen man ein Haus baut!" (Brecht, *Die Sieben Todsünden*, p. 17). It should be noted that the general scenario may be by neither Brecht nor Weill but by one of their collaborators on the work (producer Edward James, designer Boris Kochno). For simplicity's sake, though, I will refer to the work as being by Weill and Brecht. As for the stage directions, these are entirely lacking in Weill's score; the 1959 printed libretto includes them, but, since it was published after Brecht's death, it may or may not represent his own thoughts (in his last years, much less in 1933) about how the work should be staged.

48. Anna I's commentaries are "immer wieder unterbrochen von den bald pharisäischen, bald bangen Einwürfen des Quartetts des restlichen Familienrates" (Heinrich Lindlar, jacket essay to Gisela May's recording; the performance has been rereleased on CD, but with different essays).

49. There is also a current trend for countertenors to assume certain *male* (or semimale) roles writen for women: Brian Asawa, for example, plays Baba the Turk—a bearded lady role, written for a female mezzo—in a forthcoming video of Stravinsky's

The Rake's Progress (conducted by Esa-Pekka Salonen) and, it is reported, may be tackling soon the role of Cherubino in Mozart's *Figaro*. Though the novelty will surely bring added excitement, add new layers of meaning, and make good newspaper copy, female mezzo-sopranos may be less amused at this incursion into their repertory.

50. "Lucky Boettger (Anna I) war ein aasiger Mephisto im Frack, die dunkle, böse, übrigens männliche Seite der Gesamt-Anna. (Wie man sieht, spielt [der Regisseur] Torsten Fischer auch noch mit wohlfeilen Klischees.)" Kanthak, "Am lautesten klatschte."

51. Anna I's use of the whip against Anna II (the whip had a different function in the ballet's original scenario) is mentioned in two reviews: "Lucky treibt Katja wie ein Matador mit der Peitsche den Stolz aus: runter mit dem keuschen Ballerinaröckchen, rein ins Korsett, Pin-up Pose" (Eckes, "Anna wird zum Ruhm getrieben"); "Die Frau entpuppt sich . . . als die Geopferte, die sich prostituiert, weil der Mann, Dompteur [animal trainer] mit Peitsche, es so will" (Jocks, "Feminismus-Kitsch"). The phrase "feminist kitsch" in the title of Jocks's review refers, in the review itself, not to *Die Sieben Todsünden* but to Brecht's *Fatzer*, a fragmentary work that, the reviewer felt, was given a simplistic spin, with women the social conscience and "salvation" of the world.

52. I suspect that the deaths fall into the latter category, in that they reflect a fashionable and perhaps sentimental—because insincere?—vulgar Marxism. On other recent performances of *Die Sieben Todsünden*, including Angélina Réaux's semistaged reading (minus Anna II) with the New York Philharmonic under Kurt Masur (Réaux stressed, through glances, Anna's "desperate" need of the family's approval, even in "her intermittent rebellions against their authority"), audio recordings by Doris Bierett, Brigitte Fassbaender, Ute Lemper, Julia Migenes, and Anja Silja, and the Peter Sellars film with Teresa Stratas, see the various astute reviews in the *Kurt Weill Newsletter* by Nicholas Deutsch (review of Réaux just quoted), David Hamilton, and Geoffrey Burleson.

53. "Fischer räumt den Figuren mehr Facetten ein, als die Vorlage ahnen lässt"; "zarte Spuren von 'Anständigkeit' "; "wenn sich die geldbringenden Männer über sie [Anna II] beugen, wendet er sich angewidert ab." Anna II, in similar richness, is presented as being convinced of the need to chase after money: "[Anna II] scheint gelegentlich von den Gesetzen des Gelderwerbs überzeugt zu sein" (Oehlen, "Die grobe Schwester"). Another reviewer (Jocks, "Feminismus-Kitsch"), similarly, found more richness/complexity than the gender-split layout might lead one to expect: "Doch zum Glück hat diese Travestie ambivalentere Züge."

Works Cited

Abbate, Carolyn. "Opera; or, the Envoicing of Women." In Ruth A. Solie, ed., *Musicology and Difference: Gender and Sexuality in Musical Scholarship*, pp. 225–58. Berkeley: University of California Press, 1993.

———*Unsung Voices: Opera and Musical Narrative in the Nineteenth Century*. Princeton: Princeton University Press, 1991.

Acocella, Joan. *Mark Morris*. New York: Farrar, Straus, and Giroux, 1993.

Adorno, Theodor, with George Simpson. "On Popular Music." In Simon Frith and Andrew Goodwin, eds., *On Record: Rock, Pop, and the Written Word*, pp. 301–14. New York: Pantheon, 1990.

Aisenberg, Nadya. *Ordinary Heroines: Transfoming the Male Myth*. New York: Continuum, 1994.

Albright, Daniel. Review of two recordings of Kurt Weill, *Sie Sieben Todsünden*. *Kurt Weill Newsletter* (Spring 1995), 3(1): 29–30.

Allanbrook, Wye Jamison. *Rhythmic Gesture in Mozart: "Le Nozze di Figaro" and "Don Giovanni."* Chicago: University of Chicago Press, 1983.

Ashbrook, William. *Donizetti and His Operas*. Cambridge: Cambridge University Press, 1982.

———"Lucia di Lammermoor." In Stanley Sadie, ed., *New Grove Dictionary of Opera*, 3:69–72. 4 vols. London: Macmillan, 1992.

Baruch, Elaine. "Forbidden Words—Enchanting Song: The Treatment of Delilah in Literature and Music." In Lena B. Ross, ed., *To Speak or Be Silent: The Paradox of Disobedience in the Lives of Women,* pp. 239–49. Wilmette, Ill.: Chiron, 1993.

Basinger, Jeanine. *A Woman's View: How Hollywood Spoke to Women, 1930–1960*. New York: Knopf, 1993.

Bergstrom, Janet, and Mary Anne Doane, eds. *Camera Obscura* (special issue on the spectatrix; May-September 1989), nos. 20–21.

Bonynge, Richard. "The Lucia Tradition." Donizetti, Gaetano. *Lucia di Lammermoor*, pp. 7–8. With Joan Sutherland. Cond. Richard Bonynge. London, OSA 13103, 1971.

Brecht, Bertolt. *Die Sieben Todsünden der Kleinbürger*. Frankfurt-am-Main: Suhrkamp Verlag, 1959.

Bronfen, Elizabeth. *Over Her Dead Body: Death, Femininity, and the Aesthetic*. New York: Routledge, 1992.

Burleson, Geoffrey. Review of Peter Sellars's video of Kurt Weill, *Die Sieben Todsünden*. *Kurt Weill Newsletter* (Spring 1994), 12(1):24–26.

Carlson, Marvin. Review of Donington, *Opera and Its Symbols*. *Cambridge Opera Journal* (1992), 4:81–85.

Cima, Gay Gibson. *Performing Women: Female Characters, Male Playwrights, and the Modern Stage*. Ithaca: Cornell University Press, 1994.

Clément, Catherine. *Opera, or the Undoing of Women*. Trans. Betsy Wing. Minneapolis: University of Minnesota Press, 1988.

Conrad, Peter. "The Libertine's Progress." In Jonathan Miller, ed., *Don Giovanni: Myths of Seduction and Betrayal*, pp. 81–92. New York: Schocken.

——— *A Song of Love and Death: The Meaning of Opera*. New York: Poseidon, 1987.

Cusick, Suzanne. "Gender and the Cultural Work of a Classical Music Performance." *repercussions* (Spring 1994), 3(1):77–110.

Davis, Kathryn. *The Girl Who Trod on a Loaf*. New York: Knopf, 1993.

De Lauretis. *Alice Doesn't: Feminism, Semiotics, Cinema*. Bloomington: Indiana University Press, 1984.

Denby, David. "Emotional Rescue." *New York*, January 3, 1994, pp. 52–53.

Deutsch, Nicholas. Review of New York Philharmonic performance of Kurt Weill, *Die Sieben Todsünden. Kurt Weill Newsletter* (Spring 1994), 12(1):21.

Donington, Robert. *Opera and Its Symbols: The Unity of Words, Music, and Staging*. New Haven: Yale University Press, 1990.

Donkin, Ellen, and Susan Clement, eds. *Upstaging Big Daddy: Directing Theater as If Gender and Race Matter*. Ann Arbor: University of Michigan Press, 1993.

Dunn, Leslie C., and Nancy A. Jones, eds., *Embodied Voices: Representing Female Vocality in Western Culture*. Cambridge: Cambridge University Press, 1994.

Eckes, Birgit. "Anna wird zum Ruhm getrieben: Brecht-Premiere 'Die sieben Todsünden.' " *Kolnische Rundschau*. September 18, 1990. Unpaginated clipping in the Kurt Weill Foundation, New York.

Garber, Marjorie. *Vested Interests: Cross-Dressing and Cultural Anxiety*. New York: Routledge, 1992.

Gossett, Philip. "Gioachino Rossini." In Stanley Sadie, ed., *New Grove Dictionary of Music and Musicians*. 20 vols. London: Macmillan, 1980.

Greenfield, Edward, Robert Layton, and Ivan March, eds. *The Penguin Guide to Opera on Compact Disc*. London: Penguin, 1993.

Griffiths, Paul. "The Song of the Sheik." *New Yorker*, January 31, 1994, pp. 83–85.

Gruber, Paul, ed. *The Metropolitan Opera Guide to Recorded Opera*. New York: Norton, 1993.

Guinther, Louise T. "I'll Take Romance: Stanford Olsen Seduces Audiences with His Refined Style." *Opera News* (March 4, 1995), 59(12):36–39.

Hadlock, Heather. "Peering into the Queen's Throat." *Cambridge Opera Journal* (1993), 5:265–75.

——— "Return of the Repressed: The Prima Donna from Hoffmann's *Tales* to Offenbach's *Contes*." *Cambridge Opera Journal* (1994), 6:221–43.

Hamilton, David. Review of three recordings of Weill, *Die Sieben Todsünden*. *Kurt Weill Newsletter* (Spring 1994), 12(1):23–24.

Heilbrun, Carolyn. "Method in Madness: Why Lucia and Elektra Must Sacrifice Their Sanity to Preserve the Male Order." *Opera News*, January 22, 1994, pp. 18–19, 45.

Heller, Wendy. "Heroism and Allure: Women in the Opera of Seventeenth-Century Venice." Dissertation-in-progress, Brandeis University.

———"The Queen as King: Refashioning Semiramide for *Seicento* Venice." *Cambridge Opera Journal* (1993), 5:93–114.

———"Women Who Lament and Women Who Don't: Singing in and Outside the Convention in Seicento Opera." Paper delivered at the Feminist Theory and Music II: Continuing the Dialogue Conference. Rochester, N.Y.: Eastman School of Music. June 1993.

Higgonet, Anne. "Images—Appearances, Leisure, and Subsistence" and "Representations of Women." In Genevieve Fraisse and Michelle Perrot, eds., *A History of Women in the West*, 4:247–305, 306–18. 5 vols. Cambridge: Belknap Press, 1993.

Hildesheimer, Wolfgang. *Mozart*. Trans. Marion Faber. New York: Farrar, Straus, and Giroux, 1982.

Hisama, Ellie M. Review of Solie, *Musicology and Difference. Journal of Musicology* (1994), vol. 12.

Hoffmann, E. T. A. "A Tale of Don Juan." In Jacques Barzun, ed., *The Pleasures of Music.* New York: Viking, 1960. Reprinted in Julian Rushton, ed., *Mozart: "Don Giovanni,"* pp. 129–31. Cambridge: Cambridge University Press, 1981.

Hortschansky, Klaus, ed. *Opernheld und Opernheldin im 18. Jahrhundert: Aspekte der Librettoforschung: Ein Tagungsbericht.* Hamburg: Verlag der Musikalienhandlung Karl Dieter Wagner, 1991.

Jacobson, Marion S. "Who Is Turandot?" *Atlanta Opera 1994*, pp. 54–60. Atlanta: Atlanta Opera, 1994.

Jay, Claire. "Contextualizing Lulu: A Woman's Place in a Man's Opera." Unpublished paper.

Jay, Karla. "Never Mind the Ending." *New York Times Book Review*, September 19, 1993, p. 12.

Jensen, Rita Henley. "Day in Court." *Ms.* (special issue on domestic violence; September-October 1994), pp. 48–49.

Jocks, Heinz-Norbert. "Feminismus-Kitsch, manngemäss: Bertolt Brecht in Köln: 'Fatzer' und 'Die Sieben Todsünden.'" *WZ Westdeutsche Zeitung, Dusseldorfer Nachrichten.* September 19, 1990. Unpaginated clipping in the Kurt Weill Foundation, New York.

John, Nicholas, ed. *Violetta and Her Sisters—"The Lady of the Camellias": Responses to the Myth.* London: Faber and Faber, 1993.

Kanthak, Dietmar. "Am lautesten klatschte der Minister aus Bonn: Vier Premieren im Kölner Schauspiel." *General-Anzeiger für Bonn*, September 18, 1990. Unpaginated clipping in the Kurt Weill Foundation, New York.

Keathley, Elizabeth. "Re-Visioning Musical Modernism: Woman as Agent and Sign in Fin-de-Siècle Vienna." Ph.D. diss. in progress, State University of New York, Stony Brook.

Kerman, Joseph. "Reading *Don Giovanni*." In Jonathan Miller, ed., *Don Giovanni: Myths of Seduction and Betrayal?* New York: Schocken, 1990. Reprinted in Kerman, *Write All These Down: Essays on Music*, pp. 307–21. Berkeley: University of California Press, 1994.

Klinger, Barbara. "In Retrospect: Film Studies Today." *Yale Journal of Criticism* (1988), 2:131–36.

Koestenbaum, Wayne. *The Queen's Throat: Opera, Homosexuality, and the Mystery of Desire.* New York: Poseidon, 1993.

Kopelson, Kevin. "Tawdrily, I Adore Him." *Nineteenth-Century Music* (1993–1994), 17:274–85.

Kramer, Lawrence. "Liszt, Goethe, and the Discourse of Gender." In *Music as Cultural Practice, 1800–1900,* pp. 102–34. Berkeley: University of California Press, 1990.

Leicester, H. Marshall, Jr. "Discourse and the Film Text: Four Readings of *Carmen*." *Cambridge Opera Journal* (1994), 6:245–82.

Lesser, Wendy. *His Other Half: Men Looking at Women Through Art*. Cambridge: Harvard University Press, 1991.

Levin, David J., ed. *Opera Through Other Eyes*. Stanford: Stanford University Press, 1994.

Lindlar, Heinrich. Liner notes. Kurt Weill, *Die Sieben Todsünden*. With Gisela May. Deutsche Grammophon LP 139 308, 1967.

Lipking, Lawrence. "Donna Abbandonata." In Jonathan Miller, ed., *Don Giovanni: Myths of Seduction and Betrayal*, pp. 36–47. New York: Schocken, 1990.

Littlejohn, David. *The Ultimate Art: Essays Around and About Opera*. Berkeley: University of California Press, 1992.

Locke, Ralph. "Constructing the Oriental 'Other': Saint-Saens's *Samson et Dalila*." *Cambridge Opera Journal* (1991), 3:261–302.

———"Paris: Centre of Intellectual Ferment [1789–1852]." In Alexander Ringer, ed., *Music and Society: The Early Romantic Era, Between Revolutions: 1789 and 1848*, pp. 32–83. Englewood Cliffs: Prentice-Hall, 1991.

Locke, Ralph, and Cyrilla Barr, eds. *Cultivating Music in America: Women Patrons and Activists Since 1860*. Berkeley: University of California Press, forthcoming.

Lühning, Helga. "Metastasios *Semiramide riconosciuta*: die verkleidete Opera seria." In Klaus Hortschansky, ed., *Opernheld und Opernheldin im 18. Jahrhundert: Aspekte der Librettoforschung: Ein Tagungsbericht*, pp. 131–38. Hamburg: Verlag der Musikalienhandlung Karl Dieter Wagner, 1991.

McClary, Susan. *Feminine Endings: Music, Gender, and Sexuality*. Minneapolis: University of Minnesota Press, 1991.

Mc. Clary, Susan, ed. *Georges Bizet: Carmen*. Cambridge: Cambridge University Press, 1992.

———"Mozart's Women." *Hurricane Alice: A Feminist Review* (1986), 3(3):1–4.

Mattick, Paul, Jr. Review of Koestenbaum, *The Queen's Throat*. *Nation*, November 1, 1993, 504–8.

Miller, Jonathan. *Subsequent Performances*. New York: Viking Books, 1986.

Miller, Jonathan, ed. *Don Giovanni: Myths of Seduction and Betrayal*. New York: Schocken, 1990.

Milnes, Rodney. "Carmen." In Alan Blyth, ed., *Opera on Record*, pp. 461–80. London: Hutchinson, 1979.

Morris, Mitchell. "On Gaily Reading Music." *repercussions* (1992–93), 1(1):48–64.

———"Reading as an Opera Queen." In Ruth A. Solie, ed., *Musicology and Difference: Gender and Sexuality in Musical Scholarship*, pp. 184–200. Berkeley: University of California Press, 1993.

Mozart, Wolfgang Amadeus. *Don Giovanni*. Dir. Peter Sellars. London 071 511–1, 1991.

Mueller, John. "Is Giselle a Virgin?" *Dance Chronicle: Studies in Dance and the Related Arts* (1981), 4:151–54.

Oehlen, Martin. "Die grobe Schwester spielt ein Mann." *Kölner Stadt-Anzeiger*, September 18, 1990. Unpaginated clipping in the Kurt Weill Foundation, New York.

Parakilas, James. "The Afterlife of *Don Giovanni*: Turning Production History into Criticism," Journal of Musicology (1990), 8:251–65.

Poizat, Michel. *The Angel's Cry: Beyond the Pleasure Principle in Opera*. Trans. Arthur Denner. Ithaca: Cornell University Press, 1992.

Radway, Janice A. *Reading the Romance: Women, Patriarchy, and Popular Literature*. Chapel Hill: University of North Carolina Press, 1984.

Rieger, Eva. "*Und wie ich lebe? Ich lebe.* Sexismus in der Musik des 19. Jahrhunderts am Beispiel von Puccinis *La Bohème*." In Hanns-Werner Heister, Karin Heister-Grech, and Gerhard Scheit, eds., *Zwischen Aufklärung und Kulturindustrie: Festschrift für Georg Knepler zum 85. Geburtstag*, 2:121–35. 2 vols. Hamburg: Von Bockel, 1993.

Riley, Denise. *Am I That Name?: Feminism and the Category of "Women" in History*. Minneapolis: University of Minnesota Press, 1988.

Robinson, Forrest G. *Having It Both Ways: Self-Subversion in Western Popular Classics*. Albuquerque: University of New Mexico Press, 1993.

Robinson, Paul. "It's Not Over Till the Soprano Dies." *New York Times Book Review*. January 1, 1989, p. 3.

——— "The Opera Queen: A Voice from the Closet." *Cambridge Opera Journal* (1994), 6:283–91.

Rosen, Charles. "The Ridiculous and Sublime." *New York Review of Books*. April 22, 1993, pp. 10–15.

Ross, Alex. "Grand Seductions." *New Yorker*, April 12, 1993, pp. 115–20.

Rothstein, Edward. "Doting on Divas: Private Jokes, Open Secrets." *New York Times*. March 28, 1993, pp. H25, 28.

Rushton, Julian, ed. *Mozart: "Don Giovanni."* Cambridge: Cambridge University Press, 1981.

Rutherford, Susan. "The Voice of Freedom: Images of the Prima Donna." In Vivien Gardner and Susan Rutherford, eds., *The New Woman and Her Sisters: Feminism and the Theater, 1850–1914*, pp. 96–114. Ann Arbor: University of Michigan Press, 1992.

Sandow, Gregory. "Roll Over Opera: Open Letter to Will Crutchfield." *Village Voice*, June 16, 1987, p. 78.

Seydoux, Hélène. *Laisse couler mes larmes: L'Opéra, les compositeurs, et la féminité*. Paris: Ramsay, 1984.

Smart, Mary Ann. "Silencing Lucia." *Cambridge Opera Journal* (1992), 4:119–41.

——— "Verdi's Amazons." Paper presented at the Annual Meeting of the American Musicological Society. Minneapolis, November 1994.

Solie, Ruth A., ed. *Musicology and Difference: Gender and Sexuality in Musical Scholarship*. Berkeley: University of California Press, 1993.

Tambling, Jeremy. *Opera, Ideology, and Film*. Manchester: Manchester University Press, 1987.

Warner, Marina. "Valmont—or the Marquise Unmasked." In Jonathan Miller, ed., *Don Giovanni: Myths of Seduction and Betrayal*, pp. 93–107. New York: Schocken, 1990.

Weaver, William. "Puccini's Manon and His Other Heroines." In William Weaver and Simonetta Puccini, eds., *The Puccini Companion*, pp. 111–21. New York: Norton, 1994.

Weill, Kurt. *Die Sieben Todsünden*. Piano-vocal score by Wilhelm Brückner-Rüggeberg. Mainz: B. Schotts Söhne, ca. 1962.

Wheelock, Gretchen. "Schwarze Gredel: Mozart and the Engendered Minor Mode." In Ruth A. Solie, ed., *Musicology and Difference: Gender and Sexuality in Musical Scholarship,* pp. 201–21. Berkeley: University of California Press, 1993.

Wolff, Janet. "Eddie Cochran, Donna Anna, and the Dark Sister: Personal Experience and Cultural History." In *Resident Alien: Feminist Cultural Criticism,* pp. 23–41. New Haven: Yale University Press, 1995.

Wood, Elizabeth. "Sapphonics." In Philip Brett, Elizabeth Wood, and Gary C. Thomas, eds., *Queering the Pitch: The New Gay and Lesbian Musicology*, pp. 27–66. New York: Routledge, 1993.

Wright, Lesley A. "A Musical Commentary." In Nicholas John, ed., *"Carmen": Georges Bizet*. London: John Calder, 1982.

I Am an Opera: Identifying with Henry Purcell's *Dido and Aeneas*

Judith A. Peraino

Can a person identify with an opera? Not just the hero, heroine, or a secondary character, but *the opera*, with its particular situation in the scholarship, its performance and reception history, its dramaturgy, its presentation of the characters?

Henry Purcell's late seventeenth-century "miniature" opera *Dido and Aeneas* has not enjoyed the most reverent treatment at the hands of male musicologists. Indeed, prominent scholars in this field, while admitting the opera into the canon of European masterpieces, have also consistently expressed discomfort with the opera's vague history and the ambiguous or unusual elements in the plot.

The position of Purcell's opera within the present constructs of music history compares to the position of my own perceptions and experiences as a lesbian within mainstream musicology. I have, in fact, come to identify with the opera itself—as a rebellious and queer participant in an entrenched outline of history and culture. This essay sets up an analogy between traditional musicology's discussion of *Dido and Aeneas* as an "outsider" and my own outsider's subject-position as a lesbian musicologist.

My argument, or, rather, my highly subjective exegesis, follows in three parts. In part 1 I introduce the reader to the discomforts of prominent male musicologists in reaction to the opera's seemingly exceptional origin and performance history, and how these discomforts are, in turn, the source of my personal/professional identification with the opera. In part 2 I examine aspects of the dramaturgy considered flaws by these same musicologists. I will offer a "rebellious" reading of *Dido and Aeneas* showing how the very ambiguities and flaws that trouble male musicologists provide access for present-day lesbian audiences by inviting cathartic identification with either Dido or the Sorceress.

With the first two parts I hope to present a marriage of the personal and professional. The lack of concern for historical propriety in my interpretation of *Dido and Aeneas* is offered as an exceptional reading within musicology, just as the opera is itself seen as exceptional within music history. In the third part of this essay I wed the present with the past by addressing the psychological impact *Dido and Aeneas* must have had for the adolescent girls taking part in the 1689 performance. Drawing on the notion of melodrama and "body genres" developed by film critic Linda Williams and using the notions of cathartic identification and vicarious pleasure presented in part 2, I will project backward (using my lesbian hindsight) in order to reconfigure history from the perspective of the margins.

My experience as a lesbian has no doubt created a sensibility that counsels my taste in music and scholarly pursuits. The marginal, the miniature, the exceptional, and the ambiguous attract my attention, and I seem to resonate naturally to musical compositions that somehow embody these attributes. Henry Purcell's 1689 opera *Dido and Aeneas* is such a composition. Within the established discourse of music history and criticism, *Dido and Aeneas* can be likened to a tragic hero or a rebel who challenges social norms (i.e., scholarly canons and accepted constructs of history).

Before delving into musicology and its discontents with *Dido*, I shall provide a synopsis of the plot and present the few historical "facts" concerning the opera's conception. Purcell's librettist, Nahum Tate, followed only the broad outline of the original story found in book 4 of Virgil's *Aeneid*, leaving many details up to the audience and their presumed familiarity with the classical source, or simply to their imagination. Act 1 takes place at the palace of Dido in Carthage.[1] Belinda, her lady-in-waiting, and a chorus of courtiers attempt to cheer up brooding Queen Dido. Although the cause of her grief is unspecified—indeed, kept secret by Dido—Belinda assumes that Dido suffers from her love of Aeneas. Aeneas and the Trojans have come to Carthage after a series of misfortunes in their attempt to fulfill a God-given mandate to refound Troy. Dido's court urges her to marry Aeneas. Aeneas himself appears, and Dido acquiesces to be his bride. The betrothed then go on a hunting expedition.

Meanwhile, in act 2, a Sorceress and her coven of witches plot to ruin Dido by sending a spurious divine messenger to Aeneas, commanding him to leave Carthage. The witches conjure a storm that scatters the hunting party and leaves

Aeneas alone with an apparition of Mercury. Aeneas agrees to the false command with a heavy heart and the witches rejoice.

Act 3 opens with a chorus of Trojan sailors happily making preparations to ship out, followed by a triumphal celebration by the Sorceress and her coven. These two scenes of merrymaking provide a sharp contrast to the final confrontation between Dido and Aeneas. In an efficient and effective telescoping of the story, the opera dispenses with a more predictable scene of Aeneas breaking the news to Dido, jumping instead to the emotional aftermath of the news and an explosive "last goodbye." Dido expresses her despair and outrage at being left, while Aeneas attempts to appease her with a sudden decision to stay. But, for Dido, his crime of abandonment has already been committed, and she shuns him. In a final lament Dido welcomes death as an end to her misery.

Purcell's opera has survived the centuries in a precarious state. Only three records of the opera survive from before 1800, and only one of these contains music. All three sources are far removed from the hands of Purcell and Tate and are shrouded in layers of controversial interpretation. Thus, like the "hidden history" of gays and lesbians, the opera's inspiration, conception, and conditions of its premier performance must be reconstructed from sketchy evidence. When investigating "hidden histories" it is important to keep in mind a distinction between the unattainable "true" history, the "(re)constructed" history, and the history of that (re)construction. What is propagated and received as true history often masks a tangled lineage of convenient arguments and hidden agendas.

The earliest surviving record of the opera is an undated libretto that introduces the work as

> a Opera Perform'd at Mr. Josias Priest's Boarding-School at Chelsey. By Young Gentlewomen. The Words Made by Mr. Nat. Tate. The Musick Composed by Mr. Henry Purcell.

This source has enjoyed the mythic position of "authority" as the libretto for the first performance of the opera—a claim first made by musicologists in the early part of this century. The libretto has been dated 1689, based on Thomas Durfey's spoken epilogue, which refers to political events of that year, and was published the following year in 1690.[2] Indeed, no earlier record of the opera has survived. Musicologists, in their obsession for objective, quantifiable truths and tidy histories, have until recently equated the "earliest" with the "first." In the case of *Dido and Aeneas*, this equation has resulted in considerable discomfort.[3]

The earliest source for the opera's music dates circa 1775—nearly one hundred years removed from the "authoritative" libretto. To complicate matters, the eighteenth-century musical score shows discrepancies with the seventeenth-century libretto regarding text assignment and the parsing of the scenes into acts. However, the authority of this musical score has been argued and upheld on the basis of what amounts to a curiosity. For some reason, the copier of this manuscript used an antiquated style of musical notation, originally used in the late seventeenth century at the time of the "authoritative" libretto.

Could this be a coincidence, or a "true" link with some lost copy of the music contemporaneous with Purcell himself ? Of course, musicologists prefer the latter interpretation.[4] Nevertheless, in their Frankensteinian efforts to unite the authoritative music with the authoritative text, musicologists have turned to a 1700 playbook that contains the text of the opera interspersed between acts of Shakespeare's *Measure for Measure*. This source promises to bridge the temporal gap and reconcile differences, but only muddies the waters with yet a third set of discrepancies. Suffice it to say that, arguably, Purcell's *Dido and Aeneas* does not exist; all versions of the opera (text and music, copied, published, or produced) are constructions of a particular time and place.

1. Tragically Short, Rebelliously Opera

Dido and Aeneas can be regarded as a tragic hero, a "rebel" at odds with the canon of music established by music historians and critics. Though included in all standard histories of music, Purcell's opera does indeed stand in the margin of opera history. First of all, the piece is short, taking about an hour to perform. Donald Grout (*A Short History of Opera*) states: "The dramatic work of Purcell includes only one opera in the strict sense—that is, sung throughout—namely *Dido and Aeneas*. Composed for performance at a girls' school in 1689, it is on the scale of a chamber opera rather than a full stage work" (141).

Elsewhere Grout states that the "musical style and proportions" of *Dido and Aeneas* "show the influence of the Italian cantata rather than the opera" (ibid., 139). For Grout and most historians, *Dido and Aeneas* is just barely an opera—an opera qualified and compromised primarily because of its length. I cannot resist the temptation to regard the appreciation of length as a masculine aesthetic. This bias is encoded in the language of nearly every Purcell biographer and scholar of the twentieth century. Jack Westrup, whose many writings about Purcell often betray a curious disdain for his music, describes the piece as "unusually short" (*Purcell* 135), "an exception," and "a miniature" that "suffers a little from its brevity: the drama moves too rapidly for all the episodes to make their full effect, and Aeneas hardly has time to establish himself as a character."[5]

In his book *Opera as Drama*, in a chapter entitled "The Dark Ages," Joseph Kerman echoes Westrup and implicitly feminizes the opera, calling it a

> crystalline little opera . . . a unique work, innocent of any indigenous operatic traditions . . . dashed off with a cheerful incorrectness. . . . It dodges the cruel problem of making a full evening's entertainment for a court that demands a decent cut of splendor. (43)

Dido and Aeneas, if not a female opera, as Kerman might have it, unable (too weak, perhaps) to take on the job of entertaining a court (not "cut" but rather innocent and undefiled), is, at most, according to Grout and Westrup, an emasculated opera—akin to another genre: the cantata. The cantata is itself regularly described as resembling "a detached scene from an opera" (Grout, *A History of Western Music* 354). In other words, *Dido and Aeneas* only suffers in comparison to "real men" (that is, "real opera"), and is more favorably compared to the dismembered part than the whole.

The marginal position of *Dido and Aeneas* within the present-day canon of "great operas" follows logically from its exceptional (indeed, rebellious) situation in seventeenth-century English musical culture. Seventeenth-century England, preoccupied with civil war, xenophobia, and a strong tradition of spoken drama, did not produce a repertory of drama sung from beginning to end. Opera originated in Italy in the early part of the century and was later taken up by the French, but remained a foreign art form in the opinion of English critics—suitable for importation but not cultivation. English men of letters lacked appreciation for Italian and French recitative—rhythmically flexible music that attempts to imitate natural speech inflections and delivery. Writers and critics such as John Dryden and Thomas Rymer adhered to prevailing neoclassical aesthetic presuppositions that art ought to imitate nature, and condemned opera in general and recitative in particular as too unnatural for dramatic effectiveness.[6]

A second feature of English culture that worked against the cultivation of opera was the decided preference for Continental music and musicians shown by the English aristocracy and would-be aristocracy, which led to the neglect and repudiation of their native resources.[7] This was due in part to the importation of French musicians by Charles II in an effort to emulate the royal *vingt-quatre violons* of Louis XIV. Instead of opera English musicians continued to cultivate the masque—dramatically light, often allegorical spoken dramas with interpolated musical numbers and scenes[8]—and semi-operas or dramas in which music plays an important role but none of the principle characters sing. The other thoroughly sung drama was *Venus and Adonis*, composed by John Blow, c. 1681. Though most often referred to as a masque by musicologists, *Venus and Adonis* was, for all intents and purposes, an "opera" that served as a model for Purcell. As in *Dido and Aeneas*, Blow's opera concentrates on the female protagonist Venus, while Adonis simply instigates various moods. *Venus and Adonis*, by comparison to *Dido and Aeneas*, is dramatically undeveloped and discontinuous, remaining closer to the "pure entertainment" aesthetic of the court masque. Thus *Dido and Aeneas* represented a rather bold musical experiment that cut against the grain of contemporary critical and social attitudes.

• *Performance Anxiety*

Jack Westrup writes, "The peculiar circumstances under which *Dido* was produced isolate it not only from Purcell's other works but from the rest of the dramatic music of the period" (*Purcell* 135). The belief that Purcell composed *Dido and Aeneas* for young female amateurs has been the source of disappointment and embarrassment for many generations of Purcell scholars, most of whom are British. Robert Moore comments with near contempt, "It is ironic that the dramatic masterpiece of England's supreme dramatic composer should have been written not for the professional theatre but for a young ladies' school" (38). Edward Dent, a prominent figure of English musicology, postpones revealing the nature of the first performance until he has prefaced the information with remarks that "soften the blow":

> It was not composed for the professional stage, and except for a performance in 1700, where it was inserted as a masque into Gildon's adaptation of *Measure for Measure*, it seems never to have been acted in public until some two hundred years later. This accounts for its peculiar form and style, and for the fact that it never had any successors of its own kind. . . . One can easily imagine that Purcell, when invited by the dancing-master Josias Priest to compose a musical entertainment for the young ladies at his school in Chelsea, may have felt that here was an opportunity of showing himself a better composer than Grabu. (177)

This passage abounds with barely contained shame and inconsistent excuses. Dent first intimates that *Dido* was somehow not fit for the public because it was intended for amateurs—the gender of which he does not immediately reveal. Dent goes on to discuss the first professional performance of *Dido* in 1700, despite the fact that for this performance the "opera" was not treated as an opera at all but rather cut apart—reduced and demoted to a lower-ranking genre, the masque. Dent then effectively describes Purcell's opera as impotent and, in a word, *queer* ("peculiar" in form and style)—unable to sire offspring ("successors" or heirs). This impotence Dent attributes to the circumstances of the commission that emasculated it. Purcell's opera was thus unable to achieve recognition as a "real" opera for professional performers. When Dent finally gets around to mentioning the gender of the amateurs, the information is buried within a long-winded subordinate clause and suddenly glossed over as an inconsequential detail. In the last sentence of the passage, Dent offers the hypothesis that Purcell wrote *Dido* in competition with Grabu (a French musician who wrote a flop of an opera for the English court in 1685). But why would Purcell choose a private forum to compete with an unambiguous musical and commercial disaster? Dent's hypothesis seems to be a desperate attempt to redress his earlier characterization of *Dido and Aeneas* as emasculated by showing how the opera can be regarded as a weapon of male homosocial competition and thus virile.[9]

Rather than expressing embarrassment or disappointment, Westrup and Zimmermann simply deny the possibility of an entirely female and an entirely amateur cast. In his article on Purcell in *The New Grove Dictionary of Music and Musicians*, Westrup writes,

> Since Aeneas is a tenor, at least in the copies that have survived, and there are parts for tenors and basses in the chorus, the work cannot have been performed entirely by Priest's pupils; and although the music does not make any extravagant demands, some of it calls for a professional standard of technique. ("Henry Purcell" 231)

The tenor part of Aeneas does indeed pose a problem; however, as previously mentioned, the earliest source for the music is so far removed from the presumed date of the opera's premier that many important specifics regarding the cast of the first performance remain mysteries. Ellen Harris (61) suggests that the role of Aeneas could have been originally written in the treble range. Although a treble Aeneas does not occur in any of the extant musical sources, similar transpositions involving the part of the Sorceress and the Sailor who opens act 3 (the only other male role in the opera) do occur in eighteenth-century musical sources. Harris writes:

> The assumption has been that these parts have been transposed down to achieve greater vocal variety in the late eighteenth-century productions. This implies that even the Sailor was played by a female in 1689, and it leads one to question whether the role of Aeneas might not also have been transposed later. (ibid.)

Purcell's most recent biographer, Franklin Zimmermann, follows Westrup blindly in concluding that the first performance of *Dido* could not have occurred without men and professionals:

> The only known copy of the libretto may have been printed solely for the audience at the first production, as nothing beyond the following is given on the title page: "An opera perform'd at Mr. Josias Priest's Boarding-school at Chelsea by young Gentlewomen."

> As for the actual performance, this statement *scarcely represents the whole truth* because it is unlikely that the school would have provided sopranos capable of singing the parts of Dido and Belinda (not to mention Aeneas's tenor role, or the choral bass and tenor parts).[10] Nor could a girls' school have provided the orchestral players and dancers required. Hence Priest very likely would have invited as many London professionals as needed.
>
> (173; emphasis mine)

Both Westrup and Zimmermann have misrepresented history as more determined than the evidence suggests and have made unabashed, unsubstantiated conclusions about an event for which scant, if not contrary, information exists. Amateur music making was a popular pastime in England and part of the curriculum in boarding schools.[11] Compositions, as well as instruction manuals for playing instruments, improvising, and even music theory, were designed for amateurs of all levels and provided a healthy source of income for professional musicians, especially during the years of the Commonwealth (1649–1660) when the Puritan rulers forbade music in church services. The pupils of Josias Priest—a well-known dance instructor and choreographer for the London theaters—would not have been of the lowest musical caliber but rather young cognoscenti.

England also boasts a rich history of amateur theatrical production. Plays written for companies of choirboys flourished from the late sixteenth to the early seventeenth century. Eminent playwrights such as Ben Jonson and Christopher Marlowe added to this repertory. Girls' schools often revived court masques as one of many theatrical experiences provided for in the curriculum (see Zaslaw). *Dido and Aeneas* does not appear so anomalous thus situated in this tradition of amateur music and theater. Ellen Harris's observations about the opera support this view, almost directly contradicting Zimmermann's. "It is short and demands less in the way of vocal technique than the later works [Purcell's five semi-operas written for the London theaters], and its orchestra consists only of strings, whereas the dramatic operas include beautiful and effective writing for woodwinds and trumpet" (*Henry Purcell's Dido and Aeneas* 7). Given the fashionable and educated audience, the private forum, and the probable talent and amateurish enthusiasm of the young students, it is perfectly reasonable that Purcell took the opportunity to experiment and write a tragic opera "at a time when operas were hardly ever tragic and when England had no real opera" (Price, "Introduction" vii).

The most recent "attack" on the girls' school performance comes from two English musicologists, Bruce Wood and Andrew Pinnock, in an article published in 1992 entitled "'Unscarr'd by turning times'?: the dating of Purcell's *Dido and Aeneas*." The title of their article is more ironic than Wood and Pinnock might have intended, since every attempt to recover or reconstruct the history of this opera is indeed scarred by leftover and concurrent scholarly anxieties. For their part Wood and Pinnock fixate on the year 1684 and a hypothetical court performance (i.e., professional production) as the intended premiere of *Dido and Aeneas*, basing their argument on a single new piece of evidence and dizzying interpretations of barely tenable assumptions.

Their new evidence is a recently discovered libretto for a 1684 revival of John Blow's *Venus and Adonis* at the very same boarding school that put on *Dido and Aeneas* in 1689. Keep in mind that Blow's masque premiered at court in 1681.[12] Wood and Pinnock then compare the epilogue to others appended to masques revived for school productions and find, not surprisingly, stereotypic rhetoric. They then leap to the conclusion that the girls' school performance must have been a revival. Through an elaborate series of buttressing arguments concerning allegorical insinuations, musical style, and models, Wood and Pinnock argue that Purcell wrote *Dido and Aeneas* in 1684 as a sequel to Blow's *Venus and Adonis* (388).

Not surprisingly, these two musicologists do not admit the possibility that Purcell could have written his opera for Josias Priest in response to the girls' school revival of *Venus and Adonis*; they rather insist that Purcell intended his masterpiece for the professional stage, in response to a hypothetical intended professional revival of Blow's masque. For their crowning piece of scholarship to secure a 1684 composition date for *Dido*, Wood and Pinnock link accounts of the weather for that year with the meteorological rhetoric of the prologue, thus proving that musicologist will do almost anything to set the record "straight" about *Dido and Aeneas*; as if talking about the weather could save the conversation concerning the origin of *Dido and Aeneas* from falling into an uncomfortable silence.

• *No Future*

So why do musicologists—especially English musicologists—persist in apologizing for or misrepresenting the history of *Dido and Aeneas*? The answer lies in two telling passages written by Edward Dent. The first passage discusses a portion of John Blow's *Venus and Adonis*; the second appears in the concluding chapter of the book:

> Space must be found for a few bars of the hunters' music [from John Blow's *Venus and Adonis*], if only to show how Blow anticipated Weber's "wild hunt" and the hounds of *Die Walküre*. (176)
>
> What Purcell failed to achieve was not to be accomplished by the mediocre talents which survived him. There was just a moment's hope that Handel might have built up an English opera on Purcell's foundations. (230)

What Purcell's opera failed to do was to procreate—to produce heirs that might have developed into an identifiable national style to rival or take part in the evolutionary progress of instrumental music and opera. Conventional wisdom among musicologists holds that Western music reached a pinnacle in the German achievements of the nineteenth century, specifically Beethoven's symphonies and Wagner's "music dramas." In the first passage Dent makes a feeble attempt to link Blow with the great German achievement, whereas in the second passage he bemoans the failure of Purcell's composition to fulfill its "biological" function and potential by not founding an English opera with its offspring. Dent's despairing comment in the second passage actually renders the title of his book, *The Foundations of English Opera,* ironic: there is no English opera; all that exists are its foundations. Thus isolated, *Dido* lies outside the lineage of Beethoven and Wagner and the ideal of individualism coupled with nationalism their music represents.[13]

For musicologists Purcell's *Dido and Aeneas* stands as a tragic hero—a rebel who struggled against society in a failed attempt to found English opera. But musicologists also regard *Dido* with ambivalence and disappointment. Why did this "hero" of an opera have to be so short, or written for a group of female amateurs? Why did its history have to be so hidden? Why did the opera have to be so queer?

The marginal situation of *Dido and Aeneas* in music history (as it is construed by musicologists) is analogous to the situation of a lesbian in society. The lesbian's first disadvantage is that she is a woman living in a society that favors men, just as *Dido*'s first disadvantage was its nationality—an English opera within an ideology that favors German nineteenth-century achievements. Second, lesbian relationships are "biologically unnatural," that is, they do not further the reproduction of the species, nor, likewise, did *Dido and Aeneas* beget offspring in the form of English opera. Finally, lesbian history is as elusive as the performance history of *Dido and Aeneas*, and evidence regarding both is generally met with distrust and ambivalence.

2.

Thus far I have shown how *Dido and Aeneas* functions as a tragic hero and rebel within the drama of music history, and how the opera's specific history and treatment by musicologists invites me to identify readily with the opera as a lesbian. But what makes this opera a *lesbian* opera rather than just a *queer* opera? Whether due to the female cast from the girls' school or the vogue for witches in Restoration plays, the plot of the opera revolves around the actions of women (Belinda, Dido, the Sorceress and her coven) and focuses on an implicit struggle between two queens—Dido and the Sorceress. These two roles carry not only the weight of the drama, but hold all musical interest apart from the choruses.

Why might a powerful Sorceress, completely unprovoked, wish to torment Dido, the queen of Carthage? Why is Dido so unhappy at the beginning of the opera? And why is Aeneas so uncompelling? Perhaps the pupils of Josias Priest's boarding school for "young gentlewomen" had a better intuitive appreciation of these sentiments than the opera's two male composers. Both the specific social pressures of competition and conformity and the more general growing pains of adolescence must have run high in the Chelsea boarding school. No doubt the young women resonated to the dilemmas and emotions presented in Purcell's female-centered, tragic opera. So, too, might a present-day lesbian audience find in Purcell's *Dido and Aeneas* a surprisingly sympathetic work of art that escapes interpretive pigeonholes.

Musicologists have long considered Purcell's opera to be a "flawed masterpiece"—a conception based on the preoccupation of scholars with four ambiguities: 1. the reason for Dido's grief in act 1; 2. the astonishingly slight dramatic and musical weight given to the leading male character in the opera, Aeneas; 3. the unmotivated hatred of the sorceress; 4. the alteration of Virgil's story to include witches (understood to be a concession to the conventions of Restoration theater) and the resultant ambiguous presentation of the witches as both comic and dramatic.[14] It is precisely these flaws, however, that open the door and provide access to the opera for the present-day lesbian audience. The musical presentation of characters and the "flawed" dramaturgy invite cathartic identification with either Dido or the Sorceress.

• *Dido Divided*

"Ah Belinda, I am pressed with torment not to be confessed." Dido's first utterance reveals that she suffers from an unnameable grief (as, perhaps, in "the Love that dare not speak its name"), the nature of which remains a mystery in the opera. In *The Aeneid* Dido's grief has a specific cause. Despite having made a vow of chastity after the death of her husband, Dido falls in love with Aeneas and longs—indeed plans—to break that vow. Thus Dido is a woman divided against herself. Tate and Purcell, however, chose to introduce Dido in this state of internal conflict but with no clue as to its provocation. The opera opens with the courtiers and Belinda attempting to cheer Dido with her new opportunities for love and capital gain:

> BELINDA: Shake the clouds from off your brow
> Fate your wishes does allow

Empire growing
Pleasure flowing
Fortune smiles and so should you.

But Dido, psychologically withdrawn and politically out of touch with her court, responds with an opening lament.

DIDO: Ah! Belinda I am press'd
With torments not to be confess'd.
Peace and I are strangers grown,
I languish till my grief is known
but would not have it guess'd.

Within the confines of the opera Dido's grief and internal struggle appear to stem from her inability to conform to the demands of society. The court pressures Dido to marry Aeneas, and Dido (for some reason) resists. The ambiguity surrounding Dido's opening lament allows for a reading that compares Dido's plight to the plight of the lesbian in society (and the girls in the Chelsea boarding school, for that matter)—divided between maintaining personal identity and conviction in the face of intense social pressures to conform.

Belinda interprets Dido's grief as lovesickness and counsels Dido to accept Aeneas's advances:

BELINDA: Grief increases by concealing;

DIDO: Mine admits of no revealing.

BELINDA: Then let me speak; the Trojan guest
Into your tender thoughts had press'd. (1.14–17)

The motivation behind Belinda's entreaties and those of the courtiers is overtly political rather than sympathetic:

SECOND WOMAN: The greatest blessing fate can give,
Our Carthage to secure, and Troy revive

CHORUS: When monarchs unite, how happy their state;
They triumph o'er their foes and their fate. (1.18–21)

Even Aeneas seems more interested in politics than love:

AENEAS: If not for mine, for empire's sake
Some pity on your lover take;

> Ah! make not in a hopeless fire
> A hero fall, and Troy
> Once more expire. (1.54–55)

Thus Dido is not only saddled with the fate of both Carthage and Troy, she is also a pawn in the phallic economy—in the power-obsessed politics of Aeneas and her own court. After much convincing, Dido acquiesces, but only to be forsaken by Aeneas shortly thereafter.

A full third of the opera (act 1) depicts social forces (Belinda, chorus, Aeneas) pressuring Dido to conform to their political wishes. Given this emphasis and the ambiguity surrounding Dido's feelings for Aeneas, the rage, grief, and eventual death of Dido would seem to stem more from the fact of her acquiescence than from Aeneas's departure. Dido gives in to social and political pressure and thus compromises her conviction, identity, and strength. She dies not from lovesickness but from a loss of will after having suffered a complete division of self to no satisfactory end. In her final powerful lament Dido does not tell Belinda to remember and learn from the tragic events but rather asks that her "wrongs" (left unnamed) and her "fate" be forgotten.

> DIDO: When I am laid in earth may my wrongs create
> No trouble in thy breast,
> Remember me, but ah! forget my fate. (3.ii.60–3)

• *Weak Aeneas*

Any number of "historical" excuses can be invoked to explain why the part of Aeneas is so meager. The first that leaps to mind is the "girls'-school commission" hypothesis. For musicologists this provides a convenient explanation for the composer's neglect of the male hero, but at the price of swallowing the bitter pill of an intended amateur, all-girl premier. In this light Bruce Wood's and Andrew Pinnock's most recent attack on the "girls'-school commission" makes the weak role of Aeneas only more intriguing.

A second excuse is the precedent of a woman-centric masque in John Blow's *Venus and Adonis*. But whereas Adonis is the catalyst for Venus's emotional states, which then become the focus of the masque, Aeneas is little more than a pawn—clothing for the plans of the Sorceress, but ultimately a figurine controlled by Fate. Aeneas *represents* weakness and disruption in the drama. He happens upon Carthage and easily loses sight of his divinely determined destiny. Aeneas is tracked in the homosocial corporate world of men and gods, and his invasion into Dido's court disrupts both her political and emotional equilibrium. The plan of the Sorceress is a manifestation of Fate that sets Aeneas back on track but leaves Dido as a casualty of his weakness. Dido, a powerful woman, thus becomes an intolerable variable in the world of men and gods—a character who must be cleared from the screen so Aeneas can get his work done.

Purcell, however, wrote a musical score that expresses and invokes more sympathy with Dido than with Aeneas. Just as Aeneas disrupts the equilibrium of Dido's court, so his music consistently disrupts the tonal plan of the opera. Purcell organized the opera into pairs of scenes written in complementary keys. The first pair uses parallel major and minor keys, the second and third pairs use relative major and minor keys. Aeneas appears in the second of every scene pair; each of his entrances wrenches the tonality away from the tidy key scheme:

1.i. c minor (Dido's initial grief)
1.ii. C major {G major/e minor} C major (Aeneas proclaims his love)
2.i. F major/minor (Witches plot)
2.ii. d minor {D major/a minor} (Aeneas decides to leave)
3.i. B-flat major (Celebration of Witches)
3.ii. g minor {F major/C major} g minor (Aeneas and Dido argue, Dido's lament)

His one monologue (2.ii) proves most invasive by ending act 2 in the wrong key according to the scheme (a minor rather than d minor). Act 3 then begins by shifting the tonic up a half-step to B-flat (if, as the Tenebury score shows, there is no concluding dance to bring the scene back to d minor). These two keys, a minor and B-flat major, do not have any chords in common. As a result such a shift of tonic sounds truly abrupt and disorienting. Thus Aeneas's moment in the spotlight also occasions a rupture in the large-scale architecture of the opera; the greater his musical contribution, the greater the disruption.

In the final scene Dido and Aeneas engage in a musical battle of wills; as Aeneas waffles on his decision to leave Carthage, his music pulls the g minor tonality to major keys—first F, then B-flat, then C. Dido does not tolerate this, however, and mocks his musical efforts. First she ridicules his sad farewell by taking his plaintive leap of a diminished fifth (c–f#) over "we must part" and turning the motive on its head (f–c#), into a diminished fourth over the word "weeps" in the line "Thus on the fatal banks of the Nile, Weeps the deceitful crocodile."

Example 4.1.[15]

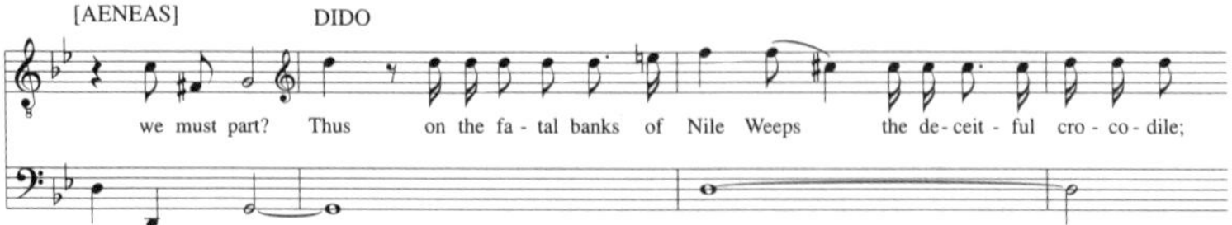

When Aeneas tries to object over a B-flat major chord ("By all that's good"), Dido mimics his line and forces the tonality back toward g minor with a half cadence ("By all that's good, no more. All that's good you have forswore").

Example 4.2.

In desperation, Aeneas changes his mind and brings the dialogue to a firm C major cadence ("I'll stay, offend the gods, and Love obey"), only to be spurned by Dido, who transposes his C major cadence to D major (the dominant of g minor) and sings the punning line "I'm now *resolved* as well as you"—literally resolving his tonal disruption with her musical and emotional resolution.

Example 4.3.

Although Dido gets the upper hand in this dialogue scene, she does not win; of course Aeneas does not make a convincing heldentenor for such a powerful queen to die for. In the words of Joseph Kerman, "Aeneas is made into a complete booby" in the opera (224).[16] So who is really the cause of Dido's suffering? The only dramatic and musical force in the opera on a par with Dido is the Sorceress. Her actions explicitly set up the conflict that drives the plot forward. But what motivates the hatred of the Sorceress; what drives her actions? Musicologists have long bemoaned this tantalizingly missing—or, better yet, hidden—element of the story.

• *Sadistic Sorceress / Masochistic Queen*

Roger Savage describes the Sorceress as "a personified aspect of Dido . . . a formidable anti-self embodying all her insecurities and apprehensions contingent on her involving herself in any deep personal relationship" (261). This intriguing interpretation implies that Dido causes her own downfall by resisting Aeneas. The motivation for the Sorceress's actions are none other than Dido's own—literally a projection of her divided self. Thus Savage attempts to explain the unstated provocation for the Sorceress's plans to torment the queen. But note the tone of anticipated delight and the persistent references to flames in the Sorceress's recitative of act 2 and air of act 3:

SORCERESS: Wayward sisters you that fright
the Lonely traveller by night
. . . Appear at my call, and share in the fame
of a mischief shall make all Carthage flame. (2.i.1–2, 5–6)

From the ruins of others our pleasure we borrow.
Elisa[17] bleeds tonight, and Carthage flames
tomorrow. (3.i.16–17)

These sentiments are echoed by the witches in a jovial little chorus:

Destruction's our delight,
delight our greatest sorrow
Elisa dies tonight,
and Carthage flames tomorrow.
Ho, ho, ho, etc. (2.i.18–19)

In three other passages the flame trope explicitly refers to desire:

AENEAS: Ah! make not in a hopeless fire
A hero fall, and Troy
Once more expire. (1.ii.54–55)

BELINDA: Pursue thy conquest, Love—her Eyes
Confess the flame her tongue denies. (1.ii.56–7)

DIDO: No repentance shall reclaim
The injured Dido's slighted flame. (3.i.44–5)

One should note, however, the flame trope appears only in association with denial ("hopeless fire," "the flame her tongue denies," "slighted flame"). Thus the flame trope links delight with destruction, desire with denial, and, by extension, pleasure with pain. The ambiguous motivation for Dido's self-absorbed grief and the Sorceress's cruelty combine with the overdetermined flame trope to suggest that Dido derives a masochistic pleasure from her state of suffering, as the Sorceress derives pleasure from tormenting her. Whether one thinks of the Sorceress as an aspect of Dido or as a separate entity, the two queens are engaged in a veiled sadomasochistic relationship.

In the course of the drama Dido and the Sorceress never encounter one another face to face, but rather the Sorceress dominates or "gets at" Dido through Aeneas—by executing a plan to persuade Aeneas that he is *bound* by destiny to leave Carthage for Italy. In this way the Sorceress *binds* Dido as well, forcing her to submit to "fate."

This erotic triangle compares to the picture of homosocial erotic triangles found in many nineteenth-century English novels as discussed by Eve Sedgwick, but as a negative thereof. In a Sedgwickian erotic triangle, two males experience an equal if not stronger bond of attraction and desire for one another expressed through their rivalry for a female. Here both Dido and the Sorceress vie for Aeneas not to gain his affection but to help satiate their own cravings. It is important to note that the Sorceress delights not in the domination of Aeneas, not in his "hopeless fire," but in the resultant suffering of Dido, in her "slighted flame." Thus the Sorceress uses Aeneas as a device in her sadistic "mischief" with Dido. Dido's suffering, however, is inevitable. Although superficially caused by the Sorceress, destiny foreordains that Aeneas leave Carthage, thereby leaving Dido to her masochistic fate. Thus destiny, in this context, can easily be understood as a case of self-fulfilling prophecy.

The music for Dido and the Sorceress underscores the sadomasochistic implications of the drama with respective submissive and dominant musical traits. Dido's music is marked by formal restriction and submission. She sings only laments and dialogues plus two declamatory interjections during Aeneas's monologues, and these are arranged symmetrically over the course of the six scenes—bound, if you will, to an exacting, abstract formal scheme:

1.i. Lament: Ah Belinda
    Dialogue: Belinda and Dido
1.ii. declamatory interjection
1.ii. declamatory interjection
3.ii. Dialogue: Dido and Aeneas
    Lament: When I am laid in earth

In contrast, the music of the Sorceress is marked by formal freedom. Although she appears in only two scenes (2.i and 3.i), these scenes weave a tapestry of recitatives, airs, duets, and choruses organized around and motivated by the declamations of the Sorceress:

2.i
Sorceress Declamation/choral response
Sorceress Declamation/choral response
Tuneful duet (two witches)
Somber chorus

3.i
Sailor Air/Sailors chorus
Sorceress Declamation/duet response
Sorceress Air
Jovial chorus

The sorceress dominates and commands these two scenes in a manner unequalled by any other character in the opera. Her part provides the musical and dramatic glue that justifies and unifies the duets and choruses. Purcell created, in effect, two scene-complexes in which music for ensembles are interpolated into what is essentially one expanded aria.[18] Although the third act opens with the sailors rather than the Sorceress, the sailors appear as evidence of her power. They sing an air celebrating deception and departure:

SAILORS CHORUS: Come away fellow sailors,
Your anchors be weighing,
Time and tide will admit no delaying.
Take a boozy shore leave
of your nymphs of the shore,
And silence their mourning
With vows of returning,
But never intending to visit them more. (3.i.1–6)

The progression of keys over the course of the opera provides another indication of the Sorceress's power and domination. Purcell contrived a key-scheme that associates the dramatic events of each scene with a specific tonal environment:

1.i. c minor (Dido's initial grief)
1.ii. C major (Aeneas proclaims his love)
2.i. F major/minor (Witches plot)
2.ii. d minor/D major/a minor (Aeneas decides to leave)
3.i. B-flat major (Celebration of Witches)
3.ii. g minor (Dido's final lament and death)

In constructing each act, Purcell used flat keys and the minor mode for scenes of grief or ill fate and the parallel or relative major mode for scenes of celebration. As the drama progresses the tonal scheme moves toward inescapable flat keys. Purcell's use of the parallel C major in scene 1.ii portrays Dido's hoped-for relief from her initial despair, but the successive scenes of celebration take place dramatically and musically in the realm of the Sorceress. One can easily read the total encroachment and eventual entrenchments of flats in the key signature as a musical analog to the increasing effect and domination of the Sorceress on the dramatic and musical events of the opera.

On the level of individual numbers the two laments that Dido sings utilize a particularly tyrannical musical technique called an ostinato or ground bass—a short cadential bass line, usually in the minor mode, that repeats obsessively throughout entire musical numbers, or large sections thereof. In Dido's two laments the grounds cycle continuously without rhythmic or melodic variation (only the first lament momentarily transposes the pitches of the ground), thus creating, in effect, musical bondage. The obsessive cycling of the bass line—often replete with chromatic inflections—produces a single controlling mood. Likewise, the short phrase pattern of the ground and its strong tonal direction furnishes a relentless set of constraints against which the vocal line struggles, only to be forced into submission at the final cadence. Thus the vocal line's denial of the bass line's relentless cadences and phrase pattern creates a self-contained play of musical domination and submission.

In the first half of her lament "Ah! Belinda," Dido sings the opening line twice, though the melodies of the two statements differ radically from one another, and neither statement coordinates with the cycle of four-bar phrases of the ground. As the bass makes its serpentine progression downward, the vocal line strains to move upward and remain in the upper register for most of the second statement, until the line comes crashing down with the leap of a fifth (accompanying the word *torment*), only to land on a succession of two dissonances (major ninths) as punishment for its impudence:

Example 4.4.

The second half of this lament shows the gradual submission of the vocal line to the ground. For the line "peace and I are strangers grown," the voice sings the head motive of the ground but positioned so as to preclude by one measure the start of a bass cycle. As a consequence the voice sounds as if it were lamenting a former state of peaceful alignment with the bass:

Example 4.5.

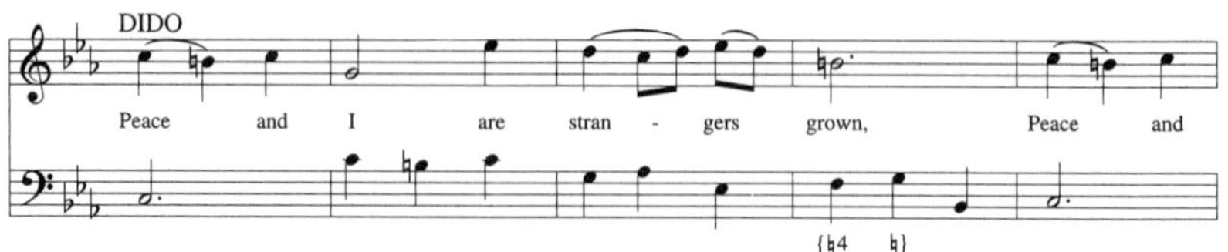

Momentarily the voice and ground are aligned but separate when the voice indulges in a long descriptive flourish upon repeating the words "I languish." As in the first half of the lament, vocal boldness is met with concluding dissonances, here falling on the word *grief.* Purcell has set this word to the same rhythmic motive that accompanied the word *torment* in the first half of the lament. With new resolve the voice leaps a tenth to begin the last line of the song, but lands on a dissonance and quickly breaks down into short chromatic, melodic fragments with appoggiaturas that displace the harmonic resolutions.

Example 4.6.

Thus the climax of the text is first withheld through the repetition and extension of the penultimate phrase "I languish until my grief is known"; then the climactic pronouncement "yet would not have it guessed" is set with a full arsenal of musical torture devices: harmonic dissonance, rhythmically weak, unsatisfying resolutions, chromatic and disjunct melody lines.

Reading this lament as a piece of musical sadomasochism merely assigns narrativity, or rather personality, to the features of ground bass laments required to create musical momentum. Laments and ground bass composition have enjoyed a strong association since the middle of the seventeenth century. The descending minor tetrachord ostinato became especially emblematic for laments, and serves as the ground for Dido's climactic lament in act 3. Ellen Rosand comments:

> It is strongly directional harmonically, moving inexorably, with stepwise melody and steady unarticulated rhythm . . . and in its unremitting descent, its gravity, the pattern offers an analogue of obsession and depression—perceptible as the expression of unrelieved suffering. (370)

Dido's lament "When I am laid in earth" is pure melodrama—a musical depiction of both emotion and event. The libretto itself does not provide an explicit cause of death; however, the music reveals an Isolde-like rapturous passing. Before the start of the lament proper, Dido sings a melodious recitative filled with chromatic inflections that musically prepare the ground bass and thus invite death to take control:

Example 4.7.

In contrast to the conflict-ridden "Ah! Belinda," Dido's climactic lament "When I am laid in earth" does not present a power play between the dominant bass and the submissive voice; instead the voice acquiesces to the hypnotic cycling of the ground. For the first half of the lament the phrases of the vocal line are coordinated with the cadential pattern of the bass. There is no struggle; all the harmonic implications of the bass are appropriately realized by the vocal line and only momentarily delayed by an expressive appoggiatura over the word *trouble* as if the word itself causes a small ripple in her composure and her intent to cause *no trouble*:

Example 4.8.

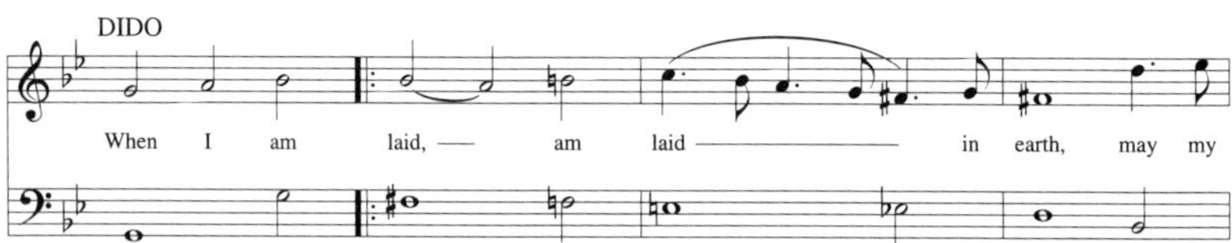

In the second half of the lament Dido's melody provides an aural equivalent to her fading consciousness. As she wistfully pleads "remember me," the melody momentarily loses contour and contact with the bass; effectively stalling on a high D, as if Dido is poised between death and life. But with renewed conviction Dido concludes her thought ("but ah! forget my fate"), bridging two cycles of the bass with a half-cadence. The expressive and rhetorical repetition of this text ends in a definitive coordination with the bass—her final submission.

Example 4.9.

In contrast to the laments of Dido, where the vocal line is chained to the cycling bass line, the music for the Sorceress is harmonically, formally, and rhythmically flexible, weaving freely between major and minor harmonies in response to her active plotting or gleeful rejoicing. The roles of the Sorceress and Dido are complementary and symbiotic. Their characters and, consequently, their music, are diametrically opposed, yet both fulfill *their* destinies—or rather, their *natures*—through a dominant/submissive interaction. This "homosexual" dyad (camouflaged by Aeneas) provides the dramatic/musical dynamic that drives the opera.

Just as the Sorceress acts as the musical and dramatic antithesis to Dido, so her coven functions as an anticourt—a "supernatural" and "uncivil" realm (a world without *proper* motives) set in opposition to the "natural" and "civil" realm of men and gods. Within her "civil" realm Dido has carved a niche with her court; the Sorceress and her coven, however, offer a way out—an alternative world with alternative rules, or, rather, no rules at all, no necessary "cause" and "effect." Passion rather than politics guides the Sorceress and governs her court.

• *Witches as a Way Out*

The Sorceress and her coven have been described variously as "the catalyst for the tragedy" (Price, *Henry Purcell and the London Stage* 231), as "symbols of the malevolence of destiny," (Westrup, *Purcell* 136), and as simply "an outrageous set of Restoration witches" inserted into the drama to follow fashion (Kerman 43). No matter what the justification, the Sorceress and her entourage contribute some of the most engaging and appealing moments in the opera. Something about *witches* inspired Purcell to characterize the Sorceress and her coven musically as complex and ultimately sympathetic. In the opera the behavior of the witches defies evaluation; on one hand their music is playful and passionate, on the other hand their motives are calculating and cruel. Did Purcell create his witches according to his own conception and interpretation of their "nature," or was he operating in line with contemporary theatrical models?

For late seventeenth-century dramatists and theater audiences, witches would have been associated with the paradigmatic "weird sisters" of Shakespeare's *Macbeth* (c. 1609). Behind this threesome, however, hang the remnants of popular Elizabethan notions about magic, witches, sorceresses, and other elements of the occult. According to church authorities, a witch or sorcerer was understood to be a person who willingly entered into a pact with agents of Satan, and thus procured supernatural powers to carry out acts of vengeful malice. Popular belief, however, made no such correlation between Satan and witches. Accusations of witchcraft were mostly predicated on seemingly malicious actions performed by eccentric neighbors; these accounts were counterbalanced by good witches practicing "white magic"—using their powers to break spells and read fortunes.

On the Elizabethan and Jacobean stage witches were most often portrayed farcically, as harmless eccentrics (Harris, *Night's Black Agents* 16). The witches in Shakespeare's *Macbeth*, however, represent a "significant dramaturgical advance," insofar as they are "effective and meaningful characters in their own right" and are portrayed as "flesh and blood creatures." These weird sisters are at once frightening and diabolical agents intertwined with the forces of Fate, yet "subject to human passions" (ibid. 47).

In Restoration theater after 1660 the vogue for operatic spectacles combined with an increasing "enlightened" skepticism toward irrational matters such as witchcraft to draw the pendulum back toward the Jacobean presentation of witches. In William Davenant's adaptation of Shakespeare's *Macbeth* (1663/64), the witches provide an occasion for songs, dances, and mechanical special effects. Momentary entertainment took primacy over dramaturgical horror and mystery. The texts of their songs further remove "the original enigma of the Sisters' identities [by] equating them with the Goddesses of Destiny" (Harris, *Night's Black Agents* 186). In this way Davenant refashions Macbeth into the more classical or neoclassical "Aeneas" mold; a hero who is less culpable, less in control of his actions than are the witches—themselves agents of destiny.

Purcell's Sorceress and her coven of witches betray their folkloric and theatrical ingredients. These witches are vengeful entities, acting upon their human passions and operating not as diabolical agents but rather as agents of destiny. Their portrayal draws upon the Jacobean tradition of comedy, the Shakespearean tradition of horror, and the Restoration tradition of neoclassicism and entertainment for its own sake.

The witches' scenes in *Dido and Aeneas* provide moments of pure escapism within the drama. Musical and special effects aside, these passionate, lawless, and deliciously malicious beings bring to life for the audience mischievous alter egos and fantasies. Furthermore, as agents of destiny, they are excused for their spiteful actions because their plot serves as a catalyst to predestined events. All in all, the witches offer a way out of the tragic world of social reality and the responsibility of personal agency.

As I have suggested, Purcell's musical portrayal of the Sorceress and her coven may betray his own reckless desire to escape to an alternative world. The worlds of Dido and the Sorceress are set up as negatives of one another, introduced separately in the first two acts and then brought together in the beginning of the third act.

1.i. Dido and her attendants
2.ii. Sorceress and her coven
3.i. Sailors depart/witches celebrate

Both the court and the coven are presented through the chorus and two subsidiary characters who serve as spokespersons for their respective societies. In the "natural" realm Belinda and an unnamed "second woman" communicate the wishes of the court/chorus; in the "supernatural" realm these two are given parallels in the form of attendant witches. The conduct of these subordinates with respect to their superiors is markedly different, however, and this difference throws into relief the opposition of the two realms. Belinda and the second woman attempt to counsel and persuade a conflicted Dido with political arguments, whereas the attendant witches act more like cheerleaders for the resolute Sorceress. In Dido's realm society holds the greatest power. Indeed, Belinda opens the opera and introduces the natural realm with surprising impertinence, telling Dido (who is queen, after all) to cast aside her emotions and get with society's program—a program that equates emotional pleasure with material wealth:

> Empire growing,
> pleasure flowing.
> Fortune smiles, and so should you. (1.i)

By contrast, in the realm of the coven the Sorceress holds all the power and is clearly in control. Indeed, her society is at her beck and call—no questioning of authority, no cajoling counselors. Purcell and Tate have tapped into a dream of the empowered individual, guided by passions themselves unmitigated by social pressure:

1ST WITCH: Say, Beldame, say, what's thy will,

CHORUS: Harm's our delight and mischief all our skill. (2.i)

Purcell's music further distinguishes the two societies. The oppressive c minor tonality of the music for the natural world in act 2.i contrasts with the flexible modality of the supernatural world, which fluctuates between F major and f minor. Not only does Purcell's choice of modes communicate different moods through the conventional association of sad with minor and happy with major, but the apparent ability of the Sorceress to effect her musical environment (plotting in minor, celebrating in major) contrasts with Dido's inability to escape her solemn and dreary musical/social circumstances; her courtiers badger her in c minor and she responds in the same key. The musical character of the choruses also adds to the opposing portrayal of the two worlds. The witches revel in their enterprise in an exuberant eighth-note patter of musical laughter and rollicking triple-time dance meters, whereas the courtiers meddle in Dido's affairs with stodgy homorhythmic, declamatory choruses.

In act 3 the natural and the supernatural worlds, heretofore kept separate and distinct, are brought together in immediate juxtaposition. First the Trojan sailors appear in joyful celebration as they make ready to leave Carthage, singing a provocative little ditty about having casual sexual relations with women while on shore:

Take a boozy shore leave of your nymphs of the shore,
And silence their mourning with vows of returning
But never intending to visit them more. (3.i)

Following this number, the Sorceress and her coven fill the stage with their own victory celebration. Aeneas, like his sailors, has forsaken Dido, his "nymph of the shore" according to their plan:

The plot has took, the Queen's forsook,
Ho, ho, ho, ho
From the ruin of others our pleasure we borrow. (3.i)

Here the two worlds are presented as strikingly similar. Purcell sets both celebrations in B-flat major, and both numbers end with rousing chorus and duple-time dances. So juxtaposed, the sadistic pleasure of the witches parallels the drunken exploits and insensitivity of the sailors (and Aeneas by extension) who celebrate making empty promises and trifling with the affections of unsuspecting young girls.

Dido and Aeneas presents the audience with a glimpse of two societies: the natural world driven by economics and politics, and a supernatural utopia, driven by pleasure and passion. Ironically, it is the witches' utopia that receives endorsement—from destiny, and from Purcell. The Sorceress and her coven win in the end; without question, they "come away" with a net gain of pleasure and no losses of any kind. As a dramatic character, the Sorceress becomes an alternative heroine—one who is not tragic but powerful and self-actualized.

In the 1970s feminists and lesbians began to search for alternatives to dominant culture: utopian social models, unconventional religions, new means of self-definition and personal empowerment. Identification with witches or as a witch became one popular solution for many women. Witches were a ready-made marginal but socially recognized subculture, with a documented history, a framework for religious practices, and a sense of community.[19] For past and present-day audiences the Sorceress and her coven in *Dido and Aeneas* offer an antidote to the natural world—a court of rebellious mischief, passion, and self-actualization juxtaposed with a court of torment, manipulation, and grief.

The physical and personal attributes of witches are suitably vague and various. After all, to be a witch is to be a "wayward sister"—to enjoy a certain amount of freedom to live outside society and, by extension, not participate in the dominant culture's power structures or its constructions of gender and sexuality. Confusion of gender and sexuality, moreover, has a long-standing association with witchcraft in English law and theater. Trying to provoke "unlawful love" became a felony connected with witchcraft under Queen Elizabeth I (Harris, *Night's Black Agents* 8). The theater, following traditional lore, often portrayed witches with both male and female traits. Shakespeare's *Macbeth* and Davenant's seventeenth-century adaptation both refer to witches' beards. Davenant's version carries the line "You should be women / And yet your looks forbid me to interpret" (Harris, ibid. 186). Furthermore, all extant sources for Davenant's adaptation of *Macbeth* cast Hecate as a baritone despite the new vogue of using women for female roles. Purcell's Sorceress, then, might have been a drag role.

Curtis Price and Irena Cholij have argued that in the professional performances of *Dido and Aeneas*, the Sorceress was, indeed, sung by a bass. As primary evidence Price and Cholij cite the Hecate travesty tradition of Davenant's *Macbeth*, regarded as the model for Purcell and Tate's Sorceress, and the 1700 playbook that includes a prompt for one [Mr.] Wilshire before the entrance of the Sorceress (616). Thus witches have a history of being identified as a third sex—both man and woman—with the choice of choosing either sex as an object for passionate obsession. The Sorceress chose Dido.

3.

• *Girls' School Drama*

Could not the same freeing ambiguities that attract modern-day lesbians to witches have attracted Purcell as well? Or, more to the point, could not the roles of both Dido and the Sorceress have provided a cathartic experience for young women at the Chelsea boarding school? I can only imagine that growing pains and competition abounded in this adolescent student body, setting off indulgences in masochistic self-pity or sadistic cruelty with little provocation. With the aid of hindsight, I want to consider the emotional charge and cathexis that the opera must have generated in these adolescent girls.

Girls' boarding-school romances in the nineteenth century have received considerable scholarly attention, and these endeavors have concentrated more on vertical (i.e., student/teacher) rather than horizontal (student/student) relationships.[20] But, as Martha Vicinus notes, "Neither the ingredients that make up an intense friendship nor its impact on the participants may have changed over time" (213). Seventeenth-century plays about girls' boarding schools satirized both cattiness and amorous intrigues, the latter occurring between students and various male instructors, such as singing or dancing masters. In fact, Thomas Durfey, who wrote the 1689 epilogue for *Dido and Aeneas*, soon after wrote the satire *Love for Money, or The Boarding School* (1690–1691). Evidence from the plot and a contemporaneous letter suggests that "there was a closely perceived connection between his play and Priest's opera production":

> Its author confesses to having gleaned material while living in a boarding school the previous summer; and the plot includes a risible dancing entertainment staged for the parents. Having established the connection, the play then demolishes the elaborate conceit of the chaste Protestant nunnery with which school masques were habitually enveloped in order to distance themselves from the reputation of the Restoration public stage. (Goldie 394)

Mark Goldie has uncovered a letter written by a Mrs. A. Buck to the wife of a leading Whig member of Parliament. The letter, which refers to both *Dido and Aeneas* and Durfey's satire, betrays a definite anxiety about the public performance of the opera, as well as an anxiety about appropriateness of school masques in general:

> [Priest] hath lately had an Opera, which I'me sure hath done him a great injury; & the Parents of the Children not satisfied with so Publick a show. . . . I cannot finde out what the children are improved in. Att present all schoolls are redicul'd: They have latly made a Play cal'd The Boarding School. (393)

Mrs. Buck's rhetoric of discomfort exposes an unconscious embarrassment at the pubic display of catharsis occasioned by the opera. Certainly Durfey's characterization of the school as a den of cattiness and amorous intrigue could have been an exaggeration of the evident unleashing of passions that a production of *Dido and Aeneas* might well inspire. Although Durfey capitalizes on the heterosexual escapades of the young women, the opera itself—with not one, but two heroines—allows for the "working out" of the underlying homosexual dynamics at play in the homosocial environment of the boarding school.

Grief and hatred, power and surrender—these are extreme emotions that affect the body and, as elements of sexual sadomasochism, involve the sublimation of sexual desire and tension. A dramatic rendition of these emotions allows for a displacement and catharsis of this tension for the performer. But what about the observers of such a performance? In "Film Bodies: Gender, Genre, and Excess" Linda Williams uses the term *body genre* in reference to films that feature displays of excessive emotion for the primary purpose of generating the same sensations in the audience. Williams proposes that the category body genre can itself be regarded as a subcategory of melodrama, which is considered to be a "filmic mode of stylistic and/or emotional excess that stands in contrast to more 'dominant' modes of realistic, goal-oriented narrative." Williams continues: "In this extended sense melodrama can encompass a broad range of films marked by 'lapses' in realism, by 'excesses' of spectacle and displays of primal, even infantile emotions" (3). This definition of melodrama and the notion of body genres seem almost tailor-made for opera. The *melo* in *melodrama* of course refers to the excess of melody—a result of emotional expression so extreme as to exceed the bounds of speech and enter the realm of song:

> A pertinent feature shared by these body genres is the focus on what could probably best be called a form of ecstasy. . . . Contemporary meanings suggest components of direct or indirect sexual excitement and rapture, a rapture which informs even the pathos of melodrama.
>
> Visually . . . ecstatic excesses could be said to share a quality of uncontrollable convulsion or spasm—of the body "beside itself" with sexual pleasure. . . . Aurally excess is marked by recourse not to the coded articulations of language but to inarticulate cries. (Williams 4).

Opera is quintessentially both melodrama and a body genre.[21] Not only is every speech act made emotionally excessive by its melodic presentation, but the distortions of the face, the quivering of the body, and the heaving chest that results from singing can be perceived as uncontrollable spasms of physical rapture. A physical catharsis for the opera audience transpires through literally sympathetic vibrations resulting from the music and the vision of the singers. This catharsis combines with the engagement of the emotions and the aesthetic experience of identification—that is, a vicarious/empathetic experience of the sentiment displayed by one or more characters. Opera is a unique artform that provides for an intertwining of emotional/physical rapture—a complete catharsis that unites the mind and the body.

• *Back to School*

Simply put, *Dido and Aeneas* presents the audience with two women who experience physical rapture on account of each other. This alone makes Purcell's opera accessible for lesbian cathartic identification. For the young girls in the seventeenth-century boarding school, and for present-day lesbians as well, struggles with self-identity, social pressures, and the dominant culture's models of womanhood result in similar pressure cooker circumstances in which expressions of sexual desire between women become veiled, ambiguous, or paradoxical.

In this article I have enumerated the various ways in which I have been able to bring together my identities as a lesbian and as a musicologist through a particular work of art. Just as performing or viewing *Dido and Aeneas* can provide a means of catharsis for lesbians, so my identification and radical exegesis of this "queer" opera—its unusual, elusive history, peculiar dramaturgy, and persuasive music—has brought about a personal catharsis by suturing the Cartesian-like split of the personal and the professional. My goal is not only to proclaim the hidden relevance of a neglected work of art for a neglected audience but also to practice musicology from a neglected though insightful perspective: the perspective of the margin. Judging from this position—a position I have come to value, and one shared by both present-day lesbians and young women in 1689—*Dido and Aeneas* should be heralded as a lesbian opera classic, perhaps one of the first and most accessible examples to be released from the annals of European music history.

Notes

1. I am following the 1689 libretto's division of the opera into three acts of two scenes each. The earliest extant musical score divides the opera into three acts of varying lengths, and inconsistantly labels the larger divisions as *parts* and *acts*.

2. See Squire, "Purcell's *Dido and Aeneas,*" p. 254.

3. See Wood and Pinnock ("'Unscarr'd by turning times?'"). I will discuss the arguments of their article in a later portion of this essay.

4. See White, "New Light on 'Dido and Aeneas,'" p. 15, and Harris, "The Design of the Tenbury Manuscript," p. 252.

5. Westrup, "Henry Purcell," p. 232. In a section following a discussion of Purcell's incidental music for the theater, Westrup writes: "The most *substantial* music is *naturally* to be found in what Roger North called 'semi-operas'" (p. 230; emphasis mine). Thus

Westrup again betrays the assumption/bias that musical weight and substance is a function of length, despite the fact that "semi-operas" were little more than disconnected musical diversions interpolated into a spoken drama.

6. English critics of the neoclassical school took many of their ideas from contemporaneous French writers such as Nicolas Boileau-Despréaux and Saint-Evremond who considered opera to be absurd and tedious (see McGeary, "English Opera Criticism," pp. 14 and 32, and Dent, *Foundations of English Opera*, pp. 159–62).

7. See Jensen, "English Restoration," pp. 206–14, and Grout, *A Short History of Opera*, p. 137.

8. After the Restoration, masques moved from the courts into the theater, becoming musical diversions inserted into plays. Ironically, English critics could tolerate all-sung masques under these conditions, but not independent full-scale operatic endeavors.

9. Moore (*Henry Purcell and the Restoration Theatre*, p. 39) echoes Dent's hypothesis.

10. The choral tenor and bass parts call into question the possibility of an all-female cast more than the part of Aeneas. Simple transposition of the bass and tenor lines results in poor voice leading and counterpoint within the four-part SATB texture of these choruses. It is beyond the scope of this essay to attempt a solution to these problems; suffice it to say, however, that the lack of evidence, especially with regard to the music, leaves the door open for many scenarios regarding original composition and later recomposition of these choruses.

11. Barbour (*Introduction to an Essay*) notes:

> When boarding schools began to flourish increasingly in the seventeenth century, it was partly because middle class and country families sought to give their daughters the extra poise and polish it would take to attract rich husbands. The curriculum emphasized singing, dancing, fashion, crafts, and all the excessive frills. (vii)

12. See Nicholas Anderson, insert, "Venus and Adonis," cond. Charles Medlam, London Baroque (Harmonia Mundi France, 901276).

13. Few big-name opera stars bother to record, let alone perform in, Purcell's opera. One notable and ironic exception is the famed Wagnerian diva Kirstan Flagstand who performed the title role in the early 1950s and recorded the part in 1952 along with Elisabeth Schwarzkopf as Belinda.

14. See Westrup, *Purcell*, pp. 135–45; Kerman *Opera as Drama*, pp. 43–47; and Price, *Henry Purcell and the London Stage*, pp. 225–62.

15. All musical examples taken from Price, *Purcell, Dido and Aeneas: An Opera* (New York: Norton, 1986), pp. 83–181.

16. Savage ("Producing Dido and Aeneas"), while criticizing Kerman for being "unjust" (267), himself makes a rather damning statement about Aeneas: "He is, in addition, so self-absorbed that he cannot see the complexities of others, certainly not of Dido. I suspect too that he is a rather selfish love-maker ('one night enjoys'), certainly too animal for the sensitive queen" (268).

17. A second name for Dido.

18. The organization of a scene-complex by a single, multisection musical number such as an aria or a trio became a frequent feature of operatic dramaturgy in the eighteenth and nineteenth centuries. A classic example is the opening scene in act 2 of Verdi's *Otello* where the music for Iago's "Credo" aria underlies the initial dialogue.

19. For a thorough discussion of twentieth-century witchcraft in America and its connections to 1970s feminism, see Margot Adler, *Drawing Down the Moon* (New York: Viking Press, 1979).

20. See Vicinus, "Distance and Desire."

21. Present-day opera is an institution marked by excess on every level, from the social profile of the audience, to the elaborate sets, to the very physical size of most opera singers.

Works Cited

Barbour, Paula. *Introduction to An Essay to Revive the Antient Education of Gentlewomen (1673), by Bathsua Makin.* Los Angeles: University of California Press, 1980.

Dent, Edward J. *Foundations of English Opera.* Cambridge: Cambridge University Press, 1928.

Goldie, Mark. "The Earliest Notice of Purcell's *Dido and Aeneas.*" *Early Music* (August 1992), 20:392–401.

Grout, Donald. *A Short History of Opera*, 2d ed. New York: Columbia University Press, 1965.

_______ *A History of Western Music*. 3d ed. New York: Norton, 1980.

Harris, Anthony. *Night's Black Agents*. Manchester: Manchester University Press, 1980.

Harris, Ellen T. "The Design of the Tenbury Manuscript." In Curtis Price, ed., *Norton Critical Scores: Purcell, Dido and Aeneas*, pp. 243–52. New York: Norton, 1986.

_______ *Henry Purcell's Dido and Aeneas*. Oxford: Clarendon Press, 1987.

Jensen, H. James. "English Restoration Attitudes Toward Music." *Musical Quarterly* (1969), 55:206–14.

Kerman, Joseph. *Opera as Drama*. Rev. ed. Berkeley: University of California Press, 1988.

McGeary, Thomas Nelson. "English Opera Criticism and Aesthetics 1685–1747." Ph.D. diss., University of Illinois, 1985.

Moore, Robert E. *Henry Purcell and the Restoration Theatre*. London: Heinemann, 1961.

Price, Curtis. *Henry Purcell and the London Stage*. Cambridge: Cambridge University Press, 1984.

_______ "Introduction." In Curtis Price, ed., *Norton Critical Scores: Purcell, Dido and Aeneas*, pp. vii–x. New York: Norton, 1986.

Price, Curtis, and Irena Cholij. "Dido's Bass Sorceress." *Musical Times* (1986), 127: 615–18.

Rosand, Ellen. *Opera in Seventeenth-Century Venice.* Berkeley: University of California Press, 1991.

Savage, Roger. "Producing Dido and Aeneas." In Curtis Price, ed., *Norton Critical Scores: Purcell, Dido and Aeneas*, pp. 255–77. New York: Norton, 1986.

Sedgwick, Eve Kosofsky. *Between Men: English Literature and Male Homosocial Desire.* New York: Columbia University Press, 1985.

Squire, William Barclay. "Purcell's *Dido and Aeneas.*" *Musical Times* (1918), 59:252–54.

Vicinus, Martha. "Distance and Desire: English Boarding School Friendships, 1870–1920." In Martin Bauml Duberman, Martha Vicinus, and George Chauncey, Jr., eds., *Hidden from History: Reclaiming the Gay and Lesbian Past*, pp. 212–29. New York: Penguin, 1989.

Westrup, J. A. "Henry Purcell." In Stanley Sadie, ed., *The New Grove Dictionary of Music and Musicians Composer Biography Series: North European Baroque Masters*, pp. 215–77. New York: Norton, 1985.

_______ *Purcell*. Rev. ed. New York: Collier, 1962.

White, Eric Walter. "New Light on 'Dido and Aeneas.'" In Imogen Holst, ed., *Henry Purcell (1659–1695): Essays on His Music*, pp. 14–34. London: Oxford University Press, 1959.

Williams, Linda. "Film Bodies: Gender, Genre, and Excess." *Film Quarterly* (1991), 44(4):2–13.

Wood, Bruce, and Andrew Pinnock. "'Unscarr'd by turning times?' : The Dating of Purcell's *Dido and Aeneas.*" *Early Music* (August 1992), 20:372–90.

Zaslaw, Neal. "An English 'Orpheus and Euridice' of 1697." *Musical Times* (1977), 118:805–8.

Zimmerman, Franklin B. *Henry Purcell, 1659–1695*. Philadelphia: University of Pennsylvania Press.

Ruggiero's Deceptions, Cherubino's Distractions

Margaret Reynolds

> Some time since I knew a woman I desired. We were friends. We were polite. I did not want to behave politely with this woman, but how to translate my rude lust into ruder action? How to make her understand? She was wise in these matters, but cautious. I was a novice, and, moreover, my circumstances required discretion . . . so I invited her to *Der Rosenkavalier.*

Everyone knows that opera is about sex. It is no accident that the opera house is furnished with velvet plush, gilded mirrors, naked cherubs, and powdered footmen, for these are the trappings of the brothel, and we go to the opera house for sex. Opera lovers are all roués. They know how to savor, how to spin out refined pleasure, how to surrender with apparent abandon, and how to contrive, calculate, cost, and regulate their pleasure. Opera is not natural, not contemporary, not real; it tells us nothing about our lives, nor does it have any truck with the trivia of the everyday. In this consecrated place we give ourselves over to the contrivances of art. And the pleasure that art offers is sophisticated and curious. It thrives on arcane rules, is wholly cerebral in the locus of enjoyment, while it is yet strangely, powerfully connected to the senses so that the body really does feel when the mind is most deeply engaged. As I say, we go to the opera house for sex.

Heterosexuals go, I suppose, for the large passions. You can see them on Saturday nights at *La Bohème*. Middle-aged businessmen in suits, who never lived in garrets or wrote a line of poetry, weep for the imagined romance of their lost youth. Their wives, all red fingernails and tight little dresses, regret the passing of their day as Mimi but comfort themselves by identifying with the full bloom of Musetta. Opera queens go for the divas and the display. Maria Callas enacting a tragic love affair in the public eye blends into Floria Tosca singing "Vissi d'arte," and both embody the flamboyance, the narcissism, the excessive behavior that began as a stereotype and became a gay choice that says "no camouflage" (Koestenbaum 86–87).

And lesbians? Why do they go to the opera?

Because where else can you see two women making love in a public place?

One of the most obvious ways in which the opera speaks of sex is in the variety of gender play. Once upon a time the Renaissance theater offered the perverse spectacle of the boy actor dressed as a woman, and played self-consciously with the contradictions of that state by drawing attention to the body in numerous undressing scenes, by making jokes around the use of stuffing or prosthetic devices, and by complicating the audience's own gendered speculation by dressing boys as girls who had disguised themselves as boys.[1] Now it is only the opera that offers this sexy tease, but with a crucial difference.[2] For today it is all about girls dressing up as boys or girls dressing up as boys and then disguising themselves as girls.

That there are so many opera roles of this kind is partly due to opera's absolute insistence upon its own esoteric rules, where voice and music come first and where realism has no place. But the number of these cross-dressing roles available to mezzo-sopranos today is also due in large part to the historic fact of the rise and demise of the castrato. That he existed once and does no longer is now a great blessing for mezzo-sopranos, who should praise the day that he stopped being made. I say *now* because the apparent obviousness of the mezzos' succession to the roles that once belonged to the castrati has not been as smooth and straightforward as it might have been. The reason? Mezzos are girls, and the castrato roles were made for men, and not all ages and cultures want to play about with gender, nor do they all have the same idea of gender hierarchy (or its absence). So far from the High Art of opera being a transcendent form where temporal ideologies have no place, the history of cross-gender roles in opera reveals just how much art—any art—is affected by fashion, social commonplaces, and contemporary cultural values.

So. Do not adjust your sex; or, how the castrato became a mezzo and what happened to the trouser role along the way. I take as my starting point the proposition that all kinds of cross-dressing in opera contribute to that peculiar alchemy where sex and tease and gender play mix. Into this analysis then go three kinds of singing roles. First, castrati roles: that is, roles originally created for a castrato or generally sung by one in early performances, whoever ends up singing them later. Second, travesti or trouser roles: where a woman sings the role of a man. And, last, disguise roles: where a woman sings the role of a woman who, for some reason to do with the plot, yet appears on stage disguised as a man. A glance through *Kobbé's* gives some idea of the cross-dressing roles available to women singers today. (Of course some of these roles are also sung by countertenors, but I shall come to them later.)

Early Italian and German opera gives a large number of castrati roles, often two male leads in the same opera. Under this heading come the roles of Nero and Ottone in Monteverdi's *L'Incoronazione di Poppea* (1642), Orpheus in Gluck's *Orfeo ed Euridice* (1762), and, especially, in a great many Handel operas, from *Julius Caesar* (l724), which included three major castrato roles in Caesar, Sextus, and Ptolemy, to *Alcina* (1735), where only Ruggiero was created for a castrato. Late castrato roles were written by Mozart in Farnace and Sifare in his juvenile *Mitridate* (1770), and he also wrote the part of Idamante in *Idomeneo* (1781) for the castrato Vincenzo del Prato. The very last notable castrato roles were both created for Giovanni-Battista Velluti in Rossini's *Aureliano in Palmira* (1814) and Meyerbeer's *Il Crociato in Egitto* (1824).

Travesti roles start with Handel, who wrote the part of Sextus in *Julius Caesar* (1724) for a female soprano voice. That character is portrayed as a young boy, and the pattern continues with Mozart's Cherubino in *Le Nozze di Figaro* (1786) and Annius in his *La Clemenza di Tito* (1791). In Rossini and Donizetti there are plenty of travesti roles, including Enrico, Pippo, Malcolm, and Arsace in Rossini's *Elisabetha Regina d'Inghilterra* (1815), *La Gazza Ladra* (1817), *La Donna del Lago* (1819), and *Semiramide* (1823), respectively, and Donizetti's Smeaton and Pieretto in his *Anna Bolena* (1830) and in *Linda di Chamounix* (1842). Other than that there are the roles of Romeo in Bellini's *I Capuleti e i Montecchi* (1830), Siébel in Gounod's *Faust* (1859), and the shepherd Andreloun in his *Mireille* (1864). Then there are the very young boys who are played by women, among them William Tell's son Jemmy in Rossini's *Guillaume Tell* (1829) and Hänsel in Humperdinck's *Hänsel and Gretel* (1893). Otherwise the travesti roles are for young boys who appear as pages, for instance Isolier in Rossini's *Le Comte Ory* (1828), Urbain in Meyerbeer's *Les Huguenots* (1836), Oscar in Verdi's *Un Ballo in Maschera* (1859), and Tebaldo in his *Don Carlos* (1867). During the course of the nineteenth century, then, the travesti role sinks to this small compass until Johann Strauss's Count Orlofsky in *Die Fledermaus* (1874), Massenet's Jean in *Le Jongleur de Notre Dame* (1902), and the title role in his *Cherubin* (1905).[3] In the twentieth century two significant travesti roles appear—Octavian in Richard Strauss's *Der Rosenkavalier* (1911) and the Composer in his *Ariadne auf Naxos* (1916).

Castrato roles, travesti roles—that leaves the disguise category, where a woman sings the part of a woman who, governed by the exigencies of the plot, appears dressed in the disguise of a man. Given the powerful tradition of this role in legend and literature it is rather surprising to find that there are in fact very few of them in opera. There is an early exponent in Handel's *Alcina* (1735) where Bradamante, following the Ariosto text, has disguised herself thus. Then there is Leonora in Beethoven's *Fidelio* (1805), Matilda in Rossini's *Elisabetha*

Regina d'Inghilterra (1815), Gilda in act 3 of Verdi's *Rigoletto* (1851), and, back to Strauss again, Zdenka in his *Arabella* (1933).

This is the cross-dressing repertoire for women that is (or some of which is) performed today. Even in this brief sketch a pattern begins to emerge, marking out the assumptions of gender construction in different periods of history. The first point to make is that, with the exception of the Composer in Strauss's *Ariadne*, not one of the noble and heroic roles listed here was created expressly for a woman singer. The numerous travesti roles that appear in the nineteenth century are not heroic; they are young men or boys, and they are very often foolish, or even portrayed as idiots. The disguise roles tend to be more elevated, but they offer a familiar model of female self-sacrifice that is not very inspiring. The fact is, because of an extraordinary quirk in history and because of changes in fashion, women singers can now exploit a superb repertoire of roles that should, strictly, have been denied them. Strangely enough, in the late twentieth century, it seems less odd that women should be singing these roles evocative of authority and power than it does to contemplate the original performances of these operas where the same butch roles were created for high voices. But it is us who are at fault here. For the twentieth century has become so locked into commonplaces of gender difference that it is hard to reassess the roles of the castrati. Yet, nonetheless, in the early days of the opera virility, authority, and power were not incompatible with a high voice. Quite the contrary.

The story of the brief reign of the castrati in opera has been told by Angus Heriot, Christian Gaumy, and John Rosselli. Castrati singers seem first to have appeared, probably from Morocco, in the Moorish courts in southern Spain and Portugal. By the fifteenth century they were singing at the court of Naples and in the papal chapel. They were welcomed into the church and justified by an interpretation of St. Paul's dictum that "women should be silent in church," and they could be heard in the Sistine choir up until 1884. At first used exclusively in church music, when the new opera form came in at the beginning of the seventeenth century they began to sing there too. And in both places the castrato voice was highly valued, not as a substitute woman's voice, nor as a substitute for the boy treble, but valued as itself and for its own qualities: its brilliance and power, its range and pitch, and its strangeness and ambiguity.

Contemporary descriptions of castrati singing remark on their projection and virtuoso skill:

> Their timbre is as clear and piercing as that of choirboys and much more powerful; they appear to sing an octave above the natural voice of women. Their voices have always something dry and harsh, quite different from the youthful softness of women; but they are brilliant, light, full of sparkle, very loud, and with a very wide range. (Brosses, cited in Heriot 14)

According to John Rosselli's modern analysis there would be a physical explanation for this exhibition of skill and strength, for here one would experience the effect of "an enlarged thoracic cavity combined with an undeveloped larynx [that] allowed a mighty rush of air to play upon small vocal chords" (33). That this voice was not feeble, like that of a child, and not forced, like that of a falsettist, meant that in many contemporary descriptions (much to the embarrassment of modern commentators) the castrato voice was often called "natural" and "genuine," which, of course, in terms of sound, it would have been.

Why the high voice, any high voice, was and is valued, is a vexing question. Brigid Brophy makes a brave attempt at it when she suggests that because the high voice is common to women, girls, and boys, it retains a powerfully direct address to our emotions both through our own experience of childhood and through the memory of the mother's authority (57). Michel Poizat points to its association with the voice of the angel—high, disembodied, otherworldly, and, above all, transsexual (116). Either or both of these explanations are relevant to the opera world of the seventeenth and eighteenth centuries. Here was a culture that operated in terms of oppositions and hierarchies where the higher is valued over the lower and associated with concepts of superiority. So the high voice is king. And, because the best high voice is supposed to be that of the castrato, the early operatic repertoire gives the main roles of kings and warriors, poets and gods to the castrato singer. So far so good. What is very peculiar, from a twentieth-century point of view, is that the hierarchy of voice value was so absolute and so important at this time that it completely overturned the oppositions of gender value. We have so thoroughly learned the lesson of the binary of "masculine" over "feminine" as a governing structure that this does seem, now, to be very surprising. But the fact is that if a theater could not get a castrato high voice to sing in their production of Monteverdi or Handel they went out and found the next best high voice and gave the part of the king or warrior, poet or god to a woman.

Angus Heriot cites a number of cases in which theaters engaged women singers as *primo amoroso* where, en travesti, they took the parts otherwise assigned to a male castrato. He quotes the case of the woman who sang the part of the ultra-macho hero Hercules in Gluck's *Le Nozze d'Ercole e d'Ebe*, and tells the story of Vittoria Tesi, who played the part of Achilles in Metastasio's *Achille in Sciro* (1737), in which the whole plot revolves around Achilles disguising himself as a woman in the harem at Scyros in order to escape the call to arms for the Trojan war. Also here is the especially strange example of Cavalli's *Eliogabalo* (1668), where the three male parts of Eliogabalo, Alessandro, and Cesare were cast for sopranos (either castrati or women), while the female part of Zenia was cast for a tenor (Heriot 33–34). Very frequently this kind of fluid casting would mean that the leading male role would be performed by a soprano (male or female), while the leading female role was sung by a lower contralto voice (male or female).

For it worked the other way round as well. I have said that the castrato voice was not a substitute for the woman's voice, and it wasn't, because it didn't need to be. Apart from the special case of Rome, where a Papal ban on women appearing on stage remained in force up to 1798, women *did* sing in opera in the rest of Italy and throughout Europe, even if they risked, like their counterparts on the stage, impudent questions about their morals. But often the female part was given to a castrato simply because that was the preferred voice for both male and female high-voice roles. At the first performance of Monteverdi's *La Favola di Orpheo* (1607), the part of the Prologue (La Musica) was sung by a castrato, as were the parts of Eurydice and the Messagiera. Just as the idea of a woman playing the part of Hercules is amusing in retrospect, so the transvestite male in a female role had some funny results. Instance the case of Manelli's *Andromeda* (1637), where the part of Venus was sung by a man.[4]

In practical terms this kind of haphazard casting meant that theaters could simply give their parts to the best qualified singer regardless of sex. As long as they had a high voice. By the eighteenth century almost all the lead roles, male and female, were for high voices, and something like 70 percent of all male opera singers were castrati. The voices that really were neglected were those natural male voices of tenor and bass who were usually consigned to the part of the old man, the nurse, the villain, or the special effects (e.g., Neptune's oracle in Mozart's *Idomeneo*).

In imaginative terms this willingness to make the demands of gendered naturalism entirely subservient to the requirements of musical fitness had some significant results. More than for its power and brilliance, more than for its range and pitch, the castrato voice was valued because it was strange and rare, because it was fabulous and other. The use of the castrato sound pointed away from the ordinary meanings of the voice, which lie in the message, and directed the listening ear to the particularities of the voice itself. Such little evidence as we have of the sound of the castrato voice confirms this point. Desmond Shawe-Taylor describes the recorded voice of the last castrato Alessandro Moreschi (1858–1922) as "curiously disembodied" (Heriot 227). Because this sound was a strange voice in the wrong body (insofar as it belonged to any natural body), it became impersonal, more a musical instrument than a voice at all. That composers saw it this way is borne out by the instrumental style of music written for the castrati. The aria "Va tacito e nascosto" from Handel's *Julius Caesar* is an example, for there the sound of the horn obbligato is mimicked by the singing voice. Similarly in "Se in fiorito ameno prato" from the same opera, the song of the lark is imitated both by the wind accompaniment and by the voice.

The effects of the universal employment of travesti (in either direction) were much the same. Again, here was the show of a voice heard, which did not match the body seen. And it was that contradiction that Goethe appreciated in the performance of the travestied castrati:

> I reflected on the reasons why these singers pleased me so greatly, and I think I have found it. In these representations, the concept of imitation and art was invariably more strongly felt, and through their able performance a sort of conscious illusion was produced. Thus a double pleasure is given.
>
> (cited in Heriot 26)

Part of this "double pleasure" and "conscious illusion" may also have come from an awareness of the sexual ambiguity that might arise when the audience looks upon women dressed as men or men dressed as women. Several of Handel's operas (*Alcina*, *Partenope*, *Siroe*, *Serse*) include scenes where sexual complications arise because of this practice. Neither does Handel seem to be averse to exploiting the presence on stage of a castrato singer to allow for teasing questions of sexuality and potency. Cleopatra's aria "Non disperar" in *Julius Caesar* is addressed to her brother—and enemy—Ptolemy, a role created for a castrato. Here a game is being offered to the audience that relies upon the discrepancy between Cleopatra's advice ("Yet why despair? Who knows? / Though kingdoms pass you by, / You'll gain a maiden's heart") and what the audience actually see, and hear, and guess at, which makes them suspect Ptolemy's sexual capacity. The music emphasizes the irony of the aria for the vocal line is accompanied by harpsichord and violins, which play rapid staccato crochets on the same note with jeering insistence, and, in the main musical passages, the strings in unison play a theme based on laughing runs and trills.

So the eighteenth-century audience was one skilled in the suspension of disbelief, but quick also to perceive the wit that might lie in a disjuncture between the real and the apparent and willing to play the game of cross-dressing trompe l'oeil. In Handel's day there was sexual anarchy on stage. Men (or ex-men) played the parts of heroes in high voices. Women, dressed up as men, sang heroes in high voices. Men, dressed up as women, played their consorts with high or low voices. And if you couldn't hire the singer of the sex required, you settled for the voice and didn't worry. Nobody cared who represented whom. Everyone knew that opera was sound, and spectacle, and they discounted all other considerations. If anyone thought at all about the gender absurdities they witnessed, the audience enjoyed the play of innuendo and suggestion.

And then. And then times changed, and the men began to wriggle in their seats.

From the middle of the eighteenth century, ideas about the immutability of sex difference began to harden. Even in philosophical works that were not about men and women at all a constructed hierarchy of "masculine" and "feminine" virtues began to appear. So Burke's aesthetic theory in the *Philosophical Enquiry Into the Origin of Our Ideas of the Sublime and the Beautiful* (1757) sets "those virtues which cause admiration" (fortitude, justice, wisdom) into the manly category of the sublime, while those that inspire love (easiness of temper, compassion, kindness, and liberality) fit into the "softer" category of the beautiful.[5] As the century went on the ideologies surrounding a constructed femininity became more insistent, and, as Nancy Armstrong has shown, increasingly the definition of "femininity" was used as a mirror to define and promote the proper dominance of "masculinity" (Armstrong 3–27). No wonder then that the castrati had to go. No wonder then that the travesti role began to shrivel.

The period of the castrati's decline is from the 1790s on, so that by the 1810s and 1820s there was a dearth of singers, and by 1844, when Pergetti appeared in London, they were all but extinct. This puts their demise at the same time as the period of the French Revolutionary and the Napoleonic wars—and with good reason. During the intense European upheaval of this time, one of the things that increasingly worried contemporary arbiters of morals was that men were no longer men and women were no longer women. Strong women in the public eye (Mary Wollstonecraft, Madame de Staël) were demanding reforms and an equality of sex in the light of the new democracies. Strong women on the streets were taking part in storming the barricades and persecuting the criminals of the revolution. And where there are strong women it follows that they must be emasculating their men.[6] The sexual anarchy once seen only on the stage was now happening all around, and the sight of a castrato on the stage became an affront. When Napoleon saw a performance by the castrato Velluti in 1810, he declared (was it a compliment?), "One must be only half a man to sing like that" (Heriot 35), and in the Italian states under Napoleonic rule, stringent measures were taken to outlaw the practice of castration.

Mozart's work comes right in the middle of this change. He wrote heroic opera seria that looked back to Handel's model in both formal shape (*recitativo secco* with da capo arias) and in its use of sex transgressive roles. But he also wrote opera buffa where the form was associative and developmental, where the subjects were romantic love, and where boys were boys and girls were girls. Even where Mozart was writing for a castrato singer the new insistences of sex difference were becoming apparent. Once the great castrato Farinelli could still be described as "manly." But when Mozart wrote the part of Idamante for Vincenzo del Prato, he said that he would have to teach the role to "mio molto amato castrato . . . as if he were a child" (cited in Brophy 36). Like Napoleon, Mozart considered del Prato "only half a man." Eventually, of course, all those half-men disappeared, and in 1786 Idamante was rewritten for a tenor.

That still left Mozart with the possibilities of sex transgressive roles for the female travesti. And one of the greatest of these is his Cherubino. But Mozart was of his time, and his Cherubino was not one of the old-fashioned, haphazard, largely innocent travesti roles where the voice was what mattered and the body beneath was irrelevant. Far from it. This time, perhaps for the first time, this young woman dressing as a man dressing as a woman was explicitly about sex.

When Beaumarchais wrote his program notes for the characters of his *Le Mariage de Figaro* (1785), upon which Mozart's *Le Nozze* is based, he said of Cherubino: "The part can only be played, as it was in fact, by a young and very pretty woman: we have no very young men in our theatre who are at the same time sufficiently mature to appreciate the fine points of the part."[7] Maybe he didn't have any promising young men in his theater, but Beaumarchais knew what he was about, and he was no stranger to scurrilous titillation. In the years leading up to and during the French Revolution, one of the more curious symptoms of a perceived sexual disorder in France was the publication (and popularity) of numerous scandalous pamphlets that attributed all kinds of sexual vices to royal wives and mistresses. Marie Antoinette suffered most, being portrayed in congress with men, with women, with animals, with her own son.[8] In 1774 Beaumarchais had been sent to London by the king to suppress one such pamphlet on Madame du Barry. When he lost his patron with the death of Louis XV, he tried his own hand at the game and traveled to Vienna saying that he was after a sex-sin pamphlet that impugned the honor of Marie Antoinette and her mother. This juicy number he presented to the empress, neglecting to tell her that he had written it himself.[9]

By the time *Le Mariage* was turned into *Le Nozze*, Cherubino was still being played by a woman and the possibilities for sex games were still present. After all, act 1 begins with the imagination of a bed, act 2 takes us into the Countess's boudoir, and act 4 shows the garden temple where amorous assignations are kept (Marie Antoinette's Petit Trianon transposed?). Dressing and undressing are activities kept constantly in the eye of the audience; when Cherubino first appears in scene 5 of act 1, he encounters Susanna carrying a dress belonging to the Countess—and is later hidden underneath this dress. In act 2 we are wound up to wonder how far Susanna and the Countess will go when undressing Cherubino in preparation for his disguise. Eventually we do see him dressed as a girl, and again he is undressed to reveal his sex—which isn't his sex at all.

Cherubino's body with its surprises and disguises is kept on show. His crossing nature as both male and female is also emphasized in his name (little cherub) and the other names that Figaro gives him (Narcissetto, "little Narcissus," Adoncino d'amor, "little Adonis of love," farfallone amoroso, "amorous butterfly"), and is especially made apparent in Figaro's aria "Non più andrai," which is a march in C major to reflect the (masculine) activity of war to which he is now being dispatched, but which includes a switch to a gavotte rhythm, with repeats from the violins on a dainty chromatic inflection, to accompany Figaro's reference to Cherubino's (feminine) interest in dress and flirtation. Cherubino's role in *Le Nozze* is an anarchic one. He crosses gender and questions sex difference. He crosses class, being both aristocratic and yet at home with servants, eventually marrying Barbarina. He is always appearing in the wrong places, much to the Count's discomfiture; thus he unsettles every social order. More than this, the music bears out his transgressive character, for when his name is simply mentioned in the finale to act 2 (bar 567), the music plunges into G minor—a key that Charles Ford argues is always associated for Mozart with anxieties, doubts, and suspicions (166). Cherubino is about mistaken identity, liminality, tease. Goethe would have appreciated this "double pleasure."

The nineteenth-century audience, however, did not. In *Either/Or* the Danish philosopher Søren Kierkegaard declared that Cherubino is Don Giovanni in his youth. The remark has been much repeated, but, of course, he isn't—he can't be.[10] Don Giovanni represents everything that lines up on the "masculine" side of constructed difference and Cherubino, whatever the dramatic personae might say, is a girl in disguise, and the audience is never allowed to forget that. Kierkegaard's mistake arises because the nineteenth century didn't want to play the gender game any more.

From Rossini onward the nineteenth-century opera became a shrine to heterosex. The tenor and baritone voices, neglected in Handel's time, were given new prominence. The lead romantic role was sung by a tenor; his rival or friend was sung by a baritone, and their voices were celebrated in the great dramatic duets that especially characterize Verdi's work. If we now interpret those duets as homoerotic we certainly weren't meant to, because the hero was supposed to get his girl. And so they did, in more ways than one. Catherine Clément's *Opera, or the Undoing of Women* is mainly about, as it has to be, the nineteenth-century romantic repertoire where women are very Women, lying on couches, dying in garrets, leaping over parapets. The high voice in the nineteenth century belonged exclusively to the female soprano, and it was the voice of an angel, not disembodied, but a Victorian angel, womanly, ethereal, self-immolating. In this new opera scene women were undone, and the cross-dressing role was entirely demolished.

There were still plenty of them, but Cherubino was the last role to offer the trompe l'oeil of sex and other sex. These new travesti roles were clean versions of the innocent young boy (Romeo, Enrico, Smeaton, Malcolm, Hansel), or else they were feminized in being gentle, poetic, and associated with nature as shepherds (Pieretto, Siebel, Pippo, Andreloun). Otherwise they play childish pages (Isolier, Urbain, Tebaldo, Oscar), or else they take the supernatural roles that are clearly asexual (Puck, the Heavenly Voice in Verdi's *Don Carlos*, the Voice of the Falcon in Strauss's *Die Frau ohne Schatten*). It should be noted here that the two great champions of heterosexuality on the operatic stage, Verdi and Puccini, give us very little in the way of cross-dressing roles. There are two boy pages played by women in Verdi (Tebaldo and Oscar). But, not surprisingly, there is nothing at all in Puccini. With two possible exceptions. The first is the role of the music master in his *Manon Lescaut* (1893). As this opera is set in an imagined eighteenth century, Puccini concedes to the demands of historical "verismo" and allows the part of the musician in act 2 (who is, apparently, a then-fashionable castrato) to be played by a (female) mezzo-soprano. The one other cross-dressing role in Puccini is, possibly, that of the Voice of the Shepherd boy at the beginning of the third act of *Tosca*. Yet he, significantly, remains unseen. And in any case, he could be sung by a real boy.

Not much tease here. This "shepherd boy" kind of casting is rather the result of a straightforward reading of woman as "undeveloped man," which means that it is perfectly proper for a woman to play a boy's part in the interests of verisimilitude. Remember that the Victorian period is the one above all others that anxiously tried to contain female sexuality by denying it altogether, by infantilizing women, and by praising—a backhanded compliment—woman's idealized association with moral and spiritual values. Remember too that while the travesti role in opera was being diminished in this way, the phenomenon of the "principal boy" was being developed in the popular theater. And, as Peter Ackroyd has explained, it was pretty and anodyne there as well: "The male impersonator, the actress in trousers, seems . . . to lack depth and resonance. . . . [She] is never anything more than what she pretends to be: a feminine noble mind in a boy's body. It is a peculiarly sentimental and therefore harmless reversal" (102).

While the travesti role atrophies in the nineteenth century, the disguise role is also curiously absent. Its early exponents (Bradamante and Leonora) dress as men in a noble cause, that of rescuing their betrothed or husband. Matilda in Rossini's *Elisabeth Regina d'Ingiliterra* is similarly protecting her husband from the queen's wrath. One might imagine that these pictures of female self-sacrifice would continue into the nineteenth century, and so they do. What stops happening, however, is the dressing up in men's clothing bit. Nice girls just don't do that sort of thing.

The disguise role, always rare after Handel, disappears altogether in the nineteenth century. Except . . . except for *naughty* girls. In the third act of Verdi's *Rigoletto* Gilda disguises herself as a man in order to flee the city, and in that shape is able to knock at the door of Sparafucile and make herself the victim who will save the life of the Duke. This selfless act lines her up with the nobility of Leonora—with one notable change. Gilda is *not* married to the Duke, but (at this point in the drama) she is a fallen woman. The lesson is clear. Within the strict dress code of Victorian morality, only bad girls dress up as men. Poor Gilda has just one odd, very late, descendant. Zdenka in Strauss's *Arabella*. She too disguises herself as a man for reasons to do with the plot, but note that she, too, in the course of the opera, becomes a fallen woman.

Strauss: Octavian. The Composer. Zdenka. Three remarkable cross-dressing roles. The travesti role, fading away through the nineteenth century, revives. Why?

Once more into the breeches, dear friend.

Throughout the second half of the nineteenth century psychologists and scientists came to unpick the Victorian platitudes of sex difference and to question the absolute split that gave "masculine" values to men and "feminine" to women. The work of the sexologists began in 1869 with Carl von Westphal and continued with Richard von Krafft-Ebing's *Psycopathia Sexualis* (1882) and Havelock Ellis's *Studies in the Psychology of Sex* (1897). These writers knew that sex difference was not inviolable, and they knew what homosexuality was. They didn't like it—they named it a sickness—but they *named* it. Pretty soon a wider public knew what it was too. In Britain the notoriety of the three trials of Oscar Wilde (1895) brought into existence a labeled homosexual identity (Weeks 21n). All this, of course, was part of a broad European phenomenon usually called decadence. It was about excess, feeling, extravagance, beauty, theater, and sex. Especially perverse sex. In this climate the travesti role came back to life.

The resurrection starts with the other Strauss, Johann, who created the role of Prince Orlovsky in *Die Fledermaus* (1874). We do not need *Kobbé*'s coy note about the "moral permissiveness" of 1870s Vienna in order to be able to see that a party, given in a theater, for the denizens of the beau monde, by a cross-dressed female who sings "chacun a son gout," is flaunting propriety and tugging at the edges of suggestion.

Serious suggestion doesn't start until Richard Strauss gets going in his post-fin-de-siècle decadence, but it is foreshadowed by the work of Massenet, who also went back to the rococo deviances of an imagined eighteenth century when he wrote *Chérubin* (1905), with its cross-dressed hero who is definitely sexually active. Curiously it is in the latter half of the nineteenth century that we also hear the one last echo of the castrati's greatness. When Wagner, who, like Verdi and Puccini, permits no sexualized cross-dressing, heard a castrato singer, he considered enticing one away from the Sistine choir at Rome in order to sing the part of the magician Klingsor in his *Parsifal* (1882).[11] Even this staunch advocate of sexual difference and strict gender roles would seem to have been affected by an atmosphere where theater's magic might allow for that most tantalizing of transformations, sex transgression.

When Richard Strauss came to write *Der Rosenkavalier* (1911) and to give the part of Octavian to a young woman, he was wily and knowing in his transgression. Of course, he was following Mozart, but this was no frilly, tinkling, childish Mozart. This was the fully aware, wicked, and saucy Mozart. For Strauss knew about sex and decadence, and just as Mozart had used a libretto from the scurrilous Beaumarchais, so Strauss too had previously used a libretto from the maligned of his own generation in his 1905 adaptation of Oscar Wilde's *Salome*.

And others knew what Strauss was doing. As in *Le Nozze di Figaro*, there are two beds in *Der Rosenkavalier*; a real one, this time, in the first act, and a secret surprise one that Baron Ochs plans to use in the third act. The first act bed caused trouble in London where the Lord Chamberlain intervened when Thomas Beecham declared his intention to stage the opera in 1912: either the bed had to go from the scene or there was to be no reference to it in the text sung by the performers. Beecham decided that the former was preferable, so the Marschallin and Octavian conducted themselves with upright propriety.[12] Singers too were worried by the erotic—the perverse erotic—of the opera. In 1909 Hugo von Hofmannsthal (Strauss's librettist) already had it in mind that the part of Octavian should be played by a woman. He wrote to Strauss: "It contains two big parts, one for baritone and another for a graceful girl dressed up as a man, à la [Geraldine] Farrar or Mary Garden" (cited in Jefferson 2). Garden had played the part of Jean, a religious fool, in Massenet's *Le Jongleur de Notre Dame* in Paris in 1904, and the part of *Cherubin* in his opera of 1905, so she was certainly not averse to dressing up in men's clothes. But . . . but she refused to sing the role of Octavian because of its implications. Its lesbian implications (Koestenbaum 218).

Octavian as a girl was Hofmannsthal's idea. But when they collaborated on *Ariadne auf Naxos* and made the second version of the piece with its backstage prologue to the opera, it was Strauss's idea to give the part of the Composer to a woman. Like Beaumarchais before him, he began by justifying that choice by reference to the absence of competent tenors: "The part of the Composer (since tenors are so terrible) I shall give to Mlle. Artôt. Only you'll have to consider now how we might further fill out the part for her. . . . I can only win Mlle. Artôt for our piece if I offer her a kind of small star part" (cited in Kennedy 64). Hofmannsthal objected furiously. He was enough of a product of fin-de-siècle decadence to enjoy erotic games in a light-hearted piece like *Der Rosenkavalier*, but he was also a man born in the nineteenth century, and he had clear ideas about what could and could not be represented by a woman. And the heroic role of artist could *not* be represented by a woman:

> Your opportunism in theatrical matters has in this case thoroughly led you up the garden path. . . . To prettify this particular character, which is to have an aura of "spirituality" and "greatness" about it . . . strikes me as, forgive my plain speaking, odious. . . . Oh Lord, if only I were able to bring home to you completely the essence, the spiritual meaning of these characters.
>
> (Kennedy 65)

Strauss had his way. And with the Composer the cross-dressing role comes full circle, as a woman is once again allowed to play the noble part of the hero, the leader, the artist, just as she had done in the eighteenth century. In many ways the terms of Strauss's decision ("A tenor is impossible . . . a leading baritone won't sing the Composer: so what is left to me except the only genre of singer not yet represented in *Ariadne*") show that he had arrived at a position where threatrical practicality and the demands of musical formality meant that sex difference and gendered realism were altogether irrelevant (Kennedy 65). If Hofmannsthal did not understand, Handel and his contemporaries certainly would have done so. Like Handel in this, Strauss's work also resembles that of his predecessor in that the voice, for him, was not so much the attribute of a particular (sexed) singer but rather an impersonal musical instrument. The singer Blanche Marchesi tells the story of how a doctor told Strauss that "I have advised all my lady singer clients to stop singing your music until it shall be written for the human voice" (Koestenbaum 218). If Strauss had had the voice of a castrato singer available to write for, then he would have done so.

Or would he? Perhaps even Strauss's acute sense of musical fitness could not have overcome the shame and embarrassment that begins to gather around the idea of the castrato in the first half of the twentieth century. An embarrassment that extended to Handel's operas, then rarely performed. Where they were performed, say during the 1920s, the shameful castrati parts were transposed and given to baritones or basses. Even the new revival, which begins in the 1950s, when Richard Bonynge was cruising the repertoire for new vehicles for Joan Sutherland, the same attitude prevails, and so in the 1959 recording of *Alcina* the part of Ruggiero is played by the tenor Fritz Wunderlich. When more scholarly revivals began to appear, giving the castrati parts to mezzos, some critics still seemed to be embarrassed, and were scathing in their amusement. Lord Harewood, for instance, describes the effect: "More or less strapping mezzos tackled the great heroes of antiquity, with results which were occasionally comic to look at and not always heroic vocally" (Harewood 30). Angus Heriot blithely declares that only "sopranos vain of their figures" volunteer to sing the "trouser roles," and he anticipates the day when " 'principal boys' in their turn have had their palmiest days and may before long be extinct" (22).

These are two very anxious boys . . . but they shall have to stay anxious, nervously clutching their mezzo-parts, because the glorious arrival of Camp means that the girls are holding firmly onto theirs.

In recent years the operas of Handel, and of his predecessors and contemporaries, have enjoyed a huge revival in opera houses all over the world. The castrati roles are back in their proper place in the scale and are sung by either countertenors or by mezzo-sopranos. In some ways that allocation of roles once again depends on who you can get. Sometimes both appear on stage, the mezzo taking the hero's role and the countertenor taking the second lead. This was the case in the English National Opera's 1984 production of *Julius Caesar*, in which Janet Baker sang Caesar and James Bowman sang Ptolemy. It also happened in the Royal Opera House production of *Mithridate* (1991), in which Ann Murray was Sifare and Jochen Kowalski was Farnace. Handel and Mozart would recognize the terms of these productions.

They would also recognize the possibility of gender tease that is now encouraged by the Camp camp. Ptolemy can be played as a raging Queen; Xerxes can be turned into a transvestite romp. And the audiences love it, for they (or at least some of them) have begun to learn the lessons so long preached by feminists and homosexuals. That is, that heterosexual identity as much as any other (*more* than any other?) is a constructed pose that can be deconstructed.

And what's in it for lesbians? Not a picture of themselves, but certainly a picture of someone playing at representing those selves. A number of recent opera productions in Britain play this game: at the Welsh National Opera Adalgisa climbs onto the pyre with Norma and Donna Anna cuddles Donna Elvira; at the Royal Opera House Cherubino lolls on the Countess's bed, and Ann Murray and Felicity Lott chuckle in publicity interviews over the wickedness of Ann Murray's nakedness as the curtain opens on *Der Rosenkavalier*. In 1762 Casanova had declared that the Roman practice of using castrati, men dressed deliciously as women, to perform the female parts in opera had the peculiar effect of forcing "every man to become a pederast" (Heriot 55). If we take this to its logical conclusion, it would seem that the much favored cross-dressing and cross-sexualizing happening on the stage today will have the interesting effect of making every woman a lesbian. I look forward to it.

All good clean fun. But the discerning lesbian reader doesn't need many saucy pointers. It's all there in the music and in the libretto, whether we are talking about Handel or Mozart or Strauss. When Handel wrote the part of Ruggiero in *Alcina* for the castrato singer Carestini, he included the puzzled aria "Mi lusinga il dolce affetto." Ruggiero is confused, and with good reason. He has been enchanted by the sorceress Alcina and dallies on her magic island forgetting all about his proper role in the real world. He neglects his honor as a warrior; he ignores his duty to his betrothed Bradamante. This is a female world, an enchanted world like that of theater, where duty, honor, and the orders of society have no place. Alcina has seduced many men before, and the whole island is littered with stones and trees and animals that were once men, who were transformed when Alcina tired of them.

At the beginning of the opera Bradamante arrives to seek her lost lover. But she is disguised in men's clothing and pretends that she is her own brother Ricciardo come to search for Ruggiero. Morgana, Alcina's sister, bored with the rampant and blustering attentions of Oronte, takes one look at Bradamante and promptly falls in love with her. To protect her disguise, Bradamante pretends to return her affection. Then . . . Oronte tells Ruggiero that Bradamante/Ricciardo is pursuing Alcina herself. Alcina decides that she'd better turn Bradamante into a stone forthwith in order to calm her jealous lover. In the midst of this accusation, plot, and counterplot Bradamante reveals herself to Ruggiero, lets her hair down in classic pantomime style, and tells him that she really is his beloved Bradamante herself. Dimly remembering his past, Ruggiero begins to recall himself, but he no longer knows what to believe. Is this another of Alcina's transformations? Or is Ruggiero himself the deceiver? "Who will help me to be sure whether I am betrayed or whether I am hearing the truth," he sings. And then,

> She deceives my gentle feelings
> With the appearance of my dearest
> Who knows? It is well to fear
> That she would deceive me to keep my love.
> But if this were really she whom I adored
> And I abandon her now, then
> I would be faithless, ungrateful, and a cruel traitor.[13]

The musical pattern of this aria underlines the alternating question as the tune moves down the scale (twice) in the opening section and climbs back up again with hesitating ornament. Even the fact of this being a da capo aria is dramatically effective here as it reiterates Ruggiero's complaint. For the contemporary audience, of course, there was another deception still, in that Ruggiero did not sing with the voice of a man, though he represented one. For the modern audience that deviant pleasure is still present when Ruggiero is sung by a woman who masquerades as a man. For the lesbian audience this is now the most tantalizing of operas, for all four main characters are played by women (Ruggiero, Alcina, Morgana, Bradamante) and all the love interest, all the wooing and the teasing, all the betrayals and reunions, happen between women.

In Mozart's *Le Nozze di Figaro* Cherubino's first aria also presents a transsexual puzzle. Like Ruggiero, he doesn't know where he is, who he is, or what he is doing. The text of the libretto is based very closely on Beaumarchais's play except for the all-important ending.

> I no longer know what I am, what I do;
> now I burn, now I freeze.
> Every woman makes me blush,
> Every woman makes me tremble.
> At the mere words "love" and "delight"
> my breast heaves and pounds,
> and there forces me to speak of love
> a desire which I cannot explain.
>
> I speak of love when I am awake,
> I speak of love when I am asleep,
> to the stream, to the shade, to the mountains,
> to the flowers, to the grass, to the fountains,
> to the echo, to the air, to the breezes,
> which bear away the sound of my fleeting words . . .
>
> And if I have no one to hear me,
> I speak of love to myself. (Carter 44)

As the text rushes hither and yon, Cherubino's distraction is mimicked in the rapid transposition through a number of associated keys. Mozart uses the sonata form, but the repetitions that express obsession and disturbance are built into the aria's development as each musical phrase is immediately repeated with small internal variations. Thus the aria presents a double strand of textual sameness, in that the libretto and the music both are about, and enact, the insistences of repetition.

This pattern is echoed when Cherubino invokes the suggestion of sexual sameness at the end of the aria ("I speak of love to myself"). Often called Narcissus in the text, Cherubino represents the doubleness, the self-reflection, of woman with woman that can easily be recuperated by a positive lesbian reading.[14]

Once one comes to *Der Rosenkavalier* all of these suggestions have been written in by Hofmannsthal. The opera begins with a visual tease of repetition, two the same, where there should be difference. Deception and distraction where there should be straight and straightforward. Where there should be hierarchy and order. And these distractions are the first matter in the libretto, for Octavian begins,

How you love! How you are!
No one knows, no one imagines! . . .
You, you!—What does "you" mean?
What "you and I"?
Does it make any sense?

Which is you? And which me? These repetitions, these doublenesses, these theatrical coups, do make sense if the lesbian viewer/reader understands textual sameness as an echo of sexual sameness. She will be familiar with Ruggiero's deceptions and Cherubino's distractions.

Ah, yes . . . and the end of the story.

We sat in the darkness of the stalls, and she watched the stage, and I watched her. She smiled as the curtain rose on Octavian's naked back; she smiled at the Presentation of the Rose. She laughed as Baron Ochs lost his wig, applauded his ignominious departure. She wept at the Trio. Afterward, in the darkness of the street, she kissed me on the mouth. She says I kissed her. Who knows?

Non so più cosa son, cosa faccio . . .

Notes

1. See Stallybrass,"Transvestism and the 'Body Beneath,' " pp. 64–83.

2. The exception, of course, is the pantomime and Peter Pan. See Garber, *Vested Interests,* pp. 176–85.

3. The part of Jean was first performed in 1902 by Charles Marechal, a tenor. In 1904 the soprano Mary Garden sang the role, as she did on later occasions. See Harewood, *Kobbé's*, p. 700. Garden created the role of Cherubin (1905).

4. See Heriot, *The Castrati in Opera*, p. 28.

5. See Jones, *Women in the Eighteenth Century*, pp. 2–4.

6. See Cameron , "Political Exposures," pp. 90–107.

7. Notes on the characters in the first edition of *Le Mariage de Figaro* (1785).

8. See Hunt, "The Many Bodies of Marie Antoinette," pp. 90–107.

9. See Heartz, *Mozart's Operas*, pp. 107–8.

10. Following Kierkegaard, Brigid Brophy suggests that "Cherubino's fluttering aria 'Non so piu' is, as it were, a soliloquy for the phallos" (106n). She is wrong, of course, for her reading takes no account of the inescapeable fact that the part is always played by a woman.

11. See Heriot, *The Castrati in Opera*, p. 21n.

12. See Jefferson, *Richard Strauss, Der Rosenkavalier*, p. 90.

13. English translation by Clifford Bartlett from EMI recording.

14. I know that accusations of narcissism are often leveled at homosexual relations in order to suggest psychological inadequacy. I also know, and agree with Michael Warner, that the most debilitating examples of narcissistic self-seeking are actually found in het-

erosexuality (see Warner, "Homo-Narcissism; or, Heterosexuality," pp. 190–206). But I do feel strongly that when it comes to women, and to lesbians, concepts of narcissism—and autoeroticism—can be used as positive images rather than otherwise. As Virginia Woolf argued long since in *A Room of One's Own* (1929), historically women have been encouraged to undervalue themselves and have been alienated from fruitful relations with other women. In the face of this negative social context, to love one's self, to love the semblance of one's self in another, can be exciting, provocative, and constructive.

Works Cited

Ackroyd, Peter. *Dressing Up: Transvestism and Drag: The History of an Obsession*. New York: Simon and Schuster, 1979.

Armstrong, Nancy. *Desire and Domestic Fiction: A Political History of the Novel*. Oxford: Oxford University Press, 1987.

Brophy, Brigid. *Mozart the Dramatist: The Value of His Operas to Him, to His Age, and to Us*. Rev. ed. London: Libris, 1988.

Brosses, Charles de. *Lettres familières sur l'Italie*. Paris, 1931.

Cameron, Vivian. "Political Exposures: Sexuality and Caricature in the French Revolution." In Lynn Hunt, ed., *Eroticism and the Body Politic*, pp. 90–107. Baltimore: Johns Hopkins University Press, 1991.

Carter, Tim. *W. A. Mozart: Le Nozze di Figaro*. Cambridge: Cambridge University Press, 1987.

Clément, Catherine. *Opera, or the Undoing of Women*. Trans. Betsy Wing. London: Virago, 1989.

Ford, Charles. *Cosi? Sexual Politics in Mozart's Operas*. Manchester: Manchester University Press, 1991.

Garber, Marjorie. *Vested Interests: Cross-Dressing and Cultural Anxiety*. London: Penguin, 1992.

Gaumy, Christian. "Le Chant des Castrats." *Opera International* (December 1984-January 1985).

Handel, George Frideric. *Alcina*. With Joan Sutherland, Jeanette van Dick, Norma Procter, and Fritz Wunderlich. Cond. Ferdinand Leitner. Verona 27011/13, 1959.

_______ *Julius Caesar* [*Giulio Cesare in Egito*]. Libretto by Nicola Haym. Trans. Brian Trowell. Cond. Charles Mackerras. EMI, 1988.

Harewood, George Henry Herbert Lascelles, the Earl of, ed. and rev. *Kobbé's Complete Opera Book*. London: Bodley Head, 1987.

Heartz, Daniel. *Mozart's Operas*. Berkeley: University of California Press, 1990.

Heriot, Angus. *The Castrati in Opera*. London: Calder and Boyars, 1975.

Hunt, Lynn. "The Many Bodies of Marie Antoinette: Political Pornography and the Problem of the Feminine in the French Revolution." In Lynn Hunt, ed., *Eroticism and the Body Politic*, pp. 108–30. Baltimore: Johns Hopkins University Press, 1991.

Jefferson, Alan. *Richard Strauss, Der Rosenkavalier*. Cambridge: Cambridge University Press, 1985.

Jones, Vivien, ed. *Women in the Eighteenth Century: Constructions of Femininity*. London: Routledge, 1990.

Kennedy, Michael. *Richard Strauss*. London: J. M. Dent, 1976.

Kierkegaard, Søren. *Either/Or*. Trans. D. F. Swenson, L. M. Swenson, and Walter Lowrie. 2 vols. Princeton: Princeton University Press, 1971.

Koestenbaum, Wayne. *The Queen's Throat: Opera, Homosexuality, and the Mystery of Desire*. London: Gay Men's Press, 1993.

Mozart, Wolfgang Amadeus. *Le Nozze di Figaro*. Libretto by Lorenzo da Ponte. Trans. Clifford Bartlett. Cond. Richard Hickcox. EMI, 1988.

Poizat, Michel. *The Angel's Cry: Beyond the Pleasure Principle in Opera*. Trans. Arthur Denner. Ithaca: Cornell University Press, 1992.

Rosselli, John. *Singers of Italian Opera: The History of a Profession*. Cambridge: Cambridge University Press, 1992.

Stallybrass, Peter. "Transvestism and the 'Body Beneath': Speculating on the Boy Actor." In Susan Zimmerman, ed., *Erotic Politics: Desire on the Renaissance Stage*, pp. 64–83. London: Routledge, 1992.

Strauss, Richard. *Der Rosenkavalier*. Libretto by Hugo von Hofmannsthal. Trans. Walter Legge. With Elisabeth Schwaarzkopf, Teresa Stich-Randall, Christa Ludwig, and Otto Edelmann. Cond. Herbert von Karajan. Philharmonia Orch. EMI 3CDX–3970, 1957.

Warner, Michael. "Homo-Narcissism; or, Heterosexuality." In Joseph A. Boone and Michael Cadden, eds., *Engendering Men: The Question of Male Feminist Criticism*, pp. 190–206. London: Routledge, 1990.

Weeks, Jeffrey. *Coming Out: Homosexual Politics in Britain from the Nineteenth Century to the Present*. London: Quartet, 1977.

Woolf, Virginia. *A Room of One's Own*. London: Hogarth, 1929.

Tancredi Continues

Hélène Cixous

I read *Jerusalem Delivered* headlong, throwing myself into lost bodies, troubled bodies, delimited bodies.

Two camps dispute the body of the Beloved. I mean Jerusalem. Two camps, always the same ones. Today just as at the time of the Crusades, and just as in Paradise.

But it is not the story of the war between the Faithful and the Unfaithful that interests me; it is the other story, the one hidden by history, the one of two beings, two others who cannot remain prisoners in their camps, do not want to win the war, but want to win life or lose it. What holds me is the story of love, in other words, the story of the other and the other's other. Not Rinaldo and Armida, Same-Couple. But the Others, the irrepressible ones, Tancredi, Clorinda, the lovers of freedom, these two singular creatures, stronger than themselves, yes, the one and the other capable of going, at the price of life, for the love of truth, for love, beyond their own forces, all the way to the other—the farthest, the nearest. The two always-others, who dare to achieve Departure. Even madder, and wiser, than Torquato Tasso, who created them much freer than himself in a dream. Stranger. Absolutely faithful—to their own human secret—to their own being more-than-man more-than-woman. With courage they do not know themselves, with nobility they do not possess themselves, with humility they do not restrain themselves, do not withhold themselves, both agree to surrender themselves, to the point of approaching the other. I no longer know whether my "they" is masculine or feminine.

What grips me is the *movement* of love. The violently described curve from one soul to the other body, from one sexed body to another gender of body, from a smile to a gaze. *Gracious* exchange (yes: it is a question of beautiful coups de grâce) from one pleasure to the other whose sex is not revealed. It is a question of the grace of genders instead of the law of genders; it is a question of dancing, of the aerial crossing of continents. It is a question before Jerusalem, *still only obscurely,* of the mystery of love, which is a question of acrobatics: fly or fall! There is no turning back, it is straight ahead. That is why it is so easy. Yes or No—there is no in-between. That is why loving is never difficult except in appearance. Because the opposite of "easy" is not "difficult": it is only *impossible.* So is love the secret of acrobatics? It is trust, yes: the desire to cross over into the other. The acrobat's body is his soul.

Is the crossing vertiginous? Like every crossing. Useless to contemplate or fathom what separates: the abyss is always invented by our fear. We leap and there is grace. Acrobats know: do not look at the separation. Have eyes, have bodies, only for there, for the other.

Tancredi-is-for-Clorinda-is-for-Tancredi.

If Tancredi is "lost for love" for Clorinda, it is for Tancredi that he is lost, but for Clorinda he is more than gained: given.

I wonder: Why can only Tancredi love Clorinda? Go as far as her? Leave the self to orient himself toward the other?

I follow Tancredi and Clorinda through forests, battlefields, the war between races, religions, over enclosures, chasms, beyond ramparts, literary genres and genders and others, as far as the wild songs of Rossini.

Then I listen to Tancredi soaring toward his inner Jerusalem on the wings of the hippogriff Music and returning to us melodiously, strangely, other . . .

For in the interval, between the unconsciouses, between the stanzas and measures, between Tasso and Rossini, the story has shifted a little:

In place of the sumptuous Clorinda, the most ardent, adorable, and vulnerable of knights, there suddenly appears a woman of equal force, but with no other armor than her soul. From the armor-clad Clorinda, Amenaide emerges utterly disarmed, impregnable in that she is so little threatening, still more powerfully woman, more strongly Clorinda.

And Tancredi? I don't know . . . I hear his voice, its sweetness, its fury, I hear the high mezzo voice of the Enigma. The Enigma? Yes: the answer: only Tancredi can love Amenaide, who lives in the heart of Clorinda. Only s(he).

Only (s)he? Yes. This Tancredi can really only be a Tancreda; this is what

Rossini feels, and I also feel it but I don't know how to speak of it. Because it is the Enigma: it doesn't explain itself, it makes itself heard.

Listen.

I say Tancreda, I'm not saying a woman; I could, but nothing is that simple.

Listen: Rossini doesn't say that the hero, in order to be Tancredi, must be haunted by a woman's voice. He performs it.

There is no explanation. There is simply singing. He makes it a condition of the body that for a man to love a woman the way Tancredi loves Clorinda or Amenaide, he must be a woman—I mean, Tancredi.

If it is enigmatic, so much the better. Because if it were not, we would no longer have the least bit of lifework to do.

We have to go around the world, around Jerusalem, lose memory, lose knowledge, in order to arrive at the depths of real love, where we never know when we love, who we love, in whom we love. Tancredi loves Clorinda. Does Tancredi not know whom in Clorinda is loved by whom in him? A moment ago it was a man; a second ago a woman; but was it really that?

One more remark before I lose myself: Clorinda "knows" that she is a "woman." Rossini's Tancred(a) does not: (she) is a Tancredi. Only God knows this, and perhaps Rossini a little—as for us, our musical body "knows" it, though we may be unaware of it.

Now I am completely lost. All I can offer you at this point is to (mis)lead you into the space where Tancredi lives and burns to be woman.

But I also want to meet a particular someone/no one and to love her beyond the true and false that mark the two extremes, ends, limits, of "reality."

I want to love a person freely, including all her secrets. I want to love in this person someone she doesn't know.

I want to love outside (the) law: without judgment. Without imposed preference. Does that mean outside morality? No. Only this: without fault. Without false, without true. I want to meet her between the words, beneath language.

I wanted to look at *Tancredi:* magical voices carried me away, whinnying, murmuring, far away from myself, far away from us, far away from the opera to the other side.

I want to meet her intimately, behind gestures, words, activities, in the region of mysteries. Still alone or alone once again. And above all uncertain, yes, always already a little strange, because it is only in society and appearance that a person of such depth presents a united, determined surface. But as soon as everyone is gone she hurries into her room, and even before changing or removing her makeup she abandons herself with joyous relief to her vital uncertainty, she collapses on the bed like a piece of scenery, and there she stretches herself and becomes, once again, she-knows-not-who.

I know that if I say "woman" or "man" one more time—and quite simply (as I have done, as we do, as we have all done, which is why I do it too)—I won't be able to shake the words off either myself or her (and we will end up no longer loving those whom we love, and we will deceive ourselves until we no longer love). I would like at least once to try to say what I am trying to think, with difficulty, already, about this question of gender: because I feel that she (this person) probably consciously inflicted it on herself, or at least mysteriously suffered from its effects: I feel it in her way of throwing herself on the bed when she is alone, as if she were leaping out of someone else, in her way of stretching herself vigorously and roaring softly, of rolling about on her long flanks, of sleeping for a while. And it is only after a dream that she shudders, goes abruptly to the bathroom mirror. And looks at herself there, asks herself, knitting her brow, whether it shows on her face that she doesn't know. And also because in the evening she, too, listens to *Tancredi* while watching the night rising through the window.

So it is a question of the mystery of *woman* and *man*. Are these words the proper names of two mysteries or of one?

I *feel* the truth of this mystery: mysterious and true. I feel its truth but I don't know how to say it truthfully.

Now, musicians have never lost the sense of the mysterious, which is the song of truth. What sings in a *man* is not him, it is her. They have always known it.

But we who speak, we lose, we lose; I am losing now.

But what suffers and rejoices under *Orpheus* is a woman's voice.

She listens to Gluck, Mozart, and Rossini because they knew too. How to live crying out with frightened joy over the pitfall of words.

Fortunately, when someone says "woman" we still don't know what that means, even if we know what we want to mean.

And so I wonder what is man and what is woman and what am I, which is what she, in the bathroom, is wondering too, while I no longer know when I say "a woman" if I am talking about a person you would call "a woman" or if . . .

In any case, she is not *a* woman. She is plural. Like all living beings, who are sometimes invaded, sometimes populated, incarnated by others, drawing life from others, giving life. Who do not know themselves.

And so, if I were to talk about a person I had met and been overwhelmed by, while she herself was also moved, and I was moved to see her moved, and she, seeing that I was moved, was moved in turn, and if this person were a she and a he and a s(he) and a (s)he and a shehe and a heshe, I would want permission not to lie, I do not want to stop her if she goes into a *transe*. I want him to, I want her to, I will follow them.

And a person who looks like a "man" full of woman hidden behind this look—what do you call such a person—and a woman full of woman in whom still another lives—I don't know—were it not for the suggestion of the look, and the name, the facial makeup, and all of the other makeups . . .

Time to listen to *Fidelio* again.

Even if I feel clearly that the more I try to say, the more I have wandered astray, far from what, beneath appearances and secretly and obscurely, I am sure I understand—I think.

I should also say that in order to know him better internally, I close my eyes, I avoid looking her straight in the face because it is not impossible that at first sight she may look a little like one of those men who are not at all feminine but who are capable of this slow inner dance, who have a loving, elastic rapport with the earth and are thus a bit f... thus in short a bit m... and thus . . .

And then I feel her so clearly and again I know without any doubt how lightly powerful she is like a man who is powerful lightly like a woman who is powerfully light like a man who is gently powerfully powerful like a woman of powerful tenderness . . .

And all I wanted to try to say is that she is so infinite.

One does not guess anything: one knows.

Before meeting the-one-whose-name-I-still-have-not-spoken I "knew" that she listens to *Tancredi*, in the evening, when she is alone, and watches the night falling through the window before her, royal, comes the night draped in her satins of dark blue steel, comes slowly toward her, pensive darkly brilliant, and the armor that covers her allows only her head to be seen; she is a Persian night. She sees her, is amazed by her blacks, by her clouds, by her swirls, and listening to the dark brilliance rising, behind her, from out of the depths of the room, of time, she hears the voice that reigns over her heart, the sea-mother-voice, which was already calling her thirty-five years ago, lulling her, awakening her.

The Third Song in *Jerusalem Delivered* takes two hours to listen to and, in reality, a day and a night. And during all this time Tancredi and Clorinda do not meet each other, do not meet each other, time almost comes to a halt.

But seen from the top of a fig tree overlooking the wall of Salem, the song can be contained in these few words:

"The Christian army approaches Salem—Clorinda overpowers the Christians—Tancredi flies to their rescue—Bouillon prepares to attack Salem."

And between times—Clorinda brushes against Tancredi—between arrows—Tancredi flies—and between words the earth disappears, time has no time, Tancredi Clorinda, seen from outside, fly (but their flight is not rapid enough, time runs out, never, seen from above, will they meet).

But inside the song God grants them all the time they need to slip toward one another, all of the time between possibility and impossibility, and inside there is no impossibility, love knows no "no," nor do desire, the text, the unconscious know what time it is. God gives them the grace to slip in between the sexes alive . . .

When they slipped into this opening, its silence vibrating, in harmony, with the sweet, muted sound of violins, then I saw them.

Tancredi haunted by Clorinda, haunted by Amenaide, haunted by Sutherland, haunted by Tancredi, haunted by Horne, haunted by Tancredi, and I, too, enchanted.

Ourselves We Do Not Owe

I did not see them come in. It was a single apparition for me, but they slipped in as if they had been coming forever or from having forever just taken shape.

I saw them slip in, one all in white, the other all in dark blues, like—not a woman—not a man—not only—like—the personification of the mystery—of humankind—like humanity in person, brooding over its own mystery, which is obviously neither man nor woman, which is two to begin with, two people, being-itself, with its mystery that is to be a question posed in the direction of the other, and only the other has the answer, has only this answer to give, to the other but not to the self, and this is how I suddenly saw them slipping down along the same musical question between them a single silence accompanied so softly, and between them a question accorded itself, answered itself, like a question that gives itself to the question that comes forth to meet it, musically grants it the ever-sought-after answer.

Because it is only the perfect harmony of two questions that will give an answer.

That is why there are so few answers in the world, there are so many questions, and so many books, so much hope, and despairing, and so many traces of error, but so few of music, of answers asking themselves, with the questions perching on their laps, eyes closed, listening, listening, there are so few. Because only two questions in perfect harmony end up composing an answer: that is, two questions moving toward each other with the same sustained rhythm, as two arrows shot forth at the same moment by two equal archers from the two sides of the mountain ascending like two alto voices soaring from the two shores of the sea above the orchestra will perhaps end up meeting above the summit, if a storm does not intervene. A storm, or history.

But first the chance of the answer is a question of body. Then of culture, history, all the rest. And in the end the truth is perhaps that only the questions that harmonize to answer each other had begun to answer from the start, had perhaps never even turned toward each other to ask, but already, committing and giving themselves to each other, had begun to rise up in reply, up through the air alongside the slopes like a bird perched on an arrow, and on the other side this unparalleled thing had also occurred, so that when the arrows at the height of their trajectory obey the laws of physics, the two birds catch sight of each other from a distance and, free, meet each other above the clouds, where we can no longer see them, but we can hear their triumphant cry very clearly.

Returning to my two precious apparitions: to tell the truth, as soon as I saw them gliding toward each other, because of the suppleness of their movement, I guessed. Perhaps because of their look of astonishment, gently astonished, remaining astonished, as if to greet each other close up as well as from far away? Gliding, yes, all in whites, one shining forth to meet the other all shimmering in deep blues, and the whites, too, created a depth, a density, like two fates: as if they felt each other inevitable. Not the way a woman walks and, graceful or awkward, she is woman-walking, and it wasn't a man who was coming closer, not simply man-approaching who came. No, before me they slipped, like two boats gliding over the water, as if each were at the mercy of the other. Drawn to each other, beholding each other with one imperceptible movement, falling lightly, with their whole body, holding each other with their eyes, holding back with a look from the brim of their eyes, wondering, asking: Why me? In the same sweet silence accompanied by twelve violins, thinking the whole time, astonished, not speaking, as if they were thinking that it was the last time they would be able to look at each other and question each other, and still not know, Who me? Why me? Who? Me who . . .

Why me? Standing, very close now, both the same height, they could have touched, there was hardly any astonishment left now, but they continued to be astonished: "Why am I in white, and the other coming night-blue to meet the day . . . ?"

"Why?" they ask each other, giving themselves as an answer, draped in many silks, and the astonishment swells their breasts, with their whole body asking each other and saying: "Because it's you," and the musical harmony of the astonishment is the answer.

(I am well aware that I am in the process of not gaining the resolve to make the evidence visible. I am afraid, I won't hide it, because I have a secret to tell that is so beautiful it dazzles me, and if I am not able to dazzle you I will have committed a crime against everything that I venerate, life, beauty, desire. Because one must reveal the secrets, but in their splendor. Otherwise, if one repeats without dazzling, one violates the secret of the secret; it is sexuality without God. Do I have enough strength to raise the secret of this story above my head? Do I have the heroic serenity, the male femininity? These are the virtues that my respect for this vision requires.)

I follow them . . .

So high, painfully trying to give herself to Tancredi, Amenaide is no more than a look. How deeply she wants to die with her eyes open, her look never leaving his eyes, to fade out in his night like the sun, and Tancredi in the same astonishment is no more than a pair of eyes, and, for a fraction of a second, together, they nearly die, they forget the world and slip into eternity.

I see them very close up then; I see their madness, their secret:

He was the most handsome of women, the most majestic of women, he was radiant with woman majesty.

And more lovely than a young man, more handsome than a knight of the faith, she was noble with heroic strength.

He the most proudly erotic of wild creatures.

She the pitiless passion, unyielding bravery of love.

Just what it was. What I saw, and what they saw, too.

Why me? were struggling now as if they were about to enter each other.

And the weapons signified: I beg of you, vanquish me but do not wound me.

Slipping toward each other like night toward the day.

Tancredi falls like the night, high up, full of dreams, and so profound and all ice on the outside, but with a burning heart, like the night that adores and does not know itself.

Falls large and delicate and male on the outside, but under the dark blue star-studded armor reigns the burning humility of a woman who loves.

And what I saw, blazing Amenaide sees it, too, even if her apparel eclipses the whiteness of the snow crowning the summit of the Alps, she is lofty only to the depth of her profound humility, if he is the woman lover, she is the man who loves . . .

This is what I wanted to say.

In a dream I saw a pure turquoise. Sobbing, I reach out and try to grasp it. It is in the middle of the sky. It is above my life, like my own external heart. I want it, I see it, I want it the way that Tancredi wants his beloved dead or alive, wants her alive to the point of death, the way human beings need the secret of their own lives. I see it shining, the splendor of my existence, my external treasure, I see above my head the meaning of my whole story. A single night separates me from it. I try to cross it. I hold out my hands, I am sobbing with rage, I have it at the tips of my fingers.

The sky is near, only one transparent night away.

Inside the turquoise gleams a fascinating pearl.

My life burns to rise above itself toward my secret. I burn my soul so that a flame will reach higher, closer, than me, but what rises highest higher closer to the turquoise is smoke, and, eyes full of tears, I sob with hope.

The why of my life is a turquoise that I could hold in my right hand. I burn for a tiny double star. Because it is so infinitely pure. My secret is the star of Evidence. At the heart of it lies a soft gleaming pearl like the flash of eternity at the heart of a moment. My star that still has no name!

My secret is no bigger than a hazelnut of eternity.

Only one night still holds back my hand.

I see what my turquoise means. A dark blue silence before my lips holds back my words in a nebula.

My turquoise contains its most precious part. An opaque pearl is the secret of its transparency. The secret of the royal blue is the infinite whiteness of its depths.

I can only sob what I wanted to say.

Tancredi leaned closer, asking himself so blue slowly as if it were the last time they would look at each other from so far away how is it that you are so white looking so closely at each other, looking closer as the adored woman looks in the mirror for the secret of this adoration, asking it, who is loved, wondering, who is she, the one who is adored in me, does not look at herself, tries to discover the secret that the other cherishes, looks painfully beneath her own features for the soul of the other, as high and noble and silent Amenaide favored by the night glides along and her heart burns contemplating the why of her life that shines blue attracts her and answers her royally blue mysterious and so close, why are you so blue?

I ask myself: One day will I understand the secret of this love that I feel and that at the touch of my fingers, at the touch of my words, fades away? One day will I understand the night? Will I know who understands me?

I saw their secret. What I am telling of it is no more than light turned to dust. He was so handsome, one felt he was beautiful. And she was not only a beautiful woman, she was handsome: I am telling what one could see:

The two of them come swooping down on each other like two enemies.

Want to have the measure of each other, urged on by desire, have elected each other,

In the darkness do not meet

(At this point, an outburst of song shook the night, and I scribbled down all that I heard, breathless phrases, on bits of paper, eyes on them, hand noting blindly):

Night day both he and she
Spring forth, still don't meet

What do you want of me, what are you bringing me
Leave you I'd rather die
Why were you searching for me, me, so ardently
As if you knew me
As if I knew you
My fiancée I beg you to tell me your name
Since fate, since destiny have so ordained
I will not reveal my name, my real name
As if you knew me
Open their arms and spring forth
If it were war they would not miss each other,
But it's not war, it's love, they brush against each other
Do not embrace, it's the war of love
Let her breathe if he can
You are no longer my sister
I am no longer your child
The anger and darkness are neither feigned nor
measured
Their feet are immobile, their souls are restless, excited,
the swords come down, broadside, or point first,
What are you fleeing, my love? Standing together. Do
not see each other . . .
Nothing separates them,
What separates them? The dark malice of History
The struggle forces them closer and closer,
Already they can't use the point anymore,
They blind each other with looks
Three times Amenaide receives Tancredi's look
Three times she breaks free from this attraction she
fears
Believe you, I'd rather die
But with my whole life, in spite of myself, I believe
you
You are no longer my child
I am no longer your sister.
Finally, exhausted, they draw back to breathe for a
moment
Attentive and silent like two adversaries
Asking themselves, who will vanquish, love, death . . .
Then what sweetness when all pain is exhausted

When anger no longer has any blood, anguish is no
  longer sustained
Then what respect.

I do not see what could separate them. Two beings, each made for the other, apparently neither sister nor brother and nevertheless of equal measure and equally without measure.

One can see that they are attuned to each other in every way, like a royal soprano to an alto capable of the highest notes, one can see that they are a match for each other in differences and in likenesses, the one enhances and brightens the other. The two of them equal in stature, in power, in richness of soul, in mobility of spirit, equal in virtue, and different in feature, in color, in resonance, like . . . like Sutherland and Horne, for example.

One sees nothing separating them. Only an imperceptible vibration. A delay, as in life.

Will they end up lips upon lips, taking each other and breathing life into each other again? I still think so. It would be a true misfortune if it were not so.

I felt a vague fear. There was an ever so light trembling in their breathing. As if they were silently struggling together against a word, a single terrible word, with all of their forces focused inward, leaning over the wall, afraid of being surprised by an enemy who was unique but as powerful and cunning as poison, who would not come from the present, but could escape, like jealousy itself, from a very ancient and unhappy time.

But thus occupied in not letting themselves be surprised by the infernal word, they had not yet had the sweet leisure to say I love you.

They look at each other a little breathlessly, their eyes begging each other with a tenderness that would turn a lioness into a faithful ally, and they lean their exhausted bodies on their swords.

Yet, with the impossible between them, do not leave
  each other,
The impossible unites them like the night
In which they lose discover themselves each other
Amie! Beloved! In your cruel destiny I will remain
  faithful to you
Why should this be impossible? Because it was night?
Because it was day? Why shouldn't it be possible?
Amie, in your faithful destiny I will remain cruel to
  you.

(And yet I felt vaguely that they were still searching, either one was weighed down or the other was losing a certain lightness. I don't know who said:

I should embrace her I can't
I should confront her I can't
I should flee from her

I do not want to know who could not keep from fleeing, from falling.

Was it misfortune? The truth is, there was mistrust. But that was in another story.)

So I do not know whom I started to love, suddenly, with all the weight of my own desire, in vain. I was in love with one with the other. With both of them. Because of the other I loved. One because the other. One for and against the other.

Yes she is the object of my passion
She, the object of my pain,
This slow passion that threatens one toward the
  other,
This tormenting hope, all growing in my heart,
This apprehension, this confidence,
This wonder, all growing,
This belief, this nonbelief,
This passion that grieves my heart and enchants me,
It is she too that I adore, I don't know why,
Love surprised me as I was watching
Two great ones look at each other for the last time,
Caught hold of me in her big, strong but delicate arms
And I fell, astonished,
In love,
Not just with the one I wanted to love,
The one I loved in advance, because she was blue and
  dark
And ardent and profound like someone I had loved
  before
But, astonished, I fell also into the musical aura
Of the one I was not thinking of, the other, white and
  gold,
The pure spontaneous and confident one, she too,
At the last moment, and because one was the answer
  that the other didn't dare hope for and with all her
  soul humbly hoped for.

Each amplifies the other, each is magnified by the other. Each all the greater and more magnificent for mysteriously understanding the other.

Is Tancredi a woman ending, or a man beginning to be a woman in order to be a man?

But my God, I am only me, I am only a woman, how can I express what is more than me? I divine what is more than a woman, what is more than a man, but above me everything sparkles and dazzles me and merges into a single person with athletic aspirations, rather tall for a woman, yes, she seems to me to be a woman, but set naturally in the bearing of a man, like my pearl in turquoise.

What do you call a person who looks rather more like a woman with dark blue eyes, an icy look in appearance, burning inside, who is large and imposing like the night, and stars nuzzle up against her full breast, closing their eyes in love, who fights like a hero, would give up her life like a mother, and who sheds tears of impatience and grief, and who dreams of destiny only as love, and who takes fortresses more easily than a kiss, and her voice is so deep and warm and moist, it sounds like the sea of human tears, and every woman not bound by the cords of marriage who hears it feels the burning need to immerse herself in it?

In this story she bore the name of Tancredi, his past, his arms. Help, Mozart, Rossini, help, number without gender, gender without limit!

When does woman begin when does one become other when continues when pursues when finally touches finally embraces?

No; I should rather ask:

Where does man begin woman begin continue?

Continues

Yet—already the last stars were paling with the first fires of dawn and yet the struggle continued forward.

Tancreda was worrying about the fatal triumph.

Continuing in an alto voice into which I wanted to pour all my tears:

Must I yield? Must I vanquish? Who?
Who are you, please, victor or vanquished, tell me, so I
  will know whom I save, whom I lose.
Speak to me: I'm not listening: Speak to me.
You alone have been loved by my heart.
How can I help believing you.
Only I must believe the impossible,
So adieu.
What do you want? To leave you. To follow you.
Two fighters. Two adversaries side by side against the
  impossible
Yes, you are the object of my pain
They do not strike. Contemplate each other.

Turn away from each other. Flee from each other.
As if they were falling upon each other.

(There are several Tancredis, which is why I have so much trouble trying not to mislead us. I promise that I will do the impossible to explain myself on this subject as soon as broad daylight arrives.)

I feel clearly that I am on the inside of the night and yet before my own night. I feel that I am before the mystery that I am destined to encounter and not resolve. Tancreda, Amenaide, these first two are the figures of my mystery. Everything that I write, it seems to me, leads me myopically to their embraces, and then I feel that everything is happening right there before my hopelessly wonderstruck eyes, the meaning of the mystery catches fire, a cry explodes in my breast—as if I were *discovering* the *truth* of *love* (all these words are smoke choking the pure point of my cry)—and—*fiat nox!*

But perhaps what is most difficult and most necessary is really to forget the judges who make us stupidly answer their stupid summons, make us justify the nonjustifiable, speak of silence, crush music under the millstone of words, lie by swearing to tell only their truth, plead guilty to a lack of absence and a lack of weakness, make excuses for every thought; really to forget, which means forgetting fearlessly, quickening the pace with a bound, without ever forgetting them in reality, flinging a glistening forgetfulness over our shoulders and making headlong for the free-soul zone into which they cannot venture because they perish on contact with pure air.

After our oppressive and inflexible era I would like to live in a time in which the tongue would not be bound, castrated, intimidated, constrained to obey fraudulent sages and genuine asses.

But sometimes I am stopped by the word police, searched, interrogated and counterinterrogated. Sometimes I am the one who stops, thinking, perhaps mistakenly, that I must show all the same that I am not afraid of the insults being hurled at us. I turn around, I respond, and the struggle begins, to the cries of Women! Women! hurled out, picked up in hatred, in love. In the din of the arguments one no longer knows what one is attacking, what one is defending, the words change in meaning depending on the speakers, now blessings, now curses.

I am well aware that the best way to defend a given truth is never to pronounce its name, never to expose it to public abuse. From so much usage the word *Jewish* is getting dry as a fossil. And this is the case with the word *Polish* at this particular moment. Yet it is a necessity of our time. At this particular moment not saying the word *Polish* is like denying a child of one's own. (This is also the case of the word *true,* accused, in our aged time, of being too good to be true.)

And at this time there are so many clandestine massacres of women that a woman has to say "woman" a dozen times a day in order to protest.

But by constantly saying "I am a woman" we end up creating various forced truths. And worst of all, the more we say it in order not to be swept far from our own banks by the current, and the more securely we moor ourselves to avoid being swept away from one another, the more we contribute to reinforcing limitations of strength, to restricting native territories and fortifying prejudices. We are closed in, we enclose ourselves, we enwoman ourselves. And worst of all, what had been the sweet and inexplicable and intimate truth—the magic hand on the heart—beneath which we could faint with joy, becomes a sentence.

So the truth, which appears inside of the night, in the warm depths of a dream, and then only, peacefully undresses before me and smiling comes slipping I do not know how over my innermost body, and caresses my heart, and—then—the sweet softness of her breasts—and this is what absolute knowledge is—(it isn't surprising if what I am writing is not sufficiently clear, since not a single word ever returns from the luminous depths where our truth lives. The few words that come close are transformed into sighs)—so the truth that lives only in the shelter of silence is forced to appear, and then is like a fish pulled from the water, thinking in a final convulsion of the sea, then, the end.

But in this night full of voices, I am bewildered between two Tancredis. Is the one the other or the same or the hidden truth or the manifest truth of the other? Here I am, between one and the other, astonished, stubbornly refusing to take my eyes off the mystery: as if I wanted to become conscious of my unconscious as I immerse myself in it. Here I am, under the sea with my lantern. I circle around inside a question like a Chinese fish in a swimming pool. I am here and I am all at sea: I imagine there is an answer outside.

"Why is it necessary for this Tancredi to be a Tancreda?"

But there is no outside. My swimming pool is infinite. It is the world.

Let's not think. Let's swim.

There are two Tancredis. They are not altogether the same, are almost the same. Tancredi of Jerusalem, is he Tancredi of Syracuse or is she not?

It is because he insisted on knowing what he was thinking that Tancredi turned against himself in an ultimate furious effort to come to grips with himself.

These are things to dream of.

I am swimming between two Tancredis, the water is almost a night starred with serenity. I am dreaming along in the very substance of eroticism, as if music had finally once more become what it was, musical wave. I am swimming between little waves of thoughts:

The enigma is cool inside, I feel good here, love glides along in pursuit of itself, from Jerusalem to Syracuse and back again, the appearance changes and reality blushes with emotion.

First of all, it is the story of a Tancredi, who loves a hero who is a woman who in reality is a hero who is a woman, and if he loves her it is because she is a woman. And so is he.

And there is a Clorinda, who is a woman with the strength to take on a man's appearance and who is all the more one because the other. In the end I am not sure. And so Tancredi is the person who loves this woman.

So Rossini guesses: for a man to love as Tancredi loves this woman who is this still and more, he had to be a woman.

I am lost . . .

So much the better . . . Tancredi can only be a woman when he is a man. Or no? Tancredi can only be a woman when she is a man?

A-man-who-loves-a-woman-as-if-he-were-a-woman has a voice that traverses life, death, walls, sands, superstitions, magnificent armor, shields, images, languages, meanings; neither race nor color, nor one gender nor another gender, hold it captive, it is made to celebrate she who inspires it. Tancredi sings a woman: a woman sings Tancredi . . .

Tancredi, a woman . . .

If I love a woman, I will call her Tancredi.

Astonished Tancredi astonished Tancreda understands Clorinda, and for Rossini, it is obvious, "Tancredi" is a woman in a man.

But for the Christians and for all Jerusalem it is Clorinda who is a woman in a man.

And there I see them hurl themselves toward each other faster than the movement of my gaze, they swoop down, their steeds raising a cloud of shining dust, I can no longer see them, I can only hear the voices measuring each other, the lioness pouncing, the eagle rending the air; I can hear two voices, one is a woman's and the other one is a woman's too, rushing headlong toward each other, one of them is not a woman, one of them is not only a woman, the one is not simply the opposite of the other.

What a secret!
O heaven you know for whom I tremble
Because he doesn't know who she is
Doesn't know he is a woman
Because with what difference

She is a woman, heaven knows,
What is the difference? It isn't only the sex,
It's the way that love loves, over the walls, despite
    armor, after the end of the world,
But I don't know how to say it.
I hear the alto wondering who
Her vast clear night full of tears
Trembles soprano and falters up there
And falls again
And at once regains breath and escapes all my questions
    that hold me below.
Higher up, the questions don't follow, there are only
    answers
Which is why women's voices are so joyful and free.

The word *woman* holds me captive. I would like to wear it out, to lose it, and to continue along on the trail of She who lives without this great worry.

All the more lovable for being more woman all the more man for being more woman and perhaps all the more woman . . .

If I loved a woman, I would call her, with my voice still moist and salty, Tancredi my Beloved.

The Lost Voice of Rosine Stoltz

Mary Ann Smart

> Read no history: nothing but biography, for that is life without theory.
>
> —Disraeli, *Contarini Fleming*

> I have chosen to write of women's lives, rather than of the texts I have been trained to analyze and enjoy. I risk a great danger: that I shall bore the theorists and fail to engage the rest, thus losing both audiences.
>
> —Carolyn Heilbrun, *Writing a Woman's Life*

Until recently women's biography and feminist interpretation of texts have traveled along irreconcilable paths, the exhaustive documentation required by biography often seeming to overwhelm efforts at interpretation, dictating that the genre remain essentially conservative and antitheoretical. This is unfortunate, if only because it is in the writing of women's lives that biography and theory may need each other most. The women whose lives we examine are sometimes minor figures, ordinary people most interesting when seen as emblematic of a broader context, and of course they rarely lived according to modern feminist principles: what does one make of a talented woman who devoted her life more to caring for men than for herself? Such situations present conundrums that simultaneously resist and require the solace of theory.[1]

A similar dichotomy has informed feminist musicology, where studies of female musicians coexist, but rarely overlap, with gendered readings of the canon. However, some recent work suggests that opera criticism, though still living somewhat on the margins of musicological respectability, has begun to explore new, synthesizing avenues, innovations perhaps propelled by the solitary, often eccentric passion of the opera fan. Catherine Clément's poetic evocations of the lives of prima donnas and Wayne Koestenbaum's queer celebration of the diva lifestyle are strong, albeit idiosyncratic examples of this trend: of operatic biography (or at least biographical anecdotes) informed by theory.

The immediacy of their prose as well as their relative freedom from footnotes and other scholarly encumbrances might lead us to conclude that writing about singers of the past will inevitably have a speculative bent, a histrionic tone designed to make us forget that immediate physical traces of a voice cannot survive. Unlike women writers, who leave their voices encoded in literary texts, singers—at least before the age of recorded sound—survive only in ventriloquistic detritus: descriptions by critics, admirers, and the like. (In this context, it seems significant that what often *does* survive is a wealth of visual evidence: engravings, costume designs, portraits allow us to recover a sense of the body, the power of these visual signs perhaps overwhelming the memory of voice even more completely.) This silence at the center of singer biography obliges us to turn to testimonies inevitably incomplete, biased, inaccurate. For the postmodern sensibility, of course, this may be less a liability than a mixed blessing: the leanings and omissions of secondhand accounts can be as revealing as "the facts"—and the difficulty (some would say impossibility) of uncovering an objective truth is hardly confined to *singers'* biographies. However, the gulf between the singer's essence—the lost voice—and the person who produced it is perhaps greater than in other fields, and it is this split between voice and bodily source, as much as the dearth of concrete evidence, that opens operatic biography to infiltration by theories.[2]

Dead singers can seem mute, then, in a way that writers cannot, but the dimension of opera that is interpretative (rather than creative) also has more positive implications, ones with particular relevance to female performers. Carolyn Heilbrun's dominant image (and Virginia Woolf's before her) of a woman writing alone in a room, and struggling, often in vain, to gain public and financial recognition must be replaced in operatic history with that of a bejeweled, well-paid prima donna accepting accolades, perhaps graciously, perhaps haughtily. To put it less positively, because female singers performed works by men, they did not have to fight to be noticed. In the nineteenth century, at least, divas enjoyed a generous professional equality: opera's celebration of the female voice ensured that they were always in demand by the male-controlled operatic establishment, their timbres and ranges essential for the romantic struggle at the center of most plots. The traditional contrast of vocal types—the competition of tenor and baritone for the soprano—might even seem to grant women added power by guaranteeing them a place at the apex of opera's triangle of romantic archetypes.

This rosy picture of female dominance can, of course, easily be inverted. The apparent advantage provided by plot and vocal hierarchies could also breed resentment, the criticism and ridicule to which divas were—and are—often subject.[3] Sopranos are routinely demonized in operatic history as greedy and ambitious, willing to sacrifice the aesthetic balance of a masterwork to satisfy their vanity with an additional showpiece aria, a few more gaudy ornaments. Male composers are not slow to provide epistolatory ammunition: Verdi's letters, for example, regularly document heroic struggles to "preserve his art" from the exhibitionistic urges of sopranos. Translated into the language of feminist theory: the soprano's power—her economic, creative, and sexual independence—seems to demand containment, and much of the rhetoric that surrounds her, whether in "primary" sources, journalistic writings, or biographies, attempts to control or limit her potential supremacy.[4]

It is in interrogating this rhetoric, and thereby diminishing its power, that modern theory can come to our rescue. Clément has notoriously launched such an attack on the language and shape of opera plots, accusing them of conspiring to diminish women by structuring plots around sopranos doomed to sacrifice and death. Michel Poizat's obscure but compelling Lacanian theory goes a step further, arguing that diva deaths are made necessary by the *sound* of the female voice: our enjoyment of the long-buried primal pleasures evoked by the soprano's highest notes must be banished violently. Objections leap to mind: Clément conveniently forgets comic opera, in which no one dies and the girl usually gets what she wants, and she gazes serenely past opera's impressive heap of dead tenors;[5] Poizat has a huge blind spot where the Italian operatic tradition should be. Whether or not one accepts the details of these particular formulations, by extending their demystifying rigor from discussions of operatic texts to the rhetoric that surrounds opera these celebrations of opera's women can provide a starting point for theorizing both their lives and the roles they play.

As Clément implies in the few pages she devotes to singers, one method of containing divas, even punishing them for being necessary to our operatic fantasies, has been to subsume their biographies into the roles they play. Her rhapsody on Maria Malibran uncovers the ways opera plots invade our chronicles, how biographies of female singers inevitably pack the messy details of life into the neat packages of art (11, 29–30 and 32–33). In Malibran's case this process emerges most vividly in the story of Rossini's *Otello*. As a girl of fifteen she sang Desdemona opposite the Otello of her father and voice teacher Manuel García, trembling with fear under the paternal threat that if she didn't reach his vocal expectations, he would *really* strangle her in the final scene. More striking than the cruelty of the threat is the tale's narrative force, the way it superimposes art on life, reads Malibran's relationship with her father through her most famous role. It is a gesture endlessly repeated, until singers' lives begin to seem as alike as opera plots.

La favorite du roi

When a biographer's romanticizing tendencies encounter a particularly willful or resistant subject, the tension between archetype and reality rises to the surface. Take the case of French mezzo-soprano Rosine Stoltz, attacked in almost every memoir of the mid-nineteenth century. She is blamed for everything: she singlehandedly ruined the Paris Opéra's box office receipts; she even drove poor Donizetti insane. Her temper tantrums in rehearsal and performance are endlessly chronicled by colleagues, composers, and journalists, all of whom attribute (with varying degrees of subtlety) the greater part of her success in Paris to her liaison with Léon Pillet, then superintendent of the Opéra. Perhaps more than that of any other nineteenth-century soprano, Stoltz's biography falls into familiar patterns, endless rehearsals: of her outbursts and the people she offended, the powerful men she married and had affairs with, the analogies between her life and the roles she played. The "real" Rosine Stoltz, like the "real" Malibran, has been buried under the weight of plots.

The role assigned to Stoltz in Donizetti's breakdown is both paradigmatic and bizarre. The background is the last days of rehearsals for Donizetti's last opera; as usual, Stoltz's temperamental antics occupy the foreground, although the murderous power attributed to them is exaggerated even within the shrill context of Stoltz demonology. Léon Escudier relates the decisive incident with indecent relish:

> Donizetti put up with an infinite number of deceptions during the rehearsals for [his last opera] *Dom Sébastien*. Many times Mme. Stoltz, who at that time had supreme power at the Opéra, created difficulties for Donizetti that deeply wounded his artistic dignity. For example, in the fifth act, Mme. Stoltz refused to remain on stage while [the baritone, Paul] Barroilhet sang his beautiful offstage barcarolle. The success that he could not fail to enjoy with this melody aroused her jealousy. . . . One evening, Mme. Stoltz insisted that Donizetti cut out one strophe of this barcarolle; the maestro, furious, grabbed his score, threw it down on the stage, and rushed out, hurling some most colorful curses at the singer. Three friends, I was among them, led him home; he could no longer speak, he let loose inarticulate rattles of fury; his mind was unhinged. Nothing could restore him to reason. Donizetti sustained a violent blow to his mind; from that day dated the dreadful illness that gradually eroded his faculties and finally bore him to the grave—alas, too young! (50–51)

There may well have been some flamboyant disagreement, although the newspapers, who made it their business to report almost everything that occurred at the Opéra, rather surprisingly carry no mention of the "event." It is easier to cast doubt on the tantrum's supposed consequences: Donizetti had probably contracted syphilis sometime in the 1830s, began to show symptoms in the mid-1840s, and by 1846 was confined to an asylum. Although early biographers hint that his true affliction was well known, whenever it suits their narrative flow they routinely blame his deterioration on emotional upheavals. After the Stoltz incident was first recounted, in Charles de Boigne's 1857 memoir of the Opéra, it became an idée fixe of Donizetti biographies for the next half century.[6]

It might seem perverse to begin a biography with a story that is almost certainly apocryphal, but the Case of the Tantrum that Killed Donizetti may tell us more than any "facts" could. Facts about Stoltz are elusive, overwhelmed by the political and personal agendas that dominated the backstage world, and were particularly acute in the troubled atmosphere of the mid century Paris Opéra. It becomes necessary, then, to scrutinize agendas, sources, biases; eventually these contexts will begin to contend for the spotlight with the life itself.

During her Parisian career Stoltz's activities were chronicled by the notoriously partisan theatrical papers, which tended to be either ruthlessly critical or blindly approving of the Opéra and its stars, depending on whether their publishers also had rights to print the new operas of the season.[7] However, the reviews transcend their biases often enough to create a believable collective image of Stoltz's voice and performance style. They are thus a doubly interesting source: early in her career they supply a much-needed musical profile; later they fill in the gossipy backstage context. Almost all notices of the 1840 premiere of Donizetti's *La Favorite*, for example, have something good to say about the soprano, and they often concur about her strengths and weaknesses. Later reports, by the mid-1840s almost uniformly negative, may have responded to a decline in her vocal powers but were probably more influenced by the intensification of political and personal rivalries at the Opéra.

Journalistic accounts are complemented by more permanent testimonies, many of them recorded after Stoltz was no longer a dominant force. Several laudatory biographical pamphlets commemorated her retirement from the Opéra in 1847.[8] An inkling of their *partis-pris* can be gleaned from Julien Lemer, who explained that the impetus for his pamphlet was a commission to write *two* accounts of Stoltz's life for a series on famous actresses. One was to be glowingly admiring, the other cruelly satirical; the publisher would wait until the singer's retirement to decide which she had earned. Outraged, Lemer rushed into print with an energetic defense, blaming most of Stoltz's problems, both of image and performance, on an unfriendly claque. All these book-length fan letters culminate in Stoltz's sentimental farewell performance and the extravagant soiree she hosted a few days later. The retirement is followed by a half century of biographical near silence: from 1847 onward only memoirs of the Opéra mention her, usually to lament her influence.[9] Her death in 1903 provoked a spate of articles revaluing her career, mostly negatively; Gustave Bord's self-styled "definitive" biography, purporting to demythologize her, appeared in 1909.[10]

Most of these accounts indulge in an obsessive blurring of art and life: biographies and even newspaper gossip columns overflow with imagined links between Stoltz and her roles.[11] By far the most common comparison is with Léonor, heroine of *La Favorite*, a role that eventually became almost her only vehicle.[12] The links were usually simple, focusing on the plot's love triangle; a rough outlines of a synopsis can provide ample context. Léonor, the mistress (or "favorite") of the king of Aragon, falls in love with Fernand, a novice who has left the monastery before taking vows because of his love for her. Unaware of Léonor's position, Fernand asks the king for her hand in marriage; surprisingly, the king agrees. But when Léonor tries to warn Fernand of her past, the king intervenes, ensuring that Fernand discovers the truth only after the wedding has taken place. Believing that Léonor has deceived him deliberately, Fernand returns to the cloister. Stricken by one of those mysterious illnesses that seem to afflict powerful sopranos, Léonor follows him and herself enters the monastery as a novice. The lovers meet, recognize each other, reconcile. As soon as Fernand forgives Léonor, she expires. Romanticizing biographers drew from this plot many ingenious and unlikely connections, but the most popular subsumed Stoltz into the labyrinthine institutional intrigues of the Opéra, as the spoilt protégée of the Opéra's director, Léon Pillet. References to her as "la favorite" were a convenient and not-too-libelous shorthand for the protection she was said to receive from the "king" of the Opéra.[13] A typical insinuation was as understated as the report in *La France musicale* of July 14, 1844: "Mme. Stoltz has departed for Baden-Baden; M. L. Pillet accompanies her." A more savage reference appeared, not surprisingly, in the satirical journal, *Le Charivari*, which called Stoltz the "surintendantesse" of the Opéra.

While this kind of reporting was common in the nineteenth century, it is perhaps more surprising that Stoltz's "romantic" connection has continued to dominate perceptions of her—even scholarly ones—up to the present. Discussing the rehearsals for *Dom Sébastien*, Philip Gossett writes that "many changes were made [in the score], some for artistic reasons, others frivolously," and that when these matters were under discussion, as in the dispute over the length of the baritone's barcarolle, Stoltz's "rights were brazenly sustained" because of her liaison with Pillet. William Ashbrook blames Pillet's lack of enthusiasm for Donizetti's *Les Martyrs* on the "unsuitability of the role for his mistress Rosine Stoltz; operas in which she could not shine were not given much attention by the management of the Opéra" (150). [14] Most emphatic of all is Steven Huebner, who repeats late nineteenth-century gossip verbatim: "During rehearsals at the Opéra for his *Dom Sébastien* . . . Donizetti had *quite literally* been driven mad by Rosina Stoltz, mistress of director Léon Pillet" (51; emphasis added). Of course, the nature of Stoltz's relationship with Pillet is unknowable; but the "truth" about her private life is less interesting than the fact that her entire career continues to be overshadowed by this single narrative.[15] The persistence of her image as "the favorite" in both the historical and modern literature is surely iconic: women have always served as allegorical symbols for institutions and abstract ideas, and Stoltz became (and has remained) a sort of statue, like the female personifications of "liberty" or "justice" that can be seen all over Paris; unlike them, however, the ideas she symbolizes are negative: power, intrigue, ambition.[16]

Professional success and sexual power can be a threatening combination; taken together with Stoltz's temperament and vocal flaws, they became overwhelming, especially when they coincided with the newly precarious artistic and financial state of the Opéra in the 1840s. The obsessive focus on Stoltz's personal life masks a deeper historical narrative, a documentation of the Opéra's decline, which was all but inevitable by the time Stoltz made her debut in 1837, but for which she nevertheless became a scapegoat. The 1830s had seen huge financial and popular success, yielding at least one successful new opera a year, including Rossini's *Guillaume Tell*, Auber's *La Muette de Portici*, Meyerbeer's *Robert le Diable* and *Les Huguenots*. Pillet's advent as superintendent in 1840 saw the Opéra's fortunes decline rapidly. After the triumph of *La Favorite* Paris's first theater slipped into disappointing premieres and lackluster revivals with singers often past their primes. Stoltz's tenure coincided with the departures of many popular artists and the vocal decline of others, including the leading tenor and pioneer of the famous high C "from the chest," Gilbert Duprez. Of course laments about vocal decline and departed great singers are a commonplace of any opera house in any season, but they had greater polemic urgency in Paris, becoming the basis for an aesthetic debate about the relative merits of the spectacular scenic effects so beloved of French grand opera and the Italian style's emphasis on voice and melody. A satirical pamphlet published in 1845 accused Pillet of alienating all the singers and composers associated with the Opéra, with the result that he had to produce operas without singers and without music—what remained were spectacular sets and costumes, which were all Pillet cared about anyway.[17]

As the unpopular superintendent's "favorite," Stoltz was a convenient symbol: since the aesthetic and political problems that haunted the Opéra were too sweeping to be confronted directly, attention could be diverted toward the smaller conflicts and disasters that could plausibly be blamed on her vanity and ambition. She was accused of sabotaging the sopranos already at the Opéra, by preventing Pillet from giving them starring roles, and of forbidding him to invite rivals to Paris. In 1845, for example, François-Joseph Fétis reported that

> a woman of talent counts among the singers at the Opéra. Although her voice is mediocre and her musical training no more than sketchy, she compensates for these disadvantages with a lively dramatic sense and an unusual intelligence. Well placed, and confined within the limits of her speciality, this actress could be very useful, but [because she is] ambitious far beyond the limits within which an artist should sensibly confine herself, she wanted to invade everything, to dominate everything, and M. Pillet's naive admiration has not left her to desire in vain the sacrifices demanded by her *amour-propre*.[18]

Baritones and tenors were not safe either: Stoltz's tempestuous behavior and insistence on the limelight is supposed to have discouraged strong male singers from remaining at the Opéra. Critics even credit her with influencing the repertoire by insisting that every work performed give the most prominent role to her particular brand of soprano.[19] Indeed, Stoltz's career was so completely synonymous with the Opéra that her vocal weaknesses were seen as influential in shaping the theater's dominant musical style. *La France musicale* charged that

> in 1772, there was a struggle between the ancient school and the modern style introduced by the Italians; [at the Opéra] today there is a struggle of the lovely school of Rossini against the bastard genre to which M. Pillet has given birth, in order to spotlight the dramatic talent of one of his employees to the exclusion of anyone else. For her melody has been sacrificed for declamation, song for pantomime.[20]

Temperament, private life and institutional crisis collide violently in accounts of the fiasco that precipitated Stoltz's retirement in 1847. By that time her professional fortunes were so closely tied to Pillet's that, when she was finally run off the stage by the intensity of public criticism, Pillet was pressured to offer his own resignation almost immediately. The turning point came in one of those public moments of humiliation commonly undergone by prima donnas. After an extended respiratory illness had required her to cancel a string of performances, she appeared in December 1846 in the premiere of Louis Niedermayer's *Robert Bruce*, a loose assembly of recycled Rossini grafted onto a plot from Walter Scott. The public's anger with Stoltz for canceling, and with the management for presenting a pastiche in the guise of a new work, was probably helped along by an especially energetic anti-Stoltz claque that night. She was violently whistled and hissed. Never noted for even temper, she tore her lace handkerchief into tiny pieces, threw them at the audience, shouted "C'est intolérable! Je suis brisée!" and stormed offstage.[21] Shreds of the handkerchief immediately became collector's items; they were acquired by a kinky English nobleman who displayed them with fetishes culled from temperamental outbursts by Malibran and Catalani (Lemer 24).

Although some say that Stoltz never again stepped onto the stage of the Opéra, she continued to perform for a few months, announcing her official retirement in a letter to the Commission spéciale des théâtres royaux in March 1847.[22] This letter, published in the *Revue et gazette musicale*, strikes a skillful balance between apology and recrimination: her recent vocal failures are due both to a lingering indisposition and to the calumnies of a biased public; her retirement is selfless, taken to avoid becoming an obstacle to the theater's prosperity.[23] Her last appearance at the Opéra (except for an unsuccessful comeback attempt in 1854) was a benefit performance on April 22, 1847, in a program of excerpts from operas she had premiered. Although gestures of goodwill seem to have prevailed—a flock of doves with colored ribbons and bouquets attached to their feet was let loose in the theater at the end of the evening—Gilbert Duprez, with characteristic bad grace, gleefully (but inaccurately) recalled that Stoltz

> was obliged to mount the performance entirely alone, because all the artists [whose participation she requested] had refused. As far as I know, this woman had never rendered a single favor to artists; she wanted to surround herself with the ornaments of Parisian society so that it would be said that she inspired sympathy among artists and so that she would leave the stage accompanied by their best wishes and regrets. Nothing. Solitude, complete isolation.[24]

A kaleidoscope of names

One tries, by juxtaposing such fragments, to tell another story, to counter the impersonal narratives that have buried Rosine Stoltz the woman. Bits and pieces culled from diaries and memoirs have a narrative immediacy that promises an antidote to overarching political and historical theories; at the same time, however, as Duprez's self-serving fictions illustrate, they demand to be considered in context, from the biographer's critical remove. Perhaps it is this undulation between reminiscence and theory, experience and context, that must shape a biography: stories crowd in, refusing to respect critical distance, but eventually mutate into narrative tropes. The tension is particularly acute in Stoltz's case because she so energetically aided the proliferation of stories around her. Her need to mythologize herself, to embroider and fabricate a persona, enlivens her narrative, but it also creates a need for theories, explanations of her unreliability as a chronicler of her own life.

Take, for example, her kaleidoscope of names. With every twist and turn of her career or personal life, Rosine took a new name, at first simply discarding the old, later accumulating them, hoarding assumed personae. By the end of her life the woman born Victoire Noël was signing her letters "Rosa Carolina, comtesse de Ketschendorf, baronne de Stolzenau, princesse de Lesignano, duchesse de Bassano, princesse de la Paix, née d'Altavilla (Rosina Stoltz)" (Bord 149). The earliest names seem ephemeral, provisional: carrying little narrative or symbolic weight, they give the impression of a young woman trying on identities until she finds one that fits. All we know of the early professional names—Rose Niva, Rosine Ternaux, and Heloise Stoltz—is that *Stoltz* may have been her mother's maiden name, while *Rosine* was probably inspired by her success in Rossini's *Barber of Seville*. Stories associated with the later, aristocratic titles are more extravagant. The ranks comtesse de Ketschendorf and baronesse de Stolzenau seem to have been "borrowed" from her son, who was granted them by his natural father, a minor German noble. Stoltz claimed to have married the prince of Lesignano on his deathbed in 1872, but this may have been fabricated. The duchesse de Bassano and princesse de la Paix derive from a genuine marriage in 1878, but her biographer Bord ungallantly stresses that this was merely a business arrangement: Stoltz agreed to bail out Bassano, a compulsive gambler, in return for his titles; immediately after the wedding the happy couple went their separate ways. Stoltz's quest for nobility reached its greatest heights in 1874, when she claimed to have discovered her natural father, the marquis d'Altavilla, and persuaded him to acknowledge her. Bord found signed documents granting Stoltz the right to use the name d'Altavilla, but the marquis's son later revealed that his father had remembered nothing about the birth, had made a highly operatic deathbed denial of paternity, and claimed to have signed the papers only because Stoltz had promised him a handsome pension that, in characteristic style, she never paid.

The stories could continue, but theory again intrudes: how can we account for all these fabrications? Her "definitive" biographer's approach was adversarial: Bord makes much of his subject's enigmatic qualities and crows with triumph whenever he uncovers one of her lies. Modern theory might offer a more sympathetic context for the self-mythologizing drive; feminist and psychoanalytic approaches suggest several mutually compatible explanations. From the chronological perspective, it is perhaps no coincidence that most of these imagined episodes date from the 1870s: after her final appearance on stage in 1860, Stoltz seems to have turned to a new kind of role-playing, an aristocratic masquerade.

But the names and their attendant stories clearly have symbolic significance as well. On one level the absurdly extravagant string of titles suggests status sought through associations with men, but it also recalls the predilection of some women writers to "re-make" themselves through pseudonyms, to achieve power and success by assuming a disguise.[25] By far the most alluring apology for self-mythologizing, and one specific to opera, is suggested by Wayne Koestenbaum, who imagines that the diva is driven to create a persona when she realizes she is marked off by the compelling voice that incomprehensibly emanates from her body.

> Her confidence that she will be a diva lifts her from an obscure, immobile, difficult childhood; the vocation of diva permits her to read her life backward and see clear meanings, hints of tremendousness, where there was once shame. . . . How can a doll be a force of nature? Only if her plastic paralyzed head conceals a masterplot. (90)

In other words, the singer's voice, emerging almost in spite of herself, alienates her both from her body and from her previous self; elaborate fictions are required to piece her together again. Koestenbaum's frequent references to the diva's invention of herself concentrate on the extravagant and self-aggrandizing gestures of the opera singer rather than on biographical fabrications, but the idea could easily be stretched to encompass a star's reshaping her past, to attempts to make her life (and her body) as grand as her voice. Perhaps Bord was grasping for something of this sort when he called Stoltz a victim of "pseudomania," her autobiographical narratives dominated by identification with her alter ego, Léonor:

> For the rest of her life she would remain "la favorite": in a perpetual quest for titles like those of Léonor de Guzman, she would seek without respite Kings of Aragon and Fernands, dramatic situations in the gardens of Alcazar or in the cloister of Monréal. Until the end of her life her favorite aria was always "O mon Fernand"; she would hum this melody constantly to evoke her past. (Bord 112–13)

As the dip back into opera plots suggests, narratives easily come unglued from attempts to ground them in broader theoretical contexts. The abstract explanations, apologies required by a subject who deliberately deceives, will always be at odds with the urge to chronicle *everything*, no matter how trivial, and to revel in the concreteness of anecdote, whether carefully authenticated or spurious. This conflict evokes once again the image of the statue—the allegorical stone figures of public art whose meanings remain abstract—but it also recalls Pygmalion's Galatea, that vessel of male creativity who surprised her creator by springing to life. Perhaps we can grant Rosine such a chance, encourage her to come alive by giving way to her stories for a few moments.

A Stoltz miscellany

- *1815: Jours de son enfance*

Conflicting stories begin at birth; the early years of the career are, if anything, even more shadowy, molded into a series of glamorous operatic climaxes. Stoltz herself claimed to have been born in Spain and brought to Paris as an orphan at early age. There she obtained the protection of the duchesse de Berri because her birthdate coincided with that of the late duc; she embarked on her musical training and convent education under the duchesse's patronage. However, biographers generally agree that Stoltz was born as Victoire Noël into a working-class Parisian family in 1815. She may indeed have been educated in a convent but, according to Bord, it was an establishment that supplied room and board for poor girls in exchange for needlework and laundry (25). Her "big break" came at about age twelve: one day, while hanging out the washing, she was overheard singing by a professor of the Paris Conservatoire, Alexandre Choron. Struck by her voice and informed that her family could not afford music lessons, he arranged for her to be taught free of charge. She studied and sang regularly in Choron's weekly concerts until she was sixteen, attracting considerable notice. Her coach and accompanist, M. Ramier, became obsessed; in addition to her vocal training, he took it upon himself to oversee her clothes, grooming, and behavior, making her his *chef d'oeuvre.*

Perhaps resisting this control, Stoltz left Paris around 1830, resurfacing as a singer and actress in Belgium and the Netherlands. Auguste Thurner's sentimental account reports that Ramier chanced upon her in Lille under a different stage name and heard her sing "Jours de mon enfance" from Hérold's *Le Pré aux clercs*. A magnificent recognition scene ensued: Ramier heard her voice, erupted into tears; when Stoltz perceived the presence of her mentor, "emotion paralyzed her voice for an instant, as she recalled the man who had been at once father and friend to her in the 'jours de son enfance' " (183–86).

After several years in provincial theaters Stoltz married a M. Lescuyer, director of the Théâtre de la Monnaie in Brussels; she began to sing principal roles. In 1836 the leading tenor of the Paris Opéra, Adolphe Nourrit, sang opposite her in Halévy's *La Juive*. Brought to tears by Stoltz's declamation of Rachel's words "Mon père, j'ai peur," just before she is burned at the stake for heresy, Nourrit urged the Paris Opéra to offer Stoltz a contract; she made her debut there the following year.[26]

- *1838: The narrow ankle, the graceful foot*

Stoltz regularly indulged in masquerade of a less sensational variety: she enjoyed some of her greatest professional success playing trouser roles. Although male impersonation was a virtual requirement for mezzo-sopranos, donning the trouser apparently often caused female singers a discomfort proportionate to the thrills it afforded their audiences. John Rosselli tells of a soprano who resisted shouted audience demands that she remove her boots to reveal her legs and later apologized: "I was a singer, and I was not going to bring myself down to that level. The women will understand" (58–59).

Stoltz seems to have had no such reservations. Théophile Gautier, generally one of her harshest critics but a connoisseur of male impersonation, was ecstatic about her cross-dressed demeanor:

> Mme. Stoltz excels in trouser roles, such as Ascanio [in *Benvenuto Cellini*] and the page Isolier [in *Le Comte Ory*], which is not to say that she is not also charming in the dress of her own sex. . . . such a beautiful voice and a lovely leg! the narrow ankle, the graceful foot, the leg as rounded and fine as that of a young Greek god!—What pleases us above all in Mme. Stoltz's performance of trouser roles is that she abstains from those equivocal simperings, those hermaphroditic ambiguities, that make the old men in the orchestra stare through their lorgnettes; she is quite thoroughly a charming boy, vigorous, petulant, spiritual, with romantic and courtly charms, a bold clown whom it would surprise no one to see wooing a pretty girl. (cited in Bord 54)

• *1878: La grande duchesse*

Stoltz's marriage to Emmanuel-Charles-Louis Godoy, prince de Bassano, took place in Pamplona, probably because the region's laws allowed quick ceremonies without a license. According to Jean Gourret's vitriolic account, the whole affair was arranged, presumably at the behest of the impecunious Bassano, by a broker in Bordeaux (78). The wedding was an unhappy affair: the bridegroom reportedly drank ammonia the night before, a gesture that left him alive but disfigured; his guests insulted Stoltz, calling her the mere purchaser of a title (Bord 153–65). Even the financial aspect went awry, since within the year Bassano ran through the one hundred thousand francs Stoltz had given him and ended up a menial worker in the casino at San Sebastien. Stoltz seems to have remained the diva throughout: Bord reports that when, at the wedding party, she sang an aria from Halévy's *La Reine de Chypre* "with incomparable brio . . . a crowd collected in the salons of the hotel and in the street outside. It became necessary to open the windows. Rosine Stoltz, duchesse de la Paix, had won a new victory. It was her last operatic success" (161–62).

• *1880: The new novice*

Late in life Stoltz turned her energies to spiritual matters, though the enthusiasm seems to have had characteristically theatrical and manipulative dimensions. Perhaps inspired by the memory of the novice Fernand in the cloister of

Monréal, she began to show marked interest in a young priest, "M.E.," whose manner of saying Mass had particularly impressed her. She took the young man under her wing, discharging his debts and arranging elocution lessons to rid him of his Provençal accent. M.E. was initially delighted by her patronage, but when he refused to sever all ties with his humble family and friends matters became difficult. The end of the affair is obscure, but there is no doubt that M.E. came off the worse, charged with theft, required to pay back Stoltz's money, and dismissed from the priesthood.[27]

- ***1903: Dictées spirites***

In addition to collecting aristocratic titles, Stoltz in retirement also wrote a pamphlet on spiritualism, *Dictées spirites*, and composed a handful of songs.[28] Not surprisingly, some mystery surrounds her death: she ended her days alone at the Hôtel Bellevue near the Opéra; according to one report, only two mourners followed her body to the grave. Although said to have died wealthy, and to have financed two funeral monuments for herself—one in Paris, one in Nice—Stoltz was buried in the cemetery for the poor at Pantin, just outside Paris.[29]

Envoicing the diva

These tales (who knows how much truth there is in them?) testify to the myths that proliferated around Stoltz, some encouraged by her penchant for fabrication, others pure biographers' invention. But the stories also fill the gap between Stoltz's voice—public property that separates itself from its source in the woman—and the rest of Rosine, the private self. To quote Wayne Koestenbaum once more: "The diva, debuting, invents herself, imposes herself on an audience unaware of her magnitude until she opens her mouth" (92). We know she is there only because she has projected a self for us to hear (Koestenbaum 86).

On one level, then, this self-mythologizing impulse alleviates the temptation to censure a biographical subject for obscuring truth and making our task more difficult. On another, Koestenbaum's construction of the diva's voice as a separable entity, available for the fan's multiplicitous pleasures, enfranchises fandom, granting it license to "read" opera in exhilaratingly personal terms. However, as Heather Hadlock has recently pointed out, this appropriation, this transformation of the diva into "a fantastic echoing mirror of the fan's life," can also work to *dis*enfranchise the singer, glorifying her voice as a free-floating object divorced from the human being who creates it (274). It is perhaps better to end by reuniting Stoltz's voice with the rest of her, to listen for her echoes rather than to let her fabrications and those of her biographers have the last word.

Voice, after all, is perhaps only as ephemeral as other realities of a life, and many descriptions of Stoltz the singer survive. They tell of power, sometimes stridency, a range of only about two octaves, very good low notes, a strong but harsh upper register. Certain common compliments and criticisms emerge: she often sang out of tune and lacked agility and technical control, but her timbre and extensive range of nuance are praised almost unanimously.[30] All agree that her greatest strength was as an actress, that the intensity of her gestures and her tragic declamation were unequalled. In the *Revue des deux-mondes* a rare attack on her acting nonetheless gives a sharp sense of extremes:

> Mme. Stoltz's pantomime proceeds much like her singing, by leaps and bounds: you see her pass in an instant from the delirium of a bacchante to the immobility of a marble statue. Never a glance, a gesture, an intention in her that suggest intelligence or the least concern for the character she is impersonating. From beginning to end, one perceives a gambler's need to risk everything, in both voice and acting.[31]

One of Stoltz's champions, Eugénie Pérignon, described her dramatic ability in a more positive—and fanciful—vein:

> One night a deaf man was seated beside me on the parterre at the Opéra: they were presenting [Halévy's] *Charles VI*. Because of his affliction, [my neighbor] could apprehend the plot of the opera only through facial expressions and gestures. He tried to translate these by writing on his program the ideas he had grasped from this or that gesture made by Stoltz. When the curtain fell, he presented me with his manuscript, and I read there, word for word, the text sung by Madame Stoltz. (25)

Such accounts rapidly collapse into the Romantic embroidery that dominates the biographies. Perhaps a better approach to the disembodied diva voice—as well as to the woman Rosine Stoltz—might be to examine the music written for her, music that must often have been shaped to suit her and may sometimes have been composed with her participation. Even more so than in Italy, the staging of a new opera in Paris was intensely collaborative, involving months of rehearsal, composition, and revision. Since rehearsals for the beginning of a work usually began long before the last acts were composed, the specific abilities of the singers engaged for the premiere—and of course the demands they made on the composer for numbers that would highlight their strengths—could be highly influential in shaping vocal style and characterization. Perhaps the great mezzo showpiece from *La Favorite*, Léonor's "O mon Fernand," calls for a style more demure than Stoltz's, but her voice (and her energy) are powerfully evoked in a passage Donizetti added to the final scene during the last stages of composition, probably at Stoltz's request.[32] It bears all the features hinted at in the reviews: sharp shifts between extremes of range, extended passages in the low register, and an emphasis on declamation through short, intense phrases. It requires not a pretty voice but a dramatic one.

Example 7.1.

These same traits are even more evident in a substitute cabaletta appended to "O mon Fernand," which in the autograph score bears the legend "Air ajouté pour Mme. Stoltz."[33] The transitional recitative with which it begins is marked by dotted rhythms and short, emphatic phrases. Both recitative and cabaletta have a jagged melodic contour, alternating stepwise motion with leaps from chest to head register. In short, the aria demands a declamatory style of delivery, juxtaposing extremes of register and volume, and avoiding legato lyricism or subtle shifts of dynamic or expression. It is appealing to think that this passage was tailor-made for Stoltz, even that Donizetti composed it while she looked over his shoulder, perhaps imperiously, perhaps seductively, offering suggestions. Could she have been there when he wrote this passage?

Example 7.2.

Or this?

Example 7.3.

Or maybe this?

Example 7.4.

The collaboration of singer and composer, not uncommon in the pragmatic world of nineteenth-century opera, hints at one way to bridge the abyss between biography and theory that concerned me at the beginning of this essay. I have dealt with evidence that might reinforce the view that women, both real and fictional, are silenced by opera, that Rosine Stoltz's reality and individuality were submerged in archetypal operatic narratives. But that image of Stoltz and Donizetti collaborating on her music offers a less gloomy prospect. Perhaps we can draw on their struggles and petty negotiations—over ornaments, high notes, and extra arias—as a basis for a new relationship between biographies of singers and the operas they performed. At the same time as their biographies were being shaped according to the romantic models of their characters, these singers' idiosyncrasies were exerting an equally strong force in shaping the characters of the women they impersonated. We are, that is, in their debt. We owe some of the individuality and vigor of opera's female characters to the humanizing touch of the demanding, fallible sopranos who were their "creators."

Notes

This article could not have been written without the help of Rebecca Harris-Warrick, who generously shared with me the press and musical material she has gathered in her work on the critical edition of La Favorite, *forthcoming with Ricordi.*

1. In the last few years, feminist biography has begun energetically and imaginatively to absorb theoretical perspectives. See Alpern et al., *The Challenge of Feminist Biography*, Ascher, DeSalvo, and Ruddick, *Between Women*, and Young-Bruehl, "The Writing of Biography" and "Psychoanalysis and Biography," in *Mind and the Body Politic*, pp. 125–54. Solie has examined theories and problems of feminist biography and musicology with sensitivity in her "Changing the Subject."

2. The difficulty of arriving at "biographical truth" is a theme of most of the essays in Alpern et al., *The Challenge of Feminist Biography*, and of Wolff's "Minor Lives."

3. See, for example, Mordden's *Demented* and McClary's discussion of the pejorative connotations of "demented" in her foreword to Clément, *Opera, or the Undoing of Women*, p. xvi.

4. For a historical view of the controls exerted over female singers since the seventeenth century, see Rosselli, *Singers of Italian Opera*, pp. 56–70.

5. See, for example, Robinson's "It's Not Over Till the Soprano Dies."

6. De Boigne, *Petits mémoirs de l'Opéra*, pp. 204–5. The incident was first picked up in Filippo Cicconetti's *Vita di Gaetano Donizetti*, although Cicconetti does not mention Stoltz, but rather blames the management of the Opéra; however, Alborghetti's and Galli's influential *Gaetano Donizetti e G. Simone Mayr*, p. 191, takes note of the incident only to dismiss it.

7. On these biases see Harris-Warrick, "Historical Introduction," in the critical edition of Donizetti's *La Favorite*, Shulman, "Music Criticism," and Gann, "Théophile Gautier: critique musicale," and "Théophile Gautier, Charles Gounod," especially n. 24.

8. The most enthusiastic of these, Pérignon's *Rosina Stoltz*, was, not surprisingly, authorized by its protagonist; Lemer's *Mme. Rosine Stoltz* and Cantinjou's *Les Adieux de Madame Stoltz* are only slightly less admiring. Copies of these pamphlets, along with various newspaper obituaries and press accounts, are preserved in Stoltz's "Dossier d'artiste" at the Bibliothèque de l'Opéra, Paris.

9. Anecdotes about Stoltz and assessments of her abilities, almost all of them negative, can be found in Duprez, *Souvenirs d'un chanteur*, Escudier, *Mes souvenirs*, and de Boigne, *Petits mémoires de l'Opéra*.

10. The obituaries included in the "Dossier d'artiste" at the Bibliothèque de l'Opéra are almost all negative. See, for example, *Les Annales* (August 9, 1903), the article by Arthur Pougin in *Le Ménéstrel* (August 2, 1903), *La Liberté* (August 1, 1903), and *Le Soleil* (July 31, 1903). The only complimentary obituary appeared in *Le Figaro* (July 31, 1903).

11. The singer herself may have participated in this process: inspired by success in Halévy's *La Juive*, she is said to have fabricated a Jewish background for herself; after her appearance in Berlioz's *Benvenuto Cellini*, she claimed to own a Christ figure sculpted by Cellini (Bord, *Rosina Stoltz*, pp. 6 and 18).

12. According to Bord, Stoltz sang Léonor in *La Favorite* 481 times. Her next most frequently performed roles were Catarina in Halévy's *La Reine de Chypre* (118 performances) and the trouser role of Lazarillo in Marco Aurelio Marliani's *La Xacarilla* (100 performances).

13. Such circumlocutions were necessary, since Pillet did not hesitate to sue journalists who attacked him openly. In the mid-1840s the Paris theatrical papers regularly reported Pillet's lawsuits. *La France musicale* of January 12, 1845, for example, gives lively details of Pillet's fight with *Le Constitutionnel*. According to Bord (*Rosina Stoltz*, pp. 80–85), in 1842 Stoltz herself launched a defamation suit against Stanislas Champein, music critic of *La Mélomanie* (later to become *Le Musicien*). In articles published between August and November of 1842, Champein accused Stoltz of eloping to Brussels with a fellow voice student, and of bearing and abandoning two children in 1833 and 1834.

14. Ashbrook concludes his biographical note with a capsule summary of Stoltz's later life: "After being mistress of the Emperor of Brazil for a while, she married in succession a baron, a count and a prince" (*Donizetti and His Operas*, p. 653).

15. A notable exception to this tendency is the biographical note in Pitou, *The Paris Opéra*, 4:1264–66.

16. A similar association between the opera star and female allegorical figures is drawn in Jean-Jacques Beneix's 1981 film *Diva*: when the starstruck fan finally connects with the diva he idealizes, they take a walk through a Paris landscape dominated by grandiose stone figures of symbolic women.

17. "Indiscrétion en trois actes et en vers par l'un des Trente-Six auteurs de la Tour de Babel" (Paris: Imprimerie de Mme. Lacombe, 1845).

18. *Revue et gazette musicale*, January 5, 1845.

19. Cantinjou, *Les Adieux de Madame Stoltz*, pp. 30–36, however, devotes a good deal of space to defending Stoltz from this accusation. He lists the sopranos who left the Opéra during Stoltz's tenure, exonerating his heroine in each case: Cornélie Falcon (the most frequently named victim of Stoltz's ambition) was already losing her voice by the time Stoltz arrived in Paris, Julie Dorus-Gras could not act, Rossi-Caccia departed to take up a prior contract in Lisbon, Sophia Loewe could never sing anyway, and Sophie Méquillet was so nearsighted that she virtually had to be led on stage by the hand.

20. De Pontecourt, "Influence de l'Académie Royale de Musique" (in the third article of a four-part series). Pontecourt continues,

> We repeat again, to firmly establish our impartiality, that we recognize in Mme. Stoltz a great dramatic talent; she feels vividly, she gives a realistic, even sometimes too realistic, expression to her gestures [*son jeu*] and to her diction; but as a singer, we must deny her that wealth of qualities that certain newspapers, indiscriminate admirers of everything admired by M. Pillet, have attributed to her. Mme. Stoltz knows neither how to place her voice, nor how to move it around. . . . [Pillet] has worn out this actress by trying to make her, and her alone, shine always and everywhere.

21. This episode is narrated, from points of view ranging from sympathetic to cruel, in almost all accounts of her life and in most obituaries. The most famous is probably Théophile Gautier's compilation of reviews, *Histoire de l'art dramatique en France*. Of the three laudatory pamphlets published in 1847, Cantinjou and Lemer recount the *Robert Bruce* incident from a sympathetic perspective, while Pérignon, the most fervent admirer of all, omits mention of it. Gautier's excerpt is reprinted in Ezvar de Fayl, *L'Académie nationale de musique 1671–1877*, p. 302.

22. See, for example, the *Liberté* obituary of August 1, 1903.

23. *Revue et gazette musicale*, March 21, 1847.

24. Journal entry of April 13, 1847. Duprez's memoirs are a gold mine of calumnies against Stoltz: the same entry accuses her of bringing his career at the Opéra to a premature end and recounts verbatim a conversation in which Stoltz blamed Pillet for all her difficulties at the Opéra (*Souvenirs d'un chanteur*, pp. 159–60).

25. Heilbrun, *Writing a Woman's Life*, pp. 109–12 and 116–18. Sandra Gilbert and Susan Gubar call the woman's pseudonym "a name of power, the mark of a private christening into a second self, a rebirth into linguistic primacy." See their *No Man's Land*, p. 241; quoted in Heilbrun, p. 110.

26. Although Nourrit's "discovery" of Stoltz is mentioned in most accounts of her

life, Louis Quicherat's comprehensive three-volume biography of Nourrit contains no mention of her.

27. The episode is recounted by Bord, *Rosina Stoltz*, pp. 173–79; he refers to newspaper accounts published in *Le Temps* (November 13, 1881) and *La Gazette des tribunaux* (July 23 and November 13, 1881) when M.E. was expelled from the church and legal proceedings initiated.

28. The title of the pamphlet is given in *Le Figaro* of July 31, 1903. Several of the songs were published; copies are preserved at the Bibliothèque Nationale (Musique). In characteristic fashion Bord (*Rosina Stoltz*, pp. 181–85) claims that the work on spiritualism is plagiarized and that Stoltz's songs are of the lowest quality, a charge partially supported by the conventional sentimentality of the ten song texts published in his appendix (pp. 223–33). However, the publication of her *Dix Mélodies* in arrangements for violin and piano, piano solo, organ, harmonium and piano four-hands attest to their popularity.

29. *La Liberté*, August 3, 1903.

30. See, for example, *Le Corsaire*, December 4 and 10, 1840; *Le Ménéstrel*, December 6; *Le Courier des théâtres*, December 8; *Revue et gazette musicale*, December 13; *La France musicale*, December 6; and *Le Moniteur des théâtres*, December 5.

31. *Le Revue des deux-mondes*, October-December 1840, p. 56.

32. Harris-Warrick, "Historical Introduction," *La Favorite*.

33. This cabaletta will be included in the appendix of the forthcoming critical edition of *La Favorite*, edited by Rebecca Harris-Warrick.

Works Cited

Alborghetti, F. and M. Galli. *Gaetano Donizetti e G. Simone Mayr: Notizie e documenti*. Bergamo: Gaffuri e Gatti, 1875.

Alpern, Sara, Joyce Antler, Elizabeth Israels Perry, Ingrid Winther Scobie, eds. *The Challenge of Feminist Biography*. Urbana: University of Illinois Press, 1992.

Anon. "Seconde crucification de la Favorite, grand opéra, en la personne de Maestro Donizetti." *Le Charivari*, March 3, 1841.

Anon. "Indiscrétion en trois actes et en vers par l'un des Trente-Six auteurs de la Tour de Babel." Paris: Imprimerie de Mme. Lacombe, 1845.

Ascher, Carol, Louise DeSalvo, and Sara Ruddick. *Between Women: Biographers, Novelists, Critics, Teachers, and Artists Write About Their Work on Women*. Boston: Beacon, 1984.

Ashbrook, William. *Donizetti and His Operas*. Cambridge: Cambridge University Press, 1982.

Bord, Gustave. *Rosina Stoltz*. Paris: H. Daragon, 1909.

Cantinjou, Corneille. *Les Adieux de Madame Stoltz*. Paris: Bretteau, 1847.

Cicconetti, Filippo. *Vita di Gaetano Donizetti*. Rome: Tipografia Tiberia, 1864.

Clément, Catherine. *Opera, or the Undoing of Women*. Trans. Betsy Wing. Minneapolis: University of Minnesota Press, 1988.

De Boigne, Charles. *Petits mémoires de l'Opéra*. Paris: Librairie Nouvelle, 1857.

De Fayl, Ezvar. *L'Académie nationale de musique 1671–1877*. Paris: Tresse, 1878.

De Pontecourt, Ad. V. "Influence de l'Académie Royale de Musique sur le sort des théâtres de la France et de l'étranger." *La France musicale*, February 9, 1845.

Duprez, Gilbert. *Souvenirs d'un chanteur*. Paris, 1880. Excerpts reprinted in *Voix d'Opéra: Ecrits de chanteurs du XIXe siècle*. Paris: M. de Maule, 1988.

Escudier, Léon. *Mes souvenirs*. Paris: Dentu, 1863.

Gann, Andrew G. "Théophile Gautier, Charles Gounod and the Massacre of *La Nonne sanglante*." *Journal of Musicological Research* (1993), 13:49–66.

———"Théophile Gautier: critique musicale et l'acceuil de Verdi en France." *Bulletin de la Société Théophile Gautier* (1986), 8:179–91.

Gautier, Théophile. *Histoire de l'art dramatique en France*. Paris: Hetzel, 1858.

Gilbert, Sandra, and Susan Gubar. *No Man's Land*. New Haven: Yale University Press, 1988.

Gossett, Philip, ed. "Introduction." Facsimile ed. of the first printed score of Donizetti's *Dom Sébastien*. New York: Garland, 1980.

Gourret, Jean. *Encyclopédie des cantatrices de l'Opéra de Paris*. Paris: Editions Mengès, 1981.

Hadlock, Heather. "Peering into *The Queen's Throat*." *Cambridge Opera Journal* (1993), 5:265–75.

Harris-Warrick, Rebecca, ed. *La Favorite. Edizione critica delle opere di Gaetano Donizetti*. Milan: Ricordi, forthcoming.

Heilbrun, Carolyn. *Writing a Woman's Life*. New York: Norton, 1988.

Huebner, Steven. *The Operas of Charles Gounod*. Oxford: Oxford University Press, 1990.

Koestenbaum, Wayne. *The Queen's Throat: Opera, Homosexuality, and the Mystery of Desire*. New York: Random House, 1993.

Lemer, Julien. *Mme. Rosine Stoltz: Souvenirs biographiques et anecdotiques*. Paris: Mme. V. Jonas, Librairie de l'Opéra, 1847.

Mordden, Ethan. *Demented: The World of the Opera Diva*. New York: Franklin Watts, 1984.

Pérignon, Eugénie. *Rosina Stoltz*. Paris: Maistresse et Wiart, 1847.

Pitou, Spire. *The Paris Opéra: An Encyclopedia of Operas, Ballets, Composers, and Performers*. 3 vols. Westport, Conn.: Greenwood, 1990.

Poizat, Michel. *The Angel's Cry: Beyond the Pleasure Principle in Opera*. Trans. Arthur Denner. Ithaca: Cornell University Press, 1992.

Quicherat, Louis. *Adolphe Nourrit: sa vie, son talent, sa caractère, sa correspondance*. Paris: L. Hachette, 1867.

Robinson, Paul. "It's Not Over Till the Soprano Dies." *New York Times Book Review*, January 1, 1989.

Rosselli, John. *Singers of Italian Opera*. Cambridge: Cambridge University Press, 1992.

Shulman, Laurie C. "Music Criticism of the Paris Opéra in the 1830s." Ph.D. diss., Cornell University, 1985.

Solie, Ruth A. "Changing the Subject." *Current Musicology* (1993), 53:55–65.

Thurner, Auguste. *Les Reines du chant*. Paris: A. Hennuyer, 1883.

Wolff, Geoffrey. "Minor Lives." In Marc Pachter, ed., *Telling Lives: The Biographer's Art*, pp. 56–72. Washington, D.C.: New Republic, 1979.

Woolf, Virginia. *A Room of One's Own*. New York: Harcourt Brace Jovanovich, 1981.

Young-Bruehl, Elisabeth. *Mind and the Body Politic*. London: Routledge, 1989.

Jenny Lind and the Voice of America

Lowell Gallagher

The arrival of Columbus in the West was a less significant event.
—*London Athenaeum* report of Jenny Lind's arrival in America.

In September 1850, P. T. Barnum brought a new attraction to America: Jenny Lind, popularly known as the Swedish Nightingale. Her tour of the major American cities was electrifying. On more than one occasion it generated a mob response, with trampled crowds and broken windows in concert halls. The reaction in Pittsburgh resulted in one reporter's naming her appearance there the "Black Friday" concert.[1] The public's desire to hear Jenny Lind was itself promoted by a tour of a different order: the circulation of prosthetic tokens—Jenny Lind hats, coats, frocks, boats, boots, shoes, night caps, tea kettles, sausages—and the publication of several books and articles that documented the soprano's life and career. The public's frenetic response, called Lindomania, signaled a desire to possess and to be possessed by an ineffable presence and authority that the Lind voice seemed to promise and that the hearing of the voice seemed to authenticate.[2] Taking the occasion of Lind's American success to distance itself from its own promotion of Lindomania, the British press derided the enthusiasm reported in the American newspapers: "Even the record of what she is supposed to say and do, must be received with great caution as reported by those who, bent on erecting her into a goddess, of course desire to exhibit her as oracular."[3] A telling oracular fantasy indeed, Lindomania acquired a notably American cast as a cipher for social and political issues in the Union at mid-century.

At the outset nothing appears characteristically American in this chapter of

Fig. 8.1. "Jenny Lind at Castle Garden," from the *Jenny Lind Almanac* (1851). *Courtesy of the Department of Special Collections, University Research Library, University of California, Los Angeles.*

the cultural history of the nation. Lindomania had already spread across Europe (in Germany as well as in England, notably, in the 1840s), and on American shores the phenomenon appears to have been isolated. Though numbers of European artists had already gained local popularity, the Lind craze was unprecedented, and it had no immediate successor.[4] The phenomenal success of Lind's American tour, in its cultic aspect, nonetheless helped develop and circulate a figure of American cultural identity and national concerns in 1850. As one review in the *New York Daily Tribune* suggested, the enthusiastic reception of Lind attested to the assimilation of Art itself by a "whole people," by a social body able to maintain, like Lind in concert, a proper control over disruptive passions, through the force of intellect and moral strength.[5] Through a collective identification with Jenny Lind, Americans could read their nation as the fertile union of domestic and foreign spheres and as the visible resolution of perceived tensions in aesthetic, moral, and social values. The urban disruption that Lind's appearances occasionally produced, like the tumult at the Black Friday concert, was only apparently at odds with the emerging Lind iconology: the ecstatic press and the frenzied public were enacting different yet convergent aspects of a politicized trope of spiritual election.

Jenny Lind's arrival from Liverpool in the fall of 1850 had been well prepared. Once the contract for the tour had been signed, P. T. Barnum hired twenty-six agents to educate the American public about the merits and established fame of the soprano. In a letter to the American press, printed in February 1850, Barnum himself stressed one of the central themes that was to emerge in the subsequent construction of Jenny Lind as an American icon in the New York press, Lind's "philanthropy":

> A visit from such a woman, who regards her high artistic powers as a gift from Heaven, for the amelioration of affliction and distress, and whose every thought and deed is philanthropy, I feel persuaded will prove a blessing to America, as she has to every country which she has visited, and I feel every confidence that my countrymen and women will join me heartily in saying, "may God bless her."[6]

As Barnum's words suggest, Lind was to be received as more than a mere vocal phenomenon. The voice had become an inspirational text, a living Christian Gospel, the typological fulfillment and counterbalance of the other "living sermon" in circulation in 1850, Nathaniel Hawthorne's Hester Prynne. At the end of *The Scarlet Letter* Hester dutifully comes to recognize the "impossibility that any mission of divine and mysterious birth should be confided to a woman stained with sin."[7] The decorousness of Barnum's quasi-allegorical description, reducing Lind's "every thought and deed" to a single edifying principle, effectively placed Lind in the kind of visionary mode of reference and "ethereal medium of joy" that Hester, the model of the virtuous but stigmatized woman, could not attain.[8] Because the soprano's identity, unlike Hester Prynne's in the romance, was primarily vocal, mediating between the material and the abstract, Lindomania was to be experienced not as a carnal seduction but rather as a spiritual *raptus*. Such a presiding perspective was important on several related fronts. It sanitized an ambivalently held art form, opera, which was a signature both of high culture and of suspect moral value. It enabled Lind to produce herself in public as a virtually disembodied voice, thus minimizing the apparent contradiction of the carnivalesque and the sacred that might be construed from the publicly paraded female exemplar of moral authority. Not least, the rapturous dimension to Lindomania charted the outline of the political trope that Lind would inhabit in the American press: the voice as the unifying resolution of opposing forces, claiming possession of those who heard it and thus rendering itself immune to critique.

The spiritually edifying quality of Lind's singing had been remarked by Continental audiences as well. One of Lind's more recent biographers points out that in the British press Lind's "greatest number of all" was not an operatic aria but rather the air "I know that my Redeemer liveth" from Handel's *Messiah*. Lind's rendition was reported to leave those who heard it with "a memory as of a sublime religious function."[9] S. P. Avery wrote an account of Lind's career, *The Life and Genius of Jenny Lind,* published in New York in 1850, that reproduced and disseminated the memory for the author's fellow Americans. Designed as a comprehensive introduction to the "distinguished songstress, whose fame has extended over the civilized world," Avery's book confirmed Lind's religious function.[10] Describing a fellow American reporter's rapture upon hearing Lind, Avery made the connection that would plot the significance of Lind's tour as an American, and Americanizing, phenomenon. Like a contagion, the Lind voice could produce in America, too, a state of rapture "inspired by its sacred influence."

Avery's book provided a cogent primer for the American public, teaching it how to naturalize its experience of the "woman with no weakness"—its Lindomania—by locating the experience in the vocabulary of several interests that characterized contemporary American society.[11] Lind's voice "would speak a language unto us all," Avery claimed, defining the soprano's voice as the font of a universal language—what Lauren Berlant has called the emergent "National Symbolic," the "order of discursive practices whose reign within a national space . . . transforms individuals into subjects of a collectively held history."[12] In a telling phrase that conflated the spiritual and humanitarian with the economic and material interests of his readers, Avery further described Lind as a "prophetess, whose whole mission, with her gold-amassing powers, seems one of pure benevolence."[13] Through Lind Americans might discover an idealized sign of their own place and stature in the world, as an indeterminate yet secure figure whose imputed "benevolence" would purify its accumulation of capital. Reading Avery, Americans might also appreciate the political corollary suggested by the resonance of Lind's voice. Situated in the American tour against a background of political upheaval abroad and the ongoing possibility of domestic fragmentation, the Lind voice created a "stream of simple, clear, *sustained* melody" (emphasis in text). Avery made the significance of the emphasis clear in a later passage, which returns to the sustaining power of Lind's legato technique: "Despite of the revolutions and revolutionary tendencies of the day," he wrote, Lind "still continues 'in power.' " The very economy of Avery's rhetoric enabled Lind's voice to appear at once as divine medium, as exponent of American political integrity, and as force of nature, able to ride over the orchestra's "hurricane of sound."

The newspapers chronicling Lind's first American concerts, in Castle Garden and in Tripler Hall, elaborated these associations. En route to Boston, aboard the steamer *Empire State*, Jenny Lind was treated to a fanciful yet telling gesture of American appreciation: "The supper-table on board was resplendent with bouquets, a model of Castle Garden in barley sugar, and a Temple of Liberty surmounted by a figure of the Swedish Nightingale dressed as the Daughter of the Regiment and bearing the Stars and Stripes."[14] How better, indeed, to announce Lind's mediating and harmonizing function than to represent her in an edible confection whose nutritive value lay in the prospect of an exemplary conceptual assimilation offered to the delighted guests. The sartorial *bricolage* of Donizetti's transvestite heroine and the American flag neatly conflated American and European values as well as male and female associations. The entire ornament produced a quasi-sacramental sign of the unifying mythos of "Liberty" itself.

The *New York Daily Tribune* was quick to point out Lind's own "deep, pervading spirituality of soul," attributing to it a scriptural and mythic dimension: "She has carried us up to Pisgah heights and we have seen at least part of the promised land, stretching away green and golden, to which all the powers and yearnings of Music point."[15] As Barnum's announcement months earlier had suggested, the potentially troublesome visuality of Lind's person on the public stage was dissipated by the attention the press gave to Lind's vocal presence as a vehicle of rapture that led to a visionary, rather than visual, experience. Lind's voice was both topical and typological; it allowed a rapt audience to envision the reassuring prospect of America itself as the fulfillment of Biblical prophecy, a "promised land" that was at once, like the Lind voice, material and abstract, a place that was also an idea: an idea of infinite extension, a horizon of limitless prospects, "stretching away" in a blur of colors, "green and golden," that yoked economic and spiritual intentions.

Apart from its scriptural pedigree, such yoking, which emphasized the spiritual character and message of Lind's voice, gained legitimacy from received aesthetic principles derived from stock tenets of elite European literary and philosophical culture, according to which art was perceived to embody an ideal beauty that could not exist, as the American literary critic George Bancroft observed, "independent of moral effect."[16] Lind's edifying effect, as the "High Priestess of Melody—the Saint Cecilia of Modern Song," was ascribed to her power to embody the virtuoso as virtuous intellectual: "all frank and real and harmoniously earnest . . . truer and the more inspiring because tempered by the intellect."[17] The "natural" quality of Lind's art was cordoned off from the unruly corporeal and material associations of the word *natural* by its representation as a quality modulated by the highest human faculty: "intellect."

Descriptions of Lind's concerts themselves recurrently evolved into theoretical discussions of the proper relation between nature and art. Thus it was that, "tempered" and chastened, Lind's singing embodied without contradiction the expressive, Romantic idea of art: her singing was construed as the natural effusion of her soul. The popular "Nightingale" epithet further encouraged an identification between Lind's art and natural processes: "The Nightingale, to which she has justly been compared," wrote one reviewer, "does not pour out its melody with more ease, its notes do not gush forth with more freedom and correctness according to Nature's pitch and scale, than do Jenny Lind's according to Art's strictest rules."[18] Postulating an artistic freedom that found itself through the normative strictures of a natural paradigm, the reviewer represented the "natural" character of Lind's singing as an apparent oxymoron that revealed itself a tautology. It was not the last time that this figuration would occur as a sign of the power of Lind's art to resolve tensions and contradictions. Even more explicit was the identification of Lind as the symbol of human perfectibility. The press reported "the inspired vitality, the hearty genuine outpouring of the whole—the real and yet truly ideal humanity of all her singing."[19]

Locating the ideal in the real and emphasizing the natural character of art were characteristic aspects of nineteenth-century aesthetic theories in circulation in America, but such ideas also defined important principles of Lind's own vocal training. Lind herself minimized the effects of formal instruction:

> To such a degree had God written within me what I had to study, my ideal was (and is) so high, that no human being existed who could in the least degree satisfy my demands. Therefore I sing after no one's method—only after that of the birds (so far as I am able); for their Teacher was the only one who responded to my requirements of truth, clearness, and expression.[20]

The very artlessness Lind claimed was in fact the product of the vocal method she had assimilated, through a process of physiological as well as mental naturalization of a rigorous technique. The principles established by her instructor, the celebrated Manuel García, enabled the singing voice to produce a seamless sound across the vocal registers, the signature of the bel canto style.[21] In the *Philosophy of Voice*, a repository of nineteenth-century vocal theory, Charles Lunn described with admiration the "Old School of Voice" that Lind represented as an entirely natural phenomenon. Such singing was "the natural outpouring of inner physical law," a "compulsory outpouring of voiced vital force."[22] Lind's "vital force," rendered in a pure tone frequently described as "angelic," allowed her public to respond to her "true voice" as the "audible vibration of her true soul."[23] Lind's true voice confirmed another current aesthetic criterion: that art, as Bancroft suggested, must be true. True in two senses: both "natural," like Lind's voice in its response to an inner "physical law," and coincidental with "virtue and moral law," as the conjunction of Lind's pure tone and reputed personal integrity suggested.[24]

Describing the harmonious vision of Art and Nature in Lind's performances was one way the American press protected Lind from charges that her art was "mechanical" and therefore unnatural. Thus one rebuttal, to the criticism that Lind showed "no feeling": "True Art supplies the place of tears by touching the emotions which are deeper and serener and not a whit less human. . . . [Her voice] is infinitely transcending the mechanical."[25] There was, of course, no denying the mechanical aspect of Lind's technique, particularly in view of her concert repertoire, dominated as it was by coloratura showpieces from contemporary grand operas by Meyerbeer, Bellini, and Donizetti. Lind did include traditional songs in her concerts, like the "Herdegossen" ("The Herdsman's Song"), and even songs written especially for her, like Taubert's "Bird Song." Such pieces conformed to the American public's reputed taste for the more accessible and decorous repertoire of folk songs and sacred hymns. Daniel Webster was not alone, then, in his stated desire—which only by a stretch could be called ethnographic—to hear more of the "simple mountain melodies of her native land."[26] The press reflected this desire to chasten the vehicles of Lind's art in its occasional demands that Lind sing more of her country's native songs, along with religious music. But the major part of her repertoire in the tour remained operatic, despite requests from the press that she temper her association with opera:

> From Jenny Lind the highest kind of music would not fall dead on the public. We ask to have more of the classic masterpieces, not merely from the one fashionable school of modern Italian opera, with a sprinkling of ballads; but also from the masters whose music her soul and her Northern genius are most kindred—from such as Mozart, Beethoven, Mendelssohn, or Franz Schubert.[27]

The press did not dwell on the fact that Lind's "Northern genius" had been nurtured by the vocal method of a Spaniard and that her voice, endowed with the agility, range, and volume characteristic of a *soprano sfogato*, was ideally suited to the musical idiom and technical requirements of the "modern" Romantic opera. Nor did the press dwell on the fact that the repertoire that enabled Lind's powers to be most acutely felt was the very repertoire that rendered her art vulnerable to criticism as mechanical.

Such reticence can be partly explained by the evidence that the mechanical aspect of Lind's singing, her technical prowess, provided a topical reference point. The emerging Lind iconology responded to contemporary concerns that "material values must necessarily outweigh spiritual" in a machine-dominated culture.[28] Lindomania helped fortify the dream of America as a pastoral Eden in the face of rising industrialism and technological culture. Thus the mechanism of the trained voice appeared as a means to a spiritual end: "These mechanical implements and arts of the bravura singer are but lifeless means of that inspired thing we call Art."[29] This teleological vision was also a typological itinerary, in conformity with prevailing cultural habits of scriptural exegesis: from the dead "letter" of vocal technique arose the inspired "spirit" of Art. Reading Lind exegetically became a way of reading the hieroglyph of the emergent culture of technology in reassuringly familiar and favorable terms. To this end the press more than once described Lind's effect as Edenic. "Yesterday," the *New York Daily Tribune* reported, "it seemed as if all the birds of Eden were piping for the first time, and glad to find themselves so gay."[30] The *Tribune* critic further described the effect of her "tones" on the atmosphere in terms of an inevitable "law" that carried both scientific and religious resonance: "The whole air had to take the law of their vibrations."[31] In a more daring flight of imagination, the same critic equated Lind's art, tellingly, with a marvel of the age: "The mechanism of art is wonderful, like the steam-engine."[32] To read Lind as her critics did was to posit a cultural space where the steam engine and Lind's vocal cords might equally be read at once as technological marvels and typological proofs. Lind's art, in other words, sanctified the presumed natural evolution of technology in industrialized society by figuring it as a recursive movement toward an originary, prelapsarian moment that confirmed the mutuality of natural and divine law.

To hear Lind was to experience the right use of technology as well as the justification of art: both were natural, both divinely inspired—and both, as the steam engine analogy suggests, were phallogocentrically oriented.[33] No less suggestive was the image that Nathaniel Parker Willis, one of Lind's contemporary biographers, found to describe her anticipated success in the far West: "When she gets to the prompt, un-crusted and foreshadowing West of this country, [she] will find her six-barrelled greatness for the first time subject to a single trigger of appreciation."[34] Like the technological culture that produced the six-barreled gun and the steam engine (literal instruments as well as symbols of conquest and possession), the rapid-fire technical virtuosity of Lind's voice seemed destined to "foreshadow" the utopian prospect of a nation in which regional differences were mitigated by the common "appreciation" of an irresistible force. From such a perspective Lind's deployment of the operatic repertoire could hardly be called suspect. The very fragmentations and dislocations that characterized her relation to her audience and to the repertoire—singing in languages the audience would not be expected to understand, singing arias taken out of context—focused attention on the technical virtuosity of the voice itself, on the effortlessness that the mechanics of its production allowed rather than on the personifications of the fictional characters it embodied.

Even the expertise of a connoisseur, it seems, could not change this basic impression. One review of Lind's performance of "Casta Diva," from Bellini's

Norma, reveals an intelligence equipped to evaluate Lind's responsiveness to the aria's musical and dramatic requirements, its particular combination of legato and coloratura cadences as well as its adroit fusion of public virtue and private transgression. Though "well selected to show the *quality* of Jenny Lind's voice," the aria comes across successfully only to those "who listened without thought of the words," for Lind's art is not equal to the dramatic *chiaroscuro* of the piece:

> On Jenny's lips, the devout purity and imploring worship and contrition, proper to the stanzas in which the Deity is addressed, are *continued throughout*; and the Roman, who has both desecrated and been faithless to her, is besought to return and sin again, with accents of sublimely unconscious innocence. . . . It was Jenny Lind, and not Norma, and she should have the air set to new words, or to an affecting and elevated passage of Scripture.[35]

It is, finally, the "sublimely unconscious innocence" of the voice itself that matters, more than the dramatic palette required to personify Norma. The sopranos "Grisi and Steffanoni," Willis acknowledges, "give better and more correct representations of 'Norma,'" but it is precisely the dramatic neutrality of Lind's vocal style that reveals a perfectly harmonized relation of person and role, of nature and art. "It is wonderful," the critic observes, "how the quality of the voice—which is inevitably an expression of the natural character and habits of mind—makes its meaning!" One might add: the ideologically preferred reading. Effortlessly Willis defines her "genius" as a characteristically "Northern genius, to be sure, which is precisely what she should have to make her greatness genuine," a greatness located in "her fresher, chaster, more intellectual, and (as they only *seem* to some) her colder strains."

The isolated pyrotechnics of Lind's preferred repertoire, together with the "quality" of Lind's voice, enabled Lind to appear as a "miraculous personation" of Voice itself, uniting art and technology, together with Northern and intellectual merit, and eclipsing the effeminized errancy of the lunatic brides and somnambulists who populated the "fashionable school" of Italian opera that Lind brought to the stage. As the *Tribune* critic put it, "The highest refinement of Art [was] not only achieved but personified before us."[36] The Nightingale epithet itself, stripped of its Ovidian association with sexual and political violence, enhanced such a claim. To personify the "highest refinement of Art" did not so much indicate the social prestige won through mastery of established protocols or, for that matter, the artist's profound identification with a particular role as it did an act of sublimation. Lind's own claim taught her public how to read the Swedish Nightingale epithet—as the emblem of a young woman who had followed "no one's method" but had, instead, found in the sound of the birds the ideal embodiment of the "requirements of truth" already divinely inscribed within her. In Lind, whose "Northern genius" distilled the particular narratives of erotic desire and suffering and loss into the abstract figure of Art, the New York public might discover an exemplary image of self-invention and release from the burden of history. What was erotic about Lind, what galvanized the phenomenon called Lindomania, was her legibility in the press as a pure sign, as a transparently self-reflexive presence that aspired to the condition of "absolute music"—that is, to the emergent instrumental and conceptless character of music associated with the "masters," notably Beethoven, to whom Lind's own apparently masculine "northern genius" was "most kindred."[37] One Mr. Dwight, a critic from Boston, distilled the essence of Lind's power in three words: "She sings herself."[38] The phrase aptly invoked the magisterial tautology of the divine name in the Hebrew Bible ("I am who I am," Ex. 3:14) as well as the rhetoric of inimitable (hence all the more desirable) heroic identity found in the epic idiom (thus Shakespeare's Cressida names Troilus: "he is himself," *Troilus and Cressida*, 1.2.71). What the phrase did not invoke was the sense of a surplus to Lind's personal history beyond the narrative requirements of the essentially hagiographical mode in which she was represented. As Mr. Dwight suggested, along with the contemporary biographers of Lind, the relation of the exemplary voice and the woman was tautological.

Secured as an authoritative exegete, the Lind voice became a vivid manifestation of the kind of theological and social prescriptions for the dissemination of Christian truth that the nation had experienced in the rise of evangelical Protestantism, in the Transcendental movement, and, more recently, in the intuitive theology and instructions for "Christian practice" propounded by Horace Bushnell in *Christian Nurture* (first published in 1846), a book that emphasized the decisive importance of enlightening example in Christian experience.[39] A seamless logic, in accord with Bushnell's principles, linked the soprano's vocal art, as a thrilling example of "moral grandeur," and her humanitarian work.[40] The press faithfully recorded Lind's many donations to charities, including the stunning information that whatever earnings Lind did not distribute among American charities she donated to the establishment of a free school system in Norway and Sweden. The imputed point was not lost on the press: "Ought not this to shame these men of wealth in our State, who are laboring to break down our Free School System?"[41] The list of American societies to which she distributed hard cash indicates the conjunction of materially sustaining and symbolically cohesive power attributed to Lind: the Fire Department Fund, the Musical Fund Society, the Society for the Relief of Indigent Females, the Lying-in Asylum for Destitute Females, the Home for Colored and Aged Persons. The "sustained melody" of Lind's legato technique found a meritorious social analog in the donations that imparted a common worthiness to the different groups literally sharing the wealth of Lind's "gold-amassing powers."

The press further delighted in recording Lind's excursions incognito into the streets of American cities, where she would sing before unsuspecting, often poverty-stricken or handicapped, individuals, then announce to the enthralled listeners that they had heard Jenny Lind.[42] In an exemplary way humanitarian work and art had indeed become one, both legitimized by the perceived clarity of Lind's voice. The voice "whose every tone in point of quality comes nearer the ideal of pure Tone, than we had thought possible" insinuated the spiritual and moral benefits of Lind's presumed artistic intentions to those who heard her: "Whoever carefully followed her singing could not fail to feel the tranquil truth of her interpretations."[43] Lind's improvisatory street singing, otherwise a bizarre footnote in the annals of American acculturation to opera, thus lent theological force to her musical proselytizing: the voice of "pure Tone" would unveil itself as the sign of the secret action of grace in the world.

Lind's proselytizing, both on- and offstage, exemplified the contemporary insistence on the broad moral imperative of women's influence, a view promulgated in particular by Catherine Beecher, author of the popular *Treatise on Domestic Economy* (first published in 1841). Following Bushnell's model, which advocated a domestic kernel of Christian nurture, Beecher maintained that women's responsibilities should be confined to the "domestic and social circle."[44] Yet Beecher's vision redefined the relation of the domestic and the social. Through female exemplars moral integrity would be "infused into the mass of the nation, and then truth may be sought, defended, and propagated, and error detected, and its evils exposed"; indeed, female exemplars became necessary guardians against "disunion, and civil wars, and servile wars."[45] Jenny Lind's appeal in 1850 demonstrated Beecher's argument. Lind was named the archetypal "Artist Woman," who symbolized the morally edifying effect of female nurture on the mass of the nation.[46] The press circumvented the oxymoronic cast of the epithet by suggesting instead its tautological character, a view enabled by Catherine Beecher's reconfiguration of the domestic and the social. As Kathryn Sklar points out, Beecher's views "politicized the traditional sphere of the home."[47] Lind's career suggested that the domestic was political because the political was domestic: the political resonances of Lind's career appeared as an epiphenomenon of an all-encompassing domestic agency.

The current estate of Lind's performing schedule lent itself to such a construction. Though she continued to sing operatic numbers, by 1850 Lind had already abandoned the operatic stage, preferring the more intimate, suggestively domestic venue of the concert hall. At least one contemporary chronicler made it clear that, whatever her venue, Lind herself possessed an essentially domestic character: "Never possibly would you meet or know any one who more thoroughly and wholly partook of all the gentler and more feminine characteristics of the homely woman."[48] The mystifying rhetoric that assimilated the oxymoron into the tautology read Lind, in effect, as the locus of a paradigm shift in the culture's reading of the female body. The relation of Lind's "gentler and more feminine characteristics" and her masculine "Northern genius" was not oppositional but mutually enabling and legitimizing.

Such rhetoric of personification enabled Lind's chroniclers to identify in her agile soprano an efficacious abstraction that exemplified broad-based social imperatives. In the *Philosophy of Voice* Charles Lunn observed that "Art is doing."[49] The virtuosic productivity of Lind's voice appealed both to the democratic mythos and to the Protestant work ethic of her audiences. One document, a chronicle from abroad allegedly written by an "Indian Chief," presents one unadulterated, "natural" voice announcing the arrival of another. The native American, embodying in his capacity as "Chief" a non-European model of royalty and authority, announced Jenny Lind to the readers of the *Tribune* as the exemplary model of the American ideal of equality: "Oh tell the poor classes all over the land," the "Indian Chief" writes, "that this far-famed vocalist was once an obscure girl—yes, a poor girl. Let them imitate such examples, and be something while they live."[50] Evidently, knowledge of Lind's personal history as "an obscure girl" helped establish Lind's value as the embodiment of an American mythology that itself obscured, if not eliminated, social and economic differences through the public's imaginative identification with an exemplar of personal transformation.

The voice of the "Indian Chief" ventriloquized in Lind's singing, *avant la lettre*, a Horatio Alger narrative of self-improvement through personal virtue and effort. This imaginative projection turned up in another article, also published before Lind ever sang a note in New York:

> She comes among us with no diadem on her brow, no scepter in her grasp, no stations at her disposal. Not hers is even the fame of dazzling beauty, nor the assumption of rare spiritual gifts, such as still binds thousands of the devout and the cultivated in either hemisphere to the memory and the teachings of her great countryman, Swedenborg. A young, untitled woman, born and educated in the useful walks of life . . . she has won her way by genius, by effort, by lofty achievement, to the society and friendship of the noblest and most eminent of her sex and to the hearts of admiring nations. . . . In the homage so widely paid to Mlle. Lind we gladly hail the dawn of a truer appreciation of well-directed Effort, no matter in what sphere. For she, too, is but a Worker, like the rest of us, though in the realm of the ideal rather than the Physical—she has well chosen her part with those whose labors are intended

> to chasten, refine, elevate, instruct, and delight. She too is but a Worker like any other, save that she has emancipated herself from the drudgery and earthliness of the laborer's lot by learning to love and rejoice in her work as well as its recompense—to find Enjoyment in Duty as well as its grosser and more palpable rewards. . . . Only let us aspire to be true Artists . . . as men who would scorn to live useless, in a world where so much needed work awaits the doing, and who would be ashamed to stand idle because none but a humble sphere of exertion was proferred them. Let us all be in the soul Artists—lovers of the benignant and the beautiful—ready wrestlers with deformity, obstruction and despair—lovers of well-doing for Humanity's sake—and Labor shall no more pace the earth with sad heart and stooping frame, but walk erect and glad-hearted, sole patent of a true nobility. Homage then to the Artist, who in a perverted and misjudging age stands forth a radiant prophecy of the good time that yet shall be![51]

In this grand prophetic vision, high and low culture, along with the preserves of "genius" and "effort," have become one. As Charles Lunn's later discussion of vocal training would suggest, Art is smoothly equated with noble Labor, a "needed work" made democratic, humanitarian, and socially progressive (not to say intuitively Marxist, given the presumed power of Lind's art to emancipate the alienated worker, and "Labor" itself, from "drudgery and earthliness"). Purged of its elitist associations, Art itself has become quintessentially American, in a sweeping vision that corroborates Russell Blaine Nye's observation of the contemporary cultural belief that "the 'mechanic arts,' " far from dehumanizing the social world and reifying class differences, "belonged within the pattern of progress decreed by the Creator."

The rubric of Lind's "homely" art sustained the politically underwritten conviction that "Art and Beauty do concern us all" and led one American commentator abroad to speculate on the intimate relationship between Art and a nation's rise to political prominence, using the case of opera in France as a negative example:

> The more I see of France, the more I am convinced that a Government which would turn the national genius from Arms to Arts, could put her at the head of nations—or at least in competition in wealth and progress with our own. . . . The [French] Republic seems to favor Art, judging from the jam at the Opéra . . . [yet] it forms no part of a national entertainment, being too expensive for the people.[52]

In the shift from "Arms" to "Arts," the mechanical or technological and the more abstractly aesthetic elements of art joined ranks as part of the same progressive impulse. By implication, the commentator advised, it was urgent that the "whole people" of America, especially the "large and intelligent middle classes," for whom "Opera is now a necessity"—thanks, in part, to Jenny Lind—continue to find artistic nourishment in their homeland.[53]

P.T. Barnum's experiment, by giving Jenny Lind to the American public, thus consecrated the "large and intelligent middle classes" of America as a modern audience ideally equipped to profit from the "modern art" of opera. The middle classes, the commentator suggested, would imbue Lind's European-bred art with egalitarian, American significance, realizing the promise that America was a land of "all true Artists," and, with the proper marketing and publicity, Lind's popularity among the middle classes would be disseminated among the masses of the people—an apparent departure from the aristocratic ethos of European nations. The success of Lind's New York concerts seemed to demonstrate that opera itself might be successfully transformed into an American icon. While Lind's concerts continued to fill Tripler Hall in the autumn months of 1850, the *Tribune* promoted the demand for "an opera house as large as Tripler Hall . . . admitting of large audiences and moderate prices."[54] Thus Willis's observation: "Opera music has, *in a couple of months*, become a popular taste" (emphasis in text). The phenomenon, he added, was "not unnatural."[55] Further considering "the Jenny Lind enthusiasm," he acknowledged that the "ear for music" might be found and cultivated anywhere in society: "the mechanic is as likely to have it as the banker—the seamstress as like as likely as the millionaire's daughter." But only in American society, he argued, would the appreciation of art "pass, with this marvelous facility, from one class to another." Glossing over the material instrumentality of print culture in promoting the rage for Jenny Lind, Willis promoted a vision of America that equalled the "sublimely unconscious innocence" he had attributed to Lind herself, in what amounted to a discursive imitation of Lind's suavely equalized vocal registers, attained through the bel canto technique. The American version of Lindomania constituted "proof of the slightness of separation between the upper and middle classes of our country—of the ease with which the privileges of a higher class pass to the use of the class nominally below"—proof, that is, of "how essentially, as well as in form and name, this is a land of equality." Mirabile dictu, opera, not baseball, was on its way to becoming the central metaphor and cultural practice defining what it meant to be American.[56]

If, in the progressive scheme thus envisioned, the political was domestic, and if the soul of the "homely woman" intersected effortlessly with the genius of the "masters," so too, where Lind was concerned, the intimate and personal were scaled to epic proportions. The first chronicles of Lind's performances in New York emphasized the unequalled "moral grandeur" of her concerts in these terms:

> To Castle Garden is reserved this sublime spectacle of a whole people as it were, worshiping at the shrine of Art, and receiving the voice of Art as that of "deep calling unto deep." Jenny Lind is evidently most herself and most inspired when she sings most for all. . . . It is only preferring the spirit to the letter of pure musical proprieties, to own that we would willingly sacrifice something of mere musical effect to have her concerts all continued on so large a scale. . . . We have never witnessed in this practical and bustling world, such an acknowledgement that Art and Beauty do most intimately concern us all.[57]

Lind's concert's provoked a rhetoric of prophetic rapture that articulated what Bryan J. Wolf has called, in a different context, an "American national sublime."[58] The project of such rhetoric—imagining the collapse of difference, enfolded into an originary One—engaged a politics of representation to which the reviewer's admixture of exegetical and democratic idioms lent force. Through the substitution, or "sacrifice," that enabled the "large scale" of Lind's concertizing to eclipse the negligible "something" of "mere musical effect," the transcendent categories of Art and Beauty, which Lind apparently embodied, became vehicles of a more pressing imperative, the enthralling spectacle of "a whole people" united, interpellated into a single identity by the "spirit" of Lind's singing. The reviewer had located an ideology of music, drawn less from theoretical or musicological insights—though these were not insignificant—than from the perceived visual and visceral effects of the large-scale containment of a social body before the production and projection of Lind's "pure Tone."

"The Northern Muse," it was said, "must sing her lesson to the world."[59] But, unlike the particular fascination associated with one of Lind's preferred heroines, the sleepwalking Amina in Bellini's *La Sonnambula*, the edifying power ascribed to her singing did not include soporific properties: if exposure to Lind's concerts infused the masses with renewed faith in their own manifest political and economic destiny, that faith was not uncritical. Press coverage of the concerts, speaking for "the world of common hearts," eventually isolated ambivalent attitudes toward the democratic experiment itself that the rhetoric of sublimity did not fully absorb.[60] An article printed in December 1850, in the wake of Lind's first concert series, seized the occasion to question the relationship in America between democracy and art. A Tocquevillian apprehension informs the writer's analysis: "Everything must be done *democratically* in this country, if it looks to popular support. This is our advantage as much as our disadvantage. . . . The tendency to equalize unhappily pulls down as well as pulls up" (emphasis in text).[61] The writer further recognizes that "the secret of the matter here, as elsewhere, is simply—*money*" (emphasis in text), money which must, in a democracy, be obtained through the channels of popular support, with the risk of "depreciating the artistic standard." The resurgent note of faith that does appear in the article belies the interpretive labor involved in establishing the harmonious union of democratic political culture and the persistently elitist resonance of Lind's art. On the one hand, the writer proclaims that democratic culture nurtures a desire for art: "No people are as ready as we to acknowledge what is genuine and to pay royally and richly for its enjoyment." On the other hand, the writer locates Lind's art in a messianic logic that makes art both crucial and irreducible to the imbricated democratic and capitalist projects: "We must trust to the hold that genuine art always has upon the genuine artist. To him, even in a world of indubitable dollars there is something solider and more golden. It is the inspiration and pursuit of that which perpetuates Art and saves Society." What the writer cannot fully acknowledge is that the "Art" of opera was a commodity as well as an intangible, inspirational value, and that these two aspects were complicitous—as the writer's ambiguous reference to the "something solider and more golden" suggests.

The messianic appeal finally prevailed over incipient cultural critique, erecting a hierarchy of interests that was nonetheless informed by the pragmatic intuition of what the democratic experiment might and might not accomplish. There was, then, "something" slightly forced in the chronicles of the enthusiasm that Lind's New York concerts generated, particularly in the last major documents to appear in the *Tribune*: in late September a final essay on Lind's first series of six concerts, and in mid-December a letter to the editor on the subject of "Jenny Lind and her True Mission." Both pieces reveal a preoccupation with questions of union and disunion, understandable questions in view of the cultural landscape in which Lind's concerts appeared. Eighteen fifty was one of the most volatile years in the antebellum period. Its calendar included the notorious Compromise of 1850, the death of J. C. Calhoun, one of the principal architects of the compromise, and Daniel Webster's personally disastrous Seventh of March speech, which promoted the compromise and provoked the wrath of the Northern abolitionists. The rhetorical and legal quid pro quos and battles that accompanied the drafting and the enacting of the compromise were no less Byzantine than the terms of the compromise itself, which included a bill admitting California as a free state, a bill establishing the Territory of Utah, with the proviso that the slavery question would be determined by popular sovereignty at the moment of statehood, a bill restructuring the boundaries of the proslavery state of Texas, by rescinding its claim to part of the New Mexico Territory, a bill prohibiting the slave trade in the District of Columbia, and the Fugitive Slave Law. Slavery and its corollary, secession, were the pivotal issues; they sharpened the political profiles and antagonisms of abolitionists and secessionists alike and lent a sense of urgency to public speculation on the nature as well as the destiny of the Union.[62]

The successful passage of the compromise bills in September seemed to acknowledge the redemptive rhetoric of one particularly forceful exponent of the compromise, Daniel Webster, whose speeches on the subject encouraged the American public and government not to risk fracturing the Union and its founding document, the Constitution, by insisting on the letter of the moral law on the slavery question. Evidence of Webster's strategy can be discerned in the Seventh of March speech, in which Webster at one point tried to disarm the abolitionists' sense of moral authority by accusing them of dealing "with morals as with mathematics . . . with the precision of an algebraic equation" and of therefore failing to "view things as they are."[63] How things were, in Webster's estimation, could be grasped by observing that the emergence in the South of slavery "as an institution to be cherished, and preserved, and extended" could be understood as a "natural" development, particularly in the light of the principal lesson "historical research" taught: that "there is no generation of mankind whose opinions are not subject to be influenced by what appear to them to be their present emergent and exigent interests." The pragmatism that guided Webster's arguments, and which helped clear the way for the passage of the compromise in Congress, was the linchpin of the paradigm shift in American political culture promoted by the very terms of the compromise: the view that the idea of union might be predicated not on commonly held values and social structures but on a constitutionally sanctioned negotiation of regional differences. Though intended to preserve the Union and the pragmatic viability of the Constitution, and generally hailed as having done so after the successful passage of the compromise, Webster's arguments, together with the legislation they endorsed, tacitly rescripted the roles of Union and Constitution, of idea and text, in the national romance called *E pluribus unum*. The events of 1850 arguably reframed the Constitution as the document that did not so much unite diverse communities in common values and goals as produce an assemblage of contradictory, finally irreconcilable, cultural practices that begged the question of the terms and the value of union itself. More of a stopgap than a solution, the compromise preserved the Union at the price of making it appear quixotic.

In this context the coincidence of the passage in the Senate of the compromise bills and Lind's arrival in New York in September is telling: the chronicles of Lind's concerts chart the inflection of a vexed political discourse in the representation and promotion of musical enthusiasm and diva-worship. Take the review essay published in late September. In the main, it recapitulates familiar topics. Lind's spiritual quality, again, infuses and justifies the mechanical. Her concerts even take on a revivalist character: they are "mass meetings." But, persistently, the rhetoric of the political crisis filters into the analysis. Lind's voice is emphasized as a union of disparate parts, the tones "each symmetrical and whole and discrete in itself," her "eyes of intellect still purged and unconfused."[64] The quality of her vocal expression appears in the loaded terms of North-South tensions: "But she has the Northern strength of intellect; she has the spiritual rather than the sensuous form of passion." The reference literally juxtaposes stereotypical Scandinavian and Latin attributes, but in 1850 could any juxtaposition of North and South fail to suggest contemporary concerns about the secession issue? Read as a sign of the ascendancy of "Northern" intellect, Lind's art became an explicit political icon, representing what the democratic experiment alone might not accomplish: "The crowds whom she delighted have, at the same time, caught something from her of the spirit of Art, which is the very spirit that must save our Republic and make earth a heaven, if that ever is to be." The vitalist character of Lind's artistic power belied the self-sufficiency of the democratic project; as the essay suggested, the Republic itself needed to be possessed by an external, transformative power in order to realize the ideal society it promoted.

The yearning for an apocalyptic resolution found an even more acute expression in the letter to the editor printed in December. The anonymous author, evidently well versed in the tropes of a Swedenborgian mysticism, begins the letter with a discussion of the "philosophy of music in general," based on a system of "seven different vibrations in the air . . . the diatonic scale, which was never invented by man, but is eternally established in NATURE."[65] His effort to consolidate, to unify discrete elements in a massive whole, generates a detailed map of how "every complete system of creation and movement in nature, however small, contains within itself the principles of the diatonic scale," including the anatomical structure of humans, the "natural classes of society," of animals, plants, geological formations and periods, and, in a final gesture of abstraction, "indeed the great System of systems generalized as one complete and universal Whole." Music, the "breathing of God through all Nature and Heaven . . the law governing the harmonious and affectionate interblending of all forms and movements," assumes an urgently needed social value: "O, could its spirit be breathed by mankind universally, what social harmony and peace would replace our present discord and distractions." Jenny Lind serves as the long-awaited messianic instrument: "In these seasons (literally speaking) of angel visitations who come to herald the millenial day, God has sent JENNY LIND as a highly qualified exponent of the natural harmonies and melodies." The letter further underscores the topical urgency of the rhetorical equipment marshaled to promote Lind's salvific power. She embodies the "gushing aspirations of the great heart of mankind at this age of moral, social, and spiritual regeneration"; "with her benevolence of soul . . . [she] is the woman who could move the world, I had almost said to its foundation, and leave a mark upon her age which could never be erased." Hester Prynne's scarlet letter had found its typological fulfillment in the "mark" imposed by the angelic visitation of Lind's voice, whose reception would be assured by its employment in the rhetoric of the "national sublime." Lind's voice alone would realize the nation's desire for an apocalyptic resolution to the tensions, the "discord and distractions," threatening the myth of political union. Together, the millenarian impulse, the pious allusions to mystical visitations, the assertions of the edifying effects of Art, and the rhetoric of sublimity provided a lens through which Lind's voice might be seen to negotiate the twin prospects of concord and historical catastrophe exemplified in the Compromise of 1850.

In this regard the "inspired vitality" and "humanity" of Lind's art mirrored the privilege attributed to the force of political oratory on the contemporary scene. Together with J. C. Calhoun and Henry Clay (to whom Lind was likened, reportedly having a "mouth like that of Henry Clay"), Daniel Webster was one of the most brilliant exemplars of an oratorical tradition that was soon to fade, the so-called elocutionary school of oratory.[66] Departing from the rule-oriented protocols of classical rhetorical theory as received in eighteenth-century America, elocutionary rhetoric favored the orator's cultivation of a personalized expression that might release the spontaneous "emotions and passions" of listeners. To this end textbooks regularly laid emphasis on the training of the orator's voice; one book, as Russel B. Nye notes, "had seven chapters on voice training alone: Emphasis, Inflection, Modulation, Personization, Expression, Articulation, and the Uses of the Pause and Slur."[67] Given the culture's responsiveness to the orator's technical mastery of vocal resources, the differences between the vocal production of Lind's bel canto art and Webster's reputed "magnificent elocution" might well seem more of degree than of kind.[68]

Nathaniel Parker Willis thought so in his account of one of Lind's Tripler Hall concerts, which Daniel Webster attended. The subject of the review is not Lind's performance per se, but rather the performance as vehicle of the encounter of the two celebrated figures. Webster enters the narrative almost as an emanation of Lind herself, whose unremarkable physiognomy was regularly depicted in terms of its "dignity of repose" and "utter simplicity of goodness."[69] Tropes of purity, austerity, and lunar beauty—the chastened iconography of the diva—fill the narrator's description of the mysterious presence, whose identity slowly comes into focus. A "white object with a sparkling dark line underneath" appears in the crowd.[70] Its "motionless" aspect prompts the narrator to imagine "a calm half moon, seen over the tops of agitated trees," then a "massive magnolia blossom, too heavy for the breeze to stir, splendid and silent amid fluttering poplar-leaves." Technology—the opera glass—at last reveals the literal identity and, through a pun, the political significance of the object. With "the eye brought nearer to the object," the narrator sees a capital (capitol): "lo! *the dome over the temple of Webster*—the forehead of the great Daniel, with the two glorious lamps set in the dark shadow of its architrave" (emphasis in text). Shared metaphorical associations of moon and classical temple—gravity, wonder, divine presence—and the erotic hint to the "massive magnolia blossom" suggest the alluring power to induce a state of rapture or possession, shared by Webster's oratorical prowess and political authority and Lind's oracular art. As the narrator observes, "our veins tingled, as veins will with the recognition of a sudden and higher presence." The reaction, produced by the "noble Constitutionist," might as easily have been observed at Lind's entrance.

Given Webster's unanticipated presence, the prevailing interest of the evening is to "see signs of the susceptibility of such a mind to the spells of Jenny Lind." As though they shared the elective affinities of celestial bodies, diva and orator have become the subject of stargazing: "slight they must be, of course, if signs were to be seen at all; but the interest in watching for them was no less exciting—very slight variations, of the 'bodies' above us, repaying fully the patient observation of the astronomer." In fact, Lind's own entrance into this planetarium occurs without comment, as though Lind's much-touted ability to produce a "sustained melody" dictated that she could not be represented *not* already in song. Lind first appears in the narrative at the moment when she decorously interrupts her program of operatic arias—the narrator calls them "those tangled skeins of music"—in order to favor a request muttered by Webster and "spirited away from the cloud-edge of his lips"—that is, quickly passed to the stage by an attendant: "Why doesn't she give us one of the simple mountain-songs of her own land?"

Lind's compliance, mingling a gesture of noblesse oblige and the protocol of female propriety, produces exactly the kind of sign of "susceptibility" in Webster that the narrator had anticipated, and it produces in the narrator an increasingly lambent style as he traces the course of the song's effect on the audience and on Webster. An erotics of the sublime infuses the description. The "loud beginning" of the "simple" song claims the "sympathy" of the audience through its simultaneous evocation of the majestic and the humble, tropes familiar to the American mythology of a national sublime. From "the bare summits that alone listen where it is supposed to be sung" the music finds a new, empathetic audience, who become Ariel to Lind's Prospero: as Lind's singing "softened," approaching the end of the song, "the audience, (as if transformed to an Ariel that 'puts a girdle round the earth,') commenced following the last clear note through the distance." The perceived effect on Webster dominates the passage:

> Away it sped, softly and evenly, a liquid arrow through more liquid air, lessening with the sweetness it left behind it, but fleeing leagues in seconds, and with no errand but to go on unaltered till it should die—and, behold! on the track of it, with the rest of us, was gone the heavy-winged intellect of Webster! We had listened with our eyes upon him. . . . The tone sped and lessened, and Webster's broad chest grew erect and expanded. Still on went the entrancing sound, altered by distance only, and changeless in the rapt altitude of the cadence—on—far on—as if only upon the bar of the horizon it could faint at last—and forward leaned the aroused statesman, with his hand clasped over the balustrade, his head raised to its fullest lift above his shoulders, and the luminous caverns of his eyes opened wide upon the still lips of the singer. The note died—and those around exchanged glances as the enchantress touched the instrument before her—but Webster sat motionless.[71]

At several turns the passage invokes elements of the discourse of the sublime, all conveying a collective enthrallment before the vistas of alterity that the single note introduces. The note's gradual dissolution is rendered as an unimpeded yet virtually unrepresentable force (the "liquid arrow" flying through "more liquid air"). Prospects of limitless extension in distance and altitude provoke a remotely necrophiliac fascination, suggested by the image of the "entrancing" note rushing to faint on the "bar of the horizon" and by Webster's own "aroused" pursuit of the note, in the course of which his body, made spectral by the dislocation of the head and the exorbitant gaze, acquires a deathlike stasis matched by the "still lips of the singer," the visible source of the note, figured as the opening to a lost point of origin.

The sepulchral union of diva and orator signals the perfection of an aesthetically and politically charged value, the resolution of difference. Such an ideal, the narrator suggests, is not to be attained through Webster alone. The narrator recalls that Webster "was only courteously attentive" to the first part of the concert, a relative aloofness he attributes to a nuance that distinguishes Webster's access to the sublime from Lind's. Giving perhaps a discreet signal of his own resistance to Webster's political agenda, the narrator proclaims Webster's own inadequate "cultivation of the voice," a lacuna Webster has compensated for with "other and sufficient advantages," which the narrator passes over in silence, except to recall the note of a Websterian sublime in the orator's voice. It is a voice "as monotonous as thunder," because "thunder has no need to be more varied and musical." Lind's singing of the mountain song arouses Webster's dormant capacity to "surpass Art with the more sudden impassioning of Nature," and, in so doing, the performance affords "her best single triumph on this side of the water, the sounding of America's deepest mind with her plummet of enchantment." The spell of Lind's voice, at once regenerative and fatal (that is, apocalyptically fated), has joined diva and orator, two differently modulated proportions of intellect and passion, in a single figure that asserts the kerygmatic power of their union to fulfill the promise the September essay found in Lind: the power to "save our Republic and make earth a heaven."

"All the stars in the Union have dimmed before the star of Jenny Lind," wrote one observer after Lind's arrival in America.[72] Like the universal enthrallment figured in the representation of Lind's "enchantment" over Webster and the entire crowd of "three or four thousand" in Tripler Hall, such rhetoric suggestively located the discourse of the sublime in the messianic political climate of 1850. One elision, principally, enabled these variations on the theme of "a whole people . . . worshiping at the shrine of Art" to resonate as politicized tropes of a "sublime spectacle." The literal subjugation at issue in the institution of slavery turned up, mystified, as the figural subjugation of a "whole people" in the idiom of diva-worship. This is not to say that Lind's reputed "enchantment" endorsed slavery, any more than Webster's pragmatic strategizing did. That is, the rhetoric of mystification at work here was at least partly enabling. Through the structural analogy that it promoted between aesthetic and political forms of enthrallment—a relation of identity *with* difference—the Tripler Hall scenario introduced the prospect of a "whole people" able to identify the dynamics of complicity that obtained between nominally disparate orbits of power in the Union.[73] The conscription of Lindomania into a politically charged rhetoric of sublimity helped sustain, then, the prospect of a politically neutral locus—the consecrated ground of a "shrine"—from which the resolution of the slavery question might be considered a national mandate without provoking the already perceptible drift toward secession. Lindomania helped a nation in crisis sustain the hope that the intractable contradictions legislated by the terms of the Compromise of 1850 might indeed "save our Republic" and that Webster's pragmatism, his "heavy-winged intellect," might prove to possess the enchantment of Lind's song.

Notes

1. Rosenberg, *Jenny Lind in America*, p. 218.

2. A brief word about Lind's background. She possessed a *soprano sfogato* of the Italian school—a voice endowed with exceptional agility, range, and volume, qualities that had been associated, generations earlier, with the castrati, who sang the female roles in the opera seria of the seventeenth and eighteenth centuries. Discussions of Lind's vocal tradition are in Chorley, *Thirty Years' Musical Recollections*, pp. 192–99. See also Pleasants, *The Great Singers,* pp. 197–204. Like many singers of her time, Lind made her debut at an early age (seventeen). Her first triumphs were in Stockholm; she became an

overnight success, and quickly rose to fame in major European cities, particularly in Berlin and in London, then the center of the operatic world.

3. Cited in Willis, *Memoranda,* p. 99.

4. Lind's success was the most sensational in the stream of European artists who were beginning to discover new horizons, and a new market, in the New World. The celebrated Maria Malibran, among others, had preceded Lind to New York. For a comprehensive view of the "migration" of European artists to America in the mid-nineteenth century, see Nye, *Society and Culture in America,* pp. 126–29.

5. *The New York Daily Tribune* (hereafter *NYDT*), September 23, 1850, p. 1. I confine myself to the reviews of Lind's New York concerts published in the *Tribune* or in contemporary biographies. Accounts of Lind's concerts in other cities—including Pittsburgh, Havana, New Orleans, San Francisco—generally rehearse the topics raised in the New York press. The most recent documentary history of Jenny Lind's career in America under the management of P. T. Barnum is Ware and Lockard, Jr., *P. T. Barnum Presents Jenny Lind.*

6. Cited in Avery, *Life and Genius of Jenny Lind*, p. 40.

7. Hawthorne, *The Scarlet Letter*, p. 185.

8. Ibid., p. 186.

9. Bulman, *Jenny Lind*, pp. 236–67. The effect of sublimity was reported by George William Curtis.

10. Avery, *Life and Genius of Jenny Lind,* pp. 3, 21. This citation includes further references in the paragraph.

11. According to N. Parker Willis, "Jenny Lind sings like a woman with no weakness. . . . There is plenty of soul in her singing, but no flesh and blood," Willis, *Memoranda,* p. 152.

12. Avery, *Life and Genius of Jenny Lind,* p. 20. For a discussion of the "National Symbolic," see Berlant, *The Anatomy of National Fantasy,* p. 20.

13. Avery, *Life and Genius of Jenny Lind,* pp. 40, 32, 20. This citation includes further references in the paragraph.

14. Bulman, *Jenny Lind,* p. 253.

15. *NYDT,* September 27, 1850, p. 1; November 6, 1850, p. 5.

16. Cited in Nye, *Society and Culture in America,* p. 83.

17. *NYDT,* September 20, 1859, p. 1.

18. *NYDT,* September 10, 1850, p. 1.

19. *NYDT,* September 12, 1850, p. 1.

20. Cited in Bulman, *Jenny Lind,* p. 54.

21. An impression of Lind's bel canto technique is in Rockstro, *Jenny Lind.*

22. Lunn, *Philosophy of Voice*, pp. 12–13.

23. *NYDT*, September 20, 1850, p. 1.

24. Nye, *Society and Culture in America,* p. 83.

25. *NYDT,* September 20, 1850, p. 1.

26. For an account of the state of the native tradition in music during the period of Lind's American tour, see Nye, *Society and Culture in America,* pp. 126–29. Webster's request is cited in Rosenberg, *Jenny Lind in America*, p. 75, and in Willis, *Memoranda,* p. 178.

27. *NYDT,* September 20, 1850, p. 1.

28. Nye, *Society and Culture in America*, p. 276.

29. *NYDT*, September 27, 1850, p. 1.

30. *NYDT,* November 11, 1850, p. 5. From other reviews: "My soul, wrapt in ecstasy, seemed borne on to the Garden of Eden," *NYDT*, September 2, 1850, p. 2; "Song is original in her; and from her singing we drink in new life," cited in Willis, *Memoranda*, pp. 122–23.

31. *NYDT,* September 12, 1850, p. 1.

32. *NYDT,* November 10, 1850, p. 5. To borrow Nye's phrase, the steam engine as "the great wonder of the age and the great hope of the future," *Society and Culture in America,* p. 272.

33. One devotee, at least, would probably have begged to differ with the comparison of Lind and the steam engine. Mrs. L. H. Sigourney wrote a celebratory poem ("The Swedish Songstress and Her Charities") that opens with these lines: "Blest must their vocation be / Who with tones of melody, / Charm the discord and the strife / And the railroad rush of life." Cited in Willis, *Memoranda,* p. 214.

34. Willis, *Memoranda,* p. 159. In referring to Lind's "six-barrelled greatness" Willis may have had the so-called pepperbox (or pepperpot) gun in mind. The pepperbox, a pistol with five or six revolving barrells, remained in widespread use after Samuel Colt patented what could be called the first true revolver, in 1835. Single-barreled, the Colt revolver utilized a revolving cylinder with several chambers. See Carman, *A History of Firearms,* pp. 143–44, with Taylerson, *Revolving Arms,* p. 4.

35. Willis, *Memoranda,* pp. 150–51. The citation includes further references in the paragraph.

36. *NYDT,* September 23, 1850, p. 1.

37. On "absolute music" see Andrew Bowie, "Music, Language, and Modernity," pp. 67–85.

38. Cited in Willis, *Memoranda,* p. 118.

39. See Bushnell, *Christian Nurture,* p. 219.

40. *NYDT,* September 25, 1850, p. 1.

41. *NYDT,* September 13, 1850, p. 6.

42. Rosenberg, *Jenny Lind in America,* p. 26.

43. *NYDT,* September 27, 1850, p. 1.

44. Sklar, *Catherine Beecher,* p. 135.

45. Ibid., 135.

46. *NYDT,* September 20, 1850, p. 1.

47. Sklar, *Catherine Beecher,* p. 135.

48. Avery, *Life and Genius of Jenny Lind,* p. 38.

49. Lunn, *Philosophy of Voice*, p. 19.

50. *NYDT,* September 2, 1850, p. 2. Willis includes the entire letter in his *Memoranda,* which identifies its author as "KAH-GE-GA-GAH-BOWH" (Otherwise George Copway)," p. 107.

51. *NYDT,* September 2, 1850, p. 4.

52. *NYDT,* September 20, 1850, p. 2.

53. *NYDT,* November 11, 1850, p. 5.

54. Ibid.

55. Willis, *Memoranda,* p. 145. The citation includes further references in the paragraph.

56. An account of the emergence of baseball as an organized sport in the 1850s is in Goldstein, *Playing for Keeps*.

57. *NYDT,* September 23, 1850, p. 1.

58. Wolf, "A Grammar of the Sublime," p. 322.

59. Willis, *Memoranda,* p. 123.

60. Ibid., p. 173.

61. *NYDT,* December 10, 1850, pp. 5–6. The citation includes further references in the paragraph.

62. A useful account of the Compromise of 1850 is in Hamilton, *Prologue to Conflict*.

63. Cited in Smith, *Defender of the Union,* pp. 168–69. The citation includes further references in the paragraph.

64. *NYDT,* September 27, 1850, p. 1. The citation includes further references in the paragraph.

65. *NYDT,* December 10, 1850, p. 6. The citation includes further references in the paragraph.

66. *NYDT*, September 2, 1850, p. 2. Peter De Bolla discusses the connection between the elocutionary method and the sublime, with particular reference to eighteenth-century Britain, in *The Discourse of the Sublime*.

67. Nye, *Society and Culture in America,* p. 142.

68. On Webster's "magnificent elocution," see Baxter, *One and Inseparable,* pp. 85–86.

69. Willis, *Memoranda,* p. 173.

70. Ibid., pp. 175–79. The citation includes subsequent references to the passage.

71. Ibid., pp. 178–79.

72. Cited in ibid., p. 95.

73. Lindomania thus suggests how the contradictions inherent in the ideology of the aesthetic—the promotion of the individual as an "abstract universality" and a "concrete particularity"—could enable a productive dialectic that might otherwise be identified as the "opposite of ideology." Terry Eagleton calls this phenomenon, tellingly, an "emancipatory critique," which brings "institutional constraints to our awareness" and which "can be achieved only by the practice of a collective self-reflection." See Eagleton, *Ideology: An Introduction,* p. 132, with Eagleton, *The Ideology of the Aesthetic*, pp. 414–15.

Works Cited

Avery, S. P. *The Life and Genius of Jenny Lind*. New York: W. F. Burgess, 1850.

Baxter, Maurice G. *One and Inseparable: Daniel Webster and the Union*. Cambridge and London: Harvard University Press, 1984.

Berlant, Lauren. *The Anatomy of National Fantasy: Hawthorne, Utopia, and Everyday Life.* Chicago: University of Chicago Press, 1991.

Bowie, Andrew. "Music, Language, and Modernity." In Andrew Benjamin, ed., *The Problems of Modernity: Adorno and Benjamin*, pp. 67–85. London and New York: Routledge, 1989.

Bulman, Joan. *Jenny Lind.* London: James Barrie, 1956.

Bushnell, Horace. *Christian Nurture.* [1861.] Grand Rapids: Baker Book House, 1979.

Carman, W. Y. *A History of Firearms From Earliest Times to 1914.* London: Routledge and Kegan Paul, 1955.

Chorley, Henry F. *Thirty Years' Musical Recollections.* [1862.] New York: Knopf, 1926.

De Bolla, Peter. *The Discourse of the Sublime: Readings in History, Aesthetics, and the Subject.* Oxford: Basil Blackwell, 1989.

Eagleton, Terry. *Ideology: An Introduction.* London and New York: Verso, 1991.

——— *The Ideology of the Aesthetic.* Oxford: Basil Blackwell, 1990.

Goldstein, Warren. *Playing for Keeps: A History of Early Baseball.* Ithaca: Cornell University Press, 1989.

Hamilton, Holman. *Prologue to Conflict: The Crisis and Compromise of 1850.* Lexington: University of Kentucky Press, 1964.

Hawthorne, Nathaniel. *The Scarlet Letter.* Ed. Sculley Bradley, Richmond Croom Beatty, E. Hudson Long, and Seymour Gross. New York: Norton, 1978.

Lunn, Charles. *Philosophy of Voice.* London: Bailliere, Tindall and Cox, 1874.

Nye, Russel Blaine. *Society and Culture in America, 1830–1860.* New York: Harper and Row, 1974.

Pleasants, Henry. *The Great Singers: From the Dawn of Opera to Our Own Time.* New York: Simon and Schuster, 1966.

Rockstro, W. S. *Jenny Lind: A Record and Analysis of the 'Method' of the Late Madame Jenny Lind-Goldschmidt, Together with a Selection of Cadenze, Solfeggi, Abellimenti, &c. in Illustration of Her Vocal Art.* Ed. Otto Goldschmidt. London: Novello, Ewer, 1894.

Rosenberg, Charles G. *Jenny Lind in America.* New York: Stringer and Townsend, 1851.

Sklar, Kathryn Kish. *Catherine Beecher.* New Haven: Yale University Press, 1973.

Smith, Craig R. *Defender of the Union: The Oratory of Daniel Webster.* New York: Greenwood, 1989.

Taylerson, A. W. F. *Revolving Arms.* New York: Walker, 1967.

Ware, W. Porter, and Thaddeus C. Lockard, Jr. *P. T. Barnum Presents Jenny Lind: The American Tour of the Swedish Nightingale.* Baton Rouge: Louisiana State University Press, 1980.

Willis, Nathaniel Parker. *Memoranda of the Life of Jenny Lind.* Philadelphia: Robert E. Peterson, 1851.

Wolf, Bryan J. "A Grammar of the Sublime, or Intertextuality Triumphant in Church, Turner, and Cole," *New Literary History* (Winter 1985), 16:321–41.

Singing in Greek Drag: Gluck, Berlioz, George Eliot

Wendy Bashant

Yes, the part suits me. Searching through hell for love is something I do all the time.

—Kathleen Ferrier's response to a compliment on her performance as Orfeo at Glyndebourne (1947)

Orfeo ed Euridice is one of the queerest operas I know. I am sure many could contest this subjective crown; there are many close seconds. Strauss's Salome, no fragile butterfly, splits her desires equally between the rigid phallic prophet and his habitation, described as a deep cavern, lake, anal or vaginal hole. "Ich will deinen Mund küssen, Jochanaan" she demands on a high F, reaching even higher to an A-flat when she says *mouth*. (Her voice falls with the triplets that follow as she desires to kiss the hole, longing to fall into that hole.) But while the diva's desires disrupt conventional sexual categories, the opera ends reinscribing gender. The Baptist is ultimately divided—head from heart, male sermon from female body.

This gendered division is preserved in the early performances of the work. The reviewer in the New York Times *(January 23, 1907) writes of Salome's dance in Strauss's opera: "It was a dance that women turn away from, and many of the women . . . last night turned away from it. Very few men in the audience seemed comfortable. They twisted in their chairs, and before it was over there were numbers of them who decided to go to the corridors and smoke." Initially the object of desire, the unbridled sexuality does not hold the male gaze. But despite this momentary confusion, gendered decorum is finally maintained. The men and women of the audience retreat to comfortable categories. Women turn away; men retreat to manly corridors and smoke. Salome, who doesn't fit either classification, is smothered.*

Other strong candidates have been mentioned in this book: Dido, whose tender final love duet is to Belinda rather than Aeneas, or Turandot's deadly desire never to marry. Even *Fidelio*, the opera dedicated to heterosexual love and marriage, has queer moments.

> *When Marcelline confesses to her father, sotto voce, how queer her feelings are, how tight her heart, how deep her desire is for Leonora "dragged-out" as Fidelio, we have our suspicions. As she begins her run up to the high G, saying how clear (es ist klar!) Leonora's love is for her, and Leonora's throaty voice moans, "O nameless, nameless, O nameless, O nameless agony!"—all of the giggling cross-dressers in eighteenth-century operas disappear, and we feel erotic love between these two women . . . until we remember that Leonora's agony is for her husband.*

Leonora dons the male britches to "stand by her man," to unearth him from the hellish hole in which he is buried by the evil and irrational governor. This is heterosexual love dressed in other clothes. The audience knows that the analytic categories of *male* and *female* will be restored by the opera's end.

And so I go back to *Orfeo ed Euridice* as the queerest. Wayne Koestenbaum elegantly sorts out the etymology of words like queer and gay in *The Queen's Throat*. He reflects: "I as a gay person do not feel 'gay.' . . . The diva's gaiety is qualified, shadowed. . . . A singer is queer because she presents the ear with unexpected bounty" (97–98). Just as the words seem flexible, elastic, accommodating, the opera too moves beyond its narrative, past its score, through its meanings. Orfeo and Euridice do not bend gender. They transform it. How many times have they been conceived? Jacopo Peri, Giulio Caccini, Claudio Monteverdi, Georg Philipp Telemann, Jean-Philippe Rameau, Franz Joseph Haydn, Christoph Willibald Gluck, Jacques Offenbach, Hector Berlioz, Claude Debussy, Darius Milhaud, Igor Stravinsky.[1] When the opera was born in 1600 (not by any means its origin—Angelo Poliziano's *pastorali*, *Orfeo*, had been around since 1472), it was unsure of its sex. *L'Euridice*? *L'Orfeo*? All of its composers seem unsure. Peri and Caccini originally collaborated, but then reneged. Both published separate scores of Ottavio Rinuccini's[2] libretto after a performance that had contained an amalgamation of both of their works. Their published prefaces suggest a rivalry. Thus, while they both conceived the musical offspring *L'Euridice*, when it was born they disowned it, dividing their love child, bickering over its parts.

Monteverdi picked up the fragmented subject, transformed the sex, and published his score: *L'Orfeo*. By subjugating himself to his librettist's words, he made it his own. Cherubino Ferrari, the Mantuan court theologian and poet, wrote of the opera:

> The poetry is lovely in conception, lovelier in form, and loveliest of all in diction; and indeed no less was to be expected of a man as richly talented as Signor Striggio.[3] The music, moreover, observing due propriety, serves the poetry so well that nothing more beautiful is to be heard anywhere. (Whenham 172)

As the words come to life—first conceived, then taking shape, and finally speaking—Monteverdi's music demurely makes itself available—"serv[ing] the poetry"—creating the beauty of this new musical form.

1. Establishing a Genealogy, Where None Is to Be Had

The queerness of the opera begins with the several narratives of the opera. Because the story is multiple Orpheus appears to be both asexual and supersexual. He is an artistic figure who creates without spouse—he invents the world through his song.[4] He must, however, also be considered one of the "urlovers" of mythology—one who is not alone but defined by his other. Similarly, Orpheus overcomes both death and the hierarchical system of the gods and yet is disciplined and divided by that same patriarchal order. On one hand, his descent into Hades is orchestrated so that he can obtain the "object" that is considered rightfully his. He enters the underworld in order to right the wrong of death, reestablish a traditional hierarchy, reinscribe sexual difference, and reinstate a heterosexual world. And, yet, in the myth he fails to restore this order. He loses Euridice by falling into the trap of men—fatally gazing at a woman's body.

Some artists, mythologists, and critics have even theorized that this "urlover" becomes pure male—a homosexual.[5] Ovid speaks of how "His life was given to young boys only" (10:82–83), causing the Maenads to tear him into pieces. Others further confuse the tale by describing how his body parts finally find their resting place on the isle of Lesbos. Orpheus becomes not-man and not-woman, a mythic figure who exaggerates the codes of sexual difference that he himself displays.[6]

> *The opening of Igor Stravinsky's ballet,* Orpheus, *creates an interesting paradox: the audience has come to see movement, but Orpheus laments Euridice, motionless; his back is turned to the audience. The opening strains also fight the audiences expectation. This is classical decorousness, a lone harp playing above the strings, floundering between Dorian and Aeolian mode. Where is Stravinsky's* Rite of Spring? *Where is Orpheus's anger at the loss? The musical violence doesn't appear until the end: Orpheus tears the bandages that were placed on his eyes during his blind pas de deux danced with Euridice in Hell. As they are separated he ascends from the underworld, and the music grows fierce, drunk, strident; the Bacchantes tear him to pieces. Stravinsky writes: "Here in the Epilogue it sounds like a kind of . . . compulsion, like something unable to stop. . . . Orpheus is dead, the song is gone, but the accompaniment goes on."*

The gendered confusion is intensified in the performance of Gluck's opera. The opera itself is unusual because it begins after the death of Euridice. Unlike Virgil's or Ovid's versions of the myth, it begins in a world without sexual differentiation. The woman has already died; the fatal snake bite has already occurred. Euridice's death, Charles Segal speculates, is crucial to Virgil's text. In the fourth *Georgic*, Euridice flees the amorous advances of Aristoeus, the bee-keeper. This setting, Segal argues, creates a foil: the sexless, disinterested productive love of the bees set next to the self-consuming, passionate love between the lovers (39). In Virgil the difference between Orpheus and the productive bees is that "Orpheus' *amor* does not further nature's aims of reproduction. He has *amor* without procreation. . . . The bees have procreation without *amor*" (Segal 47). Gluck's production begins in an even more sexually nebulous world. Set at the tomb of Euridice, the male/female distinction seems irrelevant. The difference at the opening of the opera is not sexual difference—one that will eventually produce offspring—but rather the difference between the living and the dead—one that will eventually produce song.

Berlioz's transcription of Gluck's Paris version further confused the gendered labels in the opera.[7] Gluck's title role was originally performed in 1762 by the celebrated castrato contralto, Gaetano Guadagni. When Gluck was called to Paris by Marie Antoinette in 1773, he was forced to transpose the part down a fifth so that a tenor could sing it, since the Paris opera never used castrati. In the nineteenth century the exceptionally talented Pauline Garcia-Viardot persuaded Hector Berlioz to restore Orfeo to the contralto line.[8]

> *That Berlioz was in love with Viardot seems to have been no mystery to anyone involved. Viardot writes on September 20, 1859: "Poor man! I feel very badly on his account. He is so very sick, so embittered, so unhappy! I have a great affection for him—he loves me much, I know it—he loves me only too much! . . . I feel too agitated to be able to write about it. . . . Just think; Berlioz, after a long, cordial friendship, has had the misfortune to fall in love with me all of a sudden."*[9] *Whether this love inspired Berlioz (which is the usual belief) or whether Viardot actually collaborated with him is open to argument. In a letter to a friend, Julius Rietz, written on June 7, 1859, five months before the Berlioz premier, her work seems to be more than mere inspiration. She asks for Gluck's score and then puzzles: "Is this the identical Italian partition which is sung in Berlin? In what key is the first chorus?. . . Is the role written throughout a fourth lower for tenor? Is it Euridice who sings in the second act, the air with chorus in 6/8 'Cet asile amiable et tranquille'? That strikes me as very absurd, and destroys the interest one takes in this poor Orpheus who gives himself such pains to look for his wife, while she is strolling so agreeably in the* Elysian fields *and seems to be so happy that 'here is naught to inflame the soul.' She thinks of Orpheus as if he were a nonentity. . . . I have an idea that in this scene the part of Orfeo ought to be totally different."*[10]
> (See figure 9.1.)

And nineteenth- as well as twentieth-century directors have routinely maintained a wholly female cast. While the original part of Orfeo (a castrato) further

Fig 9.1. Pauline Viardot as Orpheus.
Courtesy of Musical Quarterly.

removes the dynamic of reproductive love and replaces it with an *amor* that will never produce more of nature's division between genders, Berlioz's revision of Gluck's opera sets up a world that both is and is not reproductive. On one hand, a female Orfeo in drag is like her male counterpart: she too can produce song. Her body, however, is even more productive than his. She also can reproduce children. This doubleness is maintained in the timbre of the score. Eve Barsham claims that "the male castrato tone gave the character of [Orfeo] an 'extra-human,' mythic quality" (84). John Eliot Gardiner agrees: "Whereas the castrato voice as Gluck used it with Guadagni's talents in mind emphasized the universal and mystical qualities of Orfeo as god of song, the new setting for an *haute-contre* singing at the upper extremity of his range emphasized predominantly the heroic" (115). Although in the eighteenth century the voice of the male castrato was common on the Italian stage, a high male voice crooning to an even higher one was not a sound heard in the world beyond the theater. The castrato's natural unnaturalness, his voice that proclaims heterosexual desires and yet is not bound by copulating bodies, moves beyond the mundane world of production and reproduction.

This quality was transformed when, in Barsham's words, the "humanity of the tenor voice in the 1774 production" was introduced. She concludes that Berlioz's addition of the female voice adds "something near to the original [mythic] vocal register . . . and also the 'human' quality" (Howard 94). The revision of castrato to contralto thus creates an erotic tension between women who both are and are not women; the score makes them sound both mythic and human. *Orfeo* becomes a work that excessively reinscribes the patriarchy and yet denies the order it exaggerates.[11]

Berlioz's return not only restores the pure overtones of the trebled duets between Euridice and Orfeo, it also restores a gendered complexity to Gluck's work. The tension between the singers—castrato/female contralto and soprano—and the ambiguity created by voices that refuse to rest on their prescribed staffs have driven musicologists to battle over Orfeo's sex. Raymond Leppard said when he conducted *Orfeo* at Glyndebourne that "*Orfeo* is not an opera for purists because there is no 'correct' edition." (quoted in Rosenthal 26). Nevertheless, others continue to argue. The famous Met conductor Sir Charles Mackerras calls the original Italian version, "too short, sometimes too primitive, and often too low for the mezzo-soprano voice; the Paris version, though a great improvement in most respects, is so high that few tenors can cope with it" (Mackerras 394). He settled for an amalgamated body when he conducted Marilyn Horne in *Orfeo* at the Met in 1972—an Italian translation of the Berlioz version.

Marilyn Horne's "Che farò senza Euridice" is one of the fastest I've heard. The climbing chord in which she says "Che farò dove andro," she seems anxious to reach that final note of loneliness: "Dove andro senza il mio ben." Her 1972 Orfeo received mixed reviews. Harold Rosenthal in Opera *(January 1973) wrote that she was "a statuesque Orpheus, singing in the grand Clara Butt style. . . . If I had to criticize her performance, I would say it lacked real passion" (1983). Where he saw a static performance, however, the* New York Times *reviewer wrote of the same performance (and Horne repeats in her 1983 autobiography) "that when [Horne] went out to get Euridice, [she] 'looked for all the world like a Brooklyn matron off to a PTA meeting'" (Horne 205). When she returned to the role in L.A. (1991) in her early sixties (or late fifties, depending upon which encyclopedia you choose to believe) the reviews were even less kind. One called the production "a budget leftover. . . . As Orfeo, Marilyn Horne offered low-level projection" (Perlmutter 38). Another adds: "[her] poses looked perfunctory, and the singing was eccentric if not egocentric, laboured if not harsh" (Bernheimer 412). I, however, admire her courage. Orpheus perhaps is the role for an older woman. Rejected by society, she sings "Che farò senza . . . ": the youthful "she" is gone forever and I am left alone.*

Tom Hammond disagrees with Mackerras's conclusions. Berlioz's female Orfeo is wrong. Gluck's lover was always male: "The victorious [Orfeo] is finally transported by Cupid to the Temple of Love in Elysium . . . a pre-Wagnerian Valhalla, as it were, which is surely no place for a female warrior-hero *en travesti*." He questions the possibility of a diva's love for a woman, "however luscious of voice or noble of bearing": Can she "portray a bereaved warrior-husband with anything approaching dramatic conviction?" (Hammond 108)

> *A nineteenth-century writer would say yes. When, in 1855, George Eliot saw the performance of Gluck's and Beethoven's operas in Berlin, she wrote back to Sara Hennell in a state of ecstasy. Her initial surprise at seeing a wholly female cast of characters and her desire for the lower voices in the traditional operatic quartet are quickly replaced by acceptance and delight in hearing only the treble registers: "The scene in which Orpheus (Johanna Wagner) enters Tartarus, is met by the awful shades, and charms them into ecstatic admiration till they make way for him to pass on, is very fine. The voices—except in the choruses—are all women's voices, and there are only three characters—Orpheus, Amor and Euridice. One wonders that Pluto does not come as a Basso, and one would prefer Mercury as a tenor to Amor in the shape of an ugly German soprano—but Gluck willed it otherwise and the music is delightful" (*Letters *2:191).*

Purists, on the other hand, advocate returning to the simple, bare work of 1764. The choice, as John Eliot Gardiner puts it, is between "the pulsating intensity of the original *azione teatrale* and the sensuous allure . . . of the more heavily padded French *tragédie*" (116). While the latter is seductive, Gardiner suggests it amounts to prostitution of Gluck's talents: "Gluck, practical man of the theatre that he was . . . capitulated to French conservatism in transforming *Orfeo* to *Orphée*" (115). But many have pointed out that adopting this early version makes the piece too short for the evening. The solution? Pair it with Gluck's ballet *Don Juan*, the piece from which he stole the Furies' dance for the Paris edition. (The coupling of this pair is rife with irony: to avoid the "prostituted" version, the piece is paired with a ballet dedicated to a womanizer!) As composers and musicologists struggle over the body—*L'Euridice* or *Orfeo*, mezzo-soprano or countertenor—*Orfeo* becomes one of the queerest operas that I know, one that encompasses all realms of gendered desire.

2. A Nineteenth-Century Reading: Transforming Noble Love to Disease

But I am not interested in this queer opera for its sake alone. While the opera may seem flexible in the eighteenth century and before—male or female, austere or decorated—this opera, in a lesser known chapter in its history, marks a point at which this flexibility was frozen. I speak of the moment at which the opera moved from queer (gender-subverting) to queer (strange), the point at which desire ceased to be elastic and began to be a medical illness that the doctors longed to cure. Unbridled, gender-bending women like Salome were created by men *after* Krafft-Ebing's theories linking athletes, feminists, and "opera singers and actresses who appear in male attire on the stage by preference" were published in 1889.[12] They were *meant* to be viewed as monstrous women. (It is important to remember that in the famous Labouchère amendment, passed in England on August 6, 1885, which eventually condemned Wilde's male homosexuality to hard labor, female love is never mentioned. Ronald Pearsall theorizes that lesbian love was omitted from the amendment because "no one could think of a way to explain to Queen Victoria what homosexual acts between women were" [474].) By the time Salomé moved into Strauss's Germany, however, everyone knew what lesbian love was. The notion of a monstrous woman who desired the destruction of men was very clearly articulated in the medical literature. Lesbian love was a threat to all men: it, like Salomé, could decapitate and emasculate them, dividing them from their precious "head."[13]

Berlioz's transcription of Gluck's opera, however, marks a window during which lesbian love was not condemned as sickly, a time when one could actually envision a female warrior-husband having intense feelings for her dead wife. I therefore will now move away from the opera and introduce my closeted opera diva—George Eliot. For, despite the fact that Eliot spent twenty-four years living with one man and, at the end of her life, married another, there are places in her life where the lines between homo- and heterosexual desire overlap.

As a Victorianist I am frequently scrutinized as strange. What does my operatic collection have to do with the social "realism" of the Victorian novel. Opera is self-consciously artificial. While in opera the chant of the recitative or the soaring octaves of the aria allow relationships to work against what they initially seem to be, the Victorian novel that I teach every day always assigns the body a sex. When Lucy Snow in Charlotte Brontë's Villette *is invited to dress in drag to play the male lover in the female French boarding school play, she "retain[s] her woman's garb without the slightest retrenchment . . . assum[ing] in addition a little vest, a collar, and cravat, and a paletôt of small dimensions" (Brontë 209). Despite this seeming rigidity, however, I believe that the lover of Victorian literature and opera is not perverse. After all, the Victorian novel does have its share of arias. That same novel,* Villette, *holds Vashti's performance: "Behold! I found upon her something neither of woman nor of man: in each of her eyes sat a devil" (339); in* Jane Eyre, *silent Jane shouts from the top of Rochester's country house: "Nobody knows how many rebellions besides political rebellions ferment in the masses of life which people earth. Women are supposed to be very calm generally: but women feel just as men feel" (96). The Victorian novel, called a baggy monster by Henry James, is not that different from the bulky diva with whom we've fallen in love. It too lingers over lusciously long sentences, stories that end, only to reemerge in later chapters, lives that end single and alone, only to be rewritten with marriages and children.*

Gordon Haight describes the attraction various women felt toward George Eliot. The most well-known admirer, Edith Simcox, wrote and spoke to Eliot with hyperbolic passion. She would fall on her knees and kiss Eliot's feet. In her own copy of *Natural Law* she wrote her idol's name and added as the last sentence:

> Heaven and hell are names or visions; the earth is ours—here a hell of sensibility and hardened cruelty, there a heaven of love and wisdom, with a tender smile upon her gracious lips, and yearning prophecy in the melting depths of her unfathomable eyes,
>
> To whom
> with idolatrous love
> this book is dedicated. (cited in Haight 495)

Other women felt similar desire: Barbara Bodichon, Bessie Parkes, Mrs. Congreve, Mrs. Burne-Jones, Elma Stuart—all, at one time or another, describe intense emotions felt for the writer.[14] Haight cautions against reading these relationships as lesbian: "In reading Edith Simcox's record of her wild passion for George Eliot, we must guard against interpretations that could never have entered the writer's mind" (496). And yet the personal letters between these two women were all destroyed, suggesting the text may offer more than the biographer would like to see.[15]

This imbrication of desire is marked in Eliot's works about two operas: Beethoven's *Fidelio* and Gluck's *Orfeo*.

> *The range of the nineteenth-century diva must have been extraordinary, as many mezzo-sopranos played both roles.*[16] *Pauline Viardot's voice was artificially extended when she was trained as a youth into the soprano register. Later her voice was pushed into the realm of the contralto. Her roles included both Orfeo (she played the role over 150 times in the course of three years) and Leonora, as well as Fides (*Le Prophète*), Dido, Dalila, Lady Macbeth, and Gounod's Sapho. Johanna Wagner, the diva praised by Eliot in her letter to Sara Hennell, also boasts an impressive range. She created Elizabeth in* Tannhäuser, *Ortrud in* Lohengrin, *Lucrezia Borgia and Romeo in* I Capuleti e i Montecchi. *When she was in her late thirties, she lost her voice and appeared as an actress. It was recovered when she turned fifty, and she sang Schwertleite and the First Norn in the complete* Ring *cycle at Bayreuth (1876). She too sang both the roles of Orfeo and Leonora before her voice was lost. I strain with all of these nineteenth-century women to reach that high B-flat in the chorus at the end of act 1 of* Fidelio *when she subversively sings to the jailor that she must obey duty and he believes that this duty is to him.*

One year before she began her writing career, Eliot saw both *Fidelio* and *Orfeo* on the continent within a week of each other. Fifteen years later she incorporated the two operas into "Armgart," a poetic drama that examines creative relationships between women. Eliot's novels written in the years between the operatic performances and the poetic drama are concerned with fruitful female desire. "Mr. Gilfil's Love-Story," *Adam Bede*, "The Spanish Gypsy"—all depict women who nurture, embrace, and occasionally redeem other women. After "Armgart," however, her writing seems to pull away from the female bonds her early writing endorses. One reason, I believe, is that, at the time, the Germanic medical world was beginning to classify same-sex desire as "diseased."[17] As science divided the world into the sick and the well, the normal and the abnormal, Eliot found it desirable—perhaps even necessary—to retreat from the intimate friendships of her early novels and life.

And yet Eliot's poetic drama was written in August and September of 1870, in the midst of this discussion in Germany. "Armgart" becomes one of Eliot's final and more dramatic attempts to reconcile female friendships with the world that had already begun to condemn them. The work allows for intrasexual love in a world that was becoming more and more rigidly heterosexual. Significantly, she chooses an opera—*Orfeo*—which also allows her to write of desire between and among genders in a way that she was no longer able to do in the context of the provincial towns of England. Although the myth collapsed heterosexual and homosexual desires onto each other, it was, at the same time, readily accepted by her society; during the nineteenth century it was performed, painted, reworked, and rewritten in many different forms.[18] Thus by working within a well-known mythic structure, by using the less familiar media of opera and poetry rather than the novel, she was able to transgress against her society's notions of women loving other women while avoiding the label of medical freakishness.

George Eliot clearly was aware of *Orfeo*'s queer beginnings. She first saw the production not long after she saw *Fidelio*. While neither performance was technically perfect, the *idea* of both seems to have struck a chord. In a letter to Sara Hennell she calls the orchestra of *Fidelio* faulty, yet adds, "The divine music positively triumphs over the defects of execution" (*Letters* 2:191). Gluck's opera, heard a week earlier, seems even fresher in her mind. Although she complains of the ending—the reunification of Euridice and Orfeo for the second time and the ballet and chorus of odd-looking Greek shades—clearly the music lacked nothing at all. She raves about Johanna Jachmann Wagner's performance:

> It is one of the glories of Berlin to give Gluck's opera, and it is also something of a glory to have "die Wagner." She is really a fine actress and a fine singer; her voice is not ravishing, but she is mistress of it. I thought of you that evening and wished you could hear and see what I know would interest you greatly—I refer rather to Gluck's opera than to Johanna Wagner.
>
> (*Letters* 2:191)

This letter—particularly the final sentence of this passage—has a playful tone as she teasingly entices her friend with what was clearly viewed as an alluring performance by the female singer. Although she claims she is ravished by Gluck's *music*, one can sense, encoded in this letter, an interest in the diva as well. The tone suggests either could sweep her away.[19] The memory of this performance stayed with Eliot for a long time. Twenty years later, when she was searching for a suitable piece for Mirah Cohen to sing in *Daniel Deronda*, she considers the aria in the third and final act of Gluck's opera, "Che farò senza Euridice!": "having heard Johanna Wagner sing [it] at Berlin when in her glory there" (*Letters* 6:184).

Not only was she ravished by the female voice in this peculiar opera, she also was aware of its revolutionary beginnings. In *The History of Modern Music* (1862), John Pyke Hullah, a well-known Victorian musicologist, classified musical history into four periods. George Eliot read this work and recorded the periods in her notebook. She added that, because of its orchestra, Monteverdi's *Orfeo* (1607) initiated the second period (Gray 115). The myth of Orpheus and the music surrounding it, therefore, became fixed in Eliot's mind as music of change and revolution.

This notion of change, of course, carries over to Gluck's opera. Italian opera was famous for its empty abuses—trills, cadenzas—which showed off the acrobatic possibilities in the diva's voice. Gluck's letter to his librettist pledges to initiate a reformation, "to free music from all the abuses that have crept in either through mistaken vanity on the part of singers, or through excessive complaisance on the part of composers" (Howard 23). He wanted his operas to return music to the rhetorical function of serving poetry, rather than allowing it to compete or supersede. Once again *Orpheus* becomes a myth and opera that marks a turn from the status quo.

A reviewer of the 1859 opera speaks of Pauline Viardot's performance: "torrents of roulades . . . being flung out with such exactness, limitless volubility and majesty, as to convert what is essentially a commonplace piece of parade, into one of those displays of passionate enthusiasm to which nothing less florid could give scope."[20] *(See figure 9.2.) Although Viardot's cadenza altered the vocal part, the changes were supported by most reviewers, including Saint-Saëns. A contemporary comparison could be made to Janet Baker's Orfeo for her farewell performance (Glyndebourne 1983). A reviewer of the production says: "I do not know who had supplied the embellishments that Dame Janet used, but they certainly brought the rather musically static Act I to a rousing conclusion" (Rosenthal 27). October 1983 brought a revival of the opera to Glyndebourne; but it significantly omitted Baker's ornate line. Carolyn Watkinson's Orfeo sang as her Gluckian master would have wanted: "Looking tall, handsome and suitably distressed, she projected the character's sorrow,*

• **Fig. 9.2. Pauline Viardot's cadenza to "L'espoire renait."**
Courtesy of **Musical Quarterly** *(1916), 2:47.*

> *determination and, in the final act, torment with economical gesture and expressive face"(Blyth 1983:1312).*

It is precisely this revolutionary nature of the work—classical simplicity in which music is subservient to words—that allowed Eliot to reform her early heroines in her first novels.

Her novelette "Mr Gilfil's Love-Story," from her early *Scenes from Clerical Life*, repeatedly refers to both the opera and the myth. The tale is a conventional melodrama: Caterina, the daughter of a destitute Italian singer, falls in love with the heir of her adopted family. This shallow aristocrat, Captain Wybrow, plays with her affections but finally commits to Miss Assher, a woman of his social standing. His rejection drives Caterina to the verge of madness. Mr. Gilfil, a preacher, loves the poor daughter but seems unable to rescue her from her lunacy. Her plight reaches a crisis when she decides to kill the Captain during a clandestine meeting in the woods. Her attempt is foiled—he has already died of a heart attack, and she finds him among the weeds. Afraid of being accused of murder, she runs away to the safety of the house of the coachman's wife. She eventually returns to the manor, becomes deathly ill, and finally marries the preacher—thus saving all reputations. The heterosexual ending is thwarted, however, when she dies a few months after her marriage. The initial chapter first presents Mr. Gilfil behaving like Orpheus at the opening of the opera. Having lost his "Euridice," he has built a shrine that only Martha, his domestic, sees. He, however, never descends into Hades to rescue her.

In fact, the second chapter revises his part. We learn that the one he lost, Caterina, is actually the artist and musician who woos with song. In her first performance she even sings Orpheus's "Che farò":

> It happened this evening that the sentiment of these airs . . . [in] which the singer pours out his yearning after his lost love, came very close to Caterina's own feeling. But her emotion, instead of being a hindrance to her singing, gave her additional power. . . . Her love, her jealousy, her pride, her rebellion against her destiny, made one stream of passion which welled forth in the deep rich tones of her voice. (*Scenes from Clerical Life* 38)

This passage suggests that a male Orpheus can sing the part adequately with "*his* yearning" but a female Orpheus does it better. This passage smells of Victorian essentialism: a woman has emotion and thus can "sing her feeling." But I think there is even more. The list of qualities that create her compelling contralto finally allow the orphic song to arise from a rebellion *against* her status as a woman. In her adopted house it is an understatement to say she holds an ambiguous social position. She is part foundling, part surrogate daughter, part domestic, even part performing bird who sings on cue whenever her master asks. Thus, as she sings the role of Orpheus she certainly is not-man, but she also seems not-woman. As the character who loves, she becomes the rare voice that sings between the staffs, the "ur-lover" whose love is never returned, the creator without a spouse. To reinforce the importance of the aria and opera, the story ends with a reprise of the aria from Gluck's opera. As she comes back to life after her long illness, we hear her

> singing the very air from the *Orfeo* which we heard her singing so many months ago. . . . It was *Che farò* . . . and its notes seemed to carry on their wings all the tenderest memories of her life. The delicate-tendrilled plant must have something to cling to. The soul that was born anew to music was born anew to love. (*Scenes from Clerical Life* 186)

This final sentence creates an interesting image if one looks back at George Eliot's early letters. It recalls an address Eliot frequently used when writing to her teacher and mentor, Maria Lewis. Eliot called herself "Clematis" to signify mental beauty, and Lewis was named "Veronica," signifying fidelity (literally "true likeness)". These names moved beyond mere labels. In several letters they become images that depict a lush, sensual love: "Your letter this morning, my Veronica, was sweet to me as the early incense of the Jasmine and sent a thrill from my heart to my finger ends" (Eliot, *Letters* 1:84). Others are signed: "Your clinging Clematis," which recalls the trope that ends "Mr. Gilfil": "the delicate-tendrilled plant" that clings to the preacher. Martha Vicinus, in her article exploring the eroticized friendships in English female boarding schools, argues that this pattern is common in female relationships. The lovers "found means of speaking silently to each other, of sharing words and thoughts that could not be, and would not be talked about" outside of their private coterie (51). Eliot thus seems to borrow the private name used to encode her love for a woman to depict true love in her first novel about love between men and women. Heterosexual desire is thus palimpsestically layered on homosexual love.

*The Lyric Opera in Cleveland produced a twentieth anniversary season in 1993 that included the new and the old—*Orfeo *combined with the premier of* Mrs. Dalloway. *Libby Larsen and Bonnie Grice's thick and liquid score transformed Woolf's canvas of words into a sonic landscape. Folding the reverberating toll of Big Ben into the steady pulse of "God Save the King," the chamber ensemble that served as the orchestra became Woolf's "leaden circles." When Clarissa first sees Sally Seton, she (unlike Orfeo) can't keep her eyes off of her: "It was an extraordinary beauty of the kind that she most admired, dark, large-eyed, with that quality which, since she hadn't got it herself, she always envied" (Woolf 32). She descends her stairs in her white frock to meet her love, and she thinks (like Othello) "if it were now to die 'twere now to be most happy" When Sally kisses her on the lips, "The whole world might have turned upside down! " (Woolf 32–35). Earth becomes Hades. Incidentally, Hillary Nicholson played the role of both Sally Seton and Orfeo.*

But if Caterina plays Orpheus in this short sketch, who plays Euridice? It certainly cannot be the selfish, empty Captain Wybrow, who plays the affections of the Italian singer against the blond "rightful" mistress of the manor. Nor can it be Mr. Gilfil, who stands in the wings, in love with Caterina, waiting for his cue to bring the opera seria to a happy conclusion. In fact the only person in the story who dies, comes back to life, and dies again is Caterina.

Caterina eventually returns to the manor after finding safety with the coachman's wife. The next chapter begins:

> It is a wonderful moment, the first time we stand by one who has fainted, and witness the fresh birth of consciousness spreading itself over the blank features, like the rising sunlight on the alpine summits that lay ghastly and dead under the leaden twilight. A slight shudder, and the frost-bound eyes recover their liquid light; for an instant they show the inward semi-consciousness of an infant's; then, with a little start, they open wider and begin to *look*.
>
> (*Scenes from Clerical Life* 149)

Although Gilfil is at this moment standing nearby, he is not her Orpheus here. His song doesn't bring her out of the underworld. He is, in fact, in a decidedly unorphic posture—*dumbly* standing over her. Caterina thus seems to play both roles. Her first "death" takes her, like Euridice, into the Happy Valley of the blessed spirits: she runs away into a pastoral world to be with the coachman's wife. When Daniel, the coachman, finally seeks out Gilfil, he is described as "the most awful messenger from the land of the shades" (167). He tells the unheroic, decidedly helpless preacher how she "come t' our house. . . . Dorkis run out, for she heared the cart stop, an' Miss Sarti throwed her arms roun' Dorkis's neck an' says, tek me in, Dorkis, tek me in" (168). Caterina thus seems to leave the world of men, class, money, and patriarchy in order to embrace a woman. To reinforce the importance of this moment, the narrator repeats the story through Dorcas' eyes four pages later: "'Dear Dorcas,' says she, 'tek me in'" (172).

These echoes of Orpheus, in a decidedly heterosexual story, begin to underline the importance of a female community in Eliot's novels. Although Eliot ends the story with Gilfil and Caterina married, the love is passionless—much like the love we will see between Adam and Dinah in her next novel; indeed, in *Adam Bede* Dinah and Hetty seem to be a much more sensual couple than Dinah and Adam. The novel mirrors the plot of "Mr. Gilfil": a young girl again falls in love with a selfish, wealthy man rather than the selfless Adam who loves her. But in this novel Hetty commits a crime: she kills the child produced by this ill-matched affair. Thus rather than the meager rescue attempts of Gilfil a true savior is needed to rescue her from the underworld.

No one who saw it will forget the shudder that went through Shirley Verrett's body when Euridice (played by Elizabeth Vaughan) touches her Orfeo. The picture in Opera *(1972) does some justice: white light falling on the clenched eyes, the rest of the body is in darkness. Euridice, wrapped in gauze, is bound from our sight as she is denied Orfeo's gaze. I feel her hand on my shoulder as her falling notes implore me to look. "Che fiero momento" she sighs as she believes, cruellest of cruel, her Orfeo will not look at her again. I can hear Verrett's coppery chest-tones return: "Ecco un nuovo tormento."*

This savior comes in the form of Dinah. The opening dialogue in chapter 45 ("In the Prison") suggests the opening song between Amor and Orfeo. The jailer first tries to convince Dinah not to descend into the horrors of the prison cell, but then recognizes that she has "a key to unlock hearts" (*Adam Bede* 443). Just as Amor warns Orfeo of Jove's conditions—don't look or she will be lost to you—the man also denies sight to Dinah: "The turnkey will take you to the prisoner's cell, and leave you there for the night, if you desire it; but you can't have a light during the night—it is contrary to rules" (443–44). After Dinah's impassioned religious plea, Hetty confesses, Dinah forgives, and the two seem to become one. Not surprisingly, the farewell scene between Adam and Hetty is anemic: "Adam took the blanched wasted hand she put out to him, and they gave each other the solemn unspeakable kiss of a lifelong parting" (458). The final embrace between Hetty and Dinah, however, is passionate: "[Dinah] poured forth her soul with the wrestling intensity of a last pleading, for the trembling creature that clung to her and clutched her as the only visible sign of love and pity" (459). Once again a woman's embrace rather than a man's song saves the condemned from death.

In the decade between *Adam Bede* and "Armgart," Eliot moved from minor to major literary figure. And although her works—*Felix Holt* and *Spanish Gypsy*—became more political, she retained the vestiges of her early plots. Like the early heroines, Fedalma in *Spanish Gypsy* has the option of marrying a wealthy aristocrat. Rather than fate driving her away from men, Fedalma, unlike Eliot's earlier heroines, chooses to reject the proposal and instead lead her race to a new world. Although Eliot subverts the politics of gender to race in this poem (Fedalma is not leading *women* but her *race* of gypsies to the promised land), her critics saw through her ploy. They attacked her work because they claimed it sabotaged cherished Victorian notions about gender, marriage, and, in short, heterosexual love (Haight 405). The *Edinburgh Review* sums up their complaints:

> Whether or no it is a secret object of the poem to depress the manly and elevate the feminine character we know not, but, assuredly, Fedalma absorbs all the dramatic interest within herself. . . . She is a hero, not a heroine. . . . The advocates of the "two sexes of man" will naturally approve.
>
> ("The Spanish Gypsy" 268)

Having identified her as a man masquerading as a heroine, the reviewer ends, dismissing the book with a moral sermon:

> In the discussion respecting the equality, or rather the moral identity, of the sexes, it must never be forgotten, that whatever be the natural or social gains, the abolition of a great diversity in Nature or in Art is in itself a mighty loss, and . . . brings with it . . . monstrous and distorted combinations rather than . . . any increased completeness and more perfect whole.
>
> ("The Spanish Gypsy" 269)

This criticism would have stung Eliot. In her notes on *Spanish Gypsy* she seems to have made a conscious effort to move away from the arguments surrounding gender. She acknowledges that Fedalma is marked by difference, but stresses that this handicap is what makes her heroic: "She may be lame, she may inherit a disease, or what is tantamount to a disease: she may be a negress, or have other marks of race repulsive in the community where she is born, etc., etc." (quoted in Pinion 128). When the critic in the *Edinburgh Review* writes about the character, however, this mark of difference moves from handicap or racial marking to a gender deformity—a monstrous masculine female.

In Kathleen Ferrier's last performance of Orfeo, *the opening night was universally praised. Although she walked with a limp from the rheumatism in her hips caused by the treatments of her breast cancer, the critics praised her voice. The* New Statesman and Nation *said the dignity and nobility of her Orfeo "would be hard to match in the world." "Certain passages touch the sublime" crooned the* Manchester Guardian. *But the second performance was marked by apprehensions. Her companion Bernadine Hammond (Bernie) said, "She left for the theatre as if she were going to her own execution." In the second act disaster struck. Her femur had partially disintegrated from the medical treatments. She fell against the scenery until Euridice, in the form of Victoria Dunne, put out her palm, striking a classic Greek pose. Kathleen took it and her stage-lover walked her off. The audience claimed not to have noticed anything was wrong. Dame Eva Turner said "There was no hint of any catastrophe. We were just mesmerised by her beautiful singing." (quoted in Leonard 231–32).*

Although the notion of "monstrous" lesbian love was not a consideration at this time in Britain, it seems likely that Eliot and Lewes would have been exposed to the new theories regarding homosexuality as a pathological and physical disease in Germany. Although Krafft-Ebing's theories that linked athletes and singing divas dressed in drag weren't published until 1889,[21] the theories were probably initiated in 1870 by Dr. Karl Westphal in the *Archiv für Psychiatrie*. In one case study Westphal speaks of a woman who dressed in men's clothes in order to pursue love affairs with other women.[22] Haight's biography of Eliot mentions a Dr. Karl Westphal who met with Lewes: "Lewes spent a good deal of time at the hospitals, seeing every variety of madness talking psychiatry with Dr. Westphal, 'a quiet unpretending little man,' who was delighted with his interest in what Marian called this 'hideous branch of practice' " (424). As the scientists constructed the psychosexual model of a "mis-dressed," masculine lesbian, Eliot turned one last time to the myth of Orpheus to defend women and female friendships.

"Armgart," written late in the summer of 1870, stages *Orpheus*. The opening set picks up the references to the two operas mentioned in the 1855 letter to Sara Hennell: it is decorated with bronze busts of Beethoven and Gluck, suggesting Armgart may eventually have to choose between the roles of Orpheus and Fidelio. But at the opening Gluck's opera is the piece that has just been performed. When Armgart enters, we see a triumphant Orpheus. She is a woman of unbridled talent who sees her voice as a gift that was given to her and must in turn be given to others: "For what is fame / But the benignant strength of One, transformed / To joy of Many?" ("Armgart" 124). Although she has just played Gluck's hero, she, in fact, sees herself as the Orpheus who existed before Euridice—the singer whose music bewitched "rocks and trees and calmed primitive man at the dawn of civilization" (Kosinski 1). She speaks of how her talent charmed the banal and chaotic audience's tastes, the "roar of tropic winds that tossed / The handkerchiefs and many-coloured flowers" ("Armgart" 122). She claims it both moved rocks and ripened corn. In fact, much to her teacher's dismay, she has even transgressed from her master's score, creating her own melody by adding a trill "Gluck had not written, nor I taught" ("Armgart" 120). This deviation cannot be taken lightly, given Gluck's reforms. When Armgart adds what her mentor deems "that trill you made / In spite of me and reason," she defies the revolutionary molds of her male predecessors. She is Orpheus before Gluck's opera, before Euridice.

The rest of the play is spent questioning whether she can play this orphic role. The other three characters engage with Armgart in a contrapuntal quartet that denies this ambitious position to women. While Armgart believes her art was given to her to create worlds, Leo, her music teacher, sees her art more narrowly, as that of a performer singing before a wealthy audience. He believes the diva is merely the toy of the hour, pandering to the marketplace. He believes the trill was inserted merely to please this audience:

> Will you ask the house
> To teach you singing? Quit your *Orpheus* then,
> And sing in farces grown to operas,
> Where all the prurience of the full-fed mob
> Is tickled with melodic impudence:
> Jerk forth burlesque bravuras, square your arms
> Akimbo with a tavern wench's grace . . . (118)

Her Orpheus descended into Hades not to sacrifice himself to the gods but to sell his voice to his public in the Victorian music halls.

The Graf, the most misogynistic voice in the quartet, picks up this notion of the commodification of her voice and art. In the second scene he urges her to give up selling herself in the gross marketplace of the world. He tells a parable of a man who was too sane to spend many lonely years striving for perfection in "the mart of mediocrities." He urges her to give up this life for him because he, and he alone, can "own / The magic of your nature-given art / As sweet effluence of your womanhood" (128). His choice of the verb "own" reveals the weakness of his argument: he owns (acknowledges) her talents only if he can eventually claim ownership over her. A talented woman artist is thus in a double bind. She can either prostitute herself to her audiences or prostitute herself to her husband.

Armgart will accept neither. Her argument rests on moving herself away from the essentialist Victorian notion of "woman." When the Graf calls women "royal" because of their maternal abilities, she scornfully dismisses him. As a female Orpheus she sees herself as being above this vulgar production: "O blessed Nature! / Let her be arbitress; she gave me voice / Such as she only gives a woman child" (128). She sees herself as neither mannish female invert nor woman, both being definitions of the same symbolic order. As operatic Orpheus she is above labels of man and woman:

> Men did not say, when I had sung last night,
> "'Twas good, nay, wonderful, considering
> She is a woman"—and then turn to add,
> "Tenor or baritone had sung her songs
> Better, of course . . . " (128)

As contralto, she is not-bass, not-soprano. The Greek drag moves her out of the bind of binary gendered oppression into the world of not-man, not-woman. That is perhaps why this short piece never mentions Euridice by name. The only elliptic reference to the woman is after the Graf's proposal. Euridice's first death was caused by snakebite. Armgart refuses the Graf because, as man and wife, their opinions would "chafe the union . . . [as] little serpents biting at [the] heel" (132). The notion of marriage seems poisonous, suggesting that even an opera where a woman plays a man's part—embraces and rescues a woman as man—cannot obliterate but can merely reinforce oppression. The Graf offers his prophecy that a man will come "whose theory will weigh as nought with you against his love" (133), and Armgart corrects him saying the politics must be contingent with the love.

This lover, however, has already appeared. She is the first person on stage, Walpurga, the lame cousin whose "rare affection" for Armgart is "as tender as a sister" (116). Her lameness, as such, recalls Eliot's previously mentioned note to *Spanish Gypsy*. Although marginal to this poetic drama, she becomes the Fedalma who rescues Armgart from her silent condition. She first describes her life with Armgart the way a spouse would: "She fills my life that would lie empty else, / And lifts my nought to value by her side" (116). This description initially suggests another binary trap. It once again falls into an unequal equation: Armgart has all, Walpurga has nought.

But the second half of the play rights this imbalance. A year after the Graf's proposal, Armgart has been struck by laryngitis. A doctor is brought in to cure her and instead bungles the operation, leaving her voiceless. A rival singer takes Armgart's place.

> *The year Kathleen Ferrier died she performed* Orpheus. *Her body riddled with cancer, she stayed in bed until 10 o'clock, when rehearsals began. "Then the struggle began," says her longtime companion, Bernie. She had daily visits to the hospital in which she was showered with radium. One of the doctors recommended an oophorectomy. (Removal of the ovaries was seen as a potential cure for breast cancer.) When she*

> *consulted Dr. James Ivor Griffin, a laryngologist, about the effects this would have on her voice, he replied: "I told her that the long-term effect on the cancer would be negligible but that the effect on her voice might be disastrous. I had quite a bit of experience of the effects of hormones on the voice and I told her that it would at least alter the character of the voice. She said she regarded her voice as a divine gift and would go to the grave with the voice as it had been given her. She had this overpowering desire to sing in* Orpheus *and I said that she should go ahead. I then had a consultation with Sir John Barbirolli and Sir David Webster and I told them that I was doubtful whether she could complete the four performances. However, we decided to let her carry on"(cited in Leonard 229–30).*

A new conversation ensues between Armgart and her lame cousin. Voiceless, Armgart believes she has turned from orphic prophet to a figure as ridiculous as a man in doll's clothes ("Armgart" 144). Her transvestism becomes a body in diminutive dress. Walpurga first attempts to comfort Armgart, and then chides her mistress for treating her like a wife, a domestic, a slave: "I know joy by negatives" (145). The play ends with Armgart leaving behind the world of art, ambition, men's applause, and marriage to nurture Walpurga in her small German village. Despite the Doctor's attempt to cure her of her disease, she retreats to a world of female friendships and art. She chooses to teach—the art of Eliot's companion, Maria Lewis. The new couple—Walpurga "married" to Armgart—turns the "nought" of Walpurga and the "Poor garden" (the literal translation from German of Armgart) into something that is fruitful: "a new birth—birth from that monstrous Self" (148).

What of Armgart's rival in the opera that is played in the background? Rather than *Orfeo ed Euridice*, the new opera staged is Beethoven's *Fidelio*, the other opera marked by cross-dressing. And rather than Gluck's heroic castrato, the part Armgart's rival sings is one in which a soprano *plays* a woman disguised as a man. In this later opera the female character herself, Leonora, rather than her costumed male persona, Fidelio, is heroic.[23] Beethoven's fictional woman is allowed to be the self-abnegating, heroic savior, not merely female flesh beneath the male costume.

At the end of Eliot's career, however, she found herself revising this part. As doctors began to examine any woman dressed in male clothing, she created another singing Leonora in *Daniel Deronda*. This Leonora, Daniel Deronda's mother, is not hailed but condemned. Sacrificing everything that is important to Eliot—from family to race and religion—she becomes peripheral to the novel. She is portrayed as an artistic woman more distanced from the active life of her audience than Armgart was in *Orfeo*. She is not the orphic Armgart, who sings while everyone watches her, but instead a singer who is relegated to the backstage and bit parts.

Eliot's vision of women in drag thus becomes ambiguous. On one hand Eliot endorsed the notion of the female communities introduced in her earlier works—communities that stand apart from patriarchal structures such as marriage and the marketplace. Accordingly, Armgart escapes the busts of the male composers that frame the stage at the opening. Despite the fact that the male physicians try to cure her of her odd orphic role, and botch the operation, she triumphs over these new gods by retreating into the Elysian world of the Happy Valley with her cousin, spouse, and sister, Walpurga. Their attempt to re-form her body merely pushes her closer to female love.

And yet this female community is weaker than in the earlier novels, perhaps because of the increasing medical interest in same-sex companionships. Indeed, the physicians of the time seem to have operated on Eliot's own creativity. Their "hideous branch of practice" viewed same-sexed love as diseased and women who practiced it as oddly masculine. Her masculinely dressed Orpheus who loves Euridice thus turns into a Fidelio who loves her husband. Her central character turns from the orphic contralto to a silent governess, "praised in all the petty mimicries as doll-clothes fit the man" (144). Even the sensual embrace between women in her early novels is omitted at the end of this orphic play. Although Armgart initially claimed that she "need not crush [herself] within a mould / Of theory called nature," the psychosexual scientists—Ulrich, Krafft-Ebing, and finally Freud—have proven otherwise. These new lines—between normal and abnormal, homosexual and heterosexual, George Eliot and Marian Evans—created new molds that framed and constrained voices, voices of women who could otherwise live in the pastoral world of Euridices.

Notes

1. The titles for the pieces of these composers are: Peri, *Euridice* (1600), Caccini, *Euridice* (1602), Monteverdi, *Orfeo* (1607), Telemann, *Orfeo* (1726), Gluck, *Orfeo ed Euridice* (1762, 1774), Haydn, *L'anima del filsofo assia Orfeo ed Euridice*, unperf. (1796), Offenbach, *Orfée aux enfers* (1858), Berlioz, *Orfeo ed Euridice*, rewritten from Gluck (1859), Milhaud, *Les malheurs d'Orfée* (1925), Stravinsky, *Orpheus*, ballet (1947). I've added Rameau and Debussy to the list because both attempted to birth Orpheus, but both produced stillborn children. Rameau worked on *Orfée aux enfers* in 1740; Debussy struggled with *Orphée-roi* from 1907 to 1916.

Given the multiple titles, one runs into many difficulties when writing on the history of the opera. The title, itself, creates much of the confusion—*Orpheus*, *Orfeo*, *Euridice*, *Orfée*. As the opera is shared between countries and composers, its title becomes flexible; the gender transforms. For clarity in this essay I will try to use the title that each composer gave the work. An exception will be made in the case of Berlioz and Gluck. Although the final version of Gluck's work and Berlioz's revision was French (which would suggest Orpheus's name is Orfée), both are more commonly performed in Italian. Thus when referring to Gluck's and Berlioz's opera I will use the Italian form—*Orfeo ed Euridice* (abbreviated to *Orfeo*). Orpheus will indicate the character outside of the opera (e.g., in Virgil or Ovid). I will also use Orpheus when I speak of George Eliot's work with the opera, since that is the form that she uses in most of her letters and notes.

2. Rinuccini (1562–1621) was a Florentine librettist.

3. Alessandro Striggio (?1573–1630) collaborated with Monteverdi on several pieces: *Tirisi e Clori* (1616), *Apollo* (a lost dramatic cantata), and *Orfeo* (1607), for which he was the librettist.

4. See, for example, Apollonius of Rhodes. *Aronautica* 1:23–34.

5. In *Death of Orpheus* (1494) Albrecht Dürer labels him as "Der Erst Puseran" on the scroll in a tree. Erwin Panofsky explains the word *puseran* is used for *pederast* and is derived from the Italian word *buggerone.*

6. Contemporary lesbian and feminist theorists are helpful here. In "One Is Not Born a Woman" Wittig rejects a woman-identified lesbianism because the very notion of "woman" in a patriarchal system is subjected to domination. Matriarchies are as heterosexual as patriarchies: "It's only the sex of the oppressor that changes" ("One Is Not Born a Woman," p. 149). She concludes: "Since women belong to men . . . a lesbian *has* to be something else, not-woman, not-man" (150). In "Sexual Indifference and Lesbian Representation" de Lauretis highlights this conclusion when she labels a conceptual paradox between sexual difference and what she calls (in)difference. The latter she identifies as women wanting to be and being the same as men. The former—sexual difference—she identifies as women wanting to be or being different from men. (The problem with sexual *difference* is, of course, in Luce Irigaray's words, "*the feminine occurs only within models and laws devised by male subjects*" [Irigaray, *This Sex Which Is Not One*, p. 86].) Lesbian literature depends upon separating, isolating and yet maintaining the paradox: "Thus the critical effort to dislodge the erotic from the discourse of gender, with its indissoluble knot of sexuality . . . is concurrent . . . with a rethinking of what . . . is still, nevertheless, a gendered sexuality" (de Lauretis, "Sexual Indifference," p. 159).

7. Berlioz's score is one of many nineteenth-century adaptations of Gluck's *Orfeo.* (Others include the rendition by Liszt, who, in 1854, conducted the opera at Weimar and used his own symphonic poem *Orpheus* to replace the overture, and the very popular 1889 hybrid Italian version by the famous Ricordi publishers.) Berlioz's transcription returned the vocal registers back to the original of Gluck's Italian *Orfeo*. Although he used some of the instrumentation of that earlier version, he found most of the later French score superior, and therefore relied heavily on its shape and substance. The minimal differences between Gluck's French score and Berlioz's transcription include the loss of the third verse of Orfeo's "Objet de mon amour," the act 3 trio, and the final divertissement. He also replaced the final chorus with that of *Echo et Narcisse*, "Le Dieu de Paphos et de Gnide."

8. For an excellent summary of this history, see Eve Barsham's "The Opera in the

Nineteenth Century," pp. 84–98, in Howard's collection devoted to the opera, *C.W. von Gluck: Orpheo*.

9. Quoted in *Musical Quarterly* (1916), 2:34.

10. Ibid., p. 40.

11. The title of Ernst Krenek's *Orpheus und Eurydike* (1926), one of the many scores based on this theme, anachronistically teases the American imagination: a decorous, classical love affair joined by the title that proclaims: "you're-a-dike"

12. Quoted in Rosenthal, *Sexual Anarchy*, p. 23. In this section Elaine Showalter argues that lesbianism became a medical anomaly by the mid-eighties (*Sexual Anarchy*, pp. 22–23).

13. While most critics read Salomé's body as an expression of Wilde's male desires, her desires actually displace his. Salomé's longing for male bodies masked illicit male love—"her" body in drag allowed desire between men to flourish. While her body finally and unequivocally disciplined, the pure male body of the prophet, the virginal love between the page and Narraboth, even the love the king has for young nubile bodies are allowed to flourish. Male desire thrives while monstrous female desires are sacrificed. The critics complained. Romain Rolland wrote in a letter to Strauss: "[The subject of Salome] has a nauseous and sickly atmosphere about it: it exudes vice and literature. This isn't a question of middle-class morality, it's a question of health" (Rolland and Strauss, *Correspondence, Diary, and Essays*, pp. 82–83). In a description of the first performance of Strauss's opera in Wiesbaden, Adam Röder agrees: "We are no supporters of censorship. But if sadists, masochists, lesbians and homosexuals come and presume to tell us that their crazy world of spirits and feelings is to be interpreted as manifestations of art, then steps must be taken in the interests of *health*" (quoted in Puffett, *Richard Strauss: Salome*, p. 133). In short, by 1905, smothering the strong and desirous woman was a matter of maintaining national wellness.

14. Elma Stuart displayed a handkerchief with which she had wiped tears from Eliot's eyes, "and henceforth has reserved as a *relic*" (Haight, *George Eliot: A Biography*, p. 493).

15. In her early but influential essay "The Female World of Love and Ritual," Smith-Rosenberg explores friendships between nineteenth-century American women. She argues against the Freudian psychosexual classification of female friendships, showing how these same-sex attachments in fact undermine this binary conception of sexuality. By arguing against polar categories, she is able to conclude that, regarding female intimacy, "rather than seeing a gulf between the normal and the abnormal we view sexual and emotional impulses as part of a continuum or spectrum" (p. 28). This argument can be appropriated by critics who study a writer like Marian Evans/George Eliot. In " 'The Dark Eye Beaming' " Zimmerman examines Eliot's early novels and shows how strong female friendships undermine the male relationships of her heroines. Zimmerman argues that these early friendships pay tribute to Eliot's own relationship with her close friend and frequent companion, Sara Sophia Hennell. The critic, however, identifies a break in Eliot's writing between *Middlemarch* and *Daniel Deronda*, with the latter turning away from nurturing female bonds.

16. Patricia Juliana Smith provided much of this information about the nineteenth-

century diva in her "*Gli Enigmi Sono Tre*: The [D]evolution of Turandot, Lesbian Monster" in this volume.

17. This argument is nicely put forth in Zimmerman's article:

> Karl Heinrich Ulrich (who was read by Stephen Gordon's father in *The Well of Loneliness*) was widely read in the 1860s. . . . During the 1860s and 1870s, George Henry Lewes worked on a monumental philosophical study . . . which he called psychology. . . . His research took them to Germany, where in 1870 he had extensive discussions about psychiatry. . . . I therefore conclude that Eliot and Lewes interpreted [a masculine behaving woman and devotee of Eliot's] Edith Simcox's behavior as homosexual.

Zimmerman, "'The Dark Eye Beaming,'" p. 141.

18. See Kosinski's *Orpheus in Nineteenth-Century Symbolism*, which presents a catalogue of artistic, musical, and literary depictions of the figure.

19. As further evidence that Eliot delighted in the *jouissance* of this singer's presence as well as voice, I turn to Eliot's letters. Whenever she speaks of attending opera she speaks of *hearing* rather than *seeing* the work. In 1852 she writes of Herbert Spencer taking her "to hear William Tell" (*Letters* 2:16). In another letter at a very different point in her life, she "hears Acis and Galatea" (3:71) and, five years later, she again begins: "I am rather deaf and stupid this morning, for last night we went to hear Gounod's 'Faust'" (4:93). Even in the earlier letter to Hennell, Eliot says she *heard* Fidelio, and yet teases her friend, saying she wishes Sara could "hear and *see*" the performance of "die Wagner" (2:191).

20. Quoted in Rosenthal, *Sexual Anarchy*, p. 27.

21. Ibid., p. 23.

22. See Faderman's "Morbidification of Love Between Women," p. 77.

23. Grout describes the character as "a personage of sublime courage and self-abnegation, an idealized figure. The whole last part of the opera is in effect a celebration of Leonora's heroism and the great humanitarian ideas of the Revolution" (*A History of Western Music*, p. 524).

Works Cited

Apollonius of Rhodes. *Aronautica*. London and New York, 1921.

Barsham, Eve. "The Opera in the Nineteenth Century: Berlioz and Gluck." In Patricia Howard, ed., *C.W. von Gluck: Orfeo,* pp. 84–97. Cambridge: Cambridge University Press, 1981.

Bernheimer, Martin. "Orfeo ed Euridice." *Opera* (April 1991), 42:411–12.

Blyth, Alan. "Orfeo ed Euridice." *Opera* (July-December 1972), 23:666–68.

——— "Orfeo ed Euridice." *Opera* (July-December 1983) 33:1311–12.

Breiholz, Jochen. Review of Willy Decker's *Orfeo ed Euridice*. *Opera News* (April 11, 1992), 56:53–54.

Brontë, Charlotte. *Jane Eyre*. Ed. Richard Dunn. New York: Norton, 1987.

——— *Villette*. New York: Penguin, 1979.

De Lauretis, Teresa. "Sexual Indifference and Lesbian Representation." *Theatre Journal* (1988), 40:155–77.

Eliot, George. *Adam Bede*. New York: Scribner's, 1917.

——— "Armgart." In *Collected Poems*, pp. 115–51. London: Skoob Books, 1989.

——— *Daniel Deronda*. Ed. Barbara Hardy. New York: Penguin, 1986.

——— *Essays of George Eliot*. Ed. Thomas Pinney. New York: Columbia University Press, 1963.

——— *The George Eliot Letters*. Ed. Gordon S. Haight. 7 vols. New Haven: Yale University Press, 1955.

——— *Scenes from Clerical Life*. New York: National Library, n.d.

Faderman, Lillian. "Morbidification of Love Between Women by Nineteenth-Century Sexologists." *Journal of Homosexuality* (Fall 1978), 4(1):73–90.

Gardiner, John Eliot. "Hands Off *Orfeo!*" In Patricia Howard, ed., *C. W. von Gluck: Orfeo*, pp. 112–18. Cambridge: Cambridge University Press, 1981.

Gray, Beryl. *George Eliot and Music*. New York: St. Martin's, 1989.

Grout, Donald Jay. *A History of Western Music*. New York: Norton, 1973.

Haight, Gordon S. *George Eliot: A Biography*. New York: Penguin, 1985.

Hammond, Tom. "Orfée et Euridice: Gluck's Final Solution." In Patricia Howard, ed., *C. W. von Gluck: Orfeo*, pp. 105–9. Cambridge: Cambridge University Press, 1981.

Horne, Marilyn, with Jance Scovell. *My Life*. New York: Atheneum, 1983.

Howard, Patricia, ed. *C. W. von Gluck: Orfeo*. Cambridge: Cambridge University Press, 1981.

Irigaray, Luce. *This Sex Which Is Not One*. Trans. Catherine Porter with Carolyn Burke. Ithaca: Cornell University Press, 1985.

Koestenbaum, Wayne. *The Queen's Throat: Opera, Homosexuality, and the Mystery of Desire*. New York: Vintage, 1993.

Kosinski, Dorothy. *Orpheus in Nineteenth-Century Symbolism*. Ann Arbor: UMI Research, 1989.

Leonard, Maurice. *Kathleen: The Life of Kathleen Ferrier*. Foreward by Elisabeth Schwarzkopf. London: Hutchinson.

Mackerras, Charles. "Which *Orfeo*?" *Opera* (January-June, 1972), 23:393–97.

Ovid. *Metamorphoses*. Trans. Rolfe Humphries. Bloomington: Indiana University Press, 1960.

Panofsky, Erwin. *Albrecht Durer*. Princeton: Princeton University Press, 1943.

Pearsall, Ronald. *The Worm and the Bud: The World of Victorian Sexuality*. New York: Macmillan, 1969.

Perlmutter, Donna. "Orfeo ed Euridice." *Opera News* (January 19, 1991), 55(9):38.

Pinion, F. B., ed. *A George Eliot Miscellany: A Supplement to Her Novels*. London: Macmillan, 1982.

Puffett, Derrick. *Richard Strauss: Salome*. Cambridge: Cambridge University Press, 1989.

Rolland, Romain, and Richard Strauss. *Correspondence, Diary, and Essays*. Ed. Rollo Myers. London: Calder and Boyars, 1968.

Rosenthal, Harold. "Orfeo ed Euridice" *Opera* (July-December 1982), 33:26–30.

Segal, Charles. *Orpheus: The Myth of the Poet*. Baltimore: Johns Hopkins University Press, 1993.

Showalter, Elaine. *Sexual Anarchy*. New York: Viking Penguin, 1990.

Smith-Rosenberg, Carroll. "The Female World of Love and Ritual: Relations Between Women in Nineteenth-Century America." *Signs: Journal of Women in Culture and Society* (1975), 1(1):1–29.

"The Spanish Gypsy." *Edinburgh Review* (October 1868), 128:266–73.

Vicinus, Martha. "Distance and Desire: English Boarding-School Friendships." In Estelle B. Freedman, Barbara C. Gelpi, Susan L. Johnson, Kathleen M. Weston, eds., *The Lesbian Issue: Essays from Signs*. Chicago: University of Chicago Press, 1985.

Whenham, John. *Claudio Monteverdi: Orfeo*, Cambridge: Cambridge University Press, 1986.

Wittig, Monique. "One Is Not Born a Woman." In Alison M. Jagger and Paula S. Rothenberg, eds., *Alternative Feminist Frameworks*, pp. 148–52. 2d ed. New York: McGraw-Hill, 1984.

Woolf, Virginia. *Mrs. Dalloway*. San Diego: Harcourt Brace, 1981.

Zimmerman, Bonnie. " 'The Dark Eye Beaming': Female Friendship in George Eliot's Fictions." *Lesbian Texts and Contexts*. New York: New York University Press, 1990.

——— "George Eliot and Feminism: The Case of *Daniel Deronda*." In Rhoda B. Nathan, ed., *Nineteenth-Century Women Writers of the English-Speaking World*. New York: Greenwood, 1986.

Gli Enigmi Sono Tre: The [D]evolution of Turandot, Lesbian Monster

Patricia Juliana Smith

For a while I wanted to be an opera singer. Even though they were fat they could wear extravagant costumes, nobody laughed at them, they were loved and praised. Unfortunately I couldn't sing. But it always appealed to me: to be able to stand up there in front of everyone and shriek as loud as you could, about hatred and love and rage and despair, scream at the top of your lungs and have it come out music. That would be something.

—Margaret Atwood, *Lady Oracle*

How these stories trap you! How they latch onto your heart, there or somewhere else! How they cut you to the quick—in what unknown, innermost suffering?

—Catherine Clément, *Opera, or the Undoing of Women*

Prologue: Un' Apologia per la Vita Mia

To deflect the biographer's gaze from a personal history rife with loss and disaster and, I believe, from her lesbianism, Ivy Compton-Burnett wryly observed that she had "had such an uneventful life that there is little to say."[1] Even with far fewer sorrows than Compton-Burnett behind me, I, too, would gladly decline the impulse to autobiography, a mode I tend to distrust both in myself and others. Better to tell the story as fiction, as if it happened to someone else, and retreat behind the "objectivity" of third-person narrative. Yet unless I reveal my own bildungsroman, how, in Virginia Woolf's phrase, am I to use "all this very queer knowledge" ("Speech" xxxviii–xxxix) that I have been given? Upon what authority might I speak to explain a phenomenon so obvious that no one has noticed it or dared to speak of it?

No, no! Mai nessun m'avrà![2]

"You're too smart for your own good. No man will ever want you. You better start learning to act dumb. Otherwise, you'll never get married. Then *what'll become of you?"*

Such was the advice of my elders and betters—the married women in the mean little industrial town I called home—throughout the course of my closeted youth. While anathema to my ears, this injunction to "dummy up"—or, more accurately, dummy down*—was not without its utility, and I applied it subversively and, its seems, continuously.*

They told me that a young air force officer, visiting the home of my kinswoman, had "just fallen in love" with a high school photograph of me, displayed among the family portraits, and wanted to meet me. How unlikely, *I thought. Still dependent on them, I could not refuse the introduction, but I WOULD NOT SUBMIT. I WILL NOT SERVE.*

No! Non gettar tua figlia nelle braccia dello straniero!

When transported to the place of encounter, I engaged in what graduate school would later teach me to call Discourse. *I subjected the gallant officer and gentleman to a relentless, evening-long display of my arcane and eclectic knowledge on diverse topics. I most certainly disabused him of his ill-conceived infatuation.*

Popolo di Pekino!
La legge è questa: Turandot la Pura
sposa sarà di chi, di sangue regio,
spieghi i tre enigmi ch'ella proporrà.
Ma chi affronta il cimento e vinto resta,
porga alla scure la superba testa.

People of Peking! People of Carson, California! Hear me! I want none of this! I will not trade my purity and that vague thing called potential for a house, appliances, and an endless stream of babies, nor for the interminable drudgery and depression I see you endure! To make sure that no man who is not my equal shall have me, I will subject him to the test and have his proud and foolish head on an axe should he dare to think himself my better! (And I trust that no man who is *my equal—if he does exist—will want to engage me in such an ugly spectacle. . . .)*

In questa Reggia, or son mill'anni e mille . . .

Surrounded as I was by the spectacle of trailer parks, factories, and oil refinery smokestacks, I longed for beauty and culture. I devoured all that the local state university, my alma mater, had to offer, and still I craved for more. I embarked on an autodidactic exploration of opera. I liked Joan Sutherland—a large woman, not conventionally pretty, but nonetheless superb to the enlightened eye and ear. A big girl myself and a perpetual "fashion error" whom nothing, not even life itself, seemed to fit properly, I sought to emulate her. I bought all her recordings (by mail order, of course—there were no classical record stores in Carson), including her Turandot *(an uncharacteristic role, the critics said). Puccini, to me, was silly but okay—not thought-provoking like Wagner or Verdi, not spectacular like Rossini or Bellini. All those fragile girls who die, undone by love and the world at large, the secular versions of the virgin martyrs whose stories were among the best diversions of Catholic school. But* Turandot, *the opera about the Chinese princess who forced her suitors to solve virtually unsolvable riddles and, once they failed, had them beheaded—how incredible! I understood her. I played the record over and over, omitting—or failing to hear—the fateful, indeed fatal, ending. (But, then again, someone else wrote that after the fact. It wasn't* really *part of the opera, was it?)*

For me, as for so many others, culture and education provided the means by which to distance myself from those early ties that bound and to "come out" in a multitude of ways. Able at last to articulate who and what I always had been as well as what I had become, I could stop performing the role of Turandot la pura. *Looking at life from another perspective, I thought, with baby butch aspirations, it might be better—or at least more interesting—to play the role of Calaf the Unknown Prince.*

Tu che di gel sei cinta . . .

*My first attempt—she could have been the Crown Princess of China to my regal but deracinated soldier of fortune, so unequal were our circumstances—*seemed *successful at the outset. She was amused by my ability to untangle enigmas. Yet when it came time to force the moment to its crisis, she announced that I'd given the wrong answers all along. It was not what she meant, at all. To say she had me decapitated would be an understatement.*

Parla, parla, parla! Il nome, il nome!

The second time around, I was more savvy—I thought. I solved her riddles adroitly and directly. But she told me I was mistaken a priori—she claimed she'd never posed any enigmas, that I was merely projecting my own oppressive fantasies, although I could have sworn otherwise. And then, like Turandot, she told me my name—that the name our post-Freudian culture gives the failed suitor is not Amor *but* Ossessione.

To be decapitated twice, and yet survive! Surely St. Cecilia, that exemplary virgin martyr, had nothing on me. I dropped the persona of the romantic adventurer, for I was not Calaf, but only the feckless Principe di Persia, and I eschewed romantic epistemology altogether. I stopped playing the record—which had been superseded by a compact disc. Yet now, with the wisdom of hindsight, I must ask just what it was about Turandot that drew me to her in my closet days, if not her own, vastly more regal closet . . .

In his polemic contra *Turandot* playwright Albert Innaurato posits that Giacomo Puccini, in the creation of his last opera, "was being true to his roots in Italian machismo and the misogynistic Catholicism of Thomas Aquinas," in presenting the world with "the sort of female who appears only in the purple fantasies of heterosexual men" (11, 9). While Innaurato makes a brave attempt to define the source of the problem that most present-day audiences must almost inevitably find inherent in the opera's protagonist, he misses the most crucial causal factors of her alienation; thus, in great part, he misassigns blame and merely offers a vague hint at the enigma central to her characterization.[3]

The heart of the matter is, quite simply, that Turandot, *la principessa di morte*, is a lesbian. If this significant facet of her personality has eluded her audience for decades, it is hardly surprising. Dispossessed in the opera's libretto of the most salient aspect of lesbian identity, namely desire for another woman—or, for that matter, an appropriate woman to desire—her murderous hatred of men has become her defining trait. Yet it is hardly coincidental that fin-de-siècle medical sexologists, particularly the Italians Cesare Lombroso and Guglielmo Ferrero, envisioned the lesbian as a violent, chaotic, and chthonic force whose primary purpose was not the love of women but rather the very destruction of Western civilization.

The figure of the Turandot is, nevertheless, as old as recorded myth and predates Puccini by millennia. She manifests herself under various names and in various settings. And she has always been, according to the mores of the cultures in which she has appeared, the precursor of the lesbian. In her numerous incarnations, she shuns the institutions of heterosexuality that would entrap her. She is the riddling marriage resister of ancient legend, the Enlightenment bluestocking, and the decadent man-hater. Just as she presents her potential and unwelcome suitors with three riddles to solve, she is herself, in her historical and literary development, a tripartite enigma.

Act 1: Archetypes and Atavists

The riddling woman who puts men to the test has been with us for as long as the human imagination has been recorded, and as long as heterosexuality has been institutionalized as marriage, the marriage resister has exerted her will to evade its trap.

In the beginning there was the Sphinx. Part woman and part lion, she was hardly a prized candidate for marriage; nevertheless, she stood between men and their desires and flaunted her intellectual superiority over them. Appearing as a curse in the wake of a regicide, she blocked access to Thebes. If a man would enter the city, he must engage her in mental combat. Should he fail to outwit her, as many had, she would simply devour him. When Oedipus solved her riddle, she was "so mortified . . . that she cast herself down from the rock and perished" (Bulfinch 154). But the Sphinx had her revenge on the institutions of marriage and parenthood, for Oedipus's "reward" for the deliverance of Thebes plunged him into a family romance from which Western civilization has yet to recover.

Atalanta, the favorite of the virgin goddess Diana, was one of the earliest

❧ • **Fig. 10.1. As old as recorded myth: Puccini's princess of death (Dame Gwyneth Jones) explains herself.** *Courtesy of Winnie Klotz, Metropolitan Opera.*

mythic marriage resisters, a woman who, among other feats, killed two would-be rapist centaurs and defeated a much-acclaimed male opponent in a wrestling match (Lefkowitz 44). With a face "boyish for a girl, yet too girlish for a boy" and athletic prowess surpassing that of men, she was warned by an oracle early in life that "marriage will be your ruin" (Bulfinch 174). Her first close call with this institution came when Diana, angered at the ingratitude of the king of Calydon, sent a wild boar to wreak havoc on the land. Atalanta, the lone woman to respond to the call for hunters, was the first to wound the beast who had killed a multitude of men. When the king's son Meleager—for whom, according to some accounts, the hunt was part of a homosexual rite de passage—at last dispatched the boar, he awarded the head and hide to Atalanta.[4] Offended that such an honor would be bestowed on a woman, Meleager's uncles, who were conducting the initiatory rites (Sergent 221), snatched the trophies away, and Meleager, having become enamored of the androgynous maiden, killed his uncles in response. Meleager would have gladly married Atalanta, but his mother, distressed by the deaths of her brothers, retaliated by casting into the fire a brand, given her by deities who foretold that his life would last only as long as did this emblem. Thus Atalanta was spared the misfortunes of marriage for the nonce.

Subsequently, as she was plagued by an abundance of suitors, she established a prerequisite for marriage: a test unlike those posed by the riddling women inasmuch as it required physical rather than intellectual agility, but one whose echoes—like the cries of Turandot's ancestress Lou-ling—resound across the centuries: "No man may have me . . . unless he first defeats me in a race. Compete against me, and the one who is swift of foot will have my hand in marriage as his prize; but death will be the reward of those who are left behind" (Ovid 240). This dire imprecation, however, was to no avail; she had underestimated male rashness, as many sought their destruction at her hands. Hippomenes, knowing he could not defeat Diana's minion of his own accord, called upon Venus for assistance and was given the three golden apples of the Hesperides; consequently, the race became a struggle between the forces of the goddess of female homosociality and the goddess of heterosexuality. When his defeat appeared eminent, Hippomenes tossed an apple in Atalanta's path, then another, and another. Afflicted, presumably, by an attraction to apples peculiar to female archetypes, Atalanta stooped to retrieve them and, thus distracted, lost both the race and her freedom. Yet if Venus was triumphant over Diana in this battle, she subsequently lost the war. The newly wedded pair failed to acknowledge the goddess with appropriate gratitude. Miffed by this slight, Venus cursed her own accomplishment and provoked Hippomenes into a fit of erotomania, which he gratified upon Atalanta in the precincts of the temple of Cybele, the mother of the gods. Cybele, who required no less sacrifice than self-castration from her own priests (Frazer 403–9), punished the pair by transforming them into a pair of lions, doomed forever to pull her chariot.

Not surprisingly, the myth of Atalanta stirred not only the imagination of George Frideric Handel, perhaps the gayest of opera composers,[5] but also of Algernon Charles Swinburne and George Gissing, fashioners of the fin-de-siècle image of the female deviant. Handel, whose operas seem to the postmodern perspective nothing so much as camp critiques of received notions of heroism and romance, eschewed in his setting not only the trial Atalanta imposes on Hippomenes but also all tragic elements of the Hunt of Calydon. His *Atalanta*, "a pastoral, almost masque-like creation" that its eighteenth-century audience appreciated primarily for its stunning theatrical effects (Hogwood 131), grafts an ostensibly happy ending—a royal wedding—onto the story of Meleager and Atalanta.[6] Written rapidly in an almost desperate attempt to secure royal patronage, the opera premiered as part of the public celebrations of the nuptials of Frederick, Prince of Wales, and Princess Augusta of Saxe-Gotha, a match that produced the ill-fated future George III. Under the circumstances, Handel—who had "borrowed" the libretto from an obscure Italian source—could hardly represent Atalanta's story otherwise. Yet Handel nonetheless managed to subvert the conventions of institutional heterosexuality by casting the role of "Meleagro" for a castrato soprano—which causes further complications of gender dislocation in present-day performances in which the role is sung by a female contralto.[7] The prince, nonetheless, seems to have enjoyed the work (Hogwood 132).

More than a century later, conversely, Swinburne—whose "non-existent sexual repressions" *can*, despite Harold Nicholson's protests, be "depressing[ly] analogi[zed] to Dr. Masoch or the Marquis de Sade" (2)—elected to record *only* the tragic aspects of the hunt narrative. Despite the emphasis given to the heroine in the title of his neo-Grecian tragedy, *Atalanta in Calydon* focuses on the death of Meleager, primarily from the perspective of his aggrieved mother Alathaea, to whom the greatest portion of the speeches is given and who receives the final forgiveness of her son despite her complicity in his death. By contrast, the "strange un-sexed Arcadian virgin" against whom Alathaea warns her son is a distant and ultimately unfeeling figure who departs with "high restraint" and "fine aloofness" in the wake of the hero's demise, an agent of the "implacable cruelty of Artemis" (Nicholson 79, 88, 78). For Swinburne, who commenced *Lesbia Brandon* while composing *Atalanta in Calydon*, the myth provides an occasion to indulge in the spectacle of the "cruel" affections and desires of women, whether they be deities, mothers, or sinister androgynes.[8]

Gissing, in turn, focuses on the heroine and prominently features female physicality in his story "Fleet-Footed Hester." As in his novel *The Odd Woman*, Gissing's own peculiar and highly ambivalent admixture of admiration for and rage against the female sex leads to a scenario in which the presence of extraordinary qualities in a woman, particularly those generally deemed "masculine," make conquering her sexually and subjugating her all the more appealing.[9] Accordingly, the ability of the seventeen-year-old Cockney Hester to beat her male peers in footraces proves not only the means of gaining a desirable fiance but of losing him as well, and ultimately becomes the only means by which she is able to realize her "necessary" surrender to male authority. Gasworks foreman John Rayner, an older man with relative affluence and status in the context of Hester's world, is "excited . . . to an uneasy interest" (Gissing 291) by both the novelty and the sheer physicality of her running. Consequently, he forbids her to indulge in any display of her athletic abilities once they are engaged. Unable to resist a challenge from a neighborhood youth, she disobeys—and loses both the race and her future husband. As a result, she rejects conventional notions of courtship, leaves her family, falls into the company of "new girls of more pretentious stamp" (Gissing 294), and acts the virago whenever she encounters Rayner, until she hears of his imminent emigration to the South African colonies. Panicked at the thought of losing the one "masculine" presence in her life, she repents her behavior and must run "as if minutes meant life or death" to forestall his boarding the train that will take him to his port of embarkation, for "if John Rayner were whirled away from her into the unknown, there would be nothing left to live for" (Gissing 305). To represent this frantic feat, Gissing graphically depicts the young woman racing three miles on foot through a variety of obstacles and physical agonies in the streets of predawn London, in order to present herself, submissively in dishabille, to her conqueror.

With the possible exception of Swinburne's retroping of the myth, which seems to have little purpose other than to exult in the wonders of female cruelty to men, the didactic point of all these tales is, inevitably, that even the most rebellious woman must eventually be subsumed into the structures of patriarchy. She might be permitted to engage in her game of playing hard to get for a time; indeed, her aloofness, along with her physical (or, in later examples, intellectual) acumen makes her all the more attractive and certainly more valuable than her mundane sisters. And if she eliminates a few of the weaker males in the process—in what Gissing and his contemporaries might see as part of Darwinian natural selection—that is hardly a great loss. For when the fittest man appears, she has no choice but to submit, gladly and, as it were, naturally.

The myths of the Sphinx and Atalanta are conflated in the tale of the riddling princess, a narrative so thoroughly and deeply inscribed in the collective unconscious that it attains near ubiquity in the oral traditions of an array of cultures. Attributed to various Asian and Greco-Roman sources, the story appears in numerous reconfigurations in such collections of folk and fairy tales as the *Gesta Romanorum*, the *Arabian Nights*, *Haft Peiker* (*The Seven Pictures*) of the twelfth-century Persian poet Nezami, *Le Cabinet des fées*, *Les Mille et un jours* of Pétis de la Croix, and the *Kinder- und Hausmärchen* of the Brothers Grimm. The tale enters the realm of canonical literature—with several significant twists—with the subplot of the courtship of Portia, the lady of Belmont, in William Shakespeare's *The Merchant of Venice*.

Those who would seek the hand of this fabulous lady, who rules over a never-never land in vague proximity to Venice, must choose between three caskets, respectively of gold, silver, and lead, each inscribed with an enigmatic verse. He who correctly deciphers the riddles and chooses accordingly will become the husband of the lady and lord of her realm. That many undesired suitors, all nobles and princes, have undertaken—and failed—this test is evinced, suggestively, by Portia's initial statement: "My little body is a-weary of this great world" (1.ii.1). And that she would not willingly give her weary little body to any man who has undertaken the test thus far is abundantly evident in her early speeches. Only the penniless Bassanio, for whose cause Antonio enters into the "pound of flesh" bond with Shylock, possesses the qualities, both intellectual and personal, necessary to solve the enigmas of the caskets and win Portia as his wife—with a little help from a group of supportive musicians whose song provides a subtle clue.

On the surface this narrative follows its mythological and folkloric antecedents closely: the "special" woman who can only be won through means of some sort of trifold test, the numerous seemingly worthy but unwanted suitors, and the unlikely victor, aided by some form of metaphysical if not divine intervention.[10] The very qualities that make this version canonical, however, require certain ideological refinements. Portia, despite her protestations, is not essentially a man-hating marriage resister driven by her own unspeakable impulses to inflict harm on men. Rather, she functions as the dutiful daughter of the patriarchy, carrying out the will of her late and "ever virtuous" father by means of "the lott'ry he hath devis'd" (1.ii.27, 29). The punishment exacted upon the failed suitors, moreover, is not death; instead, the penalty for failing to win Portia—who, as a foil to the Jewish usurer Shylock, must stand as a paragon of Christian charity—is submission to a vow that the seeker is "never to speak to lady afterward / In way of marriage" (1.i.41–42). While apparently a less cruel punishment than that meted out previously by Atalanta (and subsequently by Turandot), it is nonetheless an unusual one that invokes the dire theoretical and psychological choice of "castration or decapitation" Hélène Cixous has put forth. In providing this hindrance to the future enactment of heterosexuality by the unworthy and clearly heterosexual suitors, it ironically coincides, moreover, with the pervasiveness within the play of the "classic conception of [male] bisexuality" Cixous questions elsewhere ("The Laugh of the Medusa" 254).

If, among Shakespeare's female characters, "only Portia . . . comes anywhere near [an] idea of [sexual] equality," as Maureen Duffy suggests (149), it is because she is able to perform and, to great extent, internalize the male bisexuality characteristic of central male figures in the homosocial ethos of the drama. While the respective courtships of Portia and Jessica (both played in original productions by male actors) provide a type of symmetry, the subliminal central "love story" is that of Antonio for Bassanio.[11] That Portia lovingly calls Antonio "the bosom lover of my lord" and bids Bassanio to "hence upon your wedding day," before their marriage can be consummated, to Antonio's rescue indicates not only her knowledge of her husband's dual sexual nature but also her complicity. Indeed, one might speculate that it is this particular quality, distinguishing Bassanio from the rest of the suitors, that renders him in Portia's eyes "worthy of thy praise" (1.ii.121). While we may assume that after the trial and the play's conclusion Portia and Bassanio will physically consummate their marriage and live happily ever after (possibly with Antonio) in Belmont, the metaphysical consummation of this three-way relationship comes as Portia, cross-dressed as the doctor of law, pronounces the legal loophole that saves Antonio from making good his fatal bond. Thus Portia becomes an honorary man, and is subsumed not only into institutional heterosexuality but also into cultural homosociality/homosexuality.[12] But while the bisexual Bard was willing to provide the riddling woman with a curious if nonetheless apparently satisfactory arrangement in a world in which lesbianism seems an unknown entity, such would not be her fate in her later manifestations—drawn, as they were, by men who feared the rebellion of the female sex and the chaos that must ensue.

Act 2: The Bluestocking and the Symbolic Order of Subordination

"The very word 'wife' is enough to kill me" (Gozzi 149). So says the riddling woman in her first appearance as the Princess of China, the ferocious virgin who would gladly slaughter the men who seek to possess her, in Carlo Gozzi's comedy *Turandot*.[13] Unlike Portia, whose trial by enigma is ordained by her father's will, Turandot thwarts not only the desire of her suitors but also the will of her aged father by taking language into her own hands and subverting its very meaning through the series of riddles she herself invents. In so doing, she threatens to overthrow the very foundation of the symbolic order upon which male authority—and, by extension, society and government—is constructed.[14] Such a woman must be stopped. Yet, as the daughter and sole heir of king, she cannot be destroyed, for she is vital, paradoxically, to the continuation of royal sovereignty. The attempt to resolve this dilemma lies at the heart of Gozzi's play, which elaborates the myth of the marriage resister far more vigorously than any representation heretofore.

The proud princess—and observations of her pride are constantly articulated by Gozzi's characters—resides, separated from the male sex, with her women in a "harem" guarded by eunuchs (159). As Truffaldino, the chief of her guards, observes, "If even a fly tries to buzz in there, we check if it's male or female" (159). Prior to the onstage action, her father, the emperor Altoum, pressed her to make a dynastic marriage. She balked, begged, and dissimulated: "Finally the viper fell ill from sheer rage. On the point of death, she asked her saddened but steadfast father to grant one diabolical request" (132), namely, that she be allowed to put any potential husband to the test of three riddles, marrying him should he succeed, or having her father behead him should he fail. "Diabolical" as this scheme might seem to Turandot's subjects, it is not without motive or logic. As she explained to her father in establishing this trial, "No man will dare attempt it, and I will live in peace. . . . And if any try, my father will not be blamed for carrying out a sworn public edict" (Gozzi 133). While her original intent was not wholesale slaughter but merely to ensure a life free from sexual subjugation, Turandot, like Atalanta, severely underestimated the foolhardiness of the opposite sex in the face of a challenge to subordinate a free woman.

As the play begins, the executions of her would-be spouses have become legion.[15] Calaf, the exiled Prince of the Tatars, having undergone five years of painful peregrinations since the violent overthrow of his father Timur, King of Astrakhan, anonymously enters the city of Peking, seeking his fortune as a mercenary soldier in Altoum's army. Upon his arrival he encounters his old tutor Hassan, living in Peking under the assumed name Barach, who has married the widowed inn-keeper Schirina, at whose establishment Calaf is staying. By great coincidence (in a drama depending extensively upon coincidences), Schirina's daughter Zelima is a servant in the harem of Turandot. After the two men recount their respective travails, Barach warns his former student to avoid "this grisly spectacle" of Peking's "theatre of atrocities" (Gozzi 132), the execution of the prince of Samarkand, the latest of Turandot's failed suitors. Ishmael, the tutor of the unfortunate prince, enters weeping and hurls a miniature of the princess to the ground, trampling it underfoot and cursing its subject. Despite Barach's warning that to gaze upon it "would be like gazing at the Medusa" (Gozzi 135), the curious Calaf retrieves the image and immediately falls in love;

for Turandot, unlike the stereotypical virago, is as beautiful as she is intelligent. Calaf undertakes to seek his fate in her contest and, despite the warnings of the court ministers and the emperor himself, masochistically and repeatedly resolves, "This is my choice: death or Turandot" (141–44 passim).

The princess enters flanked by her women, Zelima and Adelma. The latter, now a slave, is the former princess of Carazani. Her brother was one of Turandot's early suitors, and his execution precipitated a war between China and Carazani that resulted in the deaths of her parents and siblings and her own exile and enslavement. In this female companion Turandot places all her "love and complete trust" (Gozzi 181), while Adelma, feigning loyalty, secretly hates her. Upon seeing Calaf awaiting his ordeal, she recognizes the mysterious young man who, in the early years of his exile, served at her father's court, and with whom she is much infatuated. She therefore resolves to manipulate her mistress in whatever way possible, in order to save Calaf for herself. Meanwhile, Turandot offers her own apologia while attempting to warn away her unwanted supplicant:

> Prince, do not attempt this fatal trial. Whatever lies you have heard about me, the gods know that I am not heartless. But I abhor your sex, and I defend myself in the only way I know, so that I may remain free from men. Why should I not be as free as you are? Who forced you to come here, to make me cruel against my will. . . . Do not try to pit your skill against mine. My skill is the only thing I am proud of. God gave me intelligence and ability. If my ingenuity were beaten in this contest, I would die of shame. Go! Do not oblige me to put the riddles to you, or you will die. (144)

Yet the obsessed Calaf remains obdurate in his desire to possess her, responding, "If I had a thousand lives in this poor body, cruel princess, I would risk them all for you" (Gozzi 144).

Consequently, Turandot presents her three riddles, Calaf solves them directly and accurately, and the royal minister "sentence[s] her to marriage" (Gozzi 149). Complaining that she had not had sufficient time to prepare suitably difficult riddles and threatening her own death, Turandot pleads for a day's respite. Calaf, claiming rather incongruously that his love forbids him to cause her pain, offers her a riddle that she must solve by the next day—his name and the name of his father—if he is to set her free. But while the prince, all too eager to sacrifice himself, offers to die if she discovers his secret, Altoum, attempting to reassert some paternal control over the debacle, commutes Calaf's penalty to banishment and secretly consults with the young man.

As Turandot's own trial begins, the supposedly characteristic gossip and dissembling of women runs to chaos. Turandot, bemoaning her humiliation, plans a public suicide, while Adelma, fearing that her hated mistress will claim the man she loves, hatches her plots, suggesting that Turandot and her women issue bribes to those with knowledge of the prince; Zelima, who knows that the prince is her mother's lodger and her stepfather's acquaintance, also sets to work. Accordingly, Turandot's eunuchs arrest Barach, along with Timur, who has just arrived in Peking in search of his son, and take the men to Turandot's harem, where they are imprisoned and threatened with flogging if they fail to reveal the prince's name. Exhibiting much the same mindset as their respective student and son, Barach and Timur proclaim their preference for torture and death over safety, and are saved only by the entrance of Adelma, who warns of Altoum's approach and announces a new and better plan. She has bribed the emperor's guards who surround Calaf, and she and the other women will visit him and induce him to speak his name; Turandot exults in the thought that she will succeed so well that "no fool will ever again dare the riddles" (Gozzi 163).

Calaf is visited by a parade of Turandot's lackeys, all of whom prove inept interlocutors. Subsequently, Adelma herself appears and reveals both her identity and love to the prince, offering him escape, her rightful wealth and kingdom, and herself. Yet Calaf, able only to contemplate death or Turandot, rejects her offer, and only when she falsely informs him that Turandot will have him assassinated before he can reach the assembly at daybreak does he break down and inadvertently reveal his name and the name of his father.

Having received this information, Turandot has at her disposal the means by which to free herself from her impending marriage. Accordingly, she reveals the names at the assembly. Yet when Calaf attempts suicide in her presence, her heart is moved by the spectacle and she relents, consenting to be his wife. Thereupon the jealous Adelma grabs Calaf's dagger and, revealing her long-standing hatred of the princess, attempts her own death, which Calaf prevents. Order is then swiftly restored. Having won Turandot, and thus sovereignty over her realms, Calaf grants Adelma her freedom and restores her kingdom, Adelma graciously relents, a messenger announces that Timur has been restored to the throne of Astrakhan, and Turandot announces to the audience, as the play concludes, "May the mannerly world of men know that I love them all. For my repentance, pray let some sign of forgiveness be offered."[16]

Ted Emery characterizes Gozzi as a man obsessively concerned with maintaining "the indispensable order of subordination," a playwright who adopted to his own use the outdated conventions of the commedia dell'arte as a means of opposing the "pernicious threat to the social order of his city" and "the corrupting intellectual influence of the European Enlightenment" he deemed inherent in the works of fellow Venetian dramatist Carlo Goldoni (6, 7). As an impoverished member of the minor nobility, Gozzi had a vested interest in reasserting the patriarchal hierarchies of the status quo. Accordingly, of the various threats and "corruptions" of Enlightenment thought, few disturbed him as much as the breakdown of traditional gender roles and restrictions, and in his works, as Emery observes, Gozzi "repeatedly insists on the connection between women and social disorder" (13).

That women were engaged in the process of overturning, by means of the written word, the established order was, in fact, hardly a figment of Gozzi's imagination. In France, by the end of the seventeenth century, *Les Précieuses*, women hungry for culture, knowledge, and better treatment within the institution of marriage, had established salons and initiated much of the literature written for women and by women that would remain an influence throughout much of the eighteenth century—and, for their efforts, were roundly lampooned in a number of plays by Molière. Despite such ridicule, their influence nonetheless spread to Italy, where "learned ladies" with no other means of gaining education set up *conversazione* (Dulong 416). Clearly, the "cruel princess" is a response to their growing influence. William Ashbrook and Harold Powers observe that "Gozzi evidently intended to represent Turandot as something of a bluestocking, because she is directed to utter her first enigma 'in an academic tone,' and her resistance to marriage is prompted not only by a general contempt for the male sex but by intellectual pride as well" (47).

For Gozzi the threat of a woman appropriating language for her own purposes struck very close to home. Luisa Bergalli, the wife of his elder brother Gasparo, was not only a member of one such *conversazione* but a playwright and poet in her own right. Her attempt to start her own stage company incurred the wrath of her brother-in-law, who broke off all contact with his brother's family, and in the ensuing conflict, marked by litigation, bankruptcy, the birth of five children, and Gasparo's attempted suicide, Luisa fell victim to "melancholy," of which she died (Dulong 413). Surely some elements of the Gozzi-Bergalli conflict are reflected in the language war between the supposedly usurping Turandot and the traditionalist Calaf.

Yet an even deeper, far more fearsome threat than that posed by the literary woman attempting to seize control of the male-dominated language lurks in the subtext of *Turandot*. Who, or, more precisely, *what*, is this woman who so "abhors" the male sex and wishes only to live in her harem with other women? If the appellation *lesbian* does not appear, it is partly because the name was not yet assigned to such women and mostly because the very idea was too monstrous for men to contemplate, much less actualize through a linguistic signifier. As Terry Castle has demonstrated, the woman who loves other women has been represented throughout literary history, and while "*lesbian* and *homosexual* may indeed be neologisms . . . there have always been *other* words—a whole slangy mob of them—for pointing to (or taking aim at) the lover of women" (9). Even so, Gozzi utilizes a "slangy mob" of yet *other* words in taking his indirect aim at the lesbian by pointing to her castrated male flunkeys, who disport themselves by accusing each other, through vulgar jokes, of effeminacy, sodomy, pederasty, and flagellation (137–39). Significantly, the servants of the emperor do not partake in this banter or, presumably, engage in such actions. Thus, by evoking the "indispensible order of subordination," he indicates that the vices of the ruled are merely a reflection of those of the ruler.

In his *Memoirs* Gozzi described the societal changes stemming from the Enlightenment as a series of monstrous metamorphoses: "I watched women become men, men become women, women and men become monkeys . . . changing indecency into decency and calling anyone who disagreed a hypocrite" (cited in Emery 12). In this vision of the breakdown of gender roles, which greatly resembles the nightmares of present-day Christian fundamentalists contemplating gay and lesbian rights, we find the key to the "problem" of Turandot—she is a woman who would become a man, and thus cause men to become women.

Regardless of the name by which it was called, female homosexuality was a known practice in Gozzi's Venice. At the beginning of the eighteenth century, the aptly surnamed Italian priest Lodovico Maria Sinistrari offered an explicit (if woefully uninformed) definition of "female sodomy" in his manual of guidelines for confessors (Faderman 35–36; Brown 17–19). Gozzi's contemporary Giacomo Casanova records with libertine glee how his mistress, sent by her family to reside in a convent (the Catholic analogue, conceivably, of Turandot's harem) learned "the mysteries of Sappho [and] high metaphysics" from a nun, who was herself one of his lovers (3:622).[17] By mid-century, a decade prior to the premiere of Gozzi's *Turandot*, Giovanni Bianchi's report of Catherine Vizzani—"who followed the practices of Sappho" and seduced a number of women (including nuns) by means of a dildo, while remaining a virgin herself—was widely circulated and subsequently translated into English by John Cleland, the author of *Fanny Hill* (Trumbach 129).[18] And, finally, there was before Gozzi's very eyes the spectacle of Cecilia Zen Tron. The sister-in-law of his cousin Caterina Dolfin Tron and a major player in eighteenth-century Venetian "theater wars," she "built theaters, played the piano remarkably well, danced, rode horseback, learned fencing, prowled Venice in men's clothes and ruled her social circle with an iron hand" (Phillips-Matz 19). Such "women becoming men," whether through appropriation of language or appropriation by artificial means of the phallus (not to mention those who would dispose of the phallus altogether), clearly threatened the foundations of Gozzi's idea of order based on family, heredity, and male prerogative. It is hardly accidental, moreover, that in the character of Turandot he conflates the dangerous qualities of women of letters with those of female homosexuality; the homosocial atmosphere of the salon provided an ideal locus for generation of same-sex passion (Faderman 85–91, 125–32).

Gozzi's play provides the means by which the author can, ideologically at least, deride such women, forestall their threat to social order, and reincorporate them into traditional, hierarchical heterosexual structures. Simultaneously, as if to deny the existence of these viragos in his own culture, he displaces the offending woman into a setting as distant from Venice as possible, in China, far beyond the pale of Christendom. Gozzi's ethnocentric concern—or wish—that no *real* Italian woman would conduct herself in the manner of Turandot is articulated in the play by Altoum's secretary Pantalone, a Venetian forced to leave his country by "bad luck":

> My dear majesty, I don't know what to say. In my country . . . princes don't fall in love with portraits of girls—at least not enough to lose their heads over them. And we don't have girls like your daughter Turandot, who hate men. Not on your life! . . . If I told them about it back in Venice, they'd say, "Come off it, you old line spinner, you windbag, what are you trying to put over on us? Go tell your fairy tales to the kids." Then they'd laugh in my face and turn their backsides on me. (139–40)

Yet there apparently *were* a number of these "girls who hate men" in Gozzi's country, just as there were, we may assume, fathers like Altoum who were hard-pressed to control their daughters. How to stop such women from running amok was precisely what Gozzi needed to demonstrate. To this end the playwright calls upon nature to provide some "feminine" weakness inherent in all women—one that is merely asleep, not dead, in Turandot. This ineffable and debilitating tenderness, which has been at work in her psyche since the first sight of Calaf, causes Turandot at the moment of her ultimate victory to renounce all she has previously asserted and to avow that she does, in truth, love men.

While this protestation might be reassuring to those sharing Gozzi's worldview, such an abrupt change of philosophy, especially in character given as much interiority as Turandot, is inevitably unconvincing dramatically. Unwittingly, perhaps, Gozzi has rendered Turandot, like Milton's Satan, the most interesting—and thus the most sympathetic—character in the text; far more compelling than the bland and relatively uncomplicated Calaf. That drama is, of necessity, a polyvocal medium further undermines Gozzi's ideological ends. Turandot is given a voice of her own, and her self-justification and appeal for freedom early in the play, regardless of the attempts of the author and other characters to deem it irrational, attains a rationality otherwise absent in the text. Her manifesto therefore resonates as a far more compelling facet of the play than her subsequent, less-than-credible renunciation.

Act 3: The Lesbian Monster, or The Bride Stripped Bare by the Bachelors

Despite Gozzi's best efforts in defense of the ancient order, political revolutions and the accompanying social transformations eventually displaced much of the aristocratic privilege of his class and the moral authority of the Roman Catholic Church. As far as the condition of women was concerned, however, *plus ça change, plus c'est même chose* could hardly seem more true. While once confined to the roles of wife and mother by the divinely ordained "indispensable order of subordination," they now found themselves subordinated by the dicta of medical sexology and Darwinian evolution, which held women to be catalysts of physical, intellectual, moral, and cultural "reversion" (Dijkstra 211–13). Women who defied the norms of domestication and passivity threatened to undo the social and material progress the male sex had brought into being by the Victorian era and hurl the human race back into the condition of atavistic primitivism that would attain in a world ruled by the Amazons, the mothers of all defiant women. The virago, the feminist, the autoeroticist, the decadent, the lesbian, the bestialist, and the murderess, while logically differing quite perceptibly from one another, were deemed kindred spirits, and they were all lumped together under the same rubric of sociopathic *donne deliquente*—"female offenders" and potential annihilators of culture—by men of "science," including the Italian phrenologists Lombroso and Ferrero.

The figure of the mythological Amazon became, along with the various images of her modern-day descendants, favorite subjects of artists and writers of the late nineteenth and early twentieth centuries.[19] Dangerous women who disrupt male friendship, undermine male authority, usurp male prerogative, and take pleasure in male destruction—whether such mythic monsters as the Sphinx, the Lamia, and Lilith, or more up-to-date ones as Théophile Gautier's Mademoiselle de Maupin, Swinburne's Lesbia Brandon, and H. Rider Haggard's Ayesha (She-Who-Must-Be-Obeyed)—loomed large in the iconography of the day. As the forces of feminism grew more visible in the political realm, so did that ultimate personification of the deepest male anxieties, the female castrator qua decapitator, become a dominant figure in the artistic realm. By the fin de siècle, as Bram Dijkstra observes, "the operatic stage, in fact, [had become] one of the major stalking grounds of the headhuntresses, as well as of temptresses of every comparable sort" (376). Not only had Salome, the beheader of John the

Fig. 10.2. Turandot in the decadent imagination: the headhuntress stripped bare. Photograph of drawing by Joseph (von) Diveky (1887–1951), "Turandot" (ca. 1916). From *Idols of Perversity: Fantasies of Feminine Evil in Fin-de-Siècle Culture.* Copyright 1986 Bram Dijkstra. *Courtesy of Oxford University Press, Inc.*

Baptist (alias Jokanaan), been brought to operatic life by Richard Strauss, but so had Elektra, the dispatcher of her equally murderous mother and stepfather. Salome's own mother, Herodias, was the subject of Jules Massenet's melodrama, as were the temptress-turned-nun Thaïs (who, in the course of her pilgrim's progress, causes her monk-savior to lose his soul) and Alphonse Daudet's bisexual prostitute Sapho (who brings her middle-class male lover to the brink of suicide). While Camille Saint-Saëns immortalized the biblical barber Delilah, Giacomo Puccini canonized Floria Tosca as the most saintly of opera's homicidal heroines. The time was surely right for the return of Turandot.

In 1920 Puccini undertook the task of setting to music what he considered "the most normal and most human of all Gozzi's plays" (Carner 224). He was not the first to do so; only three years before, the Italian-German composer Ferrucio Busoni had conducted the premiere performance of his own revision of the eighteenth-century work.[20] Busoni's opera amply demonstrates what Emery has defined as the "fundamental paradox of Gozzi's posthumous success," namely, that "the ideological messages his plays were intended to transmit are rarely understood . . . by modern audiences, yet [the plays] continue to be revived and enjoyed" (2). Without changing the basic plot of the original, Busoni greatly simplified matters, eliminating Zelima, Schirina, Timur, Brighella, and Ishmael, along with the rather convoluted subplots in which they engage.[21] In this manner the narrative becomes more readily adaptable to the structures of recitative, arias, and ensembles upon which traditional opera depends. Simultaneously, this paring down extends as well to the psychology of Busoni's principals; just as the grief of characters is expressed through exclamations of "O O O O!," so are all emotions reduced to absurdities. Both the rage and resistance of Turandot and the obsession of Kalaf (as he is rendered in the composer's German libretto) become little more than stubbornness, Adelma does not burn with an old desire but tells the name in revenge for Kalaf's past slight (nor does she attempt suicide), and Turandot finally relents because "the boy" (*Knabe*), unlike the previous suitors, is "so mild and guileless" (162–63). Thus Busoni, who never forgets (or allows the audience to forget) that the work is, after all, a comedy, rids himself of most of the play's problematic sexual ideology—along with the grand passion prerequisite in opera. The result is a pleasant, moderately amusing work that, while reviving a plot potentially replete with contemporary sexual issues, is, in its relative kindness and lack of pathological behavior, completely out of synch with the zeitgeist. It is small wonder, then, that the work has received so little critical attention and so few performances.[22] But if Busoni remained true to Gozzi's plot while forfeiting Gozzi's ideology, Puccini did quite the opposite.

The now familiar 1928 Ricordi poster for Puccini's opera is an amalgam of Art Nouveau chinoiserie and Art Deco symmetry, symbolic of the opera's condition as an artifact of a belated transition from fin-de-siècle decadence to modernism. While the jewelry with which its subject is bedecked suggests femininity, the face itself lacks gender specificity and bears an uncanny resemblance to Nijinsky or Valentino, those exemplars of 1920s androgyny. Nor is the face particularly "oriental," notwithstanding the kohl mascara painted in an almond shape around the eyes. These eyes are both glazed and catlike—the eyes of a jaded yet insatiate voluptuary, deadened eyes that correspond to the phrenologist's paradigm of the autoeroticist, the lesbian, the bestialist (Dijkstra 178). The ornament on her headdress, notes Catherine Clément, is "a large red heart, upside down," inverted lest it "be confused with the heart of the Virgin of the Seven Sorrows" (98). For the heathen Turandot is the antithesis of the Catholic Mother of Sorrows; she is the antimother who rejects the biological destiny of maternity; she is the Swinburnean "Our Lady of Pain" who disdains the passive acceptance of the grief the world of men inflicts, all the while actively pouring rue upon the ranks of her male devotees. She is the embodiment of all that is unnatural, all that is fearful. Hers is the face that, if left to its own devices, would gladly undo two millennia of European progress, civilization, and evolution.

In the wake of the seemingly apocalyptic castastrophe of the First World War, the already decades-old predictions that loss of control over the female sex would bring about destruction gained currency in some influential cultural quarters. Although women, disenfranchised as they generally remained, had no power over the governments that precipitated the conflict, their sexual conduct, their vices, and, in particular, their reluctance to reproduce were construed as catalysts to this explosion of male violence. Catholic prelates drew a metaphysical causality between the growing practice of contraception and the escalation of battle deaths (Ranke-Heinemann 287–90). Similarly, a vehement disgust aimed at nonreproductive sexuality, particularly that of women, forms the continuo to the ironically childless T. S. Eliot's dirge for the war dead in *The Waste Land*, a work directly contemporary with Puccini's opera.[23] To control the sexually defiant woman, to reconcile her, somehow, to the order of the fathers, short of physically annihilating her (as was the fate of Salome), was, then, the daunting—and ultimately impossible—task facing Puccini and his librettists, Giuseppe Adami and Renato Simoni.

None of the composer's earlier female protagonists posed such a problem. Manon Lescaut might be a premodern material girl, Mimì might cohabitate with Rodolfo without ecclesiastical blessing, Floria Tosca might divulge life-or-death secrets and kill a man, and Cio-Cio-San might defy the non-European, non-Christian patriarchal authority of her kinsmen—to be sure, as Mosco Carner puts it, "girls of doubtful virtue . . . form the majority" of his heroines (275)—but none of these otherwise passive and yielding women ever blurs gender distinctions or threatens the latest configuration of the indispensable order of subordination. Together with Anna in *Le Villi* and Fidelia in *Edgar*, the earliest, most obscure of the Puccini women, they comprise a corps of martyrs of love, self-sacrificial victims of men's conflicts with other men or men's unfortunate but nonetheless expected lack of monogamist instinct, who, in a conflation of both sides of the age-old madonna-whore dichotomy, become the new type of Magdalen, the fallen woman as saint.

But as Puccini entered the latter phase of his career, the search for suitable opera plots in a cultural milieu in which "odd women" were becoming increasingly prominent slowed the composer's output. When three years had elapsed since the premiere of *Madama Butterfly* and he had yet to find a suitable libretto for a new opera, Puccini flirted seriously with the idea of setting Pierre Louÿs's *La Femme et Le Pantin* (Woman and Puppet), a chillingly dispassionate narrative of sadomasochism and an apt subject for operatic verismo.[24] Louÿs is perhaps best remembered for his Sapphically tinted *Chansons de Bilitis* (of which Claude

Debussy made two musical settings) and *Aphrodite* (which Puccini had briefly considered as an opera source nearly a decade before), but *La Femme et Le Pantin* is an anatomization of heterosexual power play and the erotics of pleasure and pain. Conchita, an oxymoronically virginal "Spanish slut" (Carner 156), sexually enslaves and debases Matteo, an older, aristocratic man, and becomes his mistress while refusing to submit to him physically. Driven by her taunts, which culminate in the spectacle of a feigned sex act with an adolescent boy, Matteo beats Conchita to the brink of death, an act that awakens her sexually and precipitates her surrender to her "master."[25]

Although Puccini and his publishers had entered into contractual negotiations with Louÿs, and a libretto, entitled *La Conchita*, was in preparation, the composer soon balked, citing the "unlovable" character of the protagonist and claiming that certain explicit scenes would be "impossible to perform" (Carner 154, 156).[26] Instead, he embarked upon *La Fanciulla del West*, the plot of which is, in essence, a nontragic *Tosca* in a Wild West setting. The theme of sexual subjugation of unruly women nevertheless stayed with Puccini. What was "impossible to perform" in the abortive *La Conchita* would be rendered allegorically in *Turandot*.

In the meantime, although he had eschewed the "unlovable" sadistic woman as his heroine, the composer developed the type in the one-act *Suor Angelica* from *Il Trittico*. Written in the interim between *La Fanciulla* and *Turandot*, it can be seen as a "practice piece" anticipating the latter work. Cruelty is personified in this opera through the character of La Zia Principessa (the Princess Aunt), a role written for a contralto, a voice for which the composer maintained a remarkable "lack of sympathy" (Carner 100). The heroine, Sister Angelica, is yet another Puccinian victim of romantic love, a once sensual young woman confined by her unsympathetic family to the female homosocial ethos of the convent as a punishment for an illicit affair and the illegitimate birth that ensued. After seven years of isolation, she receives a visitor—her cold, unforgiving aunt—who comes only to secure Angelica's signature on a family legal document. Her mission accomplished, the older woman rises to leave, but is halted by Angelica's plea for news of her predictably male child—to which La Principessa replies that he has been dead for two years. Consequently, the afflicted mother goes mad and commits botanical suicide—à la Lakmé and Selika in *L'Africaine*—but is saved from the eternal damnation Catholicism decrees for self-destroyers by the intervention of the Virgin Mary. The composer demonstrates that "lovable" fallen women are on the side of the angels, whereas their contralto (i.e., nonheterosexual) antagonists are not.[27] Thus, Turandot would have to be a soprano. Aside from the artistic consideration of the sublime rage she must express—what Dame Eva Turner, perhaps the most notable of all Turandots, has called her "ecstasy of fear" (Ashbrook and Powers 161)—and the transcendent terror that, perhaps, only the soprano voice can evoke, there is the matter of Puccini's singular struggle in the compositional process: to deny, musically and dramatically, that his heroine is really unattainable or "frigid," that these outward signs do not match her "true essence." She must, after all, be reclaimed as a sexual object by the male symbolic order. If according to the Puccinian scheme of things, she were a mezzo-soprano or contralto, her sexual "difference" would reveal her as unredeemable a priori, and there would be no opera. But in *Suor Angelica* the "woman beware woman" subplot Puccini and his librettists subsequently superimposed on Gozzi's play, a subplot that would counteract the idea that the non- or anti [hetero]sexual woman could feel compassion—much less passion—for another woman, had been set in motion.

To subdue, to "convert" the lesbian has long been a male fantasy, and to this task Giacomo Puccini devoted the last four years of his life. Throughout this period the composer issued a series of missives to Adami and Simoni, exhorting, cajoling, threatening, and pleading with them to refashion the old comedy in a manner that would culminate in the realization of his ultimate goal: to "exalt Turandot's amorous passion which she has smothered for so long beneath the ashes of her great pride" (Ashbrook 199). Complying with Puccini's instructions to "slim it down and make it effective" (Carner 224), the librettists methodically stripped Gozzi's play of seemingly extraneous matter and, in doing so, stripped Turandot herself bare of those devices by which she had, in her earlier incarnations, maintained her subjectivity and sexual difference and diffidence.

As if to strip away the primary outward sign of her lesbianism, Puccini and his collaborators effectively deny her the female companionship she had heretofore retained. Not only are Zelima and Schirina eliminated à la Busoni, but even the faithless Adelma and the large chorus of female retainers are dispatched. All that remains of Turandot's "harem," presumably for reasons of musical contrasts, is the small ensemble of handmaidens who, in act 1, scold the noisy and noisome ministers Ping, Pang, and Pong for disturbing their mistress' sleep. Only briefly can they lovingly vocalize that "darkness is filled with her fragrance" before the serenade of the *femmine ciarliere* (chattering women) is quickly silenced by the disparaging shouts of Puccini's agents of misogyny.[28]

Early in the compositional process Puccini instructed Simoni and Adami not to "make too much of those Venetian masks," the typecast character who not only provided wry commentary but acted as signifiers of unsanctioned sexuality for both Gozzi and Busoni, warning that "they must not thrust themselves on

Fig. 10.3. Turandot (Dame Eva Turner) and her women: the most salient feature of lesbian identity is reduced to a mere ensemble in Puccini's opera. *Courtesy of Royal Opera House, Covent Garden.*

the attention and be petulant." In response the librettists suggested eliminating them altogether, but Puccini relented, suggesting that they "do a little of what Shakespeare often does, when he brings in three or four extraneous types who drink, use bad language, and speak ill of the King" (Carner 227). To this end, the "Italian" masks Truffaldino, Brighella, Pantalone, and Tartaglia—each of whom had his own inclinations and worldview—are dismissed and replaced by the "Chinese" Ping, Pang, and Pong, who, as their names suggest, are virtually indistinguishable in all but their vocal ranges. Like Shakespearean clowns, the new masks are free to speak what would otherwise be unspeakable, what would be ideologically impolitic and impractical (but not imprecise) if articulated by the more "noble" characters. They are, moreover, both unquestionably heterosexual *and* misogynistic. Thus, while Turandot is effectively stripped of one more marker of her unauthorized sexuality, these cynics without conviction are able to inform the audience about just what is *wrong*—not with the king, as Puccini indicated in his instructions, but with his daughter—and predict the ultimate dire effects of her nonconformity on the fate of the nation.

Their function in their first appearance is not so much to discourage Calaf from his endeavor—their attempts in this regard are in vain—so much as to draw a portrait of the man-hating female monster, an image they subsequently enlarge, only to destroy in their collective imaginary. For the greater portion of act 2, scene 1, Ping, Pang, and Pong have the stage to themselves. In this extended ensemble they prepare for the outcome of Calaf's upcoming trial, be it a wedding or a funeral. They suggest that either, in the short run, is all the same to them. Yet these bureaucrats break off to decry that Chinese history and society, peaceful for "seventy thousand centuries," has been thrown into chaos "since the birth of Turandot," who, in the last three years has been responsible for the executions of twenty-six unfortunate princes. They then proceed to indulge in a reverie about the tranquil provincial homes and sacred books they have left behind for this boring labor, but, brought back to the present by the sound of a crowd clamoring for another execution, they return to their abiding concern—the effects of female sexual rebellion on nation and governance. If no man can subdue the stubborn princess, then "Goodbye, love! Goodbye, race! Goodbye divine issue! It's the end of China!" Such concerns would become all too common and all too strident throughout Europe within a decade, and regimes that concerned themselves with racial superiority would punish the racial "disloyalty" of women who elected not to reproduce their own kind. Yet, we can safely assume, audiences have glossed over this sentiment, displacing it with ironic if unconscious racism onto the "Chinese" notions of the masks.[29] To stave off potential national extinction, the ministerial trio pray to a supposedly Chinese deity (Tiger, "grand marshall of the sky") to "make the grand long-awaited night come, the night of surrender," in which they will prepare the wedding bed of the "vanquished and languorous" princess, who will "lie powerless in [her] husband's arms." As they anticipate their "great good fortune" on the night when "there is no longer a woman in China who spurns love," they describe for the audience's delectation the events that will occur, culminating in "the beautiful unclad body now initiated into the mystery." Thus they effectively punish and humiliate the "proud" princess through a fantasy-projection rape, one that anticipates her sexual subjugation as Calaf forcibly rips the veil from her face and kisses her in the opera's conclusion.

Puccini's most effective denuding of Turandot, however, is accomplished through the stripping away of her very subjectivity. Not only is she a woman without perceptible conscience, but one without personal history, motivation, or interiority. In Gozzi's original the task she imposed on her suitors had both motive and logic, albeit comic and skewed. If men were so self-destructive and mindless as to undertake the trial, they accordingly deserved their share of blame for their fate. Yet, in Puccini's hands, Turandot does not, cannot simply explain that she has a distaste for men and marriage; indeed, as a character more spoken about than speaking, she is deprived of the means and opportunity to express her thoughts or emotions and is thereby rendered a creature devoid of anything that resembles depth psychology. In lieu of any compelling reason for her hatred of men, Puccini and his librettists create for her an impelling history, one neither her own nor belonging to anyone's recent memory. When she finally utters a word, after half the opera has already passed, Turandot offers her justification, as it were. "Many thousand years ago," she explains, her virginal ancestress Princess Lou-Ling reigned "in silence and pure joy, defying the abhorred tyranny of man," until her empire was conquered and she was abducted, presumably raped, and murdered. (Given this history, we might be hard-pressed to figure how Turandot could be the *direct* descendant of Lou-Ling, but this incongruity only contributes to the overall impression that she is truly unreasonable.) Styling herself Lou-Ling reincarnated, she enacts her ritual humiliation and execution of men in order to take revenge "for her purity, her cry, and her death." This is, of course, a far more difficult explanation to counter rationally than "I abhor your sex, and I defend myself in the only way I know"; it is also less likely to stir any audience sympathy or empathy. Yet, in the Puccinian schemata, it is far more easily remediable, simply because it bears so little resemblance to any woman's mundane struggles or experience of reality.

Ironically, the nonlogic and the unlikeliness of Turandot's self-defense, while erasing the ostensibly lesbian motivation granted her in Gozzi's text, only serves to realign her with the lesbian according to fin-de-siècle constructs. If the story of Lou-Ling seems a figment of an overwrought imagination and an insufficient motivation for twenty-six executions and another potential one in the works, then it merely coincides with the assessment of Lombroso and Ferrero that murderous and "erotically criminal" women are possessed of a hatred of the male sex that "has no cause whatever, and springs from blind and innate perversity" (Dijkstra 325; Lombroso and Ferrero 157). If this ancestral narrative is given any credence, however, it evokes the fear of atavism and Amazonism—almost inevitably linked with lesbianism—that haunted the period. As Carner points out (460), the Lou-Ling narrative, invented and interpolated by Puccini and his librettists, resembles the story of Queen Tanais, whose land by the Black Sea was invaded by Vexoris, the King of Ethiopia. Though Tanais was forced to marry her invader, her fate was quite the opposite of Lou-Ling's; she stabbed her conqueror to death on their wedding night, which not only gave the signal to her countrywomen to follow her example and annihilate Vexoris's men, but led to the founding of an all-female state. This tale was much in circulation during the decades preceding Puccini's opera, as Penthesilea tells it to Achilles as an originary myth of the Amazon nation in Heinrich von Kleist's play bearing her name.[30] The story of Turandot's own origins, then, would not only evoke for the cognoscenti the fearful prehistorical state of "degeneration" and male subjugation but also the inexplicable and sadistic bloodlust with which Kleist characterizes the mythic Amazon defender of Troy, for whom killing and cannibalizing her bridegroom is much the same as the consummation of the wedding bed. We come to understand that Turandot, whether rational or irrational, has dangerous lesbianic tendencies, and, according to the lights of fin-de-siècle sexological discourse, is innately perverted beyond a doubt.

Although Lombroso and Ferrero would deem such women beyond remedy, Puccini, ever the romantic, believed in the curative powers of [hetero]sexual love. Thus, he provided Turandot with a role model, so she might learn the value and meaning of "Love." Liù, the slave-attendant of Timur, has no antecedant in Gozzi, and is, in almost every way, the polar opposite of the devious princess-turned-slave Adelma, with whom she shares only a past acquaintance with Calaf. Long before the audience sees or hears Turandot, Liù is present: the first solo voice, after the Mandarin's opening proclamation, to rise above the tumultuous crowd. Leading her elderly blind master through the crowd, she cries for help. When they encounter the long lost Calaf in the midst of this chaos, he does not know her. No matter, she replies, "I am nothing . . . a slave, my lord." But she remembers him "because once in the Palace you smiled at me"—and thus she is able to bear any pain or sorrow her servitude and abjection may bring. She is the opera's Mother-Surrogate of Sorrows, the heiress, as Clément notes, "to the sacrificed women Puccini could make sing their hearts out" (101). In her first aria she recounts her sorrows and declares that "Liù can bear no more," but for "the remembrance of a smile"—and for the power the powerless can attain through passive-aggressive manipulation—she will bear far more.

The opera moves along, through the first two acts, more or less in keeping with narrative expectations. Calaf solves the riddles, Turandot balks, and the Unknown Prince offers his life in exchange for her unlocking the mystery of his identity by the next dawn. But with the beginning of act 3, things fall apart. In short order Turandot's lackeys circulate the word that the public will cooperate in discovering The Name under pain of death. Seemingly oblivious to the "subdued and desperate" women's voices around him, lamenting "we shall have to die, alas, die," Calaf rapturously declares his impending victory and disdains the threats and pleas of the crowd as well as the bribes proffered by Ping, Pang, and Pong. Timur and Liù, now hostages, are dragged in by the mob. Turandot and her entourage arrive on the scene.

For a self-described "nothing," the shining moment has come—the opportunity to be Someone, to be an agent of Destiny, to throw a wrench into the plot. With an audience as captive in its way as she is, Liù announces that she knows The Name—but will not divulge it under any circumstances. Thus she offers herself up to public torture. When Turandot commands the over eager mob to stop and "let her be," the heathen virgin-martyr of unrequited romantic love demands, in quasi-religious language that recalls the Marquis de Sade's *Justine*, to be allowed her to enjoy her passion: "My secret undeclared love [is] so great that these tortures are sweet to me because I offer them to my Lord. . . . Bind me! Torture me! Let me suffer every torment as the supreme offering of my love for him!"[31] While Turandot stands "fascinated and confused," the slave confronts—affronts—the princess in words Puccini himself bestowed upon her: "You who are girded in ice . . . " (Ashbrook 207). No sooner does she make her apostrophe than she grabs a dagger from an unwary soldier and, with virtually all of Peking as her witnesses, stabs herself to death.

And *then* what happens? After a public suicide, almost anything else would be anticlimactic. *Something*, nevertheless, *must* happen—but what? The answer is ultimately and inevitably a matter of perspective. On a purely literal narrative plane, the following transpires: the ever-fickle crowd (including Ping, Pang, and Pong) goes off to bury and mourn "little Liù," leaving Turandot alone with Calaf. (Where did her attendants go?) He tears off her veil, kisses her, and tells her his name. The day dawns, and together the pair go to face Altoum and the assembly of sages. "Father," she announces, "his name is Love!" The crowd exclaims *Glo ria a te!* The opera is over.

What we can infer from the events of the last act is, as Joseph Kerman suggests, "that the way to proceed with a frigid beauty is to get your hands on her. Then she will shout 'Love' " (206). Even with the presupposition that she is "frigid," the lesbian knows this message far too well: "If only the right man . . . " Kerman senses the false logic at play:

> Puccini does nothing to rationalize . . . or illuminate the characters. . . . There is simply no insight into any emotions that might possibly be imagined in any of the situations. . . . Most damaging of all, Turandot's surrender has no motivation, except the obvious physical one. (206)

But just how "obvious" is the physical motivation for Turandot *really*? Until the last five minutes of the opera, she is still trying to make a deal with Calaf, to make him go away, to call the whole thing off. Let us try another explanation, then. "What has happened?" Catherine Clément asks, and replies, "Nothing. Just a woman who gives up and gets married" (100). Yes, Turandot gives up. But why? Is she giving into the demands of her angry subjects, who, in their collective guilt, have chosen Liù as the newest object of veneration? Perhaps, but the crowd, who constitutes a collective persona in this drama, has already demonstrated its ability to change allegiance in a moment, calling for blood and calling for clemency, in the case of the Prince of Persia, in alternative breaths. Did the example of Liù's self-destruction impress the cruel princess to the point of her enacting her own symbolic suicide?[32] *Turandot tramanta!* she cries, "Turandot is ending! . . . My glory is finished!"[33] The Turandot who was is no more. But did she jump or was she pushed? Can "Love," capitalized and all-conquering, really bring about such a sudden and uncharacteristic transformation, really be her motivation? Despite the vague metaphysical proclamation "His name is Love," she never, in fact, says that she loves Calaf. Turandot gives up and gets married, that much is true. Perhaps she does so because the old aphorism "Love conquers all" really means that the force of masculine desire that calls itself by the name brooks no dissent. Perhaps. But, more likely, she gives up because the opera has to end somehow, sometime, somewhere. And so another story, a true story, emerges . . .

If she killed twenty-six men, she killed a twenty-seventh.

For four years Giacomo Puccini struggled with the composition of *Turandot*, vascillating wildly between manic exhiliration and abject depression, wishing at times for a "charming, light, sentimental subject," threatening to return money advanced by his publishers in order to free himself from "that Chinese world" (Carner 230, 233). The work, nevertheless, went forward, and the world premiere of *Turandot* was scheduled to take place at La Scala in April 1925. In September 1924, as he set about composing the final act of Turandot, Puccini wrote to Adami, detailing his plans for the opera's *gran finale*: "It must be a great duet. These two beings, who stand, so to speak, outside the world, are transformed into humans through love and this love must take possession of everybody on the stage in an orchestral peroration" (Carner 229). Puccini would never write this duet, this transformation of the monster, the woman "outside the world," into a "human." Even as he wrote this missive, his work was impaired by the cancer growing in his throat and causing him constant pain. He composed Liù's death scene; then, before the end of the year, Puccini was dead. He was never able to reconcile the marriage-resisting princess to the institution of men that calls itself "Love." Turandot had claimed her final victim. It is at this point that the opera ended.

But the show must go on. Arturo Toscanini, whom Puccini had designated to conduct the first performance and to whom the incomplete work was entrusted, called in the hapless and now obscure composer Franco Alfano to decipher Puccini's notes and somehow make the opera presentable. But Toscanini, in the end, knew this endeavor was futile. At the world premiere of the opera in April 1926, the maestro stopped the performance after the death of Liù, announcing that at this point the composer ceased his work, that death had in this case been stronger than art.[34] It was, as Clément suggests, "the only real performance of *Turandot*" (101).

Turandot, in a sense does not, cannot end; but, ironically, the opera ends the long tradition of Italian grand opera as a genre. After *Turandot* some things, strange things, will take place on the operatic stage. A woman whose lesbianism is beyond a doubt will find a niche in a German opera, one that in its own way marks the end of operatic "decadence" and "realism." But Countess Geschwitz—like Liù—will die the self-sacrificial martyr of unrequited love.

And opera would never be able to present violent and disturbing sexual fantasies about evil and cruel women who reject the "Love" of men with the efficiency, economy, and vividness that its new rival, the cinema, could and to this day still does.[35]

Epilogue: Turandot, Present and Future

In the future Turandot will be heterosexual; not through the process of giving up and getting married, but heterosexual a priori.[36] Indeed, in many cases, she is already so. In making this observation qua prognostication, I may seem to be not only undercutting but dismissing the argument, which I have just gone to some length to present, that Turandot has always been a lesbian. Yet what I wish to point out in concluding is that while Turandot *has been* a lesbian in the past—whether we have noticed or understood it or not—she is already moving away from that orientation for a variety of complex reasons, the most salient of which have to do with the ever shifting cultural zeitgeist and changes in women's social conditions.

Semiotics, particularly those of an unspeakable or unnameable variety, rarely remain constant. Earlier, I mentioned another work contemporary with Puccini's *Turandot*, T. S. Eliot's *The Waste Land*. Teaching undergraduates in several sections of Victorian and Modern British literature survey courses in recent years, I have observed that the only students who consistently recognize and understand Eliot's polemic against nonreproductive sexuality are those of a fundamentalist Christian persuasion (who, accordingly, write papers praising the poem as "the greatest literary work in the English language" while failing to grasp the semiotics of virtually any other text on the syllabus). Students more attuned to the present (and thus, in many cases, endowed with a sort of antipathy toward history) are more apt to interpret "I had not thought death had undone so many," vis-à-vis the unappetizing sexual encounters represented in the poem, as an AIDS elegy. It would be easy—too easy—to dismiss this as just another example of naive and reductive undergraduate reader-response criticism. But consider the new status of *La Traviata*, both on stage and in the imaginary, as an AIDS opera.[37] Can *La Bohème* be far behind? Imagine Puccini's surprise . . .

But Puccini's Turandot, like Gozzi's before her, is a creation of a given culture and time. She is not a princess of timeless, ancient China; she is, rather, an artifact of 1920s European modernism. If we were to replace her privilege and her chinoiserie with poverty and ill-fitting tweeds, she would bear an uncanny resemblance to another unhappy and closeted fictional lesbian presented to the public in 1926, the suggestively named Miss Kilman in Virginia Woolf's *Mrs Dalloway*. As Woolf's frustrated scholar lacks the power or position to "kill man" literally—or, for that matter, to love woman—she turns to gluttony, religiosity, and asociality, the only means of destroying opposition and creating what feels like subjectivity she has at her disposal. Yet, as Woolf shows by contrast, the alternative to such sociopathic behavior for the repressed lesbian, that chosen by Clarissa Dalloway and Sally Seton, is to give up and get married.

At the end of the twentieth century the behaviors and choices of Woolf's characters, while more "realistic" than Turandot's, bear almost as little similarity to those of women clearly identified as lesbians as do those of the man-hating princess. It is incumbent upon the lesbian critic, however, to identify these historical semiotics and modes of conduct, regardless of how unlikely or unappealing we find them, lest, in their erasure, we find ourselves once more trapped in them, enacting them once more, imagining Turandot as a role model. For this reason, I expose Turandot's lesbian past before it slips from our sight altogether.

How these stories trap you! How they latch onto your heart, there or somewhere else!

If Turandot will soon be a lesbian no longer, it is due only in part to changing signs and significations. Perhaps she will be heterosexual because lesbians will no longer have any need to emulate her. Many years ago, I admired Turandot's *je ne sais quoi* as a means of coping with something within me that I dared not identify by any name, not even to myself. I felt this as a result of the overwhelming expectations placed on me to marry and "be normal" in a time and place where "alternative lifestyles" were not within the realm of possibilities, nor were they even spoken of, except in the most derisive terms. But as I look at young lesbians who are now the age I was then, I realize that they have no need to fantasize about annihilating men (a relatively common fantasy back in the seventies and eighties, remember?) because they will not be forced into what Adrienne Rich has so accurately termed compulsory heterosexuality. Nor, for that matter, was I, in the long run; my own need for such escapist narratives is long past.

This is not to say that heterosexual women have arrived at the same point. Perhaps women who continue to interact with men on an intimate, constant basis might continue to have Turandot-like impulses. I turn, then, to some of them for their opinions. Eva Marton, perhaps *the* Turandot of her generation, offers a contemporary and clearly heterosexual perspective on the princess' motivations:

> I see Turandot as a very simple, very normal girl. What makes her different is her power. . . . As a symbol of power she is the object of constant public adu-

> lation. It is therefore natural she shouldn't want to offer herself to any willing Tom, Dick, and Harry, regardless of their princely lineage. She will only yield to someone special, exceptional. That's all.
>
> (Matheopoulos 123)

Truly, La Marton completely dispenses with all pathology and all history in her self-described "essential view" of the role and surely her tone suggests a reaction to the suggestion that something neither "simple" nor "normal" attains nonetheless (Matheopoulos 123)—yet for a heterosexual woman interpreting what must seem an otherwise inexplicable character for a postmodern audience it is possibly her only viable option.

I look also, obliquely, to Fay Weldon, the contemporary novelist, for an explanation. If Turandot's literary counterpart of the 1920s was Doris Kilman, then in the present day it must be Ruth Patchett, the protagonist of Weldon's

Fig. 10.4. Turandot (Eva Marton). "A very simple, normal girl." Lyric Opera of Chicago. *Courtesy of Tony Romano.*

The Life and Loves of a She-Devil. While lesbianism outside the closet was not possible for Woolf's character, it is for Ruth, who dabbles in it as one of a series of experimental lives in the course of her narrative. But Ruth rejects the relative placidity of life with another woman in order to pursue the excitement only to be found in revenge and the ongoing psychological warfare between the sexes. The She-Devil, who looks to men for [in]validation and meaning, would understand a Turandot who seeks revenge and takes pleasure in decapitating men. She would also understand Liù, inasmuch as she has a similar foil and rival in Mary Fisher, a writer of popular romances who is "prone to fainting and weeping and sleeping with men while pretending that she doesn't" (6), and who fades away and dies, worn out by the harsh demands of *Love*. To Ruth and Mary, Turandot's motivations and actions would not only seem unquestionably *straight* but also sympathetic—if not enviable.

At the end of Weldon's novel, Ruth observes from a distance her lesbian daughter. "She will never make a she-devil," she snorts (264). As a lesbian she has no need to be, nor do the many young women who can be the lesbians that they are. They do not need the lesbian monster as a exemplar. But still there are those for whom the closet remains the only choice . . .

What are we to do, so far as *Turandot* is concerned, for the time being? Albert Innaurato, taking umbrage at the "values" the opera projects, comes close to suggesting that there is nothing in the work "to justify its constant repetition" (11). I do not agree, nor would I have the opera that is, in fact, Puccini's masterpiece banished from the stage or disc. I would, however, make one significant change: *leave the opera as Puccini left it*.

As Wayne Koestenbaum has so eloquently observed, Alfano's conclusion "is unsatisfying, and only reminds the listener that the opera virtually died with Puccini, that *Turandot* isn't a whole body, that Calaf never finally arrived at Turandot, and that the gong, the disc, through which we first entered Turandot's vocal universe, was just a mirror" (74). What this mirror reflects, if we look into it unflinchingly, is the fragmentation that affects us all when sexual dishonesty, deceit, and hubris is the rule rather than the exception. Thus, Puccini's opera, left in its fragmented state—with Liù dead, Calaf desiring, and Turandot unsubdued, with the plot frozen in a deadlock—is the most honest performance of the story that can be given. For as long as compulsory heterosexuality retains its force anywhere, there will be a lesbian Turandot somewhere. And, for her sake, we cannot end this opera.

Notes

This essay is dedicated with much respect and affection to Professor Violet L. Jordain, who remembers me from California State University, Dominguez Hills, in Carson, California, or son mill'anni e mille, *and knows how many years ago this essay began as a paper in an undergraduate Shakespeare course.*

1. Quoted on the flyleaf of *The Present and the Past*.

2. All citations of the libretto are from the Italian text and the English translation by Laura Mardon, both included in the booklet that accompanies the 1972 London recording. I have refrained from using the ostensibly "authoritative" original Ricordi edition, as the Italian text differs considerably, if not particularly meaningfully, from what is actually sung in virtually every recorded performance. Moreover, the K. H. B. de Jaffa English translation in this edition is not only based on a corrupt text but is, unfortunately, often more fanciful than accurate. I do, however, quote the Ricordi edition in the case of certain stage or vocal directions (e.g., "subdued and desperate," "fascinated and confused") that are omitted in Mardon's translation.

3. This is not to say that Innaurato is completely wrong. Aquinas's teachings on women and female sexuality—and on many other topics—have long been codified as official Roman Catholic doctrine, and while, as Ranke-Heinemann, *Eunuchs for the Kingdom of Heaven*, pp. 177–200, demonstrates, Aquinas is not nearly as venomously misogynistic as his teacher Albertus Magnus, one could hardly deem him "woman-friendly." Yet, as I will subsequently discuss, the misogyny of Puccini's *Turandot* is based more on nineteenth-century medical sexology and fin-de-siècle decadence than it is on traditional Catholic theology, with which the philosophy, as it were, behind most of Puccini's operas is often at odds.

4. See Sergent, *Homosexuality in Greek Myth*, pp. 173–76, 217–23, regarding the homosexual implications of the Hunt of Calydon narrative. Suggestively, Homer's representation of this episode in book 9 of the *Iliad* is a purely homosocial one, with no mention of Atalanta, who figures predominantly in Ovid's version.

5. See Thomas, " 'Was George Frideric Handel Gay?' " regarding Handel's sexuality and its influence on his music.

6. For evidence of an "opera queen" subculture that anticipates that described by Koestenbaum in *The Queen's Throat* by two and a half centuries, see Thomas Gray's 1736 letter to Horace Walpole describing a performance of Handel's *Atalanta* in its premiere season (Deutsch, *Handel: A Documentary Biography*, pp. 410–11).

7. For a Freudian interpretation of the dynamics of the castrato in "heroic" roles in eighteenth-century baroque opera, see Brophy, *Mozart the Dramatist*, pp. 73–79. Brophy also presents an affectionate postmodern spoof of Handel's perversely if not intentionally random cross-gender casting in her imaginary opera *Alitalia* (set in an airport terminal) in her novel *In Transit* (pp. 49–59).

8. Swinburne's sadomasochistic obsession with the figure of the dangerous female "invert" is well-documented by Henderson, *Swinburne: Portrait of a Poet*, pp. 95–105, Foster, *Sex Variant Women in Literature*, pp. 79–80, and Faderman, *Surpassing the Love of Men*, pp. 272–75. Nicholson, who was surely familiar with Sapphism, recoils at any discussion of the "meretricious lechery" of this aspect of Swinburne's work, based as it is on "an experience which is not only transitory but also eccentric" (*Swinburne*, pp. 104, 105).

9. For an insightful discussion of Gissing and *The Odd Woman*, see Showalter, *Sexual Anarchy*, pp. 30–34).

10. The immediate sources of Shakespeare's play, according to Bullough, *Narrative and Dramatic Sources*, pp. 457–76, 511–14, and Satin, *Shakespeare and His Sources*, pp. 120–37, are *Il Pecorone* (1378), an Italian prose narrative by Giovanni Fiorentino, and the *Gesta Romanorum* (c. 1300), a collection of folktales to which the monks who collected them added occasionally incongruous didactic morals. In the former text the trifold test the suitor must undergo is a wry variation on the bed-trick. The latter work includes not only a story of a princess who must choose between three caskets to prove herself a worthy bride to the emperor's son (pp. xliv–xlvii) but also a close variation on the Atalanta myth involving a marriage-resisting princess, footraces, and the triple distractions of a rose garland, a silken belt, and a golden ball (pp. 106–08), and the tale of another royal marriage-resister who forces her emperor father to put her suitors to a seemingly impossible trifold test (pp. 124–25), thus anticipating the actions of Turandot in Gozzi's play.

11. See Pequigney, "The Two Antonios and Same-Sex Love," for a thoughtful and insightful discussion of Shakespeare's treatment of homosexual love and desire.

12. Portia's curious relationship with the patriarchy is provocatively delineated by Leventen, "Patrimony and Patriarchy," pp. 59–79.

13. In some texts the title is rendered *Re Turandot* (King Turandot), making apparent the author's ridicule of the protagonist's pretentions to masculinity and masculine authority. The alternative spelling Turandotte is also given in some editions.

14. For an excellent, concise, and accessible Kristevan analysis of Turandot and her relationship to language and the symbolic order, see Emery, "Introduction," pp. 14–15.

15. Because Gozzi's *Turandot* has not been readily available to English-language readers and is thus relatively unfamiliar, I am providing a basic synopsis of the plot at this juncture. Since 1989 several English translations of Gozzi's major works have appeared. The best is easily the witty and lively one by Bermel and Emery (supplemented by Emery's excellent notes and introduction), which I use as the source of my citations, unless otherwise noted.

16. I cite here the translation of this passage by Ashbrook and Powers in their exhaustive study of Puccini's opera and its background, *Puccini's Turandot*, p. 51, as I find it a more accurate rendering of Gozzi's original ("Sappia questo gentil popol de' maschi, / Ch'io gli amo tutto. Al pentimento mio / Deh, qualche segno di perdon si faccia") than Bermel and Emery's less compromising "Gentlemen, I once hated your sex, but I have repented. Please give me a sign of your forgiveness" (p. 183). Indeed Gozzi, in representing Turandot's submission to and assimilation into institutional heterosexuality, does not merely allow her to declare that she no longer hates men but rather requires her to proclaim that she now loves them (and, by implication, has really done so all along).

17. See also Faderman, *Surpassing the Love of Men,* pp. 26–27. It is noteworthy that Casanova, early in his career of conquests, was a violinist in the orchestra of Teatro di San Samuele, the house with which Gozzi and his works are most closely identified (*Memoirs* 2:298–310 passim). Casanova's descriptions of the ethos of Venice in the 1740s and 1750s—the period during which Gozzi began his literary endeavors—indi-

cates that one as concerned with "maintaining good morals" as Gozzi would certainly have much to dread (Emery, "Introduction," p. 9).

18. For background in earlier (i.e., medieval and Renaissance) female homosexuality in Italy and its connections to convent life, see Brown, *Immodest Acts*. On civil and clerical punishment of lesbianism from the medieval period through the dawn of the Enlightenment, see Crompton, "The Myth of Lesbian Impunity."

19. For an exhaustive study of the iconography of "feminine evil" as well an examination of the various sexological types and their influence on the arts, see Dijkstra, *Idols of Perversity* passim. Victorian concepts of female sexual monstrosity are treated at length in Auerbach, *Woman and the Demon*, as well, while a particularly lesbian slant on literary representations of these figure is offered by Faderman, *Surpassing the Love of Men,* pp. 254–94.

20. Indeed, Turandot had had at least half a dozen operatic settings—none of which were critical or popular successes—prior to Busoni's. Several of Gozzi's other plays have served as the sources for opera, most notably *L'amore delle tre melarance* (Prokofiev's *The Love of the Three Oranges*), *Il re cervo* (Hans Werner Henze's *König Hirsch*), and *La donna serpente* (Wagner's *Die Feen*). For discussions of Busoni's *Turandot* and its lesser-known predecessors, see Ashbrook and Powers, *Puccini's Turandot*, pp. 52–58, and Beaumont, *Busoni the Composer*, pp. 76–86.

21. For Ismael, the tutor of the ill-starred Prince of Samarkand, Busoni has substituted his mother, Die Königinmutter von Samarkand, who speaks the tutor's lines with minimal alteration from the original, and who is, quite incongruously, described as "eine Mohrin," or "a negress." How or why an African—or, at any rate, a North African—woman is a monarch of a Central Asian realm is never elucidated, either in the course of her brief appearance or elsewhere (although it may be related to the "geographic confusion" of the Amazon originary myth in Kleist's *Penthesilea* [see note 30 below]), and her entourage of female retainers vocalizes a not very mournful dirge that sounds like a cross between a Native American war chant and European fantasies of "Oriental" melody.

22. Indeed, not until 1993 were commercial recordings of Busoni's *Turandot* readily available: as of this writing, both Kent Nagano's recording of the 1991 Opera de Lyon production (coupled with *Arlecchino*, Busoni's other commedia dell'arte opera) and a Berlin radio performance conducted by Gerd Albrecht. As Bill Zakariasen notes in his review of these recordings, the opera is characterized by "Italianate melody that was never to turn sentimental or sensual" (p. 50); thus, despite these deservedly praised recordings, the opera seems unlikely to inspire any significant revival.

23. With the exception of women in Scandinavian nations—which, significantly, remained neutral during World War I—European and American women were ineligible to vote at the beginning of hostilities. While many nations granted women suffrage rights during or immediately after the armistice, this was not the case in predominantly Catholic countries. French and Italian women, for example, were not enfranchised until 1944 and 1946, respectively. Echoes of *The Waste Land* resonate in Turandot; prior to the execution of the Prince of Persia, a procession of boys sings, to the traditional Chinese

tune "Mo-li-hua": "Over on the Eastern Mountains the stork sang. But April did not bloom again, the snow did not thaw. From the desert to the sea do you not hear a thousand voices whisper: 'Princess, come to me! Everything will blossom, everything will shine!' " (Là sui monti dell'Est la cicogna cantò. / Ma l'april non rifiorì, ma la neve non sgelò. / Dal deserto al mar non odi tu mille voci sospirar: / "Principessa, scendi a me! Tutto fiorirà, tutto splenderà!") Like Eliot, Puccini's librettists heterosexualize nature and, through the tacit invocation of a Great Chain of Being, place blame for infertility in nature on a lack of "natural" heterosexuality in the hierarchy of the social order (i.e., Turandot herself). As if to underscore the need for reproductive sexuality, particularly after a series of wars the unmarriageable princess has caused (vide Gozzi), these sentiments are placed in the mouths of male children. For an examination of the complex dynamics of female guilt and blame in relation to the war and the reflection of and reaction to this social and emotional manipulation in literature of the modernist period, including *The Waste Land*, see Gilbert and Gubar, *Sexchanges*, pp. 258–323. On the role of female "lack of restraint" (p. 54) in the creation of *The Waste Land*, see Bush, *T. S. Eliot,* pp. 53–58 passim.

24. Carner offers a succinct description of verismo, an influential if ultimately short-lived movement in turn-of-the-century Italian opera:

> The paramount feature of *verismo* is excess, the uninhibited inflation of every dramatic and emotional moment. Climax follows climax in swift succession and moods are no sooner established than they are destroyed. . . . Characters are presented over-lifesize and are swept along in a whirlwind of passions in which sex becomes the driving force. Erotic desire is always thrwarted and thus leads to acts of insensate jealousy and savage revenge, acts—and this is characteristic—almost invariably committed on the *open* stage so as to score a direct hit at the spectator's sensibility. (*Puccini: A Critical Biography*, p. 258)

As an artistic movement, verismo was greatly influenced by French realism and the Decadents, and many veristic plots had their sources in French literature. Whereas the often sentimental Puccini was never completely in the verismo camp, the erotic sensationalism that is present in most of his work indicates the movement's profound influence on him. For a discussion of the artistic relations between Puccini and the *veristi*, see Carner, *Puccini: A Critical Biography*, pp. 257–63.

25. Matteo suggestively claims that Conchita "decapitates" him through her insults (Louÿs, *Woman and Puppet*, p. 215). For a discussion of *La Femme et Le Pantin* in the context of the "headhuntress" as an icon in fin-de-siècle art and literature, see Dijkstra, *Idols of Perversity*, pp. 384–85.

26. While giving artistic difficulties as the official reason for his abandonment, Puccini adamantly denied in a letter to his publisher Giulio Ricordi that he had done so out of "*fear* . . . of the *pruderie* of the Anglo-Saxon audiences of Europe and America. It was not the example of *Salome* in New York" (Carner, *Puccini: A Critical Biography*, pp. 155–56; italics original). But Puccini was in New York for the Metropolitan Opera pre-

miere of *Madama Butterfly* in January 1907, when Strauss's opera, also being making its Metropolitan debut, was met with public outrage and withdrawn after one performance. It was not performed at the Metropolitan again for twenty-seven years. In an interview with the *New York Times* Puccini stated, "I haven't begun work on *La Femme et Le Pantin*. I have doubts if the American public would accept that after the treatment *Salome* recently received" (Jackson, *Monsieur Butterfly*, p. 159). Indeed, *La Bohème*, *Tosca*, and *Madama Butterfly* had all inspired a certain amount of moral protest in the United States, although nothing on such a grand scale. The ever avaricious Puccini was no doubt mindful of the disastrous financial consequences such protests entailed. Despite critical acclaim, boxholder boycotts of the 1909 Manhattan Opera production of *Salome* precipitated that company's fiscal demise (Dizikes, *Opera in America*, pp. 313–15, 333–34). Conchita nevertheless had her day (or, more precisely, days) in the cultural spotlight. Having obligated themselves legally and financially to Louÿs, Puccini's publishers salvaged the project by turning it over to Riccardo Zandonai, a promising younger composer under contract to the firm, best known subsequently for his opera *Francesca di Rimini*. Zandonai's *Conchita*, with libretto by Carlo Zangarini (who collaborated with Puccini on *La Fanciulla del West*) had its premiere in 1911, and briefly enjoyed considerable popular success (Rasponi, *The Last Prima Donnas*, pp. 298, 301). Louÿs's novel has also served as the basis for Josef von Sternberg's 1935 film *The Devil is a Woman* (starring Marlene Dietrich) and Luis Buñuel's 1977 film *That Obscure Object of Desire*.

27. Certain generalities may be observed in Puccini's usually minimal mezzo-soprano or contralto roles. Aside from the various nuns in *Suor Angelica*, they are either racial others (Tigrana in *Edgar*, Suzuki in *Madama Butterfly*, or Wowkle in *La Fanciulla del West*) or elderly (La Zia Principessa, La Frugola in *Il Tabarro*, La Zita in *Gianni Schicci*). With the curious exception of the voluptuous but masculine Tigrana—and, to lesser extent, the inarticulate "squaw" Wowkle—they are treated as nonsexual beings, and all, to Puccini's taste at least, are sexually undesirable. Suggestively, *Suor Angelica*, in which all characters other than La Zia Principessa are nuns, is the composer's only work with a predominance of lower female voices, demonstrating the "difference" between Angelica and her fellow convent-dwellers. The "lesbian" quality and appeal of the mezzo and contralto voices, which, I believe, is subliminally at work in Puccini's antipathy, has been explored by Wood, "Sapphonics," pp. 27–66, and Castle, *The Apparitional Lesbian*, pp. 200–38.

28. Curiously, although this ensemble requires two soloists, the singers are rarely given individual credit on recording or performance cast listings—while the male singer who enunciates the Prince of Persia's sole vocal contribution (the offstage cry "Turandot!") generally is credited. After Turandot's women withdraw from the stage, the next group to interrupt Ping, Pang, and Pong's diatribes are the ghosts of the unsuccessful suitors, sung in part, suggestively, by a chorus of contraltos. Although certainly not intentional on Puccini's part, this curious bit of casting would nonetheless suggest not only that decapitation and castration are indeed equivalent (vide Cixous) but that in the process the suitors became what Turandot would have preferred them to be (i.e., women).

29. The Italian libretto reads "Addio, amore, addio, razza! Addio, stirpe divina! . . . E finisce la China!" I have employed my own translation here as Mardon's vague though not inaccurate translation of these lines diminishes their more sinister racial sentiments. It is worth noting that while Nazi and Fascist regimes punished and executed male homosexuals as "sexual perverts," lesbians were subjected to persecution as "asocials," reflecting the earlier notion that their rebellion against appropriate gender roles would undo social and cultural evolution and thus indicating that lesbianism is in great part a rebellion against one's race (see Haeberle, "Swastika, Pink Triangle"). Though politically naive at best, Puccini, who became an honorary member of the Fascist Party in 1922 (while *Turandot* was in progress), cannot be held entirely blameless in matters of racialist and nationalist politics. On Puccini's political sympathies and his relationship with Fascism, see Osborne, *The Complete Operas*, pp. 250–51, Jackson, *Monsieur Butterfly*, pp. 211–27 passim, 230, 250–51, 255–56, and Carner, *Puccini: A Critical Biography*, pp. 207–11, 217–19, 234, 240–41.

30. Kleist's interpolation of the story of Tanais into a drama about Penthesilea is as anachronistic and ideologically based as that of Lou-Ling in *Turandot*. As Kleinbaum observes, the tale is "a remarkable case of geographic confusion, as well as nineteenth-century fantasies of race and sex" (*The War Against the Amazons,* p. 174). Kleinbaum's insightful discussion of Kleist's *Penthesilea* (pp. 169–80), which is part of a larger discussion of cultural appropriations and misappropriations of Amazonian myths throughout history, provides a useful analysis of the figure of the insatiate, murderous woman in Romantic epistemology, a cultural factor that surely retains much of its former influence on Puccini and his milieu. On *Penthesilea* and the sexual politics of degeneration, see Gilman, *Difference and Pathology*, pp. 193–99; for a provocative analysis of the "Voracity Syndrome," real or imagined, that male-dominated culture attempts to impose on female leaders, see Fraser, *The Warrior Queens*, pp. 11–12 and passim).

31. In his novel subtitled *Good Conduct Well Chastised*, Sade represents the eighteenth-century virgin Justine as a woman duped by an ideology dictating that passivity, suffering, and self-abnegation are the appropriate behaviors of the true Christian. Her graphic sexual torment, then, becomes both her reward and punishment, while Sade's relation of her passion becomes an uncanny and subversive—if, to some, blasphemous—mirroring of the acts of the virgin-martyr saints used as exempla to young girls in their religious and social training. As Liù merely transfers her suffering devotion to a secular (rather than divine) "Lord," it becomes fairly obvious that Puccini and his librettists are, perhaps unconsciously, synthesizing both the saints' acts and Sade's reconfiguration thereof. (See also Butler, *The Lives of the Saints.*) Here, far more than in the character of Turandot, we see in action the "Italian machismo and the misogynistic Catholicism" of which Innaurato complains (note 3 above).

32. This seems, at least, to have been Puccini's intention. He wrote to Adami that he felt "Liù must sacrifice herself because of some sorrow but I don't see how this can be developed unless we make her die under torture. And why not? Her death could be an element in softening the heart of the Princess" (Carner, *Puccini: A Critical Biography*, p. 232). Whether this desired effect has been realized, however, is another matter.

33. Translation mine.

34. Or words to that effect, at any rate. Toscanini's statement has been recorded with considerable variation from source to source.

35. We need only consider, for example, the bisexual ice pick murderess of the recent film *Basic Instincts* to test the veracity of this statement. That *Turandot* ends the grand opera tradition, which, since the 1920s, has been superannuated by the cinema, is the basic premise of Ashbrook and Powers's text (*Puccini's Turandot*, pp. 3–11).

36. Or she could become a man—a drag queen, to be precise. Vera Galupe-Borszkh (Ira Siff), of the all-male transvestive La Gran Scena Opera, offers "her" perspective on how best to cope with Puccini's problematic opera:

> It is always a source of controversy how to finish a performance of *Turandot*, as the final duet was composed by Alfano after Maestro Puccini's death. My solution? According to my contract, Calaf had to answer the riddles incorrectly and be removed. Then, instead of presenting Act III, I would descend the long staircase and give a concert of Puccini arias, which were, after all, unquestionably penned by the maestro himself. The audience always loved this, and if the tenor behaved himself I would let him sing 'Nessun dorma' while I had a glass of water.
>
> (Kellow 8)

As with most camp critiques, the suggestion has a veracity and a practicality all its own.

37. See, for example, Koestenbaum, *The Queen's Throat,* p. 45, and Román, " 'It's My Party,' " pp. 207–12. Román discusses the tacit confluence of AIDS and Verdi's opera as subtexts in Terrence McNally's play *The Lisbon Traviata.*

Works Cited

Adami, Giuseppe, and Renato Simoni. Libretto. *Turandot*. Music by Giacomo Puccini, completed by F. Alfano. Trans. K. H. B. de Jaffa. New York: Ricordi, 1926.

Ashbrook, William. *The Operas of Puccini*. New York: Oxford University Press, 1968.

Ashbrook, William, and Harold Powers. *Puccini's Turandot: The End of the Great Tradition*. Princeton: Princeton University Press, 1991.

Atwood, Margaret. *Lady Oracle*. New York: Simon and Schuster, 1976.

Auerbach, Nina. *Woman and the Demon: The Life of a Victorian Myth*. Cambridge: Harvard University Press, 1982.

Beaumont, Antony. *Busoni the Composer*. Bloomington: Indiana University Press, 1985.

Brophy, Brigid. *In Transit*. London: Gay Men's Press, 1989.

——— *Mozart the Dramatist: The Value of His Operas to Him, to His Age, and to Us*. Rev. ed. London: Libris, 1988.

Brown, Judith C. *Immodest Acts: The Life of a Lesbian Nun in Renaissance Italy*. New York: Oxford University Press, 1986.

Bulfinch, Thomas. *The Age of Fable, or Beauties of Mythology*. Ed. J. Loughran Scott. Philadelphia: David McKay, 1898.

Bullough, Geoffrey. *Narrative and Dramatic Sources of Shakespeare*. Vol. 1. 7 vols. London: Routledge, 1957.

Bush, Ronald. *T. S. Eliot: A Study in Character and Style*. New York: Oxford University Press, 1984.

Busoni, Ferruccio. *Turandot*. With Mechthild Gessendorf, Stefan Dahlberg, Franz-Josef Selig, Markus Schäfer, and Gabriele Sima. Cond. Kent Nagano. Choeurs et Orchestre de L'Opera de Lyon. *Arlecchino and Turandot*. Virgin, CDCB 7–59313–2, 1993.

Butler, Alban. *The Lives of the Saints*. Ed. Herbert Thurston, S. J., and Donald Attwater. 12 vols. London: Burns Oates and Washbourne, 1926–1938.

Carner, Mosco. *Puccini: A Critical Biography*. 2d ed. New York: Holmes, 1988.

Casanova de Seingalt, Giacomo Girolamo. *The Memoirs of Jacques Casanova de Seingalt*. Trans. Arthur Machen. Ed. and rev. Frederick A. Blossom. 8 vols. New York: Regency House, 1938.

Castle, Terry. *The Apparitional Lesbian: Female Homosexuality and Modern Culture*. New York: Columbia University Press, 1993.

Cixous, Hélène. "Castration or Decapitation?" *Signs* (1981), 7:141–55.

——— "The Laugh of the Medusa." Trans. Keith Cohen and Paula Cohen. In Elaine Marks and Isabelle de Courtivron, eds., *New French Feminisms*, pp. 245–64. Brighton: Harvester, 1980

Clément, Catherine. *Opera, or the Undoing of Women*. Trans. Betsy Wing. Minneapolis: University of Minnesota Press, 1988.

Compton-Burnett, Ivy. *The Present and the Past*. Harmondsworth: Penguin, 1972.

Crompton, Louis. "The Myth of Lesbian Impunity: Capital Laws from 1270 to 1791." *Journal of Homosexuality* (1980–1981), vol. 6, no. 17.

Dizikes, John. *Opera in America: A Cultural History*. New Haven: Yale University Press, 1993.

Deutsch, Otto Erich. *Handel: A Documentary Biography*. New York: Da Capo, 1974.

Dijkstra, Bram. *Idols of Perversity: Fantasies of Feminine Evil in Fin-de-Siècle Culture*. New York: Oxford University Press, 1986.

Duffy, Maureen. *The Erotic World of Faery*. London: Cardinal, 1989.

Dulong, Claude. "From Conversation to Creation." In Natalie Zemon Davis and Arlette Farge, eds., *Renaissance and Enlightenment Paradoxes*, pp. 395–419. Cambridge: Harvard University Press, 1993. Vol. 3. *A History of Women in the West*. Gen. ed. Georges Duby and Michelle Perrot. 5 vols. Cambridge: Harvard University Press, 1992–1994.

Eliot. T. S. *The Waste Land and Other Poems*. New York: Harcourt, 1934.

Emery, Ted. "Introduction: Carlo Gozzi in Context." In Carlo Gozzi, *Five Tales for the Theatre*, pp. 1–19. Ed. and trans. Albert Bermel and Ted Emery. Chicago: University of Chicago Press, 1989.

Faderman, Lillian. *Surpassing the Love of Men: Romantic Friendship and Love Between Women from the Renaissance to the Present*. New York: Morrow, 1981.

Foster, Jeannette H. *Sex Variant Women in Literature*. Tallahassee: Naiad, 1985.

Fraser, Antonia. *The Warrior Queens*. New York: Vintage, 1990.

Frazer, Sir James George. *The Golden Bough*. Abridged ed. New York: Collier, 1950.

Gesta Romanorum: or, Entertaining Moral Stories. Trans. and ed. Charles Swan. Rev. Wynnard Hooper. New York: Dover, 1959.

Gilbert, Sandra M., and Susan Gubar. *Sexchanges*. New Haven: Yale University Press, 1989. Vol. 2. *No Man's Land: The Place of the Woman Writer in the Twentieth Century*. 3 vols. New Haven: Yale University Press, 1988– .

Gilman, Sander L. *Difference and Pathology: Stereotypes of Sexuality, Race, and Madness*. Ithaca: Cornell University Press, 1985.

Gissing, George. "Fleet-Footed Hester." *A Victim of Circumstances and Other Stories*. Boston: Houghton, 1927.

Gozzi, Carlo. *Turandot*. *Five Tales for the Theatre*, pp. 127–83. Ed. and trans. Albert Bermel and Ted Emery. Chicago: University of Chicago Press, 1989.

Haeberle, Erwin J. "Swastika, Pink Triangle, and Yellow Star: The Destruction of Sexology and the Persecution of Homosexuals in Nazi Germany." In Martin Bauml Duberman, Martha Vicinus, and George Chauncy, Jr., *Hidden from History: Reclaiming the Gay and Lesbian Past*. New York: New American Library.

Handel, George Frideric. *Atalanta*. With Katalin Farkas, Eva Bártfai-Barta, Eva Lax, János Bándi, Jósef Gregor, and László Polgár. Cond. Nicholas McGegan. Savaria Vocal Ensemble. Capella Savaria. Hungaroton, SLPD 12612–14, 1985.

Henderson, Philip. *Swinburne: Portrait of a Poet*. New York: Macmillan, 1974.

Hogwood, Christopher. *Handel*. London: Thames and Hudson, 1984.

Innaurato, Albert. "The Gong Show." *Opera News*, February 2, 1992, pp. 8–11.

Jackson, Stanley. *Monsieur Butterfly: The Story of Giacomo Puccini*. New York: Stein, 1974.

Kellow, Brian. "Notebook." *Opera News*, November 1994, p. 8.

Kerman, Joseph. *Opera as Drama*. Rev. ed. Berkeley: University of California Press, 1988.

Kleinbaum, Abby Wettan. *The War Against the Amazons*. New York: McGraw-Hill, 1983.

Kleist, Heinrich von. *Penthesilea*. *Plays*. Ed. Walter Hinderer. New York: Continuum, 1982.

Koestenbaum, Wayne. *The Queen's Throat: Opera, Homosexuality, and the Mystery of Desire*. New York: Poseidon, 1993.

Lefkowitz, Mary L. *Women in Greek Myth*. Baltimore: Johns Hopkins University Press, 1986.

Leventen, Carol. "Patrimony and Patriarchy in *The Merchant of Venice*." In Valerie Wayne, ed., *The Matter of Difference: Materialist Feminist Criticism of Shakespeare*. Ithaca: Cornell University Press, 1991.

Lombroso, Cesare, and Guglielmo Ferrero. *The Female Offender*. Intro. W. Douglas Morrison. New York: Appleton, 1899.

Louÿs, Pierre. *Woman and Puppet*. *The Collected Works of Pierre Louÿs*. New York: Liveright, 1932.

McNally, Terrence. *The Lisbon Traviata*. *Three Plays*. New York: Plume, 1990.

Matheopoulos, Helena. *Diva: Great Sopranos and Mezzos Discuss Their Art*. Boston: Northeastern University Press, 1991.

Nicholson, Harold. *Swinburne*. London: Macmillan, 1928.

Osborne, Charles. *The Complete Operas of Puccini: A Critical Guide*. New York: Atheneum, 1982.

Ovid. *Metamorphoses*. Trans. Mary M. Innes. Harmondsworth: Penguin, 1955.

Pequigney, Joseph. "The Two Antonios and Same-Sex Love in *Twelfth Night* and *The Merchant of Venice*." *English Literary Renaissance* (1992), 22(2):201–21.

Phillips-Matz, Mary Jane. "Monsters and Maidens: Carlo Gozzi's Vivid Theatrical Fables Continue to Fascinate Audiences." *Opera News,* February 4, 1995, pp. 17+.

Puccini, Giacomo. *Suor Angelica*. With Renata Scotto, Marilyn Horne, and Ileana Cotrubas. Cond. Lorin Maazel. Ambrosian Opera Chorus. New Philharmonia Orchestra. *Il Tritico*. CBS M3K 79312, 1977.

——— *Turandot*. With Joan Sutherland, Luciano Pavarotti, Montserrat Caballé, Nicolai Ghiaurov, Tom Krause, and Peter Pears. Cond. Zubin Mehta. John Aldis Choir. London Philharmonic Orchestra. London 414 274–2, 1973.

Ranke-Heinemann, Uta. *Eunuchs for the Kingdom of Heaven: Women, Sexuality, and the Catholic Church*. Trans. Peter Heinegg. New York: Doubleday, 1990.

Rasponi, Lanfranco. *The Last Prima Donnas*. New York: Limelight, 1990.

Rich, Adrienne. "Compulsory Heterosexuality and Lesbian Existence." In Ann Snitow, Christine Stansell, and Sharon Thompson, eds., *Powers of Desire: The Politics of Sexuality*, pp. 177–205. New York: Monthly Review Press, 1983.

Román, David. " 'It's My Party and I'll Die If I Want To!' Gay Men, AIDS, and the Circulation of Camp in U.S. Theater." In David Bergman, ed., *Camp Grounds: Style and Homosexuality*, pp. 206–33. Amherst: University of Massachusetts Press, 1993.

Sade, Marquis de. *Justine. Justine, Philsophy in the Bedroom, and Other Writings*. Ed. and trans. Richard Seaver and Austryn Wainhouse. New York: Grove, 1965.

Satin, Joseph. *Shakespeare and His Sources*. Boston: Houghton, 1966.

Sergent, Bernard. *Homosexuality in Greek Myth*. Trans. Arthur Goldhammer. Boston: Beacon, 1986.

Shakespeare, William. *The Merchant of Venice. The Riverside Shakespeare*. Ed. G. Blakemore Evans. Boston: Houghton, 1974.

Showalter, Elaine. *Sexual Anarchy: Gender and Culture at the Fin de Siècle*. New York: Penguin, 1991.

Swinburne, Algernon Charles. *Atalanta in Calydon: A Tragedy. The Complete Works of Algernon Charles Swinburne*, 7:259–351. Ed. Sir Edmund Gosse and Thomas James Wise. 20 vols. New York: Russell and Russell, 1968.

Thomas, Gary C. " 'Was George Frideric Handel Gay?': On Closet Questions and Cultural Politics." In Philip Brett, Elizabeth Wood, and Gary C. Thomas, eds., *Queering the Pitch: The New Gay and Lesbian Musicology*, pp. 155–203. New York: Routledge, 1994.

Trumbach, Randolph. "London's Sapphists: From Three Sexes to Four Genders in the Making of Modern Culture." In Julia Epstein and Kristina Straub, ed., *Body Guards: The Cultural Politics of Gender Ambiguity*, pp. 112–41. New York: Routledge, 1991.

Weldon, Fay. *The Life and Loves of a She-Devil*. London: Hodder and Stoughton, 1983.

Wood, Elizabeth. "Sapphonics." *Queering the Pitch: The New Gay and Lesbian Musicology*. In Philip Brett, Elizabeth Wood, and Gary C. Thomas, eds., New York: Routledge, 1994, 27–66.

Woolf, Virginia. *Mrs. Dalloway*. New York: Harcourt, 1925.

——— "Speech Before the London/National Society for Women's Service, January 21, 1931." In Mitchell A. Leaska, ed., *The Pargiters: The Novel-Essay Portion of the Years.* New York and London: Harcourt, 1978.

Zakariasen, Bill. Review of Ferruccio Busoni's *Arlecchino* and *Turandot*. *Opera News*, May 1994, p. 50.

The Lesbian in the Opera: Desire Unmasked in Smyth's *Fantasio* and *Fête Galante*

Elizabeth Wood

> An image forms in my mind; a quickset briar hedge, innumerably intricate and spiky and thorned; in the center burns a rose. Miraculously, the rose is you; flushed pink, wearing pearls. The thorn hedge is the music; and I have to break my way through violins, flutes, cymbals, voices to this red burning center. . . . I am enthralled that you, the dominant and superb, should have this tremor and vibration of fire round you—violins flickering, flutes purring; (the image is of a winter hedge)—that you should be able to create this world from your center. Perhaps I was not thinking of the music but of all the loves and ages you have been through.
>
> —Virginia Woolf, on listening to the music of Ethel Smyth

How did Ethel Smyth, a lesbian composer, figure her lesbian desire in music—especially in opera, with its range of interactive emotions where everything can stand for something else?[1] How did she use musical codes those "in the know" could crack? How, later, do I, a lesbian scholar, decipher the codes that are only visible in certain lights, made audible only by acts of translation, so that others, and not only lesbians, can listen differently to her music?

When I began to study Smyth and her music, I planned to write a feminist biography that even mainstream musicologists might recognize. But thorny questions such as these (to graft Woolf's horticultural metaphor) have grown, like cuttings of living plants, a "red burning center" from which radiate my ideas about a lesbian history and biography, not only of Smyth but of music itself. I call this larger study of voicing and listening "Sapphonics" for a way of describing the sonic space of lesbian possibility among women who compose and perform and women who listen. If in opera I can rarely "see" representations of lesbian desire,

I know when I "hear" it —flickering, purring, a tremor, a flush—a fiery vibration in the voice that performs the text and embodies it—sung and unsung, heard and unheard, inside and outside music's boundaries and opera's conventions. I want others to hear this, too.[2]

Like Smyth's voice in her music and writing, my writing acts both inside and outside conventional musicological practices. New to academic music study, lesbian and gay work that is grounded in historical, contextual knowledge, as well as in a personal experience of music, encourages me to reconnect music's texts and scores to larger social and cultural patterns that music both mirrors and produces; to recognize the multiplicity and indeterminacy of music's meanings; to let a scholarly interpretation be improvisatory, inventive, uninhibited, speculative, polyphonic; to think of marks of gender and sexuality in music's scores and genres not as stable, universal fixtures but rather, in my *listening* to musical expressions, roles, and representations, as performed and often provisional identities.

Writing about sound begins with singing in the ears. As I experiment with ways of queering musicology, my narrative often wants to abandon linearity to leap about, wander, float. I think of a literary narrative about music as a form of sonic hypertext: a polyphonic web to be colored and connected as vividly by the listener's or reader's experience of sound as it is by my subject's and mine. If we had the technology the user of this book would be able to scan an audio text. In tune with lesbian history and lived experience, the metaphor (soon, perhaps, a reality) of the sonic hypertext represents for me the marvelous potentiality of sound and listening as modes of discourse and understanding and the liberating pleasure of putting into play (a camp improvisation, a lesbian counterpoint among my subject, myself, "our" audience of listeners and readers) both the conventional evidence of historical texts and the less conventional evidence of personal anecdata and gossip.

As I work on Smyth's musical life as a "body" of lived sound, bits and pieces flicker and ignite. I find myself wanting to pull them in: a homoerotic impulse, I think, that the writer with multiple gay identities, Baron Corvo/Frederick Rolfe, called "The Desire and Pursuit of the Whole."[3] Let me float three bits—or soundbites—that matter to my study of Smyth's operas.

- A melody haunts, ever since I found and copied it in pencil in the manuscript room of the British Library from the original score of *Fantasio*, her first opera composed in 1894. This tune has come to remind me of another, in her fifth opera, *Fête Galante*, composed thirty years later.
- In her will Smyth named as her musical executor a young neighbor, Kathleen Dale, herself a composer, to preserve and dispose of all the manuscripts. Dale

was the first woman to posthumously anatomize Smyth's complete works, including the score Smyth said she had destroyed in a 1917 backyard bonfire of all its published parts: the original manuscript of *Fantasio*. There, on pages scarred by handwritten revisions, amendments, erasures, like an old face before a lift, Dale's eye traveled first, as mine would, to parts untouched, lines not "made up." Among keys changed, words translated, melodies orchestrated Dale recognized three items she had seen before in other works by Smyth: the words and melody of an old Irish folk song, a previously published German song dating from Smyth's student days in Leipzig, and an instrumental theme from her never performed or published biblical cantata, *The Song of Love*, of 1888. How "incongruous," thought Dale, for Smyth "to resuscitate old material" for a new score when she was so inventive and fluent.[4]

- In her introduction to a collection of essays on gender and sexuality in musicology, Ruth Solie notes of my "Lesbian Fugue" that, although "the story of (Smyth's) own lesbian experience—her difference—may be encoded in her instrumental music," the plots of Smyth's operas "turn upon the vagaries of conventional heterosexual romance."[5] Reading this, I felt vaguely troubled. The essay did not mention the operas, but Ruth assured me the comment was mine. In any event, casually I let it "pass." Sometime later I recovered it, buried in something I wrote several years ago about being confronted, in Smyth's opera librettos, "with conventional romantic passion and heterosexual longing. If I imagine that autobiographical themes run, symbolically at least, behind her dramatic texts, I recall Smyth's reply to Woolf's insistence that she should write more intimately about her sexual experiences. Smyth reminded Woolf of the perils of the déclassé: that to succeed in a man's world as a woman composer, she had to identify with men."[6] On reading this now, I see that, while imagination was tuned to the possibility of a lesbian "text," I had no idea, then, how to think about, or listen for, a lesbian "sound."

How do these bits together resonate for me?

To take the last first, my straight thinking about Smyth's operas mirrors conventional ways of thinking about opera generally in musicology, in terms of its self-evident messages about gender and heterosexuality. But a newly playful musicology that risks queer pitches, feminist endings, and a lesbian . . . listening invites me to turn my comment inside out; to see that my assumption of a lesbian composer's "romance" with conventional heterosexual opera seems, in itself, to have turned on musicology's own conspiracies of silence about *opera*'s romance with the unconventional and the homosexual. As Smyth has her Pierrot sing in *Fête Galante*:

"Lovers pursue and maidens fly, ghosts that chase a phantom bliss;
Ask a wiser fool than I where the truth is, where the lie, in a stolen kiss."

When I look again at those "incongruities" Dale thought she saw in the score of *Fantasio*, I begin to see the lie.

But, first, I must tell the story of the story of *Fantasio*, before we hear the play within the play, the riddle in the riddle, and the voice inside the voice of what Smyth grandly called a "Phantastische Komoedie in zwei Acten (poetry freely adapted from the play of the same name by Alfred de Musset) with music by E. M. Smyth."[7]

On the surface, Smyth's German opera on a French play does appear to be a formulaic heterosexual fairy-tale romance. While Musset's masks, disguises, and mistaken identities suggest a comedy of errors, his play's theatrical location in Herzegovina on the Croatian border over a century ago, a site of ongoing instability in the European imagination, makes an "interesting commentary on the political consequences of masking or repressing identities."[8] In this story, a poet, Fantasio, has escaped his creditors by assuming the persona of "Jacko," court jester to the king of Herzegovina. As Jacko, Fantasio becomes the confidant of the king's daughter, the princess Danila, who is preparing to sacrifice personal happiness for the public good and marry the pompous, blustering prince of Croatia. The prince arrives incognito at Danila's prenuptial party. Fantasio, now doubly disguising himself as "the democratic prince of Zara," contends with Croatia for the princess: in part to save her from a bad union, in part to put a dissolute past behind him. With one silly ruse, which unmasks Croatia as a bald old roué, Fantasio rescues the princess and Musset ends the story with the sinister sound of the Croatian army marching on peaceful Herzegovina: for listeners a century later, a horribly prophetic note.

Smyth sensed this was no ordinary comedy. Discord, irony, the vulnerability and fragility of life and love all cloud Musset's transforming mirrors. The dance of joker and princess, a Pierrot and Pierrette, as a rescue fantasy of assumed and repressed identities and imprisoned imagination may have resonated for Smyth with a lesbian experience of desire and fantasy as closeted and fettered. Each lover sees in the other a reflection of the self. Fantasio, embodiment of excess, the dreamer who adopts the fool's disguise as outlet for poetic energy, rescues the princess to give her back to her self and restore the integrity of her father's kingdom. So doing, he frees himself from the mask of his own deceptions, the prison of a wasted life. In turn, Danila's innocence and vulnerability, which has liberated Fantasio's imagination, validates for both the power of human desire and love.

Musset's Fantasio, the character, is a projection of Musset, the playwright, a dandy fascinated by drugs and debauchery, musically gifted and a little crazy.

Songwriters, Smyth's contemporaries—Gounod, Lalo, Delibes, Bizet, Franck, Tchaikovsky—set Musset's poems, drawn to the musicality of his diction, its poetic invocation of Italian melody (especially folk song), and characters like Fantasio who sing chansons and romances. Opera composers, also contemporary with Smyth —Offenbach, Chausson, Honegger, Messager, Puccini, Leoncavallo—set Musset's plays.[9]

Musset wrote and published *Fantasio* in 1833 during the early months of his notorious love affair with George Sand, the "Sapphist" literary foremother whom Smyth worshipped. I believe he encoded within the play, as a fantasy play of life and a game between lovers, the transvestic fantasies he enacted with Sand in their private erotic partnership: his cross-dressing as maidservant to the trousered Sand, her nicknaming Musset "Fantasio" in her poem, "Elle et Lui," his role as poetic prankster who quoted and played Shakespeare's transvestic roles to amuse and seduce Sand from both her failed marriage and his male and female rivals.[10]

Given Musset's secret counternarrative, the play's concluding military effects seem less ambiguous or dramatically expedient than prophetic of personal as well as political events: the turbulent warfare and retreats that ended Musset's relationship with Sand, the collapse of Napoleon III's Second Empire to Bismarck's Prussian troops that ended the flamboyant Parisian belle epoque reflected in Musset's life and works.[11]

The play's political disturbance—perhaps, too, its personal undertones—was certainly not lost on Smyth's great friend, neighbor, and sponsor, the Spanish-born Empress Eugénie, in English exile as the widow of the "last of the Napoleons," who suggested Musset's work to Smyth in the first place. Eugénie had known both Musset and Sand and was a devotee of Offenbach's operettas during her reign, but although in exile she could not have seen the Paris premier of his *Fantasio* in 1872, she had many times delighted in the subversive, mocking mirror that Offenbach, a German, turned on the empire's glittering frivolities and political ineptness. She urged Smyth to compose Musset as English light operetta on similar lines and with spoken dialogue in the hugely popular, profitable style of Gilbert and Sullivan's political satires of the 1880s.[12] Harry Brewster, the writer who collaborated in Smyth's first three operas, concurred.

Smyth had larger ambitions. For her first attempt at opera, she said in her self-dramatizing divaspeak, "no success on the second line of effort could ever tempt me. I would far rather die (she was nearing forty) having hopelessly aimed at the best all my life than earn large sums from the second-best."[13] She created a two-act opera in eighteen scenes with a through-composed texture—a continuous narrative that refuses the internal repetitions of strophic song and the storytelling propulsions of spoken dialogue. She structured the work conventionally on brisk orchestral preludes to announce major themes, boisterous sound effects for precision-timed stage actions, trumpet fanfares and dance music for an onstage band, hearty choral numbers accompanied by full orchestra, and a recitative for the six soloists crammed with ardent and exclamatory German prose. To conclude, she feigned Musset's ominous military marches with a perfunctory marriage procession.

The sheer weight and grandeur of Smyth's design all but eclipsed Musset's delicately nuanced fantasy. When an astute musical friend, Maurice Baring, observed at its premier that "there are not enough bones in the framework to support the musical structure," Smyth was forced to agree that, for its subject, "there was far too much passion and violence" in the music, dismissed it as apprentice work, put a match to (almost) all of it, and composted *Fantasio*'s ashes in her rose garden.[14]

The score she kept in an attic cupboard interests me less for its "rescue" from apocalyptic fires or its technical miscalculations (but Smyth's alterations can tell me what she learned from what she heard in performance) than for three passages she kept intact and never changed. According to the plan of the two overture-preludes, each belongs to a secondary subject scheme, one typically more lyrical than dominant. Her "second subject," in fact, comprises those same inserted borrowings, or recyclings, that Kathleen Dale found so incongruous. Different questions now occur to me. Had materials Smyth earlier used acquired a new or different meaning for her? Had they come to have a *particular* meaning? (For her? For a particular listener?) Had they signs, carried in code, of some private, secret message?

It is right here, in these transported grafts and woven through the texture of Musset's play within the play, that I think I hear Smyth's voice in her own subjective counternarrative. Voice, and the different meanings it has in music generally, may mean an authorial presence, a musical representation specifically in opera of a particular character's point of view, a singer and her utterance, and the human voice that produces sound, perhaps *is* sound, that generates meaning in music. I use all of these meanings, but refer here specifically to Smyth's authorial presence.[15] Where Musset deploys his counternarrative in visual illusion and ironic wordplay, Smyth's inhabits actual musical structures that she inserted in the through-composed texture—thus breaking with its protocols—as an embedded narrative of self-referential, retrospective items or gestures that serve to interrupt, in effect disrupt, rather than conserve narrative unity and continuity.

How are we meant to hear this authorial voice? As an intruder? An incongruous or a subversive Other? An agent of disruption or of inclusion? Or is the voice not so much one of agency as effect? An effect, or perhaps affect, but from whom? On whom? I propose it as the affect of difference, or what I call the Sapphonic voice. How and where does this sound?

Two of these appearances come in the first act as the only autonomous "numbers" for solo singing voice in the entire opera: the first in scene 4, as Fantasio's "Freedom Song" ("Freiheit Lied"), and the second in scene 6, as Danila's Irish folk song, "Come O'er the Sea." The third occurrence (the quotations from Smyth's biblical cantata), which is more a thematic gesture than a structure, belongs to the second act and appears, first, in the orchestral prelude and, subsequently, but fleetingly, in solo-voice passages in scenes 2, 3, and 5, where it blossoms into a five-part fugal treatment arranged for mixed chorus.

Fantasio's ballad, his only extended solo expression, is a German song Smyth wrote at the age of nineteen, when newly arrived in Leipzig, on the text "Nachtreiter" by Karl Groth, for mezzo voice (her own) and piano accompaniment.[16] For the opera the only changes she made to this dashing depiction of a horserider's erotic pursuit, at dead of night, on pounding hoofs, are the key-change from her signature E major up to G to fit the male tenor voice and redistribution of the piano part among a small group of winds and strings. In the opera, however, the voice of the lied has an entirely changed context that marks something of a feminist departure from opera's heroic romance model of the male role as rescuer and seducer of women. Fantasio's tenor voice, heard alone in the entire opera only in this ballad, emerges from, and is returned to, a three-part chorus of all-female voices. In acoustic effect the male voice "comes out" of the more powerful, enveloping, sonorous web of the female "body."[17]

Danila's solo song that follows is Smyth's translation into German of an Irish folk song she herself often sang, according to listeners to thrilling effect, to her own piano accompaniment. Here it is arranged for a small chamber ensemble, the setting best designed to cherish a simple tune.[18] Where Fantasio performs his ballad in an open-air public square, in the privacy of her bedroom Danila sings only for Lady Anna, her lady-in-waiting, the very verses and melody Smyth herself had sung on first meeting Lady Mary Ponsonby, Queen Victoria's lady-in-waiting.[19] Since lesbian and gay studies celebrate and legitimate anecdotal gossip as an art form, here is that 1890 performance.

Lady Ponsonby's daughter, Maggie, had invited Smyth to dine at Windsor Castle in the family's private suite of stone rooms that in former times had been a prison inside the inner wall of the castle and overlooking the moat. On Smyth's arrival, Lady Ponsonby, aware of court gossip about the notorious foxhunting lesbian composer, made her excuses and retired, but her daughter "dragged" her back, insisting she must hear Smyth sing "Come O'er the Sea." She came, listened, the song was repeated and, spellbound, Lady Ponsonby stayed. Everafter, Smyth claimed her singing and this song had lured and won Lady Ponsonby's heart.

Come o'er the sea, maiden with me,
Mine through sunshine, storm, and snows,
Seasons may roll, but the true soul
Burns the same where'er it glows.
    Let fortune frown so we love and part not,
    'Tis life where thou art, 'tis death where thou art not,
Come o'er the sea, maiden with me,
Mine where'er the wild wind blows.

Was not the sea made for the free,
Land for courts and chains alone?
Here we are slaves! But on the waves
Love and liberty's all our own.
    No eye to watch and no tongue to wound us
    All Earth forgot, and all Heav'n around us.
Come o'er the sea, maiden with me,
Mine where'er the wild wind blows.

In the opera a solo violin doubles Danila's voice in the first verse; in the second the violin part, now coupled contrapuntally with solo flute, moves contrary to the vocal line. The song is in D major. The first four measures scarcely move; the voice, which seems self-absorbed, remains inside the boundaries of the tonic triad. The phrase is repeated. At the words "Let fortune frown," with a strange cry, and with no preparation, the voice "breaks" upward from D to E, a tone outside the octave, but the impulse to flight is brief. On "'Tis life," it begins to slip back downward, first in whole steps, then with a distracted, meandering chromatic turn (at "death where thou art not") toward triadic confinement again at the reprise of the initial four-bar phrase. A recent performance of this song produced in listeners a Sapphonic moment of border-crossing vocal breakthrough when the voice of the singer who illustrated my speech, at this designated break, literally broke down. She stopped, and had to begin over again. While the singer was appalled and apologetic (for singers are trained to cover if not control what is considered a *technical* breakdown), I was ecstatic, for she had produced exactly the effect my words, the score, and Smyth's own singing of the song had intended.

What is this "L'Invitation au Voyage," sung by a woman, addressed to a woman, to flee oppression and "come" with the singer-lover to a wild, wind-blown oceanic space of ecstasy and freedom, *doing* in a rescue fantasy of "heterosexual" romance? Is this the momentary fantasy of a female victim: a vulnerable subject facing the impossible trauma of breaking away from her predicament, the security of coming back, or of never having left? Perhaps, or perhaps something else again.

Of course, on one hand, Smyth's adaptation to opera of ballad and folk song is part of nineteenth-century musical convention, its romantic passion for historiography. Smyth's use, here, is faithful as well to Musset's interpolation of chansons in his playscripts. Throughout her career, and in other of her works, Smyth rearranged her own music for different performance contexts and refurbished for operatic use traditional and folk sources. In *Fantasio* she may merely have let a convention (the convention of intrusion) become part of the subject, in a manner similar to Mozart's insertion of his hit tune from *The Marriage of Figaro* into the seduction dance scene of *Don Giovanni*. Or Smyth may have wanted this *moment* of intrusion (since it is simultaneously a voyeuristic intrusion in a woman's bedroom of an audience of listeners) to signal some shift—in subject? in appearances? in and for certain listeners?—in the way the composer Flotow, in his opera *Martha*, adapted an Irish folk song, "The Grove of Barney," as "The Last Rose of Summer" for the aristocratic Lady Harriet's class-crossing impersonation of a country girl.

Such intrusions may, in turn, become *subject* to convention, in the way that another old chestnut, "Home, Sweet Home," became the diva Nellie Melba's regular encore in both solo and operatic performances in the 1890s. As Patti before her, Melba liked to interpolate this song in Rosina's "Lesson" scene in *The Barber of Seville* as if on impulse and always accompanying herself (to gasps of admiration) on a piano quickly wheeled onstage by stagehands waiting in the wings. For more commonplace reasons Smyth may have planned to have the ballad and folk song published separately for the British domestic sheet music market and singers wanting concert items, and thereby simultaneously promote and capitalize on an opera premier in Germany that, given her nationality and gender, was unlikely to be repeated or profitable.

What if these intrusions on the opera, their interruption of the narrative, represent Smyth's own voice, one that is not outside but inside the telling of the tale; that is, a voice not only inscribed on the score but embodied in the score, both sung and unsung, heard and not heard? After all, it is *her* voice that produces the narrative, controls it, overrides all others, and can insist that this other narrative, the story that intrudes, is the *real* story. If Musset in his narrative had found private ways to disguise and exchange erotic messages with Sand, might Smyth have meant the sound of Danila's singing to signal Smyth's lesbian desire, perhaps to authorize and legitimize a desire that certain listeners, Lady Ponsonby for one, were sure to recognize?

What, then, do we make of the opera's wordless instrumental theme in act 2: the quotation from Smyth's biblical cantata, *The Song of Love*, a forerunner of her operas, where the (originally sung) text is a rapturous cry of longing for a woman's voice?[20] Was a homoerotic "Song of Solomon" unsingable in opera because it was, like Salome's dance, too risky for words? Had Smyth also felt compelled to change to *Danila* the name of Musset's princess, *Elsbeth of Herzegovina,* because it sounded too like the name of her former lover, Elisabeth von Herzogenberg, now dead—or, perhaps, an ellipsis: the name for a lesbian scandal not yet forgotten in the German musical circles to which Smyth and Herzogenberg belonged?[21] In 1895 Smyth had even masked her own name and gender to submit *Fantasio* in Munich to an international competition for new operas as the work of one *Evald Schmidt,* a transsexual impersonation that may or may not have gained her opera an honorary mention among 110 entries by male composers.[22]

Smyth's campy delight in gossipy intrigue and fondness for speculation, especially on esoteric emanations, encourages mine. In her memoirs, where she tells the story of *Fantasio's* eventual premier in May 1898, she interpolates lesbian desire as an anonymous intrusion, an encoded and illusory impersonation of the "real." In Weimar, just as preparations for the premier began to falter, a middle-aged "woman in black," a stranger incognito, materialized as if from nowhere, took charge of the Grand Duke and his recalcitrant theater intendant, and "rescued" *Fantasio*, which opened two weeks later. Smyth reports she was entranced by this magnetic, mysterious "Countess X," her apparitional superagent, but a simple act of musicological detection lets me unveil "X" as the reclusive widowed baroness Olga von Meyendorff, at one time the lover of Franz Liszt.[23]

Dissemblance, gossip—these are the very substance of Smyth's memoirs, but also of her fifth opera, *Fête Galante*, which she described as a delicate "Dance-Dream in one act after Maurice Baring's story of that name, dramatized and composed by (now Dame) Ethel Smyth, poetic version by Edward Shanks."[24]

For 1920s listeners at its premier, *Fête Galante* may well have seemed, like Strauss's resonantly lesbian-erotic *Der Rosenkavalier* (1911), a modernist period piece nostalgic for the past, for both operas are steeped in opera's classical tradition.[25] Near contemporary scores with the same title, or theme, include Debussy's songs to Verlaine's text and several neobaroque, neoclassical opera/ballet parodies (by Poulenc, de Falla, Busoni, Tailleferre, and Stravinsky) of renaissance and eighteenth-century Harlequin theatrical and *galant* musical traditions.[26] Baring's costumed court masquerade, its courtiers in masks and dominos, a queen's betrayal of a jealous king, classical dancers, madrigal singers, puppet mimes, promenading guests, is a queer tale, as Smyth's libretto depicts, of "fickleness, betrayal, strife" with a macabre outcome. The Pierrot in a group of commedia dell'arte entertainers at the court fete is found hanged after the jealous Columbine tells the King she has recognized his Queen in a garden tryst with a Pierrot. However, this Pierrot is not the "real" Pierrot but a false identity, an intruder and impersonator: it is the Queen's illicit Lover, once banished from the court in disgrace, who has returned to the party doubly disguised in a black mask and wearing, under a dark, concealing outer cloak, a Pierrot costume. Whether in the closing scene the King's men have hung Pierrot, or Pierrot chooses death before they can, is left unclear.

Visually, as well as musically, Smyth's opera achieves a beautifully balanced architectural symmetry. A formal garden for open-air aristocratic revels (with Watteauesque vistas, promenades, temple, marble seats, bordered with hedges) defines the public site for beings seemingly manipulated by invisible puppeteers in seemingly unstructured moves and acts. Human treachery darkens the moonlit landscape; on Smyth's instruction the stage is never fully lit. The dramatic interplay of conflicts—between the illusion, in a public and external realm, of fixed and certain social order and subjectivity's disorderly interiority—is mirrored in Smyth's musical geometries. She actually constructs the effect of dissimilitude (the condition of being unlike) with explicit musical means, alternating diatonic baroque dance and vocal forms (the sarabande, musette, and waltz; an a cappella madrigal ensemble; a vocal quartet in close harmony) with solo monologues or dialogues patterned on speech and modal melodic traditions. Smyth also defines a three-dimensional, multidirectional acoustic space for dissimulation (a concealment by means of feigned semblance) in her disposition of sound among groups of on- and offstage musicians and voices that move in and out of our hearing, as well as each other's hearing.

Smyth tells us she began this work "without a shred of inspiration, and with an almost physical distaste" and, initially, without the approval of Maurice Baring, although he gave it later.[27] What did she mean by this? Baring was among her closest friends, an appreciator of her talent and lover of her music. Perhaps she feared to fail him or embarrass him. He was Lady Ponsonby's nephew, and moved in social circles that glittered with foreign ambassadors, embassy attachés, titled ladies, and endless tea and tennis parties. But Baring led a double life: a secret same-sex underlife. It is unlikely he and Smyth kept secrets from one another, for they shared too many friends in interlocking artistic and homosexual networks.

Their mutual friend, the lesbian, writer, and aesthetician, Vernon Lee, wrote perceptively of Baring's "strange, rather musical than literary talent," his detached, understated "bony dry style," his sense of the macabre, the uncanny, and the "unexpected counterpoint" in Baring's narratives, his play within the play and "quadruple arabesque," which reminded Lee of Mozart's string quartets. His characters are in no sense real, she thought: "those queer slight people, slight and unreal like a melody, and, like a melody, going to one's heart."[28]

Lee captures here the psychological masquerade of *Fête Galante* that turns on the instability of identity, of people making mistakes about identity, or assuming false identities—a troubling aura of sexual subterfuge that Smyth echoes, for instance, in the music the Queen hears while gazing at her unmasked Lover: "The music is like our love lilting and soft but with an undercurrent of sorrow and bitterness to come," she sings. A puppet quartet (in the choral singing of the musette between movements of the sarabande that opens the drama) tells in song the story the puppet-players simultaneously mime: a double narrative that tells both an onstage audience and the audience in the theater that "the world cheats, but in deceit is pleasure," that we should remember, as we watch "this painted brief deceit," that "these are but dolls, as you are in the play" (and its variation, "these are, like you, but puppets in a play").

Once the "real" play starts, as players who had formed the audience for the puppets' mimed play now themselves slip in and out of disguises, cloaks, masks, it becomes increasingly difficult to sort out who is "in" the play and what is merely "play." Taking pleasure in deceit and fooling about with identity, we seem to be told, can be a grim and dangerous thing—as it was, in life, for Ethel Smyth, Maurice Baring, Vernon Lee, and for unseen, unheard others whose "deviant" and illicit sexual identities, roles, behaviors, and expressions society and culture condemned and punished. Was it the risk of self-revelation as much as the pain of self-masking that Smyth found so physically distasteful, even frightening, as opera subject? Was composing the *Fête* no play but something terribly real for Smyth, as well for Baring?

I think Smyth's solution, once committed to the work, was to find ways simultaneously to conceal and reveal her authorial presence: to create a dissimulated web of sound, a counternarrative that would serve the dual purpose of the concealment (dissemblance) and the bursting open (dissiliency) of her own voice inside the narrative.[29] I think I hear this voice in the choral musette, first, sung onstage at the opera's very beginning; again, in its concluding bars, but now sung offstage by "distant voices" while in moonlight Columbine swoons and the Queen stands transfixed at the sight of Pierrot's body.

In its first appearance between repeated statements of the sarabande (an instrumental dance), the musette acts as an intermediating lyrical second subject in much the same manner as the interpolated quotations do in *Fantasio*:

Hushed is the world, faded the light,
O magic hour, hour of delight,
Heart against raptured heart beating.
Down through the branches the moon rains greeting,
Sighing of lovers, warm lips meeting,
Whispered vows in the night.

Musette itself has multiple meanings. In eighteenth-century French opera-ballets (or *fêtes* of poetry, music, dance, spectacle, and disguise), the musette, with its characteristic imitative bass drone, represents a pseudopastoral dance form.[30] In Smyth's opera, while male and female voices sing the musette's words very softly, dancers "execute slow, swaying movements both languid and voluptuous." In 1932 Smyth planned a production of the entire "Dance-Dream" of *Fête Galante* as a ballet after Woolf's sister, the artist Vanessa Bell, offered to design the decor and costumes. Smyth created some additional instrumental dances to form an orchestral suite, although nothing came of the ballet.[31]

The musette that figures so prominently in pastoral entertainment and ideology is also, at least metaphorically, the phallicized *instrument* of sexual pleasure: the French bagpipe. This was a small instrument popular in eighteenth-century aristocratic music making, and comprised a soft inflating, breathing windbag covered with embroidered silks and velvet, and double sets of cylindrical double-reed ivory pipes as "chanters" and "drones." The player's double action of fingering the pipes while rhythmically squeezing the windbag held against the body to prolong the breath produced a sustained, seamless harmony between the upper melody and its supporting drone.

Smyth's placement of the choral musette fore-and-aft as a framing device for "this exquisitely artificial play" suggests other possible meanings to me.[32] I think of it as a narrative *within* the narrative, one that doubles the narrative as, metaphorically, the musette's chanters are doubled by drones, or as Baring's characters play doubled roles (masked, and unmasked, as private people with public roles, puppet playthings who are also passionate human beings), or as Smyth doubles musical forms: for instance, in shadowing a polished music of classical surfaces with the undertow of romantic disillusion and sadness. The choral musette *within* the musical narrative also has the same tonal characteristics, and the same shaping strategies, as the Irish folk song of *Fantasio*. In both operas these passages are "about" desire and its potential to move the singing subject beyond whatever binds it, closets it; a desire that, in turning inward, seems only to abandon the possibility of pleasure and escape. But where, in *Fantasio's* folk song, the desiring voice momentarily breaks out, only to be returned to a "state" of desiring rather than its gratification, in the *Fête* that desire is no longer a cry "outside" the narrative. Here the anticipated break is contained: desire is neither erased nor denied but interiorized: a "sighing" of wordless longing.

The musette also acts as a coded signal for a pivotal character in the drama, the Lover, who mysteriously appears on stage during the first choral singing of the musette:

> The Queen is standing somewhat apart, near the footlights, fanning herself, and accidentally drops her handkerchief. A tall man in a domino and masked, darts forward, picks it up, and whispers a few words. The Queen starts violently, but instantly recovers herself. The mask bows low, and mingles with the company.

The Lover unmasked later abandons the Queen and vanishes from the play when he hears the puppet Pierrot sing traces of the musette to warn the Queen of the King's approach.

What is this mysterious Lover, whose identity, though visually masked, is aurally (and metaphorically) associated with a sexually ambiguous, disturbingly doubled instrumentality? Who has returned from banishment *doubly* disguised in the outward cloak of invisibility that, in turn, conceals a false identity, a Pierrot impersonation that, ironically, tragically, will be misread by everyone but the Queen and the puppet Pierrot who loves the Queen; that must inevitably destroy the "wrong," that is, the impersonated Pierrot, "for hiding where you hid, for seeing what you saw"?

And what is the meaning of the puppet Pierrot's silence about what in hiding he has secretly seen, even after he alerts the Queen? That he can't or won't "sing"? Does muteness in the opera suggest hostility to ideas and the tell-tale of hidden feelings, or that the idea itself, that Pierrot "suffers in character," is private and unspeakable?

> We are but puppets in a play, and yet in mumming, as in life,
> There is still a plot to hear: fickleness, betrayal, strife,
> The hempen cord, the bowl, the knife,
> Treacherous tale to jealous ear.[33]

To solve the riddle in the opera's riddle may be to reveal which Pierrot is the "real" Pierrot. Is it the player and mime, the human Pierrot who "keeps love hidden in his heart" and, when betrayed by fickle Columbine, silently dies to protect the Queen? Is it the Queen's illicit Lover, the visible deception who, within hearing of the King, risks betraying the Queen by revealing and voicing desire? Or are these two—the seen and unseen, the sung and unsung—one and the same?

Smyth anticipates both the riddle and its solution in her placement of an unaccompanied madrigal, sung behind the scenes by mixed male and female voices to give the effect of distance. The text of John Donne's "Song" in this arrangement by Smyth echoes and illuminates the internal doublings and thematic dissemblance of the opera as a whole:

> Soul's joy, now I am gone, and you alone, which cannot be,
> Since I must leave myself with thee and carry thee with me.

Yet when unto our eyes absence denies each other's sight,
And makes to us a constant night when others change to light,
O give way to no grief, but let belief of mutual love
This wonder to the vulgar prove, our bodies not we move.[34]

During the madrigal's performance the masked Lover becomes visible once or twice near the Queen, who waits furtively in cloak and mask; when it is over the Lover steps out. "Think you disguise will save you?" the hidden Pierrot hears the Queen whisper to the Lover in terror; "The park is full of eyes and tongues," as if to summon the voice in *Fantasio*'s Irish folk song that promises, should lovers escape their "courts and chains," "no eyes to watch and no tongue to wound us."

It seems to me, in a Lover's masquerade, in the silence of a Pierrot that the Lover inhabits and internalizes, Smyth finds musical ways to represent the risk and defiance, no less the enormous human cost of concealment, involved in revealing a desire (the "real" Pierrot) that threatens public order and may split open the social fabric if released from triadic confinement, the "tonal" closet. If the rescue fantasy of *Fantasio* was for Smyth and Musset a political as well as personal allegory of repressed identities, for Smyth and Baring the *Fête* may be an opera about the paranoia, as well as the pleasures, of the closet.

For Smyth encodes the sexual deceit and self-masking of the closet as a transvestic sonic masquerade. In an act of vocal (s)exchange and sleight of hand, she gives the Lover's singing voice to the male tenor but both the Queen's and the puppet Pierrot's singing voice to the female mezzo, Smyth's own voice.[35] In other words, and in a slyly doubled set of doublings, Smyth's author, who inhabits and controls the narrative, simultaneously envoices and embodies the singing puppet-player Pierrot, who secretly desires the Queen and "covers" her voice, the impersonated Pierrot, whom the visible singing Lover has internalized as the mute Other the Lover both covets and covers, and the Queen herself, the voice of the beloved.

The masked Lover, we are told, has been "bidden" from silence and absence into voice and presence by the sound of a woman's voice. In their forbidden "hour of delight," Queen, Lover, and Pierrot all risk discovery to voice a wondrous, constant, and forbidden "mutual love" that resonates with Smyth's lesbian desire:

The Lover: "You called, or was it but the night that feigned your voice with winds and leaves?"

The Queen: "Not winds or leaves but my own breath was sighed to slay you!"

The Lover: "It was your voice, I came. What more to say but that?" (They unmask, and gaze at each other).

At that moment of unmasking, each voice is the same, and each is Smyth's own. To hear the mezzo in the tenor, the mute Pierrot within the singing Lover, is to reveal the "real" Pierrot, the desiring Other/Lover of the narrative, as the voice of Ethel Smyth. To unmask that desire is to "hear" the Lesbian in the opera.[36]

Notes

1. Ethel Smyth (1858–1944) was an English composer, conductor, writer, and feminist. Her major works include *Mass in D* (1891), the operas *Fantasio* (1892–94), *Der Wald* (1899–1901), *The Wreckers* (1903–4), *The Boatswain's Mate* (1913–14, composed after two years devoted to the suffrage movement), *Fête Galante* (1923) and *Entente Cordiale* (1925), numerous songs, organ and keyboard pieces, chamber music, choruses (including *The March of the Women*, 1910), works for military band and orchestra, a *Concerto for Violin, Horn, and Orchestra* (1927), and a choral symphony, *The Prison* (1930).

After World War I and the onset of deafness, Smyth began to publish her memoirs, *Impressions That Remained* (2 vols., 1919), *Streaks of Life* (1921), *As Time Went On . . .* (1936), *What Happened Next* (1940), and books of critical and political polemics, travel, and portraiture including *A Three-Legged Tour in Greece* (1927), *A Final Burning of Boats* (1928), *Female Pipings in Eden* (1933), and *Beecham and Pharoah* (1935), as well as biographical studies of her friends H. B. Brewster (*The Prison,* 1930) and *Maurice Baring* (1938), and, I must add, beloved English sheepdogs (*Inordinate (?) Affection*, 1936).

Created a dame of the British Empire in 1922, Smyth's fame was enhanced by frequent public appearances as a speaker and broadcaster, two honorary degrees in music (Durham, 1910, and Oxford, 1926), her sporting skills in hunting, mountaineering, tennis, and golf, her friendships with notable musicians, writers, politicians, monarchs, and aristocrats, and her lifelong lesbian attachments to Elisabeth von Herzogenberg, Rhoda Garrett, Minnie Benson, Mary Ponsonby, the Princess de Polignac, Emmeline Pankhurst, Edith Somerville, and Virginia Woolf, among others.

2. I explore such questions in "Lesbian Fugue: Ethel Smyth's Contrapuntal Arts," in Solie, *Musicology and Difference*, pp. 164–83, and in "Sapphonics," in Brett, Wood, and Thomas, eds., *Queering the Pitch,* pp. 27–66. Earlier versions of this essay were read at the University of Virginia, the New York chapter meeting of the American Musicological Society, and Griffith University in Queensland, March-July 1993. I thank Chilla Bulbeck for inviting me to keynote the Queensland Gold Coast conference, Gender Representations in the Arts, and Suzanne Cusick, Philip Brett, Wayne Koestenbaum, and Catharine Stimpson for their invaluable comments and camaraderie.

3. The title of Rolfe's last novel, a homoerotic Venetian satire on love between Nicholas Crabbe, Rolfe's pederastic alterego, and his servant Zilda/Zildo, a transvestic figure; see A. J. A. Symons, *The Quest for Corvo*. Smyth possibly met or knew of Rolfe during his brief, violent friendship in 1905–1907 with the Catholic priest R. Hugh Benson, the youngest son of Minnie Benson, Smyth's major maternal lesbian *culte* in the mid-1880s.

4. Dale, "Ethel Smyth's Music," pp. 288–304.

5. Solie, "Introduction: On Difference," p. 10.

6. In my essay, "Music Into Words," p. 79.

7. Title page of the German libretto of *Fantasio*. The vocal score, which Smyth burned together with parts and materials belonging to the premier (and sole) performance in Weimar's Hoftheater, May 24, 1898, was also published, Leipzig: C. G. Roeder, 1899.

8. I thank the editors Corinne Blackmer and Patricia Juliana Smith for this and other helpful comments.

9. In August 1878 Smyth's gay friend Tchaikovsky had also contemplated writing an opera on a play by Musset, confiding in Madame von Meck: "How profoundly felt and fascinating is their elegance. All is written in a light hand. I delight in his truly Shakespearean anachronisms: for instance, when an imaginary King of Bavaria discusses the art of Grisi with some fantastic Duke of Mantua"; in Tchaikovsky, *Life and Letters*, pp. 315–16. Tchaikovsky's reference to the Italian opera star Grisi is probably to Giulia (soprano), more famous than her sister Guiditta (mezzo) who had retired from the stage in 1838. He may have heard Giulia Grisi's performances at St. Petersburg in 1849 before she, too, retired in 1861.

10. André Maurois, *Lélia*, p. 197. Musset and Sand, seated side by side, her hand grazing his, are portrayed in *Liszt at the Piano,* a painting by Josef Danhauser (1840), in a rapturous group of listeners (Victor Hugo, Paganini, Rossini, Marie d'Agoult) beneath the presiding bust of Beethoven. A woman composer contemporary with Smyth created a French operetta, *Elle et Lui*, on Sand's poem: Guy d'Hardelot was the nom de plume of Helen Guy (also known as Mrs. W. J. Rhodes) who, as accompanist and intimate friend of Sapphonic diva Emma Calvé, composed other "acting songs" especially for Calvé on their English and American tours in the 1890s.

11. Events that mark Napoleon III's Second Empire, 1852–1870, and his family's escape to England and exile in 1871, are explored in Kurtz, *The Empress Eugénie, 1826–1920*.

12. After meeting Smyth in 1890 and studying her early orchestral music, Sir Arthur Sullivan considered her a friend and professional colleague, offering his encouragement, contacts, and technical advice. Sullivan's scores in Smyth's personal library, from which I think she drew ideas for characters, names, and settings—especially for her comic operas—included the Savoy satires *Patience* (1881), on poets and Wildean decadence, *Princess Ida* (1884), on feminist politics and women's education, *Ruddigore* (1887), on witches, ghosts, and female madness, and *The Sorcerer* (1877), a caricature of magical thinking, the clergy, and inappropriate passions; Smyth, *Inventory* (1937), British Library Add. Ms. 49196.

13. Ethel Smyth, letter to Lady Mary Ponsonby, September 1893, as quoted in St. John, *Ethel Smyth: A Biography*, p. 89.

14. She added, "One needs absolute integrity between subject and music, like Gilbert and Sullivan," a tardy recognition that the empress and Brewster were right. Baring, *Puppet Show of Memory*, p. 216, and Smyth, *What Happened Next*, p. 85.

15. I wish to thank Joke Dame for this clarification in her recent study of theories,

myths, and meanings of the singing voice and its relations to sex, sexuality, and subjectivity.

16. Smyth's *Lieder*, Opus 4, no. 4, composed 1877 for mezzo and piano, Leipzig: C. F. Peters, 1886.

17. Kaja Silverman discusses the female and maternal voice as "acoustic envelope," *The Acoustic Mirror*, pp. 80, 84–6, and ch. 3, "The Fantasy of the Maternal Voice," pp. 101–40.

18. Philip Brett's phrase, in conversation. The last work Smyth composed was also a setting of a traditional Irish melody, a prelude for organ dedicated to her friend, Edith Somerville, and published in 1939: a short, contrapuntally intricate work having a disarmingly simple effect similar to this song.

19. Only because the name *Ponsonby* is so famous in lesbian lore do I take this opportunity to mend a tiny flaw in Blain, Grundy, and Clements, *The Feminist Companion to Literature in English*, p. 863, vide the novelist Lady Mary Emily Ponsonby (1817–1877). The name, most celebrated for an untitled Irish runaway Sarah Ponsonby (and her rustic paradise with Lady Eleanor Butler, as the Ladies of Llangollen), became the property of Lady Mary Elizabeth Bulteel (1832–1916) on marriage to Sir Henry Ponsonby. It was neither the novelist nor runaway "Lady" but *this* Lady Ponsonby, granddaughter of Lord Grey, aunt of Maurice Baring, attendant to the queen, who was passionately loved both by Smyth and Vernon Lee.

20. For instance, in part 1 of Smyth's cantata (for chorus): "The vines with the tender grapes give a sweet smell. Arise, my love, my fair one, my love, come away;" Pt. 2 (tenor solo): "My sister, my undefiled, open to me. Let me hear thy voice, thou hast ravished my heart;" Pt. 4 (soprano solo): "I sleep, but my heart waketh. Tis the voice of my beloved saying 'open to me.' " Smyth, *The Song of Love* (*Solomon's Song*), Opus 8 (1888), British Library Add. Ms. no. 46862. Smyth's lesbian erotic "Song of Songs" is thus countersubversive of Strauss's Salome, whose parodic hymn of praise for male rather than female beauty was thought a "perversion" of the same biblical text "reminiscent of Pater's *Renaissance* as well as of Wilde's predisposition," Ellmann, "Overtures to Wilde's *Salomé*," pp. 34, 53.

21. The melodrama of their passionate, tragic lesbian love, and the family conflicts that opposed and silenced it, is too convoluted to reproduce here, but see my reconstruction of Smyth's telling of these events as "Lesbian Fugue."

22. Ethel Smyth, *As Time Went On* . . . pp. 222–23.

23. Sitwell, *Liszt*, pp. 259, 270. An American pianist, Amy Fay, recorded her impression of "icy coldness and at the same time of tropical heat" on meeting the countess in Weimar with Liszt in 1873; Fay, *Music-Study in Germany*, pp. 238–40. "It was like associating with a powerful magnet," said Smyth, in her *What Happened Next*, p. 68. Her "Countess X" conjures in me the thrill and chill of Terry Castle's apparitional lesbians.

24. Her only commissioned opera, by the British National Opera in December 1921, who performed it in Birmingham and Covent Garden in June 1923, the latter produced by singer Maggie Teyte. Baring's story first appeared in his collection of fantastic tales, *Orpheus in Mayfair* (1909). After the premier of Smyth's opera Baring

reprinted his story, along with the Orpheus materials and some new, flesh-tingling terrifying tales, in *Half a Minute's Silence* (1925). This and following quotations of text and music are from Smyth, *Fête Galante*, vocal score (Vienna: Universal Edition, 1923).

25. In a published review Smyth reported feeling "spasm upon spasm of physical delight" on first hearing *Der Rosenkavalier*; in *The Suffragette*, February 21, 1913.

26. Her work precedes Poulenc's *Les Biches*, commissioned by Diagilev in 1923 and first performed in 1924, which also explores eighteenth-century *galant* music.

27. In fact, the work had several false starts. In 1919, just as Smyth sent off to publishers the manuscript of her first book of memoir (*Impressions That Remained*), she first approached Baring for permission to set his play. She hoped, she said, that *Fête Galante* would "tempt" her to work, for she had been struggling with depression brought on by the onset of deafness (the flutterings and boomings of "singing in my ears"), a loss of confidence in her music (she felt "worthless," a "fraud"), and the memory of her nervous breakdown after losing Lisl, which writing the ending of her memoir had stirred. At that time Baring found the idea of an opera repugnant, but three months later told her she could do it. By then her "mood" for it had gone. See Smyth's unpublished diary (entries for March 3, 1919 and December 15, 1921), The Harlan Hatcher Library, University of Michigan, Ann Arbor.

28. Vernon Lee, letter to Maurice Baring (June 17, 1928) as quoted in Ethel Smyth, *Maurice Baring*, pp. 137–38, 334–35, in which Smyth also reproduces a letter from George Bernard Shaw in 1937 discussing Baring's aristocratic characters (340).

29. In untangling *Charlotte's Web*, a text that is "dissimulated behind the self-evidence of its message," Marjorie Garber quotes from Jacques Derrida's essay, "Plato's Pharmacy": "The dissimulation of the woven texture can in any case take centuries to undo its web, a web that envelops a web, undoing the web for centuries"; Garber, " 'Greatness,' " pp. 252–53.

30. An example is Rameau's *Fêtes d'Hébé* (1739), whose first-act prologue opens on Sappho's island of Lesbos. Several mostly mythic *fêtes* were composed by Rameau, Lully, and Mouret.

31. "But what will become of your greatest gift (I imagine, colour) in a midnight Fête?" Smyth asked Bell (June 12, 1932), during her campaign with the Camargo Society to stage *Fête Galante* as a masked ball, with Anton Dolin as Pierrot. Bell and Duncan Grant were among several Bloomsburians associated with this dance company. Producer Lillian Baylis also wanted to use Bell's designs, if indeed these were ever completed, for an opera production of the *Fête* at the Old Vic; see Smyth's correspondence with Edwin Evans, British Library Add. Ms. no. 59814, and with Vanessa Bell, Charleston Papers, King's College Library, Cambridge. Smyth, however, seems to have preferred the operatic version by insisting the society use actor-singers, not dancers, in the roles of King and Queen.

In a Queen's Hall Prom performance Smyth herself conducted of the orchestral suite of *Fête Galante* with the B.B.C. Orchestra on January 10, 1933, she staged a kind of musical-magician's sleight of hand to produce the desired vocal effect in the musette movement. As conductor Stanford Robinson recalls,

> The minuet has a Musette in which a chorus is called for, but there was never any chorus at the Proms in those days. So Dame Ethel got several of her friends to stand in the arena and get near to the conductor's rostrum as ordinary members of the public. When the appointed moment came, she turned her back on the orchestra and with a great beaming smile conducted this utterly unexpected choir to the great delight of the audience. I shall never forget her smile on that occasion.

As quoted in St. John, *Ethel Smyth: A Biography*, p. 287.

32. The quotation is Dale, who thought *Fête Galante* Smyth's most elegant, shapely music; Dale, "Ethel Smyth's Music," pp. 302–3.

33. "I suffer in characters," says figure skating's reluctant gay diva Brian Boitano: "I'm very shy but I want audiences to feel it—what I'm feeling, in control of my body," in a CBS interview during the 1994 Winter Olympics, Lillehammer (February 16, 1994).

34. "Soul's Joy," the madrigal, is the only number from *Fête Galante* that Smyth published separately (London: Curwen, 1923).

35. In all of Smyth's operas the leading female roles are exclusively mezzo voices within her own vocal range. Until 1907 all of her solo songs are also for mezzo; later she may indicate this voice as interchangeable between female mezzo and male baritone. Her score of *Fête Galante* marks Pierrot as "light baritone," but in its most recent revival Pierrot was voiced by a female mezzo. Jennifer Barnes, who sang Pierrot and also produced the work at the Royal College of Music, June 28, 1989 (where it was first performed in 1925), heard Smyth's Pierrot, to my ears correctly, as *female* vocal masquerade.

36. The capitalized "L-word" for Smyth's opera Lover alerts this lesbian listener to the possibility of lesbian desire, just as I fancy it works for lesbian readers of Jeanette Winterson's novel, *Written on the Body*: in the narrator Lothario, the beloved Louise, and "the L that tattoos me on the inside (and) is not visible to the naked eye" (118), as much as for the love, loss, language, lies, lives, letters, and locations—the Library, the Laboratory—of lesbian lore and learning the novel maps and travels.

Works Cited

Baring, Maurice. *The Puppet Show of Memory*. Boston: Little, Brown, 1922.

Blain, Virginia, Isobel Grundy, and Patricia Clements, eds. *The Feminist Companion to Literature in English: Women Writers from the Middle Ages to the Present*. New Haven: Yale University Press, 1990.

Castle, Terry. *The Apparitional Lesbian: Female Homosexuality and Modern Culture*. New York: Columbia University Press, 1993.

Dale, Kathleen. "Ethel Smyth's Music: A Critical Study." In Christopher St. John, *Ethel Smyth: A Biography*, pp. 288–304. London: Longmans, Green, 1959.

Dame, Joke. *Het zingend lichaam: Betekenissen van de stem in westerse vocale muziek*. Kampen: Kok Agora, 1994.

Ellmann, Richard. "Overtures to Wilde's *Salomé*." In Derrick Puffett, ed., *Richard Strauss: Salome*, pp. 21–35. Cambridge: Cambridge University Press, 1989.
Fay, Amy. *Music-Study in Germany*. London and New York: Macmillan, 1887.
Garber, Marjorie. "'Greatness': Philology and the Politics of Mimesis." In Margaret Ferguson and Jennifer Wicke, eds., *Feminism and Postmodernism*. Special issue of *boundary 2* (Summer 1992), 19(2):233–59.
Kurtz, Harold. *The Empress Eugénie, 1826–1920*. London: Hamish Hamilton, 1964.
Maurois, André. *Lélia: The Life of George Sand*. Trans. Herand Hopkins. London: Penguin, 1953.
St. John, Christopher. *Ethel Smyth: A Biography*. London: Longmans, Green and Co., 1959.
Silverman, Kaja. *The Acoustic Mirror: The Female Voice in Psychoanalysis and Cinema*. Bloomington: Indiana University Press, 1988.
Sitwell, Sacheverall. *Liszt*. [1953.] New York: Dover, 1967.
Smyth, Ethel M. *As Time Went On . . .* London: Longmans, Green, 1936.
——— *Impressions That Remained*. 2 vols. London: Longmans, Green, 1919.
——— *Maurice Baring*. London: William Heinemann, 1938.
——— *What Happened Next*. London: Longmans, Green, 1940.
Solie, Ruth A. "Introduction: On Difference." In Ruth A. Solie, ed., *Musicology and Difference: Gender and Sexuality in Music Scholarship*, pp. 1–22. Berkeley: University of California Press, 1993.
Symons, A. J. A. *The Quest for Corvo: An Experiment in Biography*. [1934.] London: Penguin, 1966.
Tchaikovsky, Piotr Il'ich. *The Life and Letters of Piotr Il'ich Tchaikovsky*. Ed. Modeste Tchaikovsky. Trans. Rosa Newmarch. New York: John Lane, 1906.
Winterson, Jeanette. *Written on the Body*. London: Jonathan Cape, 1992.
Wood, Elizabeth. "Lesbian Fugue: Ethel Smyth's Contrapuntal Arts." In Ruth A. Solie, ed., *Musicology and Difference: Gender and Sexuality in Music Scholarship*, pp. 164–83. Berkeley: University of California Press, 1993.
——— "Music Into Words." In Carol Ascher, Louise DeSalvo, and Sara Ruddick, eds., *Between Women: Biographers, Novelists, Critics, Teachers and Artists Write About Their Work on Women*, pp. 71–84. [1984.] New York: Routledge, 1993.
——— "Sapphonics." In Philip Brett, Elizabeth Wood, and Gary C. Thomas, eds., *Queering the Pitch: The New Gay and Lesbian Musicology*, pp. 27–66. New York and London: Routledge, 1994.
Woolf, Virginia. *The Letters of Virginia Woolf*, 4:171–72. Ed. Nigel Nicolson and Joanne Trautman. 6 vols. New York and London: Harcourt Brace Jovanovich, 1978.

The Ecstasies of Saint Teresa: The Saint as Queer Diva from Crashaw to *Four Saints in Three Acts*

Corinne E. Blackmer

Some twenty years after the Roman Catholic Church, assenting to popular demand, canonized Teresa of Ávila in 1622, the Florentine artist Gianlorenzo Bernini, chief architect of the Baroque style and witty caricaturist, comedic writer, and younger contemporary of Claudio Monteverdi, sculpted his famous marble and bronze statue, *The Ecstasy of St. Teresa*, for the church of Santa Maria della Vittoria in Rome. The statue was inspired by the passage in St. Teresa's *Life* in which, struggling to describe her mystical "rapture" (*arrobamiento*), she strikes upon an image that compares her experience of God's overpowering visitation with arrows struck into her heart:

> [The Lord] thrusts an arrow into the deepest part of the entrails and, at times even to the heart, so that the soul does not know what ails it or what it wants. It only knows that it loves God and . . . would joyfully die for Him. One cannot exaggerate or describe the way God wounds the soul and the exquisite pain it gives; pain that makes it a stranger to itself, but a pain so delicious that no pleasure in this life can give more delight. (Lincoln 62)

Bernini, famous for his dramatic realism and his power to transform blocks of marble into vivid, almost breathing, forms, shows St. Teresa in her ecstasy with limbs akimbo, billowing habit disarrayed, eyes shut, mouth open, and head thrown back, while, in Brigid Brophy's words, "her honey-tongued, artificial-shepherd-cheeked seraph, in an act of inspired and transcendent bad taste,

• **Fig. 12.1. Gianlorenzo Bernini.** *The Ecstasy of St. Teresa*, **1645–1652. Santa Maria della Vittoria, Rome.** *One Hundred Saints: Their Lives and Likenesses Drawn from Butler's "Lives of the Saints and Great Works of Western Art."* Courtesy of Art Resource.

pierced and pierced her with his phallic spear, wearing on his honeysweet and musical lips a silly sexy simper" (*In Transit* 236). Bernini creates in sculpture an analog of Monteverdi's *stile rappresentativo*, the operatic semiotic code for representing affective states of madness, rapture, and passion (McClary 35), and shows St. Teresa's visitation as *sexual*, an ecstatic orgasm. As a *woman* mystic, St. Teresa is an ambiguous and threatening character who embodies the contradictions of voluptuous rapture and divine inspiration, religious authority and patriarchal insubordination, political shrewdness and otherworldly devotion, "masculine" initiative and "feminine" obedience, and, as such, the potential confusion of male and female. Her legend thus recollects the complexly transgendered character of the divine pagan musician in Monteverdi's *Orfeo* (1607), who oscillates between heroism and transgression, virility and effeminacy, and rationality and madness (McClary 48). Yet Bernini, in exposing her divine *arrobamiento* as sexual, seeks to master her unruly desires by representing her abandon as a distinctly feminized submission to phallic potency in a manner that recalls the eroticized madness of Lucia in Donizetti's *Lucia di Lammermoor* (1835).

For Jacques Lacan there can be no doubt that Bernini shows St. Teresa "coming" (147). But mediating uneasily between the "truth" of St. Teresa revealed in this *spectacle* and the less accessible reality of her *experience* as a mystic, Lacan cannot quite reduce this rapturous "coming," this mystical *jouissance*, either to an instance of "feminine" religious masochism or, alternately, like Freud and other materialist scientists, to questions of biological function and "fucking."

> And what is her *jouissance*, her *coming* from? It is clear that the essential testimony of the mystics is that they are experiencing it but know nothing about it. . . . Might not this *jouissance* which one experiences and knows nothing of, be that which puts us on the path of existence? And why not interpret one face of the Other, the God face, as supported by feminine *jouissance?* (147)

This mysterious female pleasure experienced by women mystics such as Teresa of Ávila, Hadewijch of Antwerp, and Thérèse of Lisieux, among others, which exceeds, *through its very inability to name itself*, what Luce Irigaray terms the "phallic economy" (*This Sex* 199) of heterosexuality and the symbolic order of masculine language, might be, Lacan implies, the very ground on which human subjectivity figures, the gift of female pleasure that sustains and guarantees the continuance of human cultural existence. Yet Lacan does not ultimately rest content with this portrait of a subject who *experiences* her jouissance but "knows nothing about it." For, as he later notes, "If the unconscious has taught us anything, it is firstly this, that somewhere, in the Other, it knows. It knows precisely because it is upheld by the signifiers through which the subject is constructed" (158).

So, Teresa, at some level, *knows* about her mystical pleasure, but she either will not tell it, or—keeping in mind that her *Life* was written under command by her confessors during the Spanish Inquisition, when she endured scandalous gossip and hostile political and ecclesiastical scrutiny for her "visitations" and her efforts to reform the Calced Carmelites (Peers 43–45)—she *refuses* to disclose it because "we," her confessors, will perversely misconstrue, since we otherwise cannot control, her meanings. Perhaps we should then, as Lacan suggests, look beyond the evidence of direct testimony to those veiled "signifiers," those embedded narratives in her *Life* where Teresa reveals, in a double movement of concealment and disclosure, the sources of her jouissance. These signifiers do not uncover the problems of which we can speak, such as errant heterosexual romance, the trials of satanic temptation, or even the concealed Jewish background of her father's family that threatened Teresa with delegitimation throughout her life (Lincoln 2–4), although they are contiguous with and, through conceptual blurring, have been *purposefully* mistaken for such sources of narrative and ideological disruption. Rather, these signifiers, filled with silences that speak, occlusions that reveal, and absences that are presences, are the textual hot spots over which official scholars have needed to erect elaborate explanations, alibis, and justifications for St. Teresa, Doctor of the Church.

Then there are those others who have been inspired by St. Teresa, the unofficial ones who, like Teresa the woman, are determined to assert themselves against threats of persecution and "exposure," are expressive and artistic but unable to speak directly, are ambitious for an approved mandate to serve others, belong to the perilous category of "not-men," are alternately sentimental and hardheaded, and often, most like her, are sincere believers ridiculed for their devotions and obstructed in their efforts to reform religious practice. These others have also homed to the narrative spaces in the *Life* that have nettled scholars, not to explain them away but rather to discover there the sources of an intense identification with her pleasure. For these others Teresa of Ávila has served as mother-goddess and heroine, a prima donna who, unlike Lucia di Lammermoor, triumphed in the end and achieved, mirabile dictu, canonization. Living behind the doors of what Eve Kosofsky Sedgwick terms the "epistemological space" (10) of the closet, these others have read her *Life* as admiring students of her bravura negotiation of the speakable and unspeakable. These others have regarded the strictly enforced homosociality of Catholic monastic life as an appealing refuge and have felt profound attractions to a religion that, as John Boswell has recently noted, regarded heterosexual marriage as a compromise with the material world that good Christians should struggle to foreswear:

> Although a thousand years after its inception Christianity would begin to emphasize the biological family as the central unit of Christian society . . . for half of its existence it was most notable for its insistence on the preferability of lifestyles other than family units—priestly celibacy, voluntary virginity (even for the married), monastic community life. (Boswell 111)

They have not approached Teresa in order to stabilize her sexuality or to reduce her writing to homoerotic ciphers that once textually "outed" can be discarded as empty shells of a now decoded "secret" erotic content. Rather, the question of Teresa's female pleasure and its relation to the motives and springs of her religious vocation has been continually posed for four hundred years precisely through an excess of unspoken knowledge and the conditions of independent living apart from men that have not only characterized the not-heterosexual monastic woman but the lesbian as well. Indeed, Edward Carpenter, the early twentieth-century advocate of homosexual rights, only said what many have long thought (and known) when he remarked that many women of the "intermediate sex" have been attracted to convent life: "Many a Santa Clara, or abbess-founder of religious houses, has probably been a woman of this type; and in all times such women—not being bound to men by the ordinary ties—have been able to work the more freely for the interests of their sex, a cause to which their own temperament impels them to devote themselves *con amore*" (36–37).

I. Saint Teresa as Queer Icon

The long line of queer devotees *con amore* at the shrine of Santa Teresa begins with Richard Crashaw (1613?–1649), who, from the evidence of his poems (as well his critics' predictable denunciations of his "effeminacy") may be termed a "prehomosexuality homosexual" (Creech 70), who sought in his conversion to Catholicism and his worship of Teresa confirmation that his androgynous or, perhaps more accurately, protolesbian-identified temperament was inborn and sanctioned by God-the-Mother.[1] The son of a noted Puritan divine, Crashaw also marked his sense of difference from his father and the nationalistic "manliness" of English Reformation Protestantism by writing in a Baroque style that subsequent scholars have accused of exhibiting "feminine devotional spirit," "cheap glitter," "continentalism," "sexual perversion," "meretricious emotionalism," and "intellectual disorder" (Roberts 16–18). As a student at Cambridge, Crashaw wrote Latin hymns to female pagan deities, and these exercises doubtless enabled him to recognize the stellar diva in Teresa of Ávila, the larger-than-life operatic heroine who, through rhetorical *sprezzatura* and heavenly inspiration, vanquishes her political enemies and emerges triumphant in her *Vida*. In the headnote to "A Hymn to Saint Teresa," she has the angelic transcendence and masculine courage associated with female opera roles en travesti: *"A woman for angelical height of speculation, for masculine courage of performance, more than a woman"* (927). Passing over the adolescent homoerotic experiences that, significantly, exercise such compelling fascination over both Teresa's later lesbian interpreters and her official scholars, Crashaw recounts her childhood aspirations to achieve martyrdom at the hands of the Moors, her adult mystical raptures, and her triumphant entry into heaven. The life he narrates, a Catholic version of the Ciceronian high style, is preeminently *heroic*. In an eloquent homoerotic (and queerly familial) retroping of the Virgin Birth, moreover, Crashaw explains how Teresa, his poetic mother, has engendered his poetic self through her spiritual union with Christ, referring to himself as one of the "Sons of thy vowes, / The virgin-births with which thy soveraign spouse / Made fruitfull thy fair soul" (167–69).

In "The Flaming Heart," Crashaw takes issue with a picture of Teresa that, like Bernini's *Ecstasy*, shows a boyish seraph piercing the heart of a passive Teresa who seems like "Some weak, inferiour, woman saint" (26). The speaker asks readers to disregard this image and interpret her character not through misleading visual pictures but rather through his verbal portrait that, inspired by her vigorous writings, reveals the inward "flaming heart":

> Readers, be ruled by me, and make
> Here a well-placed and wise mistake;
> You must transpose the picture quite,
> And spell it wrong to read it right;
> Read him for her and her for him;
> And call the saint the seraphim
> Painter, what didst thou understand,
> To put her dart into his hand?
> See, even the years and size of him
> Shows this the mother seraphim. (7–16)

Crashaw associates Teresa with the masculine symbols of energetic passion and fire and amends the painter's emasculating portrait by endowing Teresa with phallic potency through the prosthetic device of a dart, with which she "pierces" lesser mortals with divine rapture. He makes Teresa the aggressor and gives the diminutive seraph the impotent veil and the chastised "red cheeks" of a feminized "rivaled lover" (43–44) who has been vanquished in this gendered contest between quasi-classical, quasi-Catholic symbolism. In his masculine arrogance, the painter has interpreted her ecstasy as a sign of her sexual subordination to mortal men. But far from exhibiting feminine acquiescence, Teresa's writings express "manly flame" (24), resolute spirit, and "large draughts of intellectual day" (97).

In these Baroque paeans, Crashaw, crossing operatic and religious queendom, creates Teresa as the sublime goddess, the more-than-a-woman Catholic diva. Thus, by the twentieth century, gay and lesbian culture has enshrined Teresa of Ávila in the pantheon of queer saints that include, among others, the martyrs St. Sebastian, pierced by arrows, and St. Joan of Arc, burned at the stake for transvestism, as well as St. Ursula, accompanied by her eleven thousand virgins, and St. Teresa's fellow Discalced Carmelite, the contemplative St. John of the Cross. But the battle over what the *Life* or the figure of St. Teresa "really means" becomes both more intense and complex as homosexuals challenge official hagiographers and as more specific (and intimate) differences between gay men and lesbians over appropriate interpretations of St. Teresa emerge. In *The Eagle and the Dove* (1943) Vita Sackville-West, whom her lover Virginia Woolf described as "a pronounced Sapphist" (235), takes the opportunity afforded by this dual biography of Teresa of Ávila and Thérèse of Lisieux to defend herself against her scandalous public reputation as a lesbian adventuress and to take aim at her predecessor Richard Crashaw, whom she accuses of popularizing the image of Teresa as "the prototype of the hysterical woman writhing in a frenzy of morbid devotion at the foot of the Crucifix" (14). In this description, filtered through three centuries of embarrassed misreadings of Crashaw, Teresa sounds like an unholy admixture of Puccini's Floria Tosca and Hindemith's Sancta Susanna.[2] Sackville-West, the descendant of an ancient English family (and a Spanish Catholic gypsy dancer), treats Crashaw like a seventeenth-century version of her contemporary, the novelist Ronald Firbank, a parvenu homosexual convert to Catholicism. Like Crashaw an adept of devotional cults and a sapphically identified queer man, Firbank once told his friend Carl Van Vechten, "I am a *spinster* sir, & by God's grace, intend to stay so" (quoted in Brophy, *Prancing Novelist* 82). In his high-camp novels queer female saints, both historical and invented, along with lesbian nuns and modern Sapphists, are represented with unabashed comic gusto.

For instance, in *Valmouth* (1919), Mrs. Hurstpierpoint and Mrs. Thoroughfare are two widows who enjoy an eroticized romantic friendship along with elaborate Catholic devotions aimed, in part, at converting their friend Lady Parvula de Panzoust from her "fallen" conditions as heterosexual and Protestant. Residing in the health resort Valmouth, a town presided over by the black bisexual masseuse Mrs. Yajñavalkya, they include among their collection of sacred relics the tooth of the invented St. Automona di Meris, the "especial friend" of St. Teresa, who, according to "the astonishing life" recorded in the works of Père Pujol, "seeing a young novice yawning, suddenly spat into her mouth. . . . Some ninety hours afterward the said young novice brought into the world the Blessed St. Elizabeth Bathilde, who, by dint of skipping, changed her sex at the age of forty and became a man" (188). In Firbank's last novel, *The Eccentricities of Cardinal Pirelli* (1926), the title character embroils himself in considerable trouble with the Papal authorities for baptizing (in crème de menthe) the police dog puppy of a lesbian countess. Pirelli retreats to the monastery of the Desierto where, "Theresa of Ávila, worn and ill, though sublime in laughter, exquisite in beatitude, had composed a part of the *Way of Perfection*" (319). Inebriated, he receives a vision of St. Teresa (who has been haunting the Desierto in search of a lost sheet of the manuscript of the *Way*), and he cries out: " 'Teach me, oh, teach me, dear Mother, the Way of Perfection' " (328). In other words, Pirelli asks St. Teresa the Way, both artistically and religiously, to be queer with impunity; but, tragically, he escapes from the papal authorities only by dropping dead shortly thereafter while chasing a choirboy around his cathedral.

Sackville-West, whom Firbank caricatured in *The Flower Beneath the Foot* (1922) as "Mrs. Harold Chilleywater," a writer of "artistic and literary novels" under her maiden name "Victoria Gellybore-Frinton" (543), found Firbankian Catholic camp déclassé in the extreme—and a contributing factor to the public images of lesbians that exacerbated the scandal surrounding her own life.[3] Hence, she blames Crashaw's "excesses" on the position he shares with Firbank as a religious parvenu overwhelmed by the "coruscation of his own conversion" (14). Unlike her own properly "discreet" homosexual husband, Harold Nicholson, these belletristic religion queens made Teresa into an image of their own quasi-hysterical and flamboyant sexual perverseness. While Crashaw's influence is discernible in the title of her book, culled from "The Flaming Heart," Sackville-West divides the attributes of "the eagle and the dove," which Crashaw had used to describe the simultaneously masculine and feminine, transcendent and nurturing aspects of Teresa's character, between two saints, making Teresa of Ávila pure eagle and Thérèse of Lisieux pure dove. Sackville-West thus rehabilitates Teresa by reemphasizing her powerful intelligence, and, most important, by interpreting her mysticism not, as would Lacan, as an "incoherent" and "irrational" language but rather as a manifestation of higher instinct and an anticipation of evolutionary process. Teresa becomes, in terms that recollect the experimental projects of lesbian literary modernists such as Virginia Woolf and Gertrude Stein, a woman ahead of her time who speaks in an original, evolved, and therefore difficult language and who succeeds in integrating her mystical visions into the patterns of everyday life (Raitt 118–20). Teresa, like many lesbian icons, becomes a *survivor* and harbinger of the future development of women rather than an isolated figure whose exceptionalism "proves" the general rule about her sex.

Beneath this grousing about Crashavian "excesses" rests less readily articulable complaints about the representations of sapphists as languorous femmes fatales, "carnivorous flowers" (Faderman 293–98), and, in the words of Ronald Firbank, "artificial princesses" in much fin-de-siècle male homosexual (and heterosexual) literature. As is often the case, Sackville-West's biography of Teresa is in large measure an allegorical autobiography, and in it she extracts herself and Teresa from cultural disrepute, categorical confusion, and the well-publicized scandal attached to her own earlier affair with the lesbian writer Violet Trefusis by reducing Teresa's *sexual* manifestations of lesbianism to "youthful indiscretions" and showing the adult Teresa, although still lesbian-oriented, subsuming her sexual energy into respectably platonized, or, in Lillian Faderman's words, "romantic" friendships with other nuns and into the furtherance of her religious and intellectual goals (17).

Published two years after Virginia Woolf's suicide in 1941, in patriotic support of the war effort against fascism, *The Eagle and the Dove* is soberly cognizant of the analogies between the Spanish Inquisition and the Nazi persecution of Jews and, as well, of the precarious yet salvational presence of visionaries like Teresa who reform the societies that would persecute them. The main attributes that enable Teresa, whom she describes as "that sane, vigorous, intelligent, humorous Spaniard" (14), are high-hearted faith and intellect, qualities Sackville-West found indispensable in negotiating the paradoxes of her own position as an aristocratic British Catholic lesbian mother of ancient heritage married to a homosexual diplomat and anxious to vindicate her reputation as an eminently reasonable woman. Thus, unlike the affectionately campy, cross-gendered portrait of her in Woolf's *Orlando* (1928), Sackville-West presents herself, through Teresa, as a woman who "tried hard to appear as a normal person in her outward life" (51).

Sackville-West focuses her discussion of Teresa's "sex variance" (Foster 13)[4] on an incident described in chapter 2 of her *Life* when, in the company of a female cousin with "vain" habits and "frivolous" conversation, she indulges in certain unnamed "sins" with "otra que tenia la misma manera de pasatiempos" [another person given to the same manner of pastimes] (La Fuente 25). Both her father and mother find this friendship distressing but, abetted by corrupt servants and, most important, willing to commit a sin that will enable her to protect her "honor" (i.e. chastity) and good name, Teresa "did not see" that, in disporting herself with this *persona*, "I was losing my honour in quite a different way" (27). As Sackville-West points outs, this description makes it difficult to determine what Teresa really did, but since she blames herself so bitterly and uses condemnatory words such as "mortal sin" and "blinded passion," she cannot be simply referring to an enjoyment of the salacious conversation of older girls or to a heterosexual cousinly flirtation. For Sackville-West the strongest proof that Teresa is probably describing a homoerotic attachment lies in her use of the purposefully ambiguous word *persona:*

> Whatever her apologists may say, for three months something very dark was taking place in Teresa's life; something so dark according to her views that she never brought herself to be explicit on paper. It is to be noted that this "other," so ambiguous in English, appears in the feminine in the Spanish original; and, since few things are more distasteful than veiled hints, it may also be outspokenly noted that in her own country the name of Teresa has been associated with that of Sappho. . . . Nobody in their senses or with any knowledge of this most misunderstood aspect of natural psychology would dream of comparing the organized orgies of Lesbos with the rudimentary experimental dabblings of adolescent girls, sciolists whose tentative essays may wither with maturity. (25–26)

At this point, Sackville-West, representing herself as an expert who does indeed know the difference between adolescent homoerotic experimentation and mature lesbian passion, *seems* to acquiesce in the outlines of the interpretation of this episode offered by the mid-twentieth-century Spanish editor of Teresa's *Life*, Don Vicente de la Fuente. In a lengthy, anxiety-ridden footnote to this passage, La Fuente ruefully admits the homoerotic nature of this episode, but, taking umbrage at the "salacious imaginations" of certain French authors (who also, not coincidentally, presided over the creation of Sappho as *the* decadent lesbian), distinguishes St. Teresa from Sappho in terms of unabashed moral outrage: "El amor divino, puro, sublime, hermoso y sobrehumano, que durante toda su vida, excepto en tres mese escasos, ocupó el corazon de Santa Teresa, no admite comparación con el amor lascivo, torpe y desenfrenado de Safo, sino en el concepto en que pueden compararse antitéticamente Cristo con Mahoma, la luz con las tinieblas, ó los panales de la abeja con los de la abispa" (26) [The divine, pure, sublime, beautiful, and superhuman love of Saint Teresa, which filled her heart and lasted throughout her life with the exception of this three-month period, only admits comparison with the lascivious, lewd, and unbridled loves of Sappho inasmuch as one might antithetically compare Christ with Mohammed, the light with darkness, or the honeycombs of the bee with those of the wasp].

Despite these elaborate disclaimers and qualifiers, the contest over Teresa's sexuality does not end here. Victoria Lincoln, a contemporary biographer determined to rescue the "ordinary woman" in Teresa from the historical incrustations of sanctimonious hagiographers and aberrant rumor mongers alike, calls Sackville-West an "over-innocent" translator, and notes with considerable pique that "*persona* is an invariable feminine" in Spanish (Lincoln 24). Sidestepping the authoritative figure of La Fuente, she focuses her attack on the more vulnerable Sackville-West and reduces her homoerotic interpretation to an instance of "wishful thinking" (24). For Lincoln the coupling of the names of the pagan lesbian poet Sappho and the Catholic heterosexual saint Teresa not only reveals Sackville-West's childishness and ignorance of "real" adult sexuality but also

> fits no part of Teresa's story, least of all that passionate outpouring of grief in which, remembering her profession at the end of that novitiate, she mourns for her faithlessness to Him who had made her His bride. The man was probably Garcia de Toledo. . . . It is only during the second and third times of association that he can be firmly placed, but we can say at least that Teresa would have found no *devoto* more flattering and few men more endearing. When their "fondness" (*afición*) first began, Teresa says, she did not think it wrong. Such associations were the accepted thing, and she did not stop to think that while such intimacies "might be harmless to those who were naturally good, it was a great danger to me." (24)

Lincoln makes valiant efforts to stabilize Teresa's sexuality by transforming her into a "normal" (read *heterosexual*) woman, casting aside variant interpretations as self-serving, and discovering, on slender evidence, the requisite heterosexual alibi for Teresa in the unlikely person of Garcia de Toledo. Lincoln herself not only engages in "wishful thinking" but in dishonest scholarship as well, for the "sexual orientation" of this adolescent episode is, in fact, *ambiguous*. More important, the claim that homoeroticism "fits no part" of Teresa's *Life* is, quite simply, incorrect. The adolescent episode would, in itself, not be especially worthy of note were it not that the images and situations used therein are repeated in subsequent contexts marked far more clearly as homoerotic. Although Sackville-West mentions (somewhat slyly) these later episodes, she clearly wants to contain Teresa's sexuality within her adolescence, at a time when her gender identity is still in unresolved suspension. This differs considerably from Crashaw's understanding of the heroic *constancy* of her gender-transcending character from childhood to adulthood and Firbank's fictional elaboration of an adult homoerotic alliance between Sts. Teresa and Automona di Meris.

To take only a few of the many examples in the *Life*, after her adolescent "sin" with *una persona*, which is responsible for ushering the fourteen-year-old Teresa into an Augustinian convent for "girls like myself . . . although there were none there as depraved as I" (28), she discusses her intimate friendship with one Doña Juana Suárez, a nun at the (Calced or Unreformed) Carmelite convent of the Encarnación whose companionship Teresa so craves that she insists on joining her order, "more intent on the gratification of my senses and my vanity than on the good of my soul" (30). What might passages such as these and many others like them, which mingle the "errors" of *vanitas* (i.e., self-love or, in modern parlance, narcissism) and sensual gratification, mean? Does Teresa refer to indulgences in gossip, to shared hankerings after the feminine fineries of perfume, jewelry, and embroidered dresses, to the sensual nature of her intimacies with Doña Juana, or to all of the above? Tentative answers to these questions emerge in both the radically unstable definitions and moral status of "lesbian" sexuality within Roman Catholic theology and in Teresa's complaints, related from the vantage point of hindsight after her "conversion" at the age of thirty-eight, about the pernicious ignorance of her half-educated confessors, who, as she notes, "have done my soul great harm" (40). In the context of her adolescent adventure, Teresa comments that her confessor informed her "that in many respects I was not offending God" (29). In reference to her friendship with Doña Juana, she is told that what she eventually comes to recognize as a "venial sin" was, in reality, "none at all" (40). Still later, she bemoans the fact that she once told her nuns that they were in "no danger" because there was "nothing wrong" in these practices: "This I did in blindness, for I would not have deceived them deliberately" (54).

In their work on lesbian nuns, Rosemary Curb and Nancy Manahan offer the official Catholic definition of "particular friendships," such as apparently existed between Teresa and Doña Juana, as those "between two sisters which exclude others . . . considered harmful to community living and prelude to Lesbian relationship" (369). Yet the "sinful" nature of these friendships can, under certain conditions, be discounted. Eve Kosofsky Sedgwick, in her analysis of the deployment of lesbian sexuality in Denis Diderot's *La Religieuse* (1760), terms the power to ignore such meanings the "privilege of unknowing" (103). In this tragicomic novel the novice Suzanne pretends not to "know" what is really "happening" when she submits, in incoherent transports of delight, to the seductions of her Mother Superior. Despite her purported "innocence," however, Suzanne eventually "outs" her Mother Superior to the male authorities and thereby destroys her. The bizarre turns in an epistemological plot that features the angelic "innocence" of young women on the one hand and the demonic "ignorance" of the Church on the other become evident in the autobiographical narratives Curb and Manahan present of nuns who have genital sex with other nuns but do not regard themselves or their activities as belonging to the "sinful" category of lesbianism, a term they apparently connect with identity, politics, and "lifestyle." Lacking an appropriate language or dismissing categories they do not believe to fit themselves, such nuns do not, moreover, regard their behavior as "incompatible with the vows of chastity" (xxvii).

In these views of the blamelessness or, perhaps more accurately, *moral indeterminacy* of female homoeroticism, such nuns are supported by the official dogma of the Catholic Church, for the *Modern Catholic Dictionary* offers a telling guideline by which to define the blessed state of virginity essential to monastic life:

> Strictly speaking, a person is physically a virgin unless he or she has had sexual intercourse with a person of the opposite sex. Moral virginity means the absence of any willful consent to venereal pleasure; again, strictly speaking, with a person of the opposite sex. Virginity is factual when, de facto, a person has not in the past sought or indulged in sexual pleasure; it is intentional when a person intends never to experience such pleasure, according to the distinctions made. (563)

Even a cursory reading of this elucidation indicates that the "distinctions made" would allow those who experience "venereal pleasure" only with those of the *same* sex, or, for that matter, those who do not take pleasure in sexual commerce with those of the opposite sex, to retain their virginity and thus advance on their progress toward sanctity.

The types of acts included under the category "female homoeroticism" have the virtue of making sense of an otherwise inexplicable state of affairs in which Teresa can regard herself as committing an unnameable sin *in her very zeal to protect her chastity.*[5] But the blessed state of virginity that, in Teresa's case, can be maintained and protected on such pleasurable terms hardly qualifies an ordinary nun in the sixteenth-century for the exalted condition of sainthood. What, then, is an ambitious girl, living in an era when the newly propounded Lutheran heresy was making inroads against an indolent and corrupt Catholic Church, to do? Teresa had no taste and, in her historical period, little use for the masochistic rigors of female martyrdom pictured with quasi-pornographic abandon in the *Lives of the Saints.* These accounts, set in the early centuries of Church history, follow an almost invariable pattern: a young woman who, having chosen to remain a lifelong virgin, encounters a "pagan" man who "outs" her as a Christian to the authorities, takes her captive, and asks her to reconsider, often forcing her to be exposed naked among prostitutes. When these efforts fail, she is subjected to ingenious tortures such as flogging, maiming, mutilation, beating, exposure to wild beasts, suffocation in steam baths, or burning at the stake. Divine intervention often renders these torments ineffective; nevertheless, the protagonist is subsequently translated into the joys of heaven, virginity *intacta*, via the generally (but not always) fatal means of beheading or some variation thereof (Smith 3)

In her historical moment Teresa had to discover another narrative pathway to religious immortality. The opportunity came when, at the age of thirty-eight, having enjoyed her *pasatiempos* with other nuns for twenty-four years, apparently (or conveniently) ignorant of any wrongdoing, she chanced to read St. Augustine's *Confessions*, which narrates his journey from lascivious pagan immorality to spotless Christian chastity. At this point Teresa experiences what she calls her conversion and, although she remains at the convent of the Encarnación with her companion Doña Juana for another seven years, sets out on the spiritual pathway that eventually leads her to become the Reformer of the Order of Our Lady of Carmel (Rohrbach 144–47). Thus, along with her numerous chronic ailments, her miraculous escapes from life-threatening illnesses, and her levitations and raptures, Teresa's *Life* narrates a movement from *ignorant* sinfulness to *enlightened* sanctity on which both her status as religious reformer and her eventual canonization depend. In a moment of supreme irony in lesbian and feminist cultural history, the breakthrough into *significance* for Teresa occurs when, in addition to her reading of Augustine's *Confessions*, she encounters well-educated confessors, such as her close friend Father Gracian, acquainted perhaps with the injunctions against "lesbian" sexuality in Sts. Paul, Ambrose, John Chrysostom, Anselm, Thomas Aquinas, and Antoninus (Brown 3–20).[6]

But even here the linkages between female homoeroticism and sinfulness remain, as Teresa's *Life* testifies, simultaneously incoherent and unspeakable, existing in an epistemological space that defines them, on the one hand, as insignificant and, on the other, as so potentially threatening and disruptive that they cannot even be *named* as sins. For instance, Augustine defines as "unnatural and sinful those sexual acts in which intercourse did not take place in a vessel fit for procreation" (9–51). While this broad definition could conceivably include lesbian sexuality, which blasphemes the telos of Christian cosmology by allowing the pleasures of sexual activity without the consequences of biological reproduction, Augustine *sees* sex as an entity defined by penetration and the presence of the penis, and he specifically decries male homosexuality and anal intercourse between heterosexuals. If women do not cross-dress, use prosthetic devices, or, most important, attempt to usurp male prerogative, the sensual "things" they do together fall into the nebulous category of "vain," or, rather, useless and unmeaning (and quintessentially *female*) activities that, although "pleasing to the senses," are not-*quite*-real, not-*quite*-sinful "nonsex." Indeed, the only allusion Augustine makes to something that might be termed *lesbian* sexuality appears in the context of a letter to his sister advising her on the governance of a monastic order, and his tone is vaguely admonitory rather than explicitly condemnatory.[7]

Thus, recalling that Teresa first joined an Augustinian and, later, an Unreformed Carmelite convent (an order that had, over the centuries, received numerous mitigations of the original Primitive Rule), her ignorant confessors may be excused for excusing her homoerotic pasatiempos as innocent diversions. But Teresa must avoid the self-cancelling extremes of either naming her monstrous "sin" directly or reducing it to an insignificant vanitas, lest she lose the leverage required to narrate her transformation from sinner to saint in an orderly manner. Hence, her criticisms of uneducated confessors and her gratitude for the learned men who, metaphorically, "open her eyes" to the wrongfulness of the practices of the unreformed convents where, in the words of Sackville-West, "fashionable topics of culture, philosophy, music, literature, and even, more dangerously, Platonic love, came under lively discussion" (62). Teresa is more direct than her later lesbian biographer about the nature of these "Platonic" loves:

> The way of true religion is so little used that friars or nuns who begin truly to follow their calling have more to fear from members of their own communities than from all the devils. They have to be more cautious and exercise greater dissimulation when speaking of the friendship that they wish to have with God, than on the subject of those other friendships or desires that the devil ordains shall flourish in religious houses. (53)

This passage, an eloquent and masterful example of what James Creech calls "closet writing" (56), which, like the entire *Life*, has compelled both the sentimental identification and intellectual admiration of Teresa's subsequent queer readers, exercises, despite her perhaps tongue-in-cheek professions to the contrary, a much more complex dissimulation in discussing the erotic friendships in religious life than the union between herself and Jesus Christ, on which she lavishes lengthy (and somewhat tedious) descriptions throughout the *Life*. Yet the homoerotic eros rampant in monastic communities provides what D. A. Miller terms the "instances of disequilibrium, suspense, and general insufficiency," the "incitements to narrative" and "underlying impulsions" (ix) that render St. Teresa's narrative *narratable*. In any case, an intellectually bored and frustrated Teresa eventually decides that it would be worthier (and certainly more interesting) to be a sinner on a par with men than to be an insignificant (or, literally, vain) woman. Hence, her *Life* is a notable instance of the manner in which, as Elizabeth Petroff remarks of the *Lives* of Italian women saints, "transgression gets shaped into nontransgression . . . into, in fact, a virtuous and compelling act . . . an event [that] is both transgressive and divinely sanctioned" (162).

This skillful management of an autobiographical narrative grounded in an experiential homoeroticism over which her symbolic union with Jesus Christ both *figures* and triumphs is not an easy act to follow, as Firbank and his character Cardinal Pirelli, who are both searching—with the ghost of St. Teresa—for the lost page of her *Way of Perfection*, know all too well. The social alienation and isolation of queers and, moreover, the acute invisibility of lesbians in the mid-twentieth century contributes materially to the Irish lesbian author Kate O'Brien's somewhat melancholy and self-abjecting placement of Teresa within an economy of lesbian cultural scarcity in her poignant biography, *Teresa of Ávila* (1950). O'Brien, writing in an uncomfortable transitional period when the imaginative space within the closet had considerably shrunk and when discernible queer writers and audiences were an event in the then still distant future, had to practice her craft in an inimical cultural environment of intolerance, antimodernist backlash, and provincialism. Two of her books were banned by the Irish Censorship Board for their "immorality" (Dalsimer xvi). Thus, she faced more rigorous penalties for following the Teresian injunction to treat the inner life as sacrosanct (Flanagan vii) than Teresa, whose writings received, despite the machinations of powerful detractors such as the Princess Eboli (who objected to the rigor of Teresa's reforms and about whom O'Brien wrote a novel, *That Lady* [1946]), the favorable judgment of the Holy Office of the Inquisition.

Mary Lavelle (1936), which includes a portrait of unrequited homoerotic passion for the title character, set in the context of contemporary Irish and Spanish political upheaval, committed the sin of describing heterosexual sex in explicit terms. *The Land of Spices* (1942) was banned for a sentence in which the main character, Helen Archer, discovers the homosexuality of the father she had once idolized as the "perfect man." In a reaction that mirrors that of the Irish Censorship Board, Helen is traumatized and horror-struck and decides to bury her secret knowledge. She makes the impulsive decision to become a nun and, eventually, the English Reverend Mère Marie-Hélène at the aptly named *Couvent de la Compagnie de la Sainte Famille*. Helen "turns her back upon herself, upon talents, dreams, emotions—and undertook the impersonal and active service of God" (18)

The narratives of unrequited homoerotic passion in *Mary Lavelle* (1936), homosexual panic in *The Land of Spices* (1942), and the political machinations of Teresa's archrival Princess Eboli in *That Lady* (1946) may be seen as preludes to her two last, explicitly lesbian novels, *The Flower of May* (1953) and *As Music and Splendour* (1958). Following the general rule that it is better to ignore than to admit the reality of lesbianism, neither were banned by the Irish Censorship Board. But before taking on these more intimate and self-revealing narratives, O'Brien turned, in preparation, to a biography of her beloved St. Teresa, which implicitly revolves around the following conundrum: If ordinary lesbians seem a scarce commodity in a patriarchal culture determined to keep women both passively obedient and sexually ignorant, then how much rarer are lesbians or, in the code O'Brien employs, "women" of genius who enjoy canonical status?

Indeed, in the entire course of western culture, there have been only three: Sappho, Emily Brontë, and Teresa of Ávila, the last to whom O'Brien, as a devout (if, obviously, dissenting and unconventional) Catholic, looks as an inspiration and role model. O'Brien restates the connection between Teresa and Sappho made by Sackville-West (and the "salacious" French scholars whom La Fuente derides) and adds to this stellar pair Emily Brontë, around whom an extensive (and now well-documented) lore of homoerotic passion involving an adolescent companion had long circulated (Foster 129–35).

Thus O'Brien, as an opening gesture in the search for lesbian community and readership (and, as well, for lesbian interpretations of cultural history), socializes Teresa among belletristic women stars and, differing somewhat from Sackville-West's emphasis on mystical intelligence and political savoir faire, transforms Teresa into an exemplary Romantic genius. But what, for O'Brien, constitutes a woman of genius, and why are such extraordinary women invariably nonheterosexual? She finds female heterosexuality and (in the those times prior to birth control) the related duties of wifehood and motherhood incompatible with the imaginative and personal freedoms required for creation. Moreover, none of these women geniuses write heterosexual narratives of courtship (like, for example, the ironic Jane Austen, whom O'Brien allows to gossip wittily with Madame de Sévigné in, metaphorically speaking, the kitchen of the House of Great Women Authors, while the three *prime donne* discourse on weightier matters in the main parlor). Since O'Brien finds romantic love (whether homosexual or heterosexual) disconnected from larger artistic, political, or religious projects invariably disappointing, insipid, and a meager measure of human worth, she cannot include among lesbian writers of genius those such as Radclyffe Hall, whose *The Well of Loneliness* is, after all, an "inverted" version of an unhappy courtship narrative. Rather, lesbian literary geniuses are those fortunate women daring enough to self-consciously understand (before their societies would explicitly term them *lesbian*) their own "sex variance," yet who lived in less scrutinizing pre-Freudian times, and who, like Sappho and Brontë, were "lucky in the shortness and the veiledness of their lives" (28).

Whereas Sackville-West sees Teresa as an artist forced by sixteenth-century Spanish culture to direct her ambitions to religion, O'Brien preserves religion as the central philosophical component of Teresa's practical genius. Although she writes an "easy, living Castilian" (28), Teresa is principally a "genius in her living," who "lived several lives, and lived each one intensely and to its fullest exaction" (28). In other words, Teresa, who disported herself with her "gay" (29) (a word O'Brien uses in both senses) companions as an adolescent and young nun, *self-consciously knows the meaning* of her homosexual experiences, "and we need not seek, as some of her pious biographers do, to shield her from her own cool accusations" (31).[8] After she "elopes" to the convent against her father's wishes, she attains an independent status and undertakes a protracted search for the *Way of Perfection* that involves, along the way, ongoing erotic relations with her sister nuns:

> She is not explicit in her writings about the particular "pastimes of the senses" to which she confesses her long addiction, but we may take her cool word for it that she knew as well what she talked of in their regard as she did in other contexts. . . . These friendships which in her youth delighted and in her young womanhood as a professed nun so much troubled and impeded her, prepared her in great measure no doubt for that part of her life which from her cell in the Encarnación was not to be foreseen. In order to become a saint she had to overcome and forego them; but in order to become the Reformer of the Order of Our Lady of Carmel, it was perhaps necessary for her to have known them, and through them all that of herself and of human nature which they revealed to her. (37)

Genius in women, then, is the complex product of historical possibility, sexual (and social) nonconformity, and the resourcefulness and determination to discover solutions to problems others regard as intractable. Sappho had the good fortune to live in a culture that permitted the relatively unabashed expression of female homoerotic passion (connected, significantly, to religious worship). Brontë expressed what might be termed her protolesbian *butchness* through her masculine identification with her antihero Heathcliffe in *Wuthering Heights*. Teresa moves from enclosed homoerotic passion to celibate sainthood, but employs the knowledge she gained through her earlier experiences as the foundation on which to construct her religious reforms.

What inspiration and, more important, assistance in solving aesthetic problems involving the representation of lesbianism can Kate O'Brien, writing in the historical moment of the mid-twentieth century, derive from the writings of her exalted predecessors? More specifically, what wisdom can she cull from the life and figure of Teresa of Ávila, whom she regards as sharing with her the same religion and a similar sexual "temperament" and dissatisfaction with placing romantic eros of whatever persuasion at the center of human existence? For O'Brien the salient aesthetic problems revolve around the issue of sexual innocence and knowledge and, collaterally, the question of narrative form. Like the later *As Music and Splendour* (1958), her first lesbian narrative, *The Flower of May* (1953), is an explicit *künstlerroman* that intersects the growth of the author's own artistic temperament with that of her characters. In this novel O'Brien returns to turn-of-the-century Ireland to explore the atavistic sexual innocence of Fanny Morrow and Lucille de Mellin, both of whom reject the conventional narratives of heterosexual romance and marriage and, surpassing the adolescent *schwärm* of schoolgirl infatuations (to which Sackville-West had essentially confined Teresa), establish a serious commitment to an adult existence together. That Lucille has an impenetrable "secret" she promises to tell Fanny but never does indicates her hidden knowledge of her lesbianism. But Fanny never has any inkling of the sexual nature of her feelings for Lucille. While this innocence (although a pretense for Lucille) shields both of them from disillusionment and enables them to pursue unconventional lives without any sense of "sinning" against their Catholic faith, this protracted and artificial (and, indeed, somewhat cloying and unconvincing) innocence also limits the narrative form to an incomplete bildungsroman, as neither character can develop further self-understanding or insight into the power of society that stunts them in a perpetual childhood. In this last breath of somewhat desperate and wishful innocence, both Kate O'Brien and her characters sound like early twentieth-century transcriptions of Teresa in her mid-thirties in the convent of the Encarnación, enjoying sensuous caresses with Doña Juana and other nuns, but wondering, like Peggy Lee, "Is that all there is?"

Unlike Teresa, however, O'Brien finally discovers that the *Way of Perfection* for contemporary lesbians lies not in self-closeting or religious transcendence but rather in self-conscious, deliberate *imperfection* and the "musical" arts of blatant sexual and operatic sinning (and singing). Just as Richard Crashaw had portrayed Teresa as a poetic version of the larger-than-life operatic diva, so does she reappear as the behind-the-scenes *spiritus mundi* in *As Music and Splendour*, in which the problems inherent in fitting lesbians into conventional narrative patterns are eliminated by jettisoning those forms and substituting the distinctly artificial (shades of Firbank) and nonmimetic topoi of operatic plotting. All the characters in this novel have heterosexual or homosexual *affairs de coeur* outside of marriage, so the Irish Clare Halvey and Spanish Luisa Carriãga are not, as sophisticated lesbian lovers, any more "sinful" than anybody else within their milieu whose erotic passions rival in their complications and intricacies the best of Handelian or Mozartian opera. As Elizabeth Wood eloquently notes, the "plot" of *As Music and Splendour* tracks the path of two "Sapphonic" female voices that "meet and bond in travesty duets, endure tests in travesty lament, are avenged and reunited 'as one' in warrior-goddess roles, and part only as two solo careers demand" (37). When Clare plays Euridice to Luisa's en travesti Orfeo, they become offstage lovers for whom the public performance of Berlioz's version of Gluck's *Orfeo ed Euridice* (1762) both masks and enables their private lesbian passions. Subsequently, when the men in their lives threaten to separate the lovers, they sing the lament of Pergolesi's *Stabat Mater* (1729), originally written for paired castrati. At last Luisa weeps as she hears Clare sing

"Casta Diva" from Bellini's *Norma* (1831), in which the Druid warrior-priestess prays to the moon goddess for peace between the warring Romans and Gauls. Soon after, however, Norma discovers that her Roman lover Pollione has been unfaithful, thus representing the anxieties of the two women that the men in their lives, and, more important, their solo careers as divas will separate them. But perhaps, O'Brien implies, Clare and Luisa will have the final song and eventually be reunited, for "Casta Diva" precedes the rapturous duet between Norma and Adalgisa, "Mira, O Norma," one of the most eloquent expressions of romantic friendship between women in opera. The two women, who had once been rivals for the love of the faithless Pollione, renounce men and pledge their eternal fidelity to one another:

> Yes, you will have me as your friend
> until your last hour;
> the world is large enough
> to be a shelter to both of us together.
> With you I shall set my face
> firmly against the shame which fate may bring
> as long as I feel your heart
> beating on mine . . . (43–44)

II. Saint Teresa Goes to the Opera

> Singing is the only occasion to express a truth
> which would otherwise be inaudible.
> —*Soeur Marie Keyrouz*

If, as Kate O'Brien finally suggests, aesthetic representations of lesbian lives are not reducible, without politicized distortion and cloying diminution, to the commonplace private romances of bourgeois heterosexuality but discover, rather, their "true reflection" in the resplendent artifice of art forms such as opera, how then, to go one step further, might St. Teresa herself be represented in opera? Can the conventions of *dramma per musica* be shaped and expanded to portray the mysticism and heroic resolve (as with Crashaw) and the religious accomplishments and practical intelligence (as with Sackville-West and O'Brien) of a queer female saint? Given that Sackville-West and, in particular, O'Brien, were avid opera fans with wide and eclectic literary tastes, it may seem curious, at first glance, that neither mentions their sister lesbian modernist Gertrude Stein in their reviews of important writers on Teresa. Yet here, as in so many other ways, Stein was an artistic pioneer whose libretto, *Four Saints in Three Acts* (1927), offered novel solutions to the problems inherent in representing female sainthood later faced by those who implicitly followed her lead in installing Teresa in the gallery of twentieth-century lesbian icons. Perhaps because of her originality, few men or women of any sexual persuasion have known quite what to do with Stein, either as an individual woman or, as becomes increasingly apparent, the most far-reaching modernist innovator of American English. The temporal lapse between when Stein actually wrote and when her so-called experimental (DeKoven xiii) writings began to be read with informed understanding is so great that it has become fashionable to explain this lag by calling Stein a postmodernist before her time, whose works are characterized by (to name but a few attributes) "radical suspension of narrative form . . . disruption of narrative hierarchies . . . promotion of acausality, nonteleological motion, fragmentation, open structures, indeterminacy, mise-en-abyme, dispersion, randomness, principles of nonselection and other modes for producing discontinuity" (Barry 4).

While these abstract terms do describe crucial aspects of the Steinian oeuvre, they can disconnect Stein from her historical and intellectual milieu and, more important, obscure recognition of the aesthetic concerns she shared with her fellow queer modernists, not the least of which was her admiration for St. Teresa and her fascination with Spanish Catholic culture, which rendered her, as lesbian and Jew, *doubly* socially marginal and symbolically central. As Wendy Steiner notes in reference to Steinian verbal portraiture, her writing project constitutes an intellectual effort to achieve "exact resemblance," and thus "the experience of reading Stein—of really reading her . . . is striking in its coherence" (27). Just as Sackville-West complained (well before Lacan) about persistent impulses to reduce Teresa's mystical writing to incoherent raptures, so with Stein it cannot be overstressed that, as Catherine R. Stimpson cogently remarks, "her literary language was neither 'female,' nor an unmediated return to signifiers freely wheeling in maternal space. It was instead an American English, with some French traits and a deep structure as genderless as an atom of plutonium" (79). Since the lives of saints are, by their very nature, miraculous and extraordinary, an artistic "exact resemblance" of Teresa and her community of Spanish mystics, such as Stein endeavors to body forth in *Four Saints*, must invariably "disrupt" the conventions of realism and narrative paradigms of conflict and resolution. Here, as elsewhere in her writings (which range in style from the chattily accessible *Everybody's Autobiography* to the densely abstract *How to Write*), Stein accommodates her treatment to the nature of her medium and subject matter.

Ironically, in part because literary critics almost never approach it as a text to be *sung* in *performance*, the libretto of *Four Saints* has a history as singular and original (and, one is tempted to add, as queer) within twentieth-century American literature as Virgil Thomson's richly consonant and hymnodical setting within American opera. *Four Saints* received very favorable reviews when first performed under the auspices of the Friends and Enemies of Modern Music at the Avery Memorial Hall in Hartford, Connecticut, in 1934 and, later that year, in New York City.[9] According to Carl Van Vechten, Thomson chose an all-black cast because, while attending a performance of the "Negro"-themed choral play *Run, Little Chillun*, he decided that black singers alone "possess the dignity and the poise, the lack of self-consciousness . . . [and] . . . the rich, resonant voices essential to the singing of my music and the clear enunciation required to deliver Gertrude's text" (7).[10] Although widely recognized as the two finest examples of American opera, neither *Four Saints* nor *The Mother of Us All* (which concludes with a secular, quasi-Buddhistic apotheosis of suffragist Susan B. Anthony) have achieved a secure position in standard operatic repertoires, although this situation has begun to change in recent years.[11] In some measure because her literary executor Carl Van Vechten included *Four Saints* in his 1946 edition, *Selected Writings of Gertrude Stein*, to exhibit the wide range of genres in which Stein worked, this text has achieved, unlike virtually any other libretto, with the possible exception of Oscar Wilde's text translated and appropriated for Richard Strauss's *Salome*, an independent status as an important work of *literary* modernism, where it is regularly treated as an entity wholly apart from (and, sometimes, antagonistic to) Thomson's musical setting.[12]

Thus, in choosing the drama of the canonization of "saints" as the respective topics of their operas and as allegories of their working lives as artists, Stein and Thomson not only consciously play on the various connotations of sainthood but also, as the performance history of their two operas attest, unintentionally reveal both the politics behind operatic canonization and the divisions enforced by academic specialization and disciplinary boundaries as well. Moreover, "canonical" operas had, since the early nineteenth century, almost invariably intersected tragic heterosexual love with various political, nationalistic, or cultural conflicts, so that, to take the representative case of the operas of Giuseppe Verdi, the private "mirrors" the public realm. As Catherine Clément has noted, the words that accompany (and should equally complement) opera are, significantly, like the *prime donne* in these works, overwhelmed, subordinated, and menaced by the sensuous onrush of music, performance, and spectacle.

How does Stein rescue herself as librettist and Teresa as female mystic (and diva) from an analogous fate of operatic obliteration, and how does Thomson subsequently rework the musical conventions for representing the relationship between the "personal" and the "religious" that had governed secular opera prior to *Four Saints?* In the eighteenth century and, in Italy, much of the nineteenth century, direct representations of God (or Christian religious and biblical characters) were not permitted onstage. Thus, pagan deities were regularly (and, perhaps, gleefully) substituted or, in the case of Mozart's *Die Zauberflöte* (1791), the evil seductiveness of the Catholic Church was allegorized in the figure of the Queen of the Night. Giacomo Meyerbeer's mid-nineteenth-century depictions of religious and cultural conflict in *Les Huguenots* (1836) and *L'Africaine* (1865) and religious madness in *Le Prophète* (1849) helped pave the way for the "polite" religious eroticism that characterizes Jules Massenet's *Hérodiade* (1881), *Manon* (1884), and, in particular, *Thaïs* (1894)—the last of which, significantly (like Massenet's *Sapho* [1897]), much influenced and delighted Ronald Firbank. In this opera the young Cenobite monk Athanaël decides to "convert" the lascivious courtesan Thaïs, who in an interlude of narcissistic delight sings the famous aria "Dis-moi que je suis belle" in front of her mirror. The conversion succeeds all too well, and Thaïs, now happily sanctified, becomes a nun (and eventually a saint), leaving Athanaël, ironically, frustrated and erotically obsessed in a state of damnation.

Sexually inflected Jewish religious themes make their appearance in Camille Saint-Saëns's *Samson de Dalilia* (1877), in which the seductive Philistine maiden Dalila ruins the Israelite hero. Samson's self-immolating destruction of the Temple anticipates the ending of Richard Strauss's deliberately shocking *Salome* (1905), in which the soldiers crush to death the seductive Salome, who, angry that Jokanaan (John the Baptist) has spurned her advances, has him beheaded and uses his "detached organ" to masturbate. But this overall picture of perverse or heterosexualized "religiosity," in which transcendent religious "desire" is unmasked as or reduced to sado-masochistic sexual desire, reaches its pinnacle with, not surprisingly, Giacomo Puccini and his excruciatingly sentimental *Suor Angelica* (1918). The hapless and "sinful" if, indeed, lovable and pathetic title character is forced into a convent against her will for having a child out of wedlock, and the one-act scenario ends with Suor Angelica committing suicide by drinking a concoction of poisonous flowers, but sees, as a sign of her ultimate forgiveness, a vision of the Virgin Mary.[13]

Stein and Thomson discard (and parody) the narrative and musical vocabularies in these operas of religious exposé sensationalism, prurient decadence, and masochistic sentimentality in part because their respective positions as a lesbian and gay man officially outside the pale of Christian moral dogma prompt them to create an opera simultaneously meditative and whimsical and serious and rapturous in tone and structure. Teresa's sexuality is not treated as an "incitement" to narrative or as a prurient secret to be unveiled for the delectation of her spectators, as would occur in traditional grand opera. Neither is it an occasion for high-camp frolics (as in Firbank), an adolescent "effusion" (as in Sackville-West), or a fruitful learning experience en route to chaste sainthood (as in O'Brien). Indeed, *Four Saints* recalls Richard Crashaw's focus on the "inner light" of Teresa's heroic grandeur and her innate capacity to transcend gender categories. Perhaps reflecting the unbroken continuity of Stein's own life as a lesbian, Teresa and her sensuous pleasure remain *constants* throughout *Four Saints*. In a witty reinterpretation of the "sins" of vanitas detailed in Teresa's *Life*, these amusements become the enabling substratum and context in which Teresa, as in the peaceful domestic relations between Stein and Alice Toklas, builds her character and does her arduous saintly (i.e., artistic) work. Indeed, much of the opera *is* an aesthetic-religious pasatiempos, which, in combining Christian symbolism with legend, and with homoerotic and magical elements, makes it a quasi-comic version of Wagnerian *Bühnenweihfestspiel* (a festival of consecration on the stage). Teresa's predicament does not reside in her sexuality but rather in her secondary status as a "forgotten" (581) saint, as dramatized by the obstacles placed in her path (that she must overcome) by the Jesuit St. Ignatius, who introduces the elements of tragedy and destabilization in *Four Saints* by insisting on the fundamental differences between the sexes and the superiority of men.

Stein, herself until recently a relatively "forgotten" artist in a modernist landscape dominated by male "saints" such as James Joyce (an Irish Catholic on whom she probably modeled St. Ignatius) and T. S. Eliot, clearly looks to Teresa as the model of the devoted artistic woman who achieved prominence later in life. In this opera, then, historical and fictional saints achieve "canonization" precisely by rejecting the narratives of heterosexual conflict and spiritual desublimation that characterize canonical opera plots. Thus, the process of artistic *bildung* that occurs in *Four Saints* comments indirectly on the inability of such queer operas to achieve an established position within grand opera. The peaceful if arduous efforts of their company of female and male mystics to discover the Teresian *Way of Perfection* becomes the vehicle for an exploration of the creative lines and, as Stein says, the "situations" (*Four Saints* 588) in Western culture and religion, of Thomson and Stein, who appear, appropriately—and humorously—enough, in the stage-managing roles of the *commère* (female gossip) and *compère* (accomplice).

In referring to the tenor of Stein and Thomson's long friendship, artistic collaboration, and opera as *queer,* this term assumes what can best be described as "utopian" connotations and attests to the power of the figure of St. Teresa to generate passionate interest and to create common interpretative ground between gay and lesbian artists. In the case of the collaboration of *Four Saints*, this ground of mutual cooperation and admiration was prepared by Thomson's reading of Stein's *Tender Buttons* (1911) and *Geography and Plays* (1922) while an undergraduate at Harvard, an experience that he said "changed his life" (42). Soon after first meeting his older compatriot in Paris in 1926, Thomson set two playfully erotic Steinian portraits, "Susie Asado" and "Preciosilla" (both 1913), as well as her allegorical description of the battle for preeminence among four provincial capitals, *Capital Capitals* (1923), which he then performed at the homes of the lesbian literary salonists Natalie Barney and the Duchesse de Clermont-Tonnerre. While Stein apparently appreciated these settings, the decisive moment of her growing trust and estimation of Thomson occurred when he played Erik Satie's symphonic drama *Socrate* (comp. 1919) for her and Toklas.[14] Herself a highly knowledgeable and longtime opera fan who nonetheless found most music an "adolescent" art form, Stein was impressed by Thomson's modesty and lack of excessive emotionality as he sat before the piano playing conductor, orchestra, and vocal soloist. On her way back home she commented to Toklas that Thomson was "singularly pure *vis-à-vis* his art," which, reflecting her own artistic convictions, seemed to mean to him "discipline, humility, and loyalties rather than egocentric experience" (quoted in Hoover and Cage 62).

While Thomson suggested the topic of saints and Stein decided upon the Spanish figures of Sts. Teresa and Ignatius, he marshaled the other collaborators and, most important, the financial backers to ensure eventual performance. According to Thomson, Stein, in her turn, provided him through her example with an innovative approach to the compositional process that "avoid[ed] the premeditated" and combined disciplined concentration with "spontaneity that . . . well[ed] up from a state of self-containment" (Hoover and Cage 124). In Stein Thomson perceived a writer intensely aware of the elective affinities between language and music and through whom he could "break, crack open, and solve for all time anything to be solved, which was almost everything, about English musical declamation. . . . With meanings already abstracted, or absent, or so multiplied that choice among them was impossible, there was no temptation toward tonal illustration" (Hoover and Cage 90). Moreover, Thomson had uncanny insight into the inherent limitations of both music and language, which meant that they *needed* each other to achieve artistic fruition:

> What gave this work [*Four Saints*] so special a vitality? The origin of that lay in its words, of course, the music having been created in their image. Music, however, contains an energy long since lost to language, an excitement created by the contest of two rhythmic patterns, one of lengths and one of stresses. . . . Together, and contrasted, they create a tension and release; and this is the energy that makes music sail, take flight, get off the ground.
>
> (Hoover and Cage 105)

John Cage eloquently describes the result in *Four Saints* as a perfect "marriage" and, "as with successfully married couples, one wonders what either partner would be like without the other" (Hoover and Cage 157). If "divorced," both would be diminished and impoverished. The thematic musical relationships "function insufficiently as architecture to produce an independent work," while the thematic structures and forward momentum of music "makes the ambiguity of the text less baffling, more immediately enjoyable" (158)

Thus, through their "perfect marriage" as queer collaborators Stein and Thomson create a dynamic symmetrical balance between elements usually characterized by intimate antagonism (as between the homosexual Firbank and the lesbian Sackville-West) or arranged according to patterns of dominance and subordination (as in music *over* words, masculine *over* feminine, or gay man *over* lesbian). In the relations of mutually influencing and non-narcissistic communion between libretto and setting and male and female "sainthood" (and artistry), who or what is "active-top" or "passive-bottom" is in a continual state of flux, transformation, and exchange. In his setting Thomson achieves an analogous intermixture of "high" and "low," French and American, and avant-garde and demotic musical motifs. He combines the sonorous gravitas of liturgical plainchant and antiphonal choruses with the humorous quasi campiness of the brass choir and harmonium of an American revivalist Salvation Army (perhaps an ersatz version of the Church Militant). With these elements and others such as madrigals, popular ballads, dance tunes, anthems, and nursery rhymes, Thomson integrates an ironically Sateian but serious treatment of standard operatic conventions including soaring arias, rousing oratorio, pastoral ballet music, and meditative recitative. John Cage, once again resorting to the metaphor of marriage to describe the Stein and Thomson collaboration, notes that *Four Saints* simply "defies analysis" and that "to enjoy it, one must leap into . . . the world in which the matter-of-fact and the irrational are one, where mirth and metaphysics marry to beget comedy" (157). In this "saintly" panoramic world *queer sexuality* is no longer a noun that belongs to the identity of the paradigmatic "gay man" or "lesbian," it rather describes a dynamic musical-theatrical mode of socially organizing and dramatically performing erotic pleasure and intimacy in which *power freely circulates and is freely exchanged*.

The prologue, *A Narrative of Prepare for Saints*, opens with the two choirs of saints, as well as the female Sts. Settlement and Sarah and the male Sts. Plan and Stephen and the commère (mezzo) and compère (bass) preparing for the entry of Teresa in act 1.[15] The opera begins with a snare drum roll that segues into an "oompah" waltz rhythm, which gives the opening the whimsical musical atmosphere of a circus merry-go-round. The full chorus sings a rousing melody that is, in essence, a Teresian version of the Catholic catechism's meaning of life ("To know Him, to love Him, and to serve Him in this world") and also invokes the fish symbolism of Christ, the preparation of Sacrament, and the miracle of the fishes:

To know to know to love her so
Four saints prepare for saints.
It makes it well fish.
Four saints it makes it. well fish. (Stein 581)

To know Teresa means to love her, but she has remained a "forgotten saint" (Stein 581), never properly known, remembered, or, therefore, loved. Thus, the prologue not only dramatizes All Saints Day, designed to commemorate those unnamed saints who have gone to heaven, but also evokes Advent, the season of preparation. The commère and compère, as well as the aptly named Sts. Plan and Settlement, must artistically and philosophically "settle" or determine how this opera "plans" to portray St. Teresa. This preparation begins when the commère, in a chant ending in melody, narrates one version of peaceful saintly (and artistic) life as the seasonal cycles of activity and contemplation reminiscent of Stein's *Lucy Church Amiably:*

> We had intended if it were a pleasant day to go to the country it was a very beautiful day and we carried out our intention. We went to places that we had been when we were equally pleased and we found very nearly what we could find and returning saw and heard that after all they were rewarded and likewise. This makes it necessary to go again. (Stein 582)

The compère responds in greater length in an abstract (and, in the score, emotionally wrought) philosophical discourse about the impossibility of representing in temporal narrative the nature of the eternal. The commère, realizing that such speculations will not "do" in an opera, simply says: "This is how they do not like it" (Stein 582). At this point the commère and compère take up the difficult task, which occupies them throughout much of the opera, of imagining and stage-directing how Teresa and the other three principal saints (Teresa's "special friend" St. Settlement, and St. Ignatius and his aide-de-camp St. Chavez) will be incarnated and "prompted" into dramatic existence during the opera. Indeed, much of the opera is a (re)enactment of the work of writing an opera. Since it is easier "to be land" (ibid.), or to have an embodied spatial presence than to be pure spirit, they begin their work by imagining where the saints will be seated: "Imagine four benches separately. . . . Four benches used separately" (ibid.). While this does not eliminate the problem of portraying saints, who exist in eternity, within the spatial and temporal dimensions of an opera, Stein renders time a meaningless measurement by transforming performance into static tableaux and, hence, action into a quality. In a central passage in the prologue sung in successive parts by Sts. Settlement, Stephen, and Sarah, the temporal function of memory is evoked only to be dismissed: "It is very easy in winter to remember winter spring and summer it is very easy in winter to remember spring and winter and summer it is very easy in winter to remember summer spring and winter it is very easy in winter to remember spring and summer and winter" (583). While sublunary mortals can remember former winters or compare present with past seasons, perhaps only saints (who are themselves "frozen" in time) can remember "winter in winter," for one cannot remember something one exists "in." Saints are beyond the functions of history, memory, and identity, so that in this "narrative to plan an opera" (Stein 584) Stein transforms temporal "habits" into a tableau of a way of life and mode of dress that typify the changeless existence, both playful and serious, of monastics and, by implication, artists: "A croquet scene and when they made their habits. Habits not hourly habits habits not hourly at the time that they made their habits not hourly they made their habits" (584).

Having temporarily "settled" or set forth the paradoxes of representing characters in time who exist outside of time, the opera invokes (to the dramatic accompaniment of the chorus) the arrival of Pentecost (the descent of the Holy Spirit) and the sexual "panic" induced in nature by the Greek god Pan: "Come panic come. . . . Rejoice saints rejoin saints recommence some reinvite" (585). Stein turns to the miracle of the Communion of Saints in which saints of different times and places are brought together ("Four saints were not born at one time although they knew one another" [585]), often represented in Renaissance art through the pictorial convention of the "sacred conversation" that occurs in heaven among the blessed. But Teresa, "not knowing of other saints" (585), has not yet achieved secure status among these saints in an Aristotelean heaven of the unities of time, place, and action, so Stein simultaneously conflates and synchronizes the "past" of writing and rehearsing and the "present" of performing this opera. Significantly, Teresa's inability to achieve at once a "perfect" place in heaven (which occurs in act 4) allows Stein to make her presence felt as a librettist, for she *impedes* the dramatic and sensuous flow of operatic performance by calling attention to the slower processes of contemplation and planning that not only enable that performance but also characterize the first part of Teresa's life. During that period Teresa not only engaged in homoerotic vanitas with other nuns but also developed a new method of "inward" or "mystical" prayer, which Stein perceives as the artistic creation of a new mode of "language" through concentrated self-recollection. Hence the playful references to "Tanglewood," the location of the music festival in Massachusetts where this opera *might* be performed, and the comment that Teresa *might* be "something like" (Stein 585) the American anthem, "My country 'tis of thee sweet land of liberty of thee I sing" (ibid.), which the chorus does sing, and which Americans sing regularly. Thus, before beginning an opera that shows Teresa beginning to be a saint, the commère and compère provide a chanted litany of subsequently canonized (e.g., Sts. Teresa and Ignatius) and fictional saints (e.g., Sts. Electra, Martyr, and Cardinal) reminiscent of Ronald Firbank. As queers are constantly accused of doing, these saints may not "breed," but they certainly "recruit" Teresa into their blessed company.

Act 1, which takes place in Ávila, portrays the *Life* of St. Teresa as a series of seven tableaux, which are posed by Saint Teresa II (contralto), while Saint Teresa I (soprano) enacts for the edification of the audience and saints these autobiographical scenes. Here as elsewhere the commère prompts St. Teresa I by speaking her first line: "A pleasure April's fools day a pleasure" (Stein 586). Of course, "not April's fools day" means Easter, and Teresa, who is alone, or "seated and not surrounded" (ibid.), has her first epiphany of a world greater than herself and her environment in a repeated refrain ending with a melodic phrase of piercingly transcendent beauty: "There are a great many places and persons close together" (Stein 587). Teresa is depicted as a social nun who is "visited by very many" and is "half inside and half outside outside the house," which not only alludes to her "unsettled" (and unsettling) situation as a female mystic but also to her numerous trips to found convents (ibid.) and secure "situations" for herself and her nuns. She also makes her first acquaintance with her mature and complementary self: "How do you do," St. Teresa I says. "Very well I thank you" St. Teresa II graciously replies (ibid.).

But what, then, does *Four Saints* make of the sexuality of St. Teresa apart from the homosocial milieu in which she lives? The visual mirroring of St. Teresa I and II and the musical complementarity indicated by Thomson of female soprano and mezzo voices implies an an intensely autoerotic Teresa whose two "lips speak together," in the words of Luce Irigaray. Moreover, the original choreographer, Frederick Ashton, for whom, according to Thomson, "the saints moved gaily with decorum" (Stein and Thomson 406), posed one young woman embracing another from behind outside the pavilion where the two Teresas are becoming "acquainted" with one another (ibid.), thus implying that a social context of female homoeroticism informs Teresa's self-knowledge. That Teresa does not connect her contemplativeness or homoeroticism with conscious conceptions of sorrow or self-division until the intervention of her "confessor" and fellow saint Ignatius is made apparent near the end of act 1. In the preceding tableaux Teresa, with the help of the commère and her "special friend" St. Settlement (who recalls Doña Juana), decides to join the convent or "settle a private life" (Stein 587), and is photographed with a dove, symbol of the Holy Spirit, "having been dressed like a lady and then they taking out her head changed it to a nun" (Stein 588). St. Ignatius, who had been hovering in the background, attempts a kind of heterosexual seduction by kneeling before her

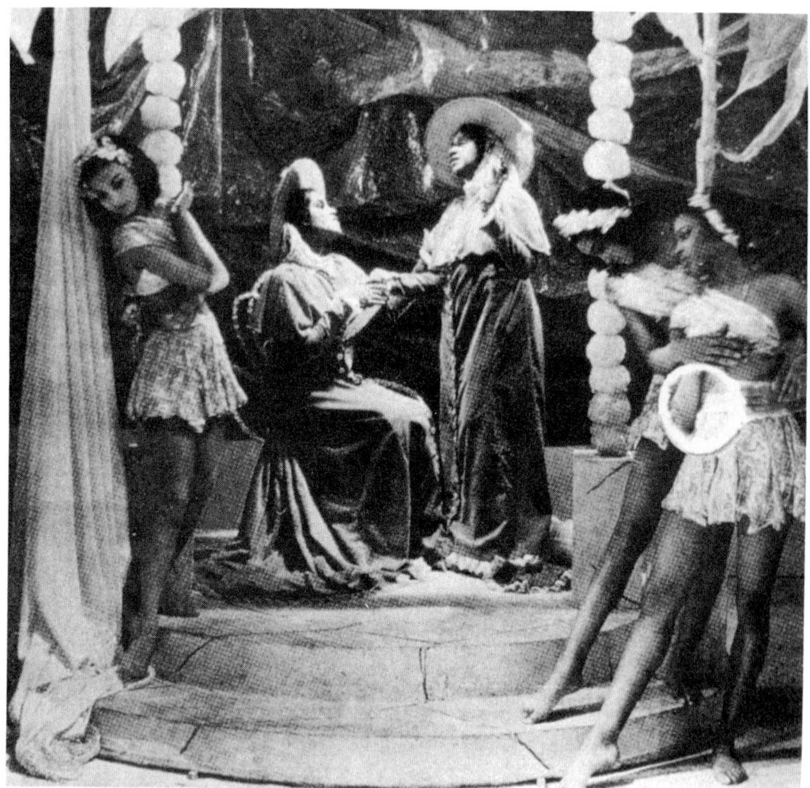

• **Fig 12.2. The younger and elder Saint Teresa become "acquainted" while angelic female lovers hover nearby.** *Courtesy of John Herrick Jackson Music Library, Yale University.*

and "wooing" her by playing guitar, presenting her with flowers, and showing her a model of the Heavenly Mansion. While St. Ignatius becomes more ominous near the end of *Four Saints*, here he is both an intrusive and helpful figure. He shows Teresa the way to her "ecstasy," but neither Stein nor Thomson interpret this moment as an irrational excess of possessed emotionality. Rather, in an angelically somber and contemplative soprano aria, Teresa in her "ecstasy" accepts with poignant dignity the painful truth that "there can be no peace on earth with calm with calm" (Stein 591). In other words, Teresa must learn to accept with equanimity the disruptiveness inherent in human power relations and the potentially divisive desires of others such as St. Ignatius if she is to remain focused on her own creative endeavors. In the final tableau St. Teresa, represented as a type of the Virgin Mary, pretends to hold a baby in her arms, having been made artistically "fruitful" by her ecstasy. She has achieved mature philosophical awareness, and self-consciously knows "the difference between singing and women" (Stein 583), or between the voice and the sensual body that produces artistic expression. In a mournful song recalling the *Agnus Dei* from Verdi's *Requiem*, the trio of St. Teresa I and II and St. Ignatius lament their newly acquired knowledge of their ignorance, both of themselves and of each other:

> They never knew about it green and they never knew about it she never knew about it they never knew about it they never knew about it she never knew about it. Planting it green means that it is necessary to protect it from the sun and from the wind and the sun and they never knew about it and she never knew about it and she never knew about it and they never knew about it.
> (593)

Here they describe the loss of innocence that transforms "not knowing" into a pernicious form of ignorance about natural processes of procreation, which prevents them from protecting their "knowledge" as one would a young green plant from excessive exposure to wind and sun. But in their preoccupations with the differences and potential divisions between male and female, they ironically reveal themselves as "innocent" creatures who want to maintain their gendered identities in the condition of unresolved suspension of childhood, as the subsequent nursery rhyme indicates: "One two three four five six seven all good children go to heaven" (Stein 594).

By act 2 St. Ignatius has become "well known" (ibid.) and St. Teresa is "in place" and "happily married" (Stein 596) to Christ. Thus securely ensconced in their sainthoods, Teresa continues to oversee the building of her Reformed Carmelite Order (and her *Foundations*) and both saints join the commère and compère in watching the Dance of the Angels. Still later Teresa I and II look and listen (and join their voices) in delight as the commère and compère (i.e., Stein and Thomson) enact a queer love duet that transcends "sense-making" in purely sensual aesthetic play and represents the perfect accord between rhyming words and harmonic music:

> Scene eight. To Wait.
> Scene one. And begun.
> Scene two. To and to.
> Scene three. Happily be.
> Scene Four. Attached or.
> Scene Five. Sent to derive. (Stein 596)

The other saints join in these rhyming and echoing games of musical "round robins" until St. Plan arrives with a telescope through which the saints see a vision of the Heavenly Mansion ("How many doors how many floors and how many windows are there in it" [Stein 602]), invoked by their beatific musical and verbal play. But St. Ignatius, in an indication of darker things to come in act 3, "Withdrew with with withdrew" (603) the telescope, thus preventing the disconsolate Teresa I from enjoying a picture of this Mansion or, by implication, of her place in the heavenly scheme. In act 3 St. Ignatius, having failed to bend St. Teresa to his wishes or dominate her mystical visions, has withdrawn from this happily mixed company of queer saints, along with his exclusively male companions, and enforced the tragic divisions of gender separatism: "This is how young men and matter" (Stein 604). In his famous aria, "Pigeons on the grass alas" (Stein 605), he uses his sorrow over mutability and the passage of time to exclude women from his Communion of Saints: "Fundamentally and saints fundamentally and saints and fundamentally and saints" (Stein 607). St. Ignatius has his vision of Final Judgment: "Around is a sound around is a sound around is a sound and around. Around differing from anointed now" (Stein 608). The frightened saints enter in a procession accompanied by the *Dies Irae*-like dirge of the commère and compère, "in wed in dead in dead wed led in led wed dead in dead in led in wed in said in said led wed dead wed" (Stein 609), which, partly in consequence of St. Ignatius's gender hierarchy, interprets the meaning of human existence as a somberly tragic and repetitive round of leading, marrying, vowing, and dying.

To this oppressively melancholy vision of sainthood, which completely excludes queers, the chorus and principals ask for supplementary "vine time," punning on "vain time" (recollecting Teresa's long interlude of presumably "vain" homoerotic activity) but also connoting the ripening time that allows things to mature and bear fruit (and the sacramental wine), which exceeds the exigencies of purely biological survival and enables the central ceremony of Christian worship. The Church, dominated by dirges and hymns, *does* need its queers, and they arrive, after a musical pastoral interlude with flute accompaniment, in the persons of Sts. Stephen and Settlement, the paired male and female saints who had invoked the "narrative of prepare for saints" (Stein 581) in the prologue. They are the younger saints (and artists) who serve the pleasurable function of building and adorning the Church, attracting admiration and future saints, providing "windowing" or new ways of looking at religious worship, and spending time in seemingly purposeless contemplation:

> Let it be why if they were adding adding comes cunningly to be additionally cunningly in the sense of attracting attracting in the sense of adding adding in the sense of windowing and windowing and frames and pigeons and ordinary trees and while while away. (Stein 609)

Thus, queers are the indispensable supplementary to the reductive vision of St. Ignatius, and the commère and compère reenter in the prologue to act 4 to inquire into the state of completion of their work and how many saints are in it, to which they now reply "four or more" (Stein 611), implying that the fictional saints have made their way into artistic immortality and that they need "Act four" (ibid.) to represent their translation into heaven. The curtain rises, and all the saints, including Teresa and Ignatius, are assembled in heaven, where Teresa rehearses the progression of tableaux beginning with "to place" and ending with "bread" (Stein 612), or starting with her efforts to become a saint and finishing with a sacramental meal. Lest we forget the librettist, Stein puts her famous signature on the piece, "When this you see remember me" (ibid.), sung by the full chorus, and after some final rearranging of the saints (which implies that St. Chavez, the follower of St. Ignatius, will "care" for Teresa), the opera closes with the "Last Act" and the chorus and principals shout in an emphatic finale: "Which is a fact" (ibid.).

III. Coda: St. Teresa as Holy Relic

This is not a story my people tell.
—*Laurie Anderson,* Langue d'Amour

On October 15, 1582, Teresa of Ávila died in the arms of Blessed Anne of St. Bartholomew, exclaiming, "O my Lord, now is the time that we may see each other!" (*One Hundred Saints* 247). So much, as Stein implies about all endings in *Four Saints*, is "fact." According to Catholic legend her corpse resisted corruption and exuded an intoxicating fragrance. Convinced that they had lived in the presence of an anointed saint, her male confessors and aristocratic admirers enacted the process of mourning her departure and taking possession of her legacy by dismembering her body and translating it into a collection of holy relics. Her once beloved confessor Father Gracian began the desecration by cutting off her left hand. Later, Father Gregorio de Naciancene inserted his knife into the truncated arm and, as he exclaimed in rapturous tones, the blade passed through the flesh like "cheese." Choosing for himself her shroud, he gave this relic to Teresa's nuns who, however grief-stricken and horrified they might have been over this spectacle of mutilation, were apparently powerless to halt this inexorable parceling out of her body. Indeed, over three hundred years later, this left forearm of the patron saint of Spain became the beloved possession of Generalísimo Francisco Franco, who kept it in his bedroom to ward off would-be assassins. Others, perhaps initially more timid, followed suit, ripping away fingers, her right foot, part of her jaw, pieces of her breasts and skin, and several ribs. Fragments of her bones, fingernails, and teeth were auctioned off or sold to the aristocracy. Her head, with the left eye gouged out, was severed from the body and laid on a satin cushion embroidered with silver and gold. At last, her "flaming heart" was torn out and placed in a reliquary. The organ bore a darkly colored wound that was seen as proof God had indeed "pierced" her heart but probably indicated that Teresa had suffered an acute myocardial infarction. Sackville-West notes that sometime after her death the Bishop of Ávila and his suite at San José, who came to inspect the "evidence" of her saintliness, were offered the macabre spectacle of a "withered and mummified image, the colour of dates, which could be propped upright by a hand placed between the shoulders" (97). This quasi-resurrected and puppetlike semblance of the former Discalced Carmelite nun did not appall but rather deeply impressed the Bishop and, subsequently, the papal authorities. In 1622, a mere forty years after her death, Teresa of Ávila was canonized by a Church that, in the midst of the Counter-Reformation, was in desperate need of saints who inspired the faith of common people. In 1970 she was called upon once again to rescue the Church from the consequences of its dogmatism and corrupt institutional practices. Teresa was made the first women Doctor of the Church in some measure as an ineffectual gesture to quell increasing complaints about the secondary status of women in the Catholic Church.

To paraphrase Laurie Anderson, this is not the story of Teresa of Ávila that queer people have told. If they have reflected mournfully upon the violence the official Church has visited upon the canonical Saint Teresa, it has mainly been to resist such death-enamoured sanctification by resurrecting the buried memories and reincarnating the unruly pleasures of the once living woman. Nor has this seemingly perpetual queer task of re-remembering, reinterpreting, and reuniting the body and soul of Teresa ended. Perhaps it is both fitting and inevitable, given the long history of queer admiration of Teresa, that the contemporary Chicana lesbian writer Gloria Anzaldúa should turn, in a poem dedicated to Vita Sackville-West, to the figure of Teresa of Ávila as *the* symbol of the queers of all nations, sexes, and colors who have resisted obliteration even as they continue to endure social isolation, dispersion, and silencing:

> We are the holy relics,
> the scattered bones of a saint,
> the best loved bones of Spain.
> We seek each other. (159)

Notes

1. The term *protolesbian* is used here to indicate Crashaw's intense identification with a female saint who, as such, has no sexual dealings with men and who has quasi-masculine *virtù*. The person of Teresa apparently suggests to Crashaw the notion articulated by Aristophanes in Plato's *Symposium* that human beings are, ideally, androgynous wholes

and that human perfection is only obtainable apart from sexual difference. Moreover, in her study of the inscriptions of gender and body in Christian women in late antiquity, Castelli quotes the noncanonical collection of sayings of Jesus, the apocryphal *Gospel of Thomas*, in which Jesus says, "Behold, I myself shall lead her so as to make her male, that she too may become a living spirit like you males. For every woman who makes herself male will enter the kingdom of heaven." Castelli notes that this text articulates the new "idea that women can gain access to holiness and salvation by 'becoming male' " (" 'I Will Make Mary Male,' " p. 30).

2. The diva Tosca, a devout Catholic, prays and offers devotions to the Madonna during an interlude in her amorous attentions to her lover, the painter Cavaradossi. In Hindemith's *Sancta Susanna* (1922) the title character has a series of religious raptures that are presented as distinctly sexual in nature. Giselher Schubert notes that the performance history of the latter opera is

> a chronicle of unprecedented scandal. Fritz Busch refused to conduct the premier of *Sancta Susanna* in fear of "open conflict." It was finally performed on 26 March 1922 in Frankfurt under the direction of Ludwig Rottenberg and led to public protests to the point of a meditation of expiation by the "Frankfurt League of Catholic Women" as a "sign of protest and distress at the disgraceful spectacle on the Frankfurt stage." ("About *Sancta Susanna*," pp. 17–18)

During the Nazi period, in 1934, Hindemith withdrew the piece and for the rest of his life refused to permit performances.

3. There are several intriguing (and perhaps unanswerable) questions posed by Firbank's extensive use of lesbian characters in his fictions, including the possibility that it might constitute an instance of the so-called Albertine strategy. In *A la Recherche du temps perdu* Proust transposed the male homosexuality he did not dare treat openly onto the lesbian character Albertine. See Brophy, *Prancing Novelist* (passim), for an alternate interpretation, which argues that Firbank on occasion "transposed" but, much more frequently, expressed an identification with and interest in lesbians as such. In any event, fin-de-siècle male homosexual writers' extensive use of lesbian characters (whether as stand-ins for gay men or not) obviously nettled Sackville-West, in part because they "outed" and represented in sensationalistic or kitsch-campy ways the particular nature of lesbianism or lesbian Catholic religiosity. See Auerbach, *Ellen Terry*, pp. 405–17, and Glasgow, "What's a Nice Lesbian Like You?" for discussions of the large number of early twentieth-century lesbians involved in the arts who converted (sometimes on their deathbeds) or found refuge in Catholicism, including Violet Shiletto, Renée Vivien, Una Troubridge, Radclyffe Hall, "Layde" Mabel Veronica Batten, Christopher St. John, Vita Sackville-West, Kate O'Brien, and Alice B. Toklas. Perhaps overstating the case, at least in the twentieth century, Glasgow argues that since Roman Catholicism perceives sex as something that happens between men or between men and women, then "lesbians were indeed innocent. And from all the evidence, it seems clear that their sexuality was seen as innocent by the church. Lesbian sexuality did not exist as a Catholic reality"

(251). Although such "innocence" might *seem* convenient, the actual results of this reluctance to acknowledge the meaning or reality of lesbian sexuality was anomie, self-alienation, and ontological crisis.

4. In her invaluable and, for scope, still unparalleled study, *Sex Variant Women in Literature* (1956), the pioneering lesbian literary historian Jeannette Foster defines as *variant* that which differs from the generally accepted standard of "adequate heterosexual adjustment" (p. 11). Hence, this term encompasses "not only women who are conscious of passion for their own sex, with or without overt expression, but also those who are merely obsessively attached to other women over a longer period or at a more mature age than is commonly expected" (p. 12).

5. In the "Polemical Introduction" to her study *The Apparitional Lesbian: Female Homosexuality and Modern Culture* (New York; Columbia University Press, 1993), Terry Castle notes that prior to the terms *lesbian* and *homosexual,* a "whole slangy mob" of words for describing the lover of women—"*tribade, fricatrice, sapphist, roaring girl, amazon, freak, romp, dyke, bull dagger, tommy*" (p. 9)—were commonly used. Other code terms (e.g., pasatiempos and vanitas) are employed in Teresa's *Life* (as well as in writings of other female monastics), and one of the central tasks of gay and lesbian criticism is the uncovering of the embedded meanings of these various "prehomosexuality" vocabularies and narratives and their possible address to readers capable of discerning or decoding them.

6. In her valuable review of the patristic literature and biblical sources of Christian views on "lesbian" sexuality, *Immodest Acts*, Brown notes that St. Paul's reference (Romans 1:26) to pagans who rejected Christian monotheism, "God gave them up unto vile affections: for even their women did change the natural use into that which is against nature," was interpreted, although the exact meaning of his words is unclear, as a reference to sexual relations between women. According to St. Ambrose, "He testified that, God being angry with the human race because of their idolatry, it came about that a woman would desire a woman for the use of foul lust." St. John Chrysostom found this sin particularly pernicious, because "it is even more shameful that the women should seek this type of intercourse, since they ought to have more modesty than men." St. Anselm interpreted this passage as "the women themselves committ[ing] shameful deeds with women." Peter Abelard argued that such behavior was sinful because "women's genitals [were created] for the use of men . . . and not so women could cohabit with women." St. Thomas Aquinas listed "copulation with an undue sex, male with male and female with female" under his four categories of vices against nature. Yet, despite these injunctions, the relative neglect of lesbian sexuality (as opposed to homosexual activity among men) in law, theology, and literature suggests, as Brown argues, "an almost active willingness to *dis*believe" and, hence, to condemn. Although, during the Spanish Inquisition, Gregorio Lopez extended the death penalty to women for "unnatural sex" ("Women sinning in this way are punished by burning according to the law of their Catholic Majesties which orders that this crime against nature be punished with such a penalty, especially since the said law is not restricted to men, but refers to any person of whatever condition who has unnatural intercourse"), his contemporary Antonio Gomez believed that death should be the penalty only if "a woman has relations with

another woman by means of any material instrument." All in all, these injunctions betray an ignorance of what women "do" with one another erotically, and how to fit such behavior into sexual categories defined principally by penetration. Moreover, the late sixteenth-century French scholar Brantôme (in whose *Les Dames galantes* Sappho personifies the threat of female same-sex love) perceived "lesbianism" as an effort on the part of women, held to be naturally inferior to men, to emulate the superior sex:

> It is better that a woman give herself over to a libidinous desire to do as a man, than that a man make himself effeminate; which makes him out to be less courageous and noble. The woman, accordingly, who thus imitates a man, can have a reputation for being more valiant and courageous than another.
>
> (Brown, *Immodest Acts,* p. 12)

For Brantôme, lesbianism becomes a way for women to "improve" their inferior condition, but which simultaneously asserts the indelible superiority of men (of whom lesbians are, at best, a pale imitation). See Brown, *Immodest Acts,* pp. 7–8, 9, 14.

7. "The love which you bear one another ought not to be carnal, but spiritual: for those things which are practiced by immodest women, even with other females, in shameful jesting and playing, ought not to be done even by married women or by girls who are about to marry, much less by widows or chaste virgins dedicated by a holy vow to be handmaidens of Christ."

Augustine, *Letters*, 32:211 (New York: Fathers of the Church Series, 1956).

8. O'Brien offers a refreshing departure from the disavowals of wrongdoing (at least in terms of Catholic morality) of many English lesbian writers. As late as 1962, a year before her death, Lady Una Troubridge, the longtime lover of Radclyffe Hall, when asked by a friend how she and John (i.e., Radclyffe Hall) reconciled their "inversion" with their Catholicism, and how they approached this topic in confession, replied, "There was nothing to confess" (Baker, *Our Three Selves*, p. 357).

9. According to Kathleen Hoover, the Hartford premiere was successful because the production

> was that delectable rarity, a perfect musico-theatrical creation, forged at the white heat of total artistic co-operation. By the consistency, high quality, and painstaking preparation of all the contributing elements it shows, as only the ballets of Diaghilev had shown, that the Wagnerian ideal, divested of its Victorian erotico-philosophic paraphernalia, could still be realized. (p. 82)

10. Thomson notes that although he had chosen an all-black cast "purely for beauty of voice, clarity of enunciation, and fine carriage," their "surprise gift to the production was their understanding of the work. They got the spirit of it, enjoyed its multiple meanings, even the obscurities, adopted it, spoke in quotations from it." ("About 'Four Saints').

11. *Four Saints* employs, relative to grand opera, a fairly modest (and original) orchestral ensemble, consisting of violins, violas, bass, flute, oboe, clarinet, bassoon,

two horns, trumpet, trombone, percussion, as well as accordion and harmonium. Thus the opera has benefited from the recent revival of Baroque operas, which also employ small orchestras, and which can be staged quite successfully in smaller performance spaces with (at the discretion of the director) simple sets.

12. It would be more accurate to term the text of *Four Saints* that appears in the *Selected Writings* a "polyvocal play to be sung," since Stein does not regularly indicate the singing parts or the scenario. According to Thomson, when Stein gave him the completed text she said, "Do anything with this you like; cut, repeat, as composers have always done; make it work on stage" ("About 'Three Saints'"). Although Thomson did very little cutting or repeating, he assigned singing parts to the various saints Stein named in her original text. Maurice Grosser subsequently added a scenario to facilitate the staging. Stein was apparently pleased with the results of this collaborative effort, for she later noted that "Maurice understands my writing" ("About 'Four Saints'"). For an example of a literary reading of *Four Saints* that portrays Stein and Thomson (and libretto and setting) in an antagonistic relationship, see Jane Palatini Bowers, "The Play as Langscape," in *"They Watch Me as They Watch This": Gertrude Stein's Metadrama* (Philadelphia: University of Pennsylvania Press, 1991). Objecting to Thomson's comment that *Four Saints* is about " 'the working artist's life' as symbolized by the saints," Bowers states that the only artist is Gertrude Stein, who represents her work in the writing of this play. Thomson purportedly "obscured" this fact "by parceling out the authorial commentary of two figures. . . . Even at that, however, they discuss not so much the performance of the play—the stage business—as they do the composition—the business of writing. Thomson divided Gertrude Stein, but he did not conquer her" (50–51). While these comments do suggest some of the techniques Stein employed to secure the equal status of her libretto with Thomson's setting, they also reveal, I would argue, the bias that often accompanies academic specialization. Bowers not only questions the very possibility of artistic collaboration but also the nature of opera as *dramma per musica*.

13. Although this list is scarcely exhaustive, it does point to a fairly ubiquitous pattern in opera of using female characters (usually sinful, irrational, or victimized) to "expose" the hidden sexual nature of religious devotions. A more complex example of this phenomenon, which also (once again) poses the question of patterns of "transposition" and "identification" of gay male artists onto their nonheterosexual female mystic subjects occurs in Francis Poulenc and Georges Bernanos's opera, *Dialogues des Carmèlites* (1957), after Gertrud von Le Fort's novel *The Song of the Scaffold*. The opera returns to the French Revolution and the Carmelite Convent at Compiègne (significantly, the order founded by St. Teresa) to examine how a group of nuns deal with their persecution and martyrdom by the (male) French secular authorities. During the time Poulenc was composing this opera, he was undergoing a breakdown, occasioned by his agonizing love affair with a young man named Lucien Robert, who was suffering a terminal illness. According to Wilfrid Mellers, "The case of *Dialogues des Carmèlites* suggests that, if private anguish was an impulse to creation, salvation accrued from the very process of composition" (*Francis Poulenc*, p. 103). Indeed, Poulenc appears both to lend aesthetic expression to his "unspeakable" pain and to compensate for his lack of what

might be termed a faithfully devoted and institutionally sanctioned homosocial/homosexual community through the representation of the tragic ordeals of these nuns.

14. Perhaps the two most discernible musical-dramatic precursors of *Four Saints* are Satie's *Socrate* and Claude Debussy's *Le Martyre de Saint Sébastien* (1911), both of which, significantly, employ women singers to portray Christian or Greek male homosexual martyrs. *Socrate* (with four sopranos and orchestra), moves from Alcibiades' praise of Socrates, to his walk with Phaedrus, to the narration of his death by Phaedo. *Le Martyre de Saint Sébastien*, originally intended as a lavish theatrical production after the five-act play by Gabriele D'Annunzio (with soprano, two contraltos, chorus, and orchestra), narrates in tableaux the story of the "closeted" Christian Sebastian, a young and handsome officer of the Praetorian guards who, according to tradition, Diocletion ordered to be killed by his own archers because of his secret sympathies for persecuted Christians. Moreover, despite the widely acknowledged artistic merit of both these works, neither has achieved a place in standard repertoires because of their innovative intermixture of traditional genres and, perhaps, their subject matter.

15. Although my interpretation of the narrative of *Four Saints* follows the scenario of Maurice Grosser (approved by Stein), Grosser states that other interpretations than his would also be valid. See Hoover and Cage, *Virgil Thomson*, p. 64.

Works Cited

Anzaldúa, Gloria. *Borderlands/La Frontera:The New Mestiza*. San Francisco: Spinsters/Aunt Lute, 1987.

Auerbach, Nina. *Ellen Terry: Player in Her Time*. New York: Norton, 1987.

Augustine. *Treatises on Marriage and Other Subjects*. Vol. 27. Fathers of the Church Series.

Baker, Michael. *Our Three Selves: The Life of Radclyffe Hall*. New York: Morrow, 1985.

Barry, Ellen E. *Curved Thought and Textual Wandering: Gertrude Stein's Postmodernism*. Ann Arbor: University of Michigan Press, 1992.

Bellini, Vincenzo. *Norma*. Libretto by Felice Romani. Trans. Kenneth Chalmers. With Joan Sutherland, Marilyn Horne, John Alexander, and Richard Cross. Cond. Richard Bonynge.London 425 488–2, 1965.

Boswell, John. *Same-Sex Unions in Premodern Europe*. New York: Villard, 1994.

Brophy, Brigid. *In Transit*. London: Gay Men's Press, 1989.

——— *Prancing Novelist: A Defense of Fiction in the Form of a Critical Biography in Praise of Ronald Firbank*. New York: Harper and Row, 1973.

Brown, Judith C. *Immodest Acts: The Life of a Lesbian Nun in Renaissance Italy*. New York: Oxford University Press, 1986.

Carpenter, Edward. *The Intermediate Sex: A Study of Some Transitional Types of Men and Women*. London: George Allen and Unwin, 1908.

Castelli, Elizabeth. "'I Will Make Mary Male': Pieties of the Body and Gender Transformation in Christian Women in Late Antiquity." In Julia Epstein and Kristina Straub, eds., *Body Guards:The Cultural Politics of Gender Ambiguity*, pp. 29–49. New York: Routledge, 1991.

Crashaw, Richard. "A Hymn to Saint Teresa" and "The Flaming Heart." In Alexander M. Witherspoon and Frank J. Warnke, eds., *Seventeenth-Century Prose and Poetry*. 2d ed. San Diego: Harcourt, 1982.

Creech, James. *Closet Writing / Gay Reading: The Case of Melville's Pierre.* Chicago: University of Chicago Press, 1993.

Curb, Rosemary, and Nancy Manahan, eds. *Lesbian Nuns: Breaking Silence*. Tallahassee: Naiad, 1985.

Dalsimer, Adele M. *Kate O'Brien*. Boston: Twayne, 1990.

DeKoven, Marianne. *A Different Language: Gertrude Stein's Experimental Writing*. Madison: University of Wisconsin Press, 1983.

Faderman, Lillian. *Chloe Plus Olivia: An Anthology of Lesbian Literature from the Seventeeth Century to the Present*. New York: Penguin, 1994.

——— *Surpassing the Love of Men: Romantic Friendship and Love between Women from the Renaissance to the Present*. New York: William Morrow, 1981.

Firbank, Ronald. *Five Novels*. New York: New Directions, 1981.

Flanagan, Mary. "Introduction." *The Land of Spices*. London: Virago, 1990.

Foster, Jeannette H. *Sex Variant Women in Literature*. London: Frederick Muller, 1958.

Glasgow, Joanne. "What's a Nice Lesbian Like You Doing in the Church of Torquemada?: Radclyffe Hall and Other Catholic Converts." In Karla Jay and Joanne Glasgow, eds., *Lesbian Texts and Contexts: Radical Revisions*, pp. 241–54. New York: New York University Press, 1990.

Hardon, John A., S. J. *Modern Catholic Dictionary*. New York: Doubleday, 1980.

Harewood, George Henry Hubert Lascelles, Earl of, ed. *The Definitive Kobbé's Opera Book*. New York: Putnam, 1987.

Hoover, Kathleen, and John Cage. *Virgil Thomson: His Life and Music*. Freeport, N.Y.: Books for Libraries, 1959.

Irigaray, Luce. *This Sex Which Is Not One*. Trans. Catherine Porter, with Carolyn Burke. Ithaca: Cornell University Press, 1985.

——— *Speculum of the Other Woman*. Trans. Gillian C. Gill. Ithaca: Cornell University Press, 1985.

Lacan, Jacques. *Feminine Sexuality*. Ed. Juliet Mitchell and Jacqueline Rose. Trans. Jacqueline Rose. New York: Norton, 1985.

La Fuente, Don Vicente de, ed. *Escritos de Santa Teresa*. Vol. 1. Biblioteca de Autores Españoles. Madrid: Hernando, 1930.

Lincoln, Victoria. *Teresa: A Woman: A Biography of Teresa of Ávila*. Ed. Elias Rivers and Antonio T. de Nicolás. Albany: State University of New York Press, 1984.

McClary, Susan. *Feminine Endings: Music, Gender, and Sexuality*. Minnesota: University of Minnesota Press, 1991.

Mellers, Wilfrid. *Francis Poulenc*. Oxford: Oxford University Press, 1993.

Miller, D. A. *Narrative and Its Discontents: Problems of Closure in the Traditional Novel*. Princeton: Princeton University Press, 1981.

O'Brien, Kate. *The Flower of May*. London: William Heinemann, 1953.

——— *The Land of Spices*. London: William Heinemann, 1941.

——— *As Music and Splendour*. London: William Heinemann, 1958.

——— *Teresa of Ávila*. *Critic* (Winter 1975), no. 2, pp. 26–51.

——— *That Lady*. London: William Heinemann, 1946.

One Hundred Saints: Their Lives and Likenesses Drawn from Butler's "Lives of the Saints" and Great Works of Western Art. Boston: Little, Brown, 1993.

Peers, E. Allison. *Handbook to the Life and Times of St. Teresa and St. John of the Cross*. London: Burn Oates, 1954.

Petroff, Elizabeth Alvilda. "The Rhetoric of Transgression in the *Lives* of Italian Women Saints." In *Body and Soul: Essays on Medieval Women and Mysticism*. New York: Oxford University Press, 1994.

Raitt, Suzanne. *Vita and Virginia: The Work and Friendship of V. Sackville-West and Virginia Woolf*. Oxford: Clarendon Press, 1993.

Roberts, John R. *New Perspectives on the Life and Art of Richard Crashaw*. Columbia: University of Missouri Press, 1990.

Rohrbach, Peter-Thomas O. C. D. *Journey to Carith: The Story of the Carmelite Order*. New York: Doubleday, 1966.

Sackville-West, Vita. *The Eagle and the Dove: A Study in Contrasts, St. Teresa of Ávila, St. Thérèse of Lisieux*. London: Michael Joseph, 1943.

Schubert, Giselher. "About *Sancta Susanna*." Trans. John Patrick Thomas. Paul Hindemith and August Stramm, *Sancta Susanna*. Wergo 60 106–50, 1986.

Sedgwick, Eve Kosofsky. "Privilege of Unknowing." *Genders* (Spring 1988), 1:102–24.

Smith, Patricia Juliana. "Better to Burn Than to Marry: The Narratives of the Virgin Martyrs." Paper delivered at the Center for the Study of Women Graduate Research Conference. University of California, Los Angeles. May 17, 1993.

Stein, Gertrude. *Four Saints in Three Acts*. In *Selected Writings of Gertrude Stein*, pp. 581–612. Ed. Carl Van Vechten. New York: Random House, 1945.

Stein, Gertrude, and Virgil Thomson. *Four Saints in Three Acts: Complete Vocal Score*. Scenario by Maurice Grosser. New York: Music Press, 1948.

Steiner, Wendy. *Exact Resemblance to Exact Resemblance: The Literary Portraiture of Gertrude Stein*. New Haven: Yale University Press, 1978.

Stimpson, Catherine R. "The Somagrams of Gertrude Stein." *Poetics Today* (1985), 6:1–2.

Thomson, Virgil. "About 'Four Saints.'" Libretto. *Four Saints in Three Acts*. Elektra Nonesuch, 9 79035–2, 1982.

——— *Four Saints in Three Acts*. Libretto by Gertrude Stein. With Betty Allen, Gwendolyn Bradley, William Brown, Clamma Dale, Benjamin Matthews, Florence Quivar, and Arthur Thompson. Cond. Joel Thome. Orchestra of Our Time. Elektra Nonesuch, 9 79035–2, 1982.

——— *Virgil Thomson: An Autobiography*. New York: Dutton, 1985.

Teresa of Ávila. *The Life of Saint Teresa of Ávila by Herself*. Trans. J. H. Cohen. Harmondsworth: Penguin, 1957.

Van Vechten, Carl. "Introduction." In *Four Saints in Three Acts: An Opera to be Sung*. New York: Random House, 1934.

Wood, Elizabeth. "Sapphonics." In Philip Brett, Elizabeth Wood, and Gary C. Thomas, eds., *Queering the Pitch: The New Gay and Lesbian Musicology*, pp. 27–66. New York: Routledge, 1994.

Woolf, Virginia. *The Diary of Virginia Woolf: 1920–1924*. Vol. 2. Ed. Anne Olivier Bell. 5 vols. San Diego: Harcourt Brace Jovanovich, 1980.

Admiring the Countess Geschwitz

Mitchell Morris

Lulu! mein Engel!
"Lulu! my angel! appear once more! I am near you! will stay near you! in eternity!"

1.

Why is it so moving to me, this death? There are hundreds of deaths, after all, in opera: glorious, tragic, ironic, unnoticed; Catherine Clément could turn the deaths of women in the mainstream operatic repertory into a picture of continuous "undoing." I go to the opera, or I listen at home, and women die, men die—the losses are more often than not an aesthetic gain, and they frequently persist in the memory for a while, but they don't haunt me the way this death does.

I admire the Countess. Her passionate commitment to Lulu calls forth my respect and wonder as a listener, particularly as a queer listener familiar with love that is condemned as well as unrequited. Not that respect for the Countess is something especially new in writings on Berg's opera. Douglas Jarman, for instance, accounts for the end of *Lulu* in this way:

> We are finally compelled, through the intensity and the power of the music, to feel pity for and to identify not only with Lulu and Geschwitz, whose sexually "abnormal" but self-sacrificing love is presented as a positive alternative to the brutal, uncomprehending and possessive sexuality of the male figures, but with all the characters helplessly trapped in this grotesque Totentanz. It is through that act of identification that we are made to feel our moral responsibility for the society depicted on stage. (*Alban Berg: Lulu* 98)

But this is not enough for me. Even a small difference in subject position matters here. Though I am a white man of the class background typical of academics, I am supremely far from straight. My queer identity moves me to qualify Jarman's assessment, for Lulu interests me less than the Countess, whose patterns of desire feel almost uncomfortably akin to mine; rather than pass over the rhetoric of "abnormality" with scare quotes, I insist on confronting it in its historical contexts. I feel perhaps less implicated in Berg's condemnation of his (our) society's sexual constructions because I am outside, like the Countess.

This essay aims to work out some of the conditions of my feeling and its consequences, both for myself and, I hope, for other audience members with queer affinities. On the one hand, the Countess Geschwitz is first a literary and then an operatic character, invented by Frank Wedekind and Alban Berg successively. Her sex and character are constituted in a historical milieu that I think still needs to be worked through more deeply. On the other hand, the Countess as a theatrical or operatic character exists fully only in performance, and the resulting "female authorial voice" and body thus escape her creators.[1] And to complicate matters, I write as a queer musicologist doing queer musicology—a person and genre still being formed—at the same time that I am trying to construct as a listener a partial account of my passion for the most unreal person of an operatic character. My writing here is meant to move between these poles.

2.

Frank Wedekind's two Lulu plays, *Erdgeist* (*Earth Spirit*, 1895) and *Die Büchse der Pandora* (*Pandora's Box*, 1902), occasioned government censorship from the time of their first performance. Charges of obscenity circulated freely enough around the plays—particularly around *Pandora's Box*—that by 1906 Wedekind was moved to write a foreword rebutting the charges against his work. The most important part of the defense was Wedekind's claim that his critics, as represented in three German court cases against him, had misunderstood the play's moral center; although the character of Lulu seems to dominate *Pandora's Box*,

> The central tragic figure of the play is not Lulu . . . but Countess Geschwitz. Apart from an intrigue here and there, Lulu plays an entirely passive role in all three acts; Countess Geschwitz on the other hand in the first act furnishes an example of what one can justifiably describe as super-human self-sacrifice. In the second act the progress of the plot forces her to summon all her spiritual resources in the attempt to conquer the terrible destiny of abnormality with which she is burdened; after which, in the third act, having borne the

> most fearful torments of soul with stoical composure, she sacrifices her life in defense of her friend.
>
> That I chose the fate of a human being burdened with the curse of abnormality as the theme of a serious dramatic creation was not pronounced inadmissible in any of the three judgments. It is a matter of fact that the chief protagonists in the old Greek tragedies are almost always beyond the pale of normality. . . . That is to say: in spite of a spiritual development inspiring enough to transport their audience to the summit of human happiness, they are unable to shake off the unholy inheritance by which they are dominated; instead, unfit for human society and in extreme torment they succumb to their fate. As far as the audience is concerned abnormality as such could hardly be more tellingly stigmatised. If at the same time the spectator derives aesthetic pleasure from this presentation as well as unqualified spiritual gain, then the presentation is lifted out of the realm of morality into that of art. (103–4)[2]

What is Wedekind doing? He had planned Lulu's play *Earth Spirit* to be the first installment of the larger play called *Pandora's Box*; in the 1906 preface he claims that in the last half of the work the central character is the Countess. Yet the plot of *Pandora's Box* always revolves around Lulu, whose escape from prison, financial and social ruin, and miserable fate as a streetwalker provide the matter for the three acts successively. Wedekind can assert that Lulu's action is restricted to "an intrigue here and there," but he will be believed mostly by those who have not read the play. To judge by number of lines, the Countess is definitely one of the crucial supporting characters, but she is no more important than Alwa, Schigolch, or Rodrigo.

Wedekind's claim is surely a subterfuge. Taking his readers' minds off the character of Lulu, whose tendency to "commercial love" was one of the censor's chief complaints, seems to be Wedekind's main design. In focusing on the Countess, he picks the one character whose behavior is not tied to traffic in women. (For that matter, she is the only character in the drama to love anyone else nonabusively; this may partially account for the "Countess and Christ Figure" overtones of his apologia.) Furthermore, by placing the Countess at the center of his drama, Wedekind can associate himself with the serious legal and humanitarian efforts of the German homophile movement, at that time just beginning its activities to end discrimination.

Dr. Magnus Hirschfeld and two of his associates had formed the *Wissenschaftlich-humanitäres Komittee* (Scientific-humanitarian committee) in 1897 in Berlin to argue for the repeal of Germany's Paragraph 175, which penalized homosexual relations. From the beginning the committee's work was strongly linked to medical discourse, as it sought to use the prestige of disinterested science to counter homophobia. Hirschfeld himself was the founder and director of the Institute for Sexual Science in Berlin, editor of the *Jahrbuch für sexuelle Zwischenstufen* (Yearbook for intermediate sexual types) from 1899–1923, and a proponent of Karl Heinrich Ulrichs's theory of the "third sex." Arguing that homosexuality was a congenital state that ought to be met with tolerance rather than criminalization, Hirschfeld and others campaigned vigorously for freedom from persecution, at one point even submitting a supporting petition signed by over three thousand doctors and intellectual leaders (including Thomas Mann, Arthur Schnitzler, and Gerhart Hauptmann) to the German government.[3]

At least a hint of the committee's position is contained in Wedekind's preface. Making some allowance for the rhetoric of abnormality—he is writing for a presumably hostile audience, after all, so he must clearly separate the Countess's feelings from theirs—Wedekind nevertheless insists on Geschwitz's spiritual superiority, comparing her to a Greek tragic hero. Her implicit placement within the third sex model also allows her to be taken more seriously in the context of the time as a quasi-masculine figure whose suffering deserves attention—a strategy that can also be seen in Otto Weininger's *Geschlecht und Charakter* (*Sex and Character*) and Aimée Duc's *Sind es Frauen?* (Are they women?). "Sympathy and compassion" are Wedekind's aims.

When taken with the preface the text of *Pandora's Box* suggests Wedekind's allegiance, at least as a writer, to a model of homosexuality as an "intermediate sexual type." Lulu's cruel dismissal of the Countess in act 2, for instance, uses the language surrounding accounts of the third sex to construct an image of monstrosity: "You were uncompleted in your mother's womb, either as a man or a woman. You're not a human being like the rest of us. There wasn't enough material to make a man of you and for a woman you've got too much brain" (Wedekind 138). The Countess agrees with Lulu that she is "not human," though she maintains that she has "a Human soul." But for her alienness is something to be grateful for, since it separates her from the brutishness of the people around her (Wedekind 169–70). Breaking free of the savage customs of heterosexual love, she comes off as uncommonly decent. So, from the perspective Wedekind wants to establish in the preface, the Countess is indeed superior to her sordid compatriots.

And yet separating the Countess so far from the "us" that Wedekind projects risks reducing her to an object of sentimental appropriation. The (presumably bourgeois) audience can weep all the more because it knows that it is, unlike her, "normal"; its vicarious experience of the Countess's suffering places it under no obligation to question itself. Given the vicious irony that characterizes much of Wedekind's work, we might wonder whether we are meant to take the invitation to sentimentalize implicit in the preface at all seriously. Consider the prologue of *Earth Spirit*, given here in Berg's redaction:

> Step this way into the menagerie,
> You proud gentlemen, you merry ladies,
> With hot pleasure and with cold shudders
> To look at the soulless creatures
> Tamed by human genius.
> What do you see in comedy or tragedy?!
> House pets, that feel so civilized,
> Vent their anger on vegetarian fare
> And feast with comfortable bawling,
> Like those others under the Parterre . . . [4]

Spoken by an animal tamer who describes the beasts that the audience (themselves tamer beasts) will view, venting their rage and complacent tears, Wedekind's prologue announces a stagey display of jokes at the expense of his audience. Couldn't the 1906 preface be a joke as well, on the bourgeois public likely to be swayed by the censor's claims? We cannot easily decide. But even if it is facetious, it points to a way that the character might escape her creator as well as the play she inhabits.

For escape she did; by the time of the Weimar republic the figure of the Countess Geschwitz was the archetype of the lesbian in German drama. As censorship eased and more and more important actors became interested in creating roles in the Lulu plays, Wedekind's lesbian became so well-known that at least one writer could speak of "coming out" as "absconding to the Geschwitzian region" (Schäfer 180). Perhaps the Countess's popularity depended on the paucity of lesbian representations in general before the veritable explosion of homophile culture in the Weimar republic.[5] But equally as important, I think, was her decency and strength. That she dies in the end matters less than how beautifully and movingly she lives.

3.

The Countess escaped into the sum of her representations on the German stage. When Berg came to set the Lulu plays, he wove her into an even more intense network of representations. All the characters in Berg's *Lulu* seem to live more violently and passionately than they do in Wedekind's plays, inscribed as they are within the immediacy-effects of the music.[6] This liveliness depends on *Lulu's* intertwining of musical immediacy and theatricality. For the most part Berg's (and Wedekind's) characters are creatures of stagey entrances and exits (as in the opening words of the prologue given above or the first words of act 1: *Darf ich eintreten?* [May I come in?]); the characters live most intensely in their protestations of love or lust, variously gaudy, violent, even sincere. And of course, in opera, these are exactly the features most likely to feel authentic—or at least convincing—to all of us "under the Parterre."

Lulu herself possesses the most radiant moments of acts 1 and 2: the brilliant melodrama accompanying the Closing Theme of the act 1 Sonata Form in scene 2, "Wenn ich einem Menschen auf dieser Welt angehöre, gehöre ich Ihnen" (If I belong to anyone in the world, I belong to you; mm. 615–624); and the glorious entrance of act 2, scene 2, "O Freiheit! Herr Gott im Himmel!" (Oh Freedom! Lord God in heaven!; mm. 1000–1040).[7] Both of these are moments of coming out, where Lulu's inner nature seems to be revealed with an irresistible glamor and force. Berg marks Lulu's act 1 declaration of eternal attachment to Dr. Schön, in which her love reveals itself for the first time in the drama, with all the pathos at his command, as if insisting to his audience that one so capable of love is well worth dying for. And in Lulu's act 2 paean to freedom, tonal closure, register, orchestration, and dramatic circumstance conspire to make the moment overwhelming, drowning the listener's thought in the conviction of pure presence. In the parterre we thus mimic the characters of the drama, who shine most brightly in Lulu's presence.

But at first the Countess stands back from the others.[8] She is actually preparing to leave the stage as the curtain rises on act 2, and when she stealthily returns it is only to hide for most of the rest of the scene. The second half of act 2 is a variation on this "theme," with the Countess departing after the scene's opening in order to be talked about later on. She seems to be background only, mere exotica, for most of act 2 as well—and her music is rather subdued—but at the very end of the opera, the last ten minutes of the final act, she suddenly ascends to musical glory, assuming a moral force previously absent in the opera. For my ears, at least, this music carries an uncanny authority that dominates the opera in retrospect. How fine a woman Lulu must have been, I think to myself, if such a transcendent personality as the Countess would consent to die for her, and yet how strangely finer the Countess remains. I am almost shocked to find myself thinking of Wedekind's phrases—"super-human self-sacrifice" and "spiritual gain." But that is how it feels.

Berg accomplishes this effect by taking advantage of the habits of ears and minds accustomed to the language of late Romantic tonalities; he expected his audience to have been submerged in Wagner, Strauss, and Mahler, and to have acquired not only appropriate strategies for following the flow of musical arguments but also a set of associations between musical gestures and affects.[9] That is, though Berg wrote *Lulu* in a "post-tonal" idiom he derived mostly from Schoenberg, he also deliberately resurrected the sounds (and consequently, the habits) of late Romantic tonality.

To be sure, all of Berg's music courts tonal reference to some extent. George Perle, describing the overall musical language of *Lulu*, notes that

> harmonic formations derived from *various* twelve-tone sets are components of a pervasive harmonic texture to which the sets themselves are subordinate and which comprises non-dodecaphonic elements as well. How far this texture departs from that of other twelve-tone music is suggested in the character of the outer voices, and especially of the bass line, whose linearity and directed motion imply a significant affiliation to traditional tonal music in spite of the radical difference in harmonic content. (86)

Although the harmonic structures Berg favors are always more complex than triads, our ears infer harmonic roots with surprising frequency, and we can even imagine functional relationships from time to time. Two of the spots of quasi tonality thus created, with their sudden presentation of audible functional relationships, correspond exactly to the lyric highpoints most often noted in the drama: the Closing Theme of the Sonata Form and Lulu's act 2, scene 2 Entrance.[10]

But the Countess has her own tonal voice, and it comes at the end of the opera, launching what is frequently called her *Liebestod*, her apostrophe to the dead Lulu. My analysis begins a few measures before the Countess sings. Example 13.1 shows the meandering figures left to the orchestra as Jack the Ripper prepares to leave the stage.

Example 13.1.

His last words are addressed to the dying Countess: "It'll be over for you soon, too." The music seemingly lacks the strength to argue. It only repeats itself. But as Jack exits, the music gathers itself to state the tone row that characterizes him and Dr. Schön, his double from the first half of the opera (see example 13.2).

Example 13.2.

The presence of the row is obvious in its vehemence, since each pitch is given in its primary order, in equal note values; the very simplicity of the row's presentation argues that its manner of presentation is meant to carry a strong dramatic significance. It doesn't seem to me to be simply a summation of the identity of Dr. Schön and Jack, nor an epitome of the course of heterosexual male desire, though both these interpretations are present. More important, it seems to act as a kind of exorcism of Jack's presence, for with the row's completion the music relaxes into a clouded but genuine V-I cadence preparing the Countess's final address to Lulu (see example 13.3).

Example 13.3.

It is worth noting that there is no third degree in the A triad implied by the bass A-natural and the E-natural just above it. The Countess's most characteristic sonority in the opera is the interval of an open fifth, ghostly and ambiguous in meaning (major? minor?). When the open fifth appears here, it is masked over with another open fifth (A-flat/E-flat) a tritone away that seems to suggest a major seventh chord with a suspended sharp fourth degree; the movement of the E-flat down to D-flat (C-sharp) in the next measure reinforces this hearing. As the Countess's *Liebestod* continues, however, it becomes clear that the apparent tonic of measure 1315 is beginning to turn into something else (see example 13.4a):

Example 13.4a.

an elaborate pre-dominant chord (a species of ii) moving toward V⁹/G by dropping a half-step down from a variety of flat-VI chord a tritone away from its point of origin. The movement of the bass line shows, however, that this move is only temporary. The V^9/G sounds like part of a feint towards the subdominant side of the key of A; it acquires its own flat-VI chord, but then the pattern breaks open. The first part of the music of the *Liebestod* enacts its text—"Lulu! my angel! appear once more!"—by reaching out from its tonal foundation toward a goal that turns out to be unattainable: an arrival somewhere on the subdominant side of A, one last glimpse of Lulu. After this the bass motion settles down by third through E-ish and C-ish areas back to the A-natural/E-natural fifth that began the process (see example 13.4b),

Example 13.4b.

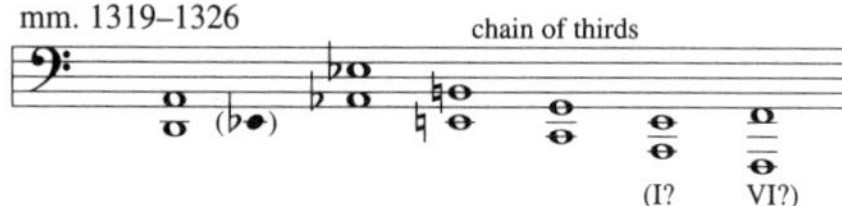

and the implicit tonality evoked is securely on A. Above the bass motion successive phrases drop down, ever lower, through the orchestra. This dying fall accompanies the Countess's final declarations: "I am near you! will stay near you! in eternity!" All that is left is the close, which, by filling in the ambiguous third of the A-natural/E-natural fifth, complicates matters further: the antepenultimate chord is A major, and the penultimate is A minor, both over an F-natural bass (these were the chords that ended acts 1 and 2, and were associated with Dr. Schön and Alwa respectively). The chord that concludes the opera has F-natural as its root, and in this context it evokes flat-VI of A.

What does this close mean? If the A major and minor are fillings-in of the Countess's fifth, then perhaps the close is meant to create a space for us to compare the love she shows toward Lulu to the love shown by Dr. Schön and Alwa. On the other hand, Perle, among others, suggests that the final three chords are meant to recall Dr. Schön, Alwa, and the Countess in turn, in which case only the very last chord applies to the Countess's character and fate. Whatever the choice, it seems to matter less to me than the overall tonal character of the final section.

All these tritones. And, although I haven't emphasized it, all these half-steps. It seems somehow fitting that after the large cloudy V-I that sets the Countess's Liebestod going, the most distinctive bass motions and harmonic intervals should be these most ambiguous and distant pitch relationships in tonal practice. Theodor Adorno, at one time Berg's composition student, observed in a monograph on his teacher that "in musical material nothingness has its equivalent in the half-step that extends barely beyond the tone itself, yet establishes no melodic profile of its own—still this side of the plasticity of intervals and therefore ever ready to fall back into amorphousness (3)." The presence that we hear in Berg's tonality, then, is grounded on an almost nothingness; its delight is all the more touching because of its fragility.

The tonal associations implicit in the Countess's death song, however, are not the only defining aspects of its structure. Rather, it is a concatenation of important nontonal motives and rows—the so-called Basic Cell I, the Countess's row and her trope (see example 13.5)

Example 13.5.

—which offers the most organizing power because of its constant presence in her earlier music and because of the way that the tonal references are articulated around its framework. This doubling of function, where the same music can be heard in multiple ways, is equally apparent in the other tonal incidents in *Lulu* and raises an interesting question: if we assume that the twelve-tone organization of the score, because of its priority in the composition, its continuous presence throughout the opera, and its demonstrable "rule" over tonal passages, constitutes the law of the opera's "world," would we not be entitled to assume that the presence of tonal reference in the score could be understood in this case as a marker for the transcendent suspension of the opera's "reality"? What does this mean?

Let me suggest at least a partial answer by leaving *Lulu* for the moment to return to two striking passages in act 3 of Berg's earlier opera *Wozzeck*. The first is from scene 1, where Marie, remorseful over her affair with the Drum Major, reads the Bible and cries out her repentance in alternation. The music is ungoverned by any strong tonal sense until, when she attempts to tell her child a fairy tale, it relaxes into an elegiac Mahlerian F minor. Unquestionably the presence of tonality here is meant to signify "once upon a time," to evoke a nostalgia for a thing that perhaps never really was, or never even could have been. And the story Marie tells is horribly depressing: "Once upon a time there was a poor child who had no father and no mother—everyone was dead and there was no one in the world, and he was hungry and cried day and night." Tonality is used to speak pain and loss. The second case is the great D minor Interlude between scenes 5 and 6. Marie is dead, Wozzeck is dead, and the curtain is down to allow the composer to comment on the action through the orchestra by recalling significant leitmotives. Again, tonality speaks pain and loss.[11]

This is true of *Lulu* to an important extent as well. The Closing Theme of the Sonata Form in act 1, for instance, appears repeatedly at crucial points in the drama: at Lulu's first declaration of love and indebtedness to Dr. Schön (1, mm. 615–624), the climax of their verbal battle (1, mm. 666–668), Dr. Schön's surrender to Lulu (1, mm. 1356–1361), and Lulu's arrangements with Jack the Ripper (3, mm. 1193–1199 and 1235–1261). As many critics have observed, this music represents the relationship between Lulu and Schön—in the terms of the play, a liaison foredoomed to appalling failure. The music here speaks in the accents of what is impossible; everything is driven toward loss in death. The Countess's possession of (or is it by?) tonality is even more dependent on loss: first (3, mm. 1174–1187), the loss we seem likely to experience because of her very probable suicide; second (3s, mm. 1315–1326), her actual death from Jack's assault. Adorno commented on Berg's taste for tonality in *Lulu*:

> The way . . . in which the *imagerie* of the nineteenth century stirs within Berg is forward-looking. Nowhere in this music is it a matter of restoring a familiar idiom or alluding to a childhood to which he seeks a return. Berg's memory embraced death. Only in the sense that the past is retrieved as something irretrievable, through its own death, does it become part of the present.
>
> (*Alban Berg* 21)

But mixed in with the tragedy in each case I have cited from both *Wozzeck* and *Lulu* is something more exciting, more lofty. This intense exaltation, an instance of the sublime, comes about because our attention has been so carefully trained in the difficulties of Berg's nontonal style that when he shifts into a tonal style we become more conscious of its force than we are in styles where tonality is the norm. The ears and the mind must work very hard indeed to follow the details in Berg's music—motivic, contrapuntal, rhythmic, orchestrational—because the tonal habits we are likely to possess as nonspecialist listeners rarely apply. This level of attention may lessen somewhat when tonal function and genuine triads come to the fore, but it does not disappear entirely; since all of our established habits become useful as well, we in effect overcome our normal perceptual abilities. The immediacy-effects of music are immeasurably heightened at these moments of cognitive overload, and I don't think this is only my own reaction; even in the midst of my own paroxysms I have observed others responding with involuntary spasms of voluptuous delight at just these moments in Berg's operas, their minds temporarily captured by the music's mix of pain and pleasure.

I have mentioned the sublime because it seems to me to provide a further understanding of the Countess's appeal. At least three of *Lulu*'s deaths are governed or influenced by an understanding of the sublime in terms of the philosophical work that mattered more to musicians of Berg's milieu than any other: Schopenhauer's *The World as Will and Representation*. To review briefly the relevant points of Schopenhauer's position, the primary characteristic of the phenomenal (perceptible) world is suffering, which occurs because of the ceaseless striving of the universal Will; death, which dissolves the individual back into the noumenal world, is the only permanent relief of suffering, but there are nevertheless useful ways to ease the pain of life by denying the Will; through the contemplation of art, in which "significant forms" possess a "hostile relation to the human will in general," for instance, it is possible to suspend the operations of the Will; this relief brings about a feeling of exaltation that we call the sublime. Furthermore,

> every case of death presents itself to a certain extent as a kind of apotheosis or canonization. . . . Dying is certainly to be regarded as the real aim of life; at the moment of dying, everything is decided which through the course of life was only prepared and introduced. Death is the result, the *résumé*, of life, or the total sum expressing at one stroke all the instruction given by life in detail and piecemeal, namely that the whole striving . . . was a vain, fruitless, and self-contradictory effort, to have returned from which is a deliverance.
>
> (Schopenhauer 636–37)

Berg writes the music for the deaths of Dr. Schön and Lulu as if to provide an audible representation of the process Schopenhauer describes. Dr. Schön's characteristic tone row, described by Berg as derived from the basic row of the opera, is drawn back into the basic row as he dies.[12] That is, Schön's individual will becomes submerged in the primary organizing principal, or Will, of the opera. Lulu's famous *Todesschrei* is accompanied by a tremendous fortississimo (*fff*) chord containing all twelve pitch-classes—the basic material of the opera's musical universe.

But Berg did not read Schopenhauer without reservations. Judging in favor of Wagner over Schopenhauer, he wrote to his fiancée: "[Wagner] recognized that we can and must look forward to the future with optimism. He's much more *modern* than Schopenhauer because, like Ibsen and Nietzsche, he 'says yes to life'" (38). I think that the death of the Countess shows Berg writing somewhat against Schopenhauer. The Countess's last words are the products of desire—tokens of love and loyalty, however tempered by her ebbing strength—and it seems that her words and music are so powerful that they resist being pulled back into the stuff of the opera and instead only submit to the three chords that summarize the human drama.[13] The Countess remains individualized at least in part because her greatest activity occurs in the final scene: she contemplates suicide, but, working through her despair, she decides to return to Germany to study law and struggle for women's rights; finally, she dies trying to save Lulu from Jack's violence. And she dies within tonality, unlike any other character in the opera.

She dies within tonality, though in some ways she is already dead. To begin with, act 2, scene 2 is haunted. Berg wrote the roles of Lulu's johns to be sung by her husbands from the first two acts, and they return trailing the music with which they were previously associated.[14] Jack the Ripper in particular, as the uncanny double of Dr. Schön, brings with him two *leitsektionen* of Schön's (and Lulu's) music: the Closing Theme of the sonata form and the cavatina of act 2, scene 1. The immense pathos of the Closing Theme in particular casts an exquisitely creepy pall over the spectacle of serial killer and whore/husband and wife arguing over the price of an encounter. Death-driven.

And when Jack murders Lulu and mortally wounds the Countess, the opera is essentially over. Lulu's *Todesschrei*, as I have mentioned, encompasses the musical universe of the opera in its total chromatic saturation; what occurs after it is in some sense outside the opera. First, there is a view from the world of men in the form of a brutal postscript by Jack, himself only barely a man even though he is the essence of the opera's masculinity: "That was a piece of work!" And then the Countess speaks, outside time and the opera's end where she seems to persist, outside the humanity that has been explicitly denied her as a being of the third sex. She doesn't die as the Schopenhauerian Schön and Lulu do—it may be that she doesn't exactly die at all, but remains even after the end of the opera, hovering.[15] Queer to the end, her detachment from the sordid rounds of heterosexual exploitation makes her a noble ghost. The queer qualities of this kind of existence become all the more obvious if you think about what kinds of sexuality are most likely to be called un- (or is it super- ?) natural.

4.

Berg's Countess, then, is exactly what Wedekind had described in his preface to *Pandora's Box*—"the central tragic figure" of the drama. But though this reading was always possible, it was not inevitable. The Lulu plays were given an influential interpretation, for instance, by Berg's intellectual idol, the Viennese critic Karl Kraus, in a 1905 lecture just before a performance of *Pandora's Box* that Berg attended; in Kraus's view the central matter of the plays is the savage relationship between the sexes. The Countess is praised in the lecture, but Kraus falls into a nasty bit of homophobia (or is it misogyny?) when he describes the relationship between the Countess and Jack: "The only way he could get satisfaction from her would be to cut out her brain."[16] Why should Berg have created a figure so much more sympathetic?

Berg developed his version of the Countess between 1927 and 1935, in a time when homosexual rights were fiercely contested throughout German-language culture; his personal circle was strongly homophilic. Most generally, alongside and out of the homosexual emancipation movement centered in Germany had arisen a significant body of apologetics in literature and theater, but also in the new art of film. Richard Oswald's *Anders als die Anderen* (Different from the others) of 1919 was as much an instrument of Magnus Hirschfeld's committee as it was a story of homosexual tragedy; there were other films, such as *Michael* (1924) and *Geschelcht in Fesseln* [Sex in bondage] (1928), but the main characters were men. The great lesbian films were of course G. W. Pabst's *Die Büchse der Pandora* (1929) and Leontine Sagan's *Mädchen in Uniform* (1930).[17] It is likely that Berg, keenly interested in the new art form (he recommended *Der blaue Engel* to his mentor Arnold Schoenberg in a letter, and he was to put a short film at the very center of *Lulu*), would have known at least some of these works. Though the homosexual characters die in each case (even in one of the two version of *Mädchen*), their deaths are meant to rouse the compassion of the viewers in a way more than a little reminiscent of Berg's Countess. Then, too, between 1905 and 1907 Karl Kraus had mounted in his journal *Die Fackel* a defense of homosexuality that not only emphasized its status as an individual peculiarity not to be meddled with by the law but also interpreted it as a "widening of the capacities for pleasure" that was the right of artists to pursue (Rode 89–90).

But the most important homophilic context for Berg was his family: his sister, Smaragda, lived most of her life as an open lesbian. In a famous letter of 1910, written to the disapproving father of his fiancée Helene Nahowski, Berg mounted an eloquent defense of Smaragda:

> I have . . . a sister whose abnormal condition and Lesbian inclination is her family's desperate sorrow. But alas, there is no sanatorium for her . . . no

> place where these tendencies could be cured, where she might be saved from the dangers they carry with them, and from other people's malicious gossip.
>
> So we have come to the root of your attacks against my family. Had I the time, I would make this long letter twice or three times as long, and deal in detail with homosexuality: those afflicted by it and those who, because they are not so afflicted, treat these sick people as criminals. Perhaps your slurs, if I hear any more of them, will one day force me to take the matter up.
>
> (110)

The rhetoric of teratology is strong in this passage, but Berg is, after all, writing to his conservative prospective father-in-law. It is worth noting that Smaragda's "abnormal condition" might be something other than homosexuality (her "Lesbian inclination").[18] An examination of his other letter clarifies his position.

As early as 1907, the beginning of his correspondence with Helene, Berg refers very casually to his sister's relationships with her girlfriends; Berg seems quite at ease with Smaragda's sexuality even when it is on public display. In a letter of 1908 he writes to Helene, complaining of boredom in her absence and contrasting his situation to the fun his sister is having: "Smaragda is in a circle of beautiful women enjoying herself with Altenberg and Karl Kraus. And when she gets home at three in the morning with Ida [a girlfriend], I expect she'll come into my bedroom and regale me with her conquests and ecstasies" (32). Describing a collection of houseguests:

"One is a real officer's-daughter type, would-be aristocratic, terribly slim and chic, with quite fine features and gracious-to-stiff movements—she's the one Smaragda's in love with" (41). Furthermore, Berg seems to have treated Smaragda's long-term girlfriend May Keller as one of the family.[19] There is no sorrow over Smaragda in these passages at all; in fact, besides the letter to Helene's father, the only remarks in Berg's correspondence that can be interpreted as at all antihomosexual are a passing reference to the "ghastly horde of homosexual Wagnerians" at Bayreuth (presumably men, and is it their homosexuality or their brand of Wagnerism that is "ghastly"?) and a brief description of Smaragda's "small, stunted soul" that probably has less to do with her sexuality than with her personality in general (*Letters to His Wife* 90, 102).

This matters to me. I began by admiring an operatic character, but my search in the opera's historical context has brought me to the opera's composer. In my imagination the Countess and Berg overlap. Isn't his defense of Smaragda at least a little like the Countess's defense of Lulu? And when I look there are other things that bring my sympathy closer to Berg. To explain, let me swerve in my account for a moment.

Immediately after I read an earlier version of this essay at the 1991 Conference on Feminist Theory and Music at the University of Minnesota, I was approached by a highly regarded music theorist who has worked extensively on the music of the Second Viennese School (Schoenberg, Berg, and Anton Webern). In the course of our conversation the theorist mentioned that there were supposed to be some unpublished letters in the Berg archives suggesting that Berg had been sexually involved with other men. The campaign of censorship carried out by Helene Berg to "protect her husband's memory" (actually, an idealized portrait of their marriage) is quite well known: Frau Berg, in addition to preventing the completion of the third act of *Lulu* during her lifetime by keeping it from public view and misrepresenting its state at the time of Berg's death (it was almost finished), also sought in her will to keep the third act out of sight after her death; she systematically suppressed any information about an extramarital liaison between Berg and Hanna Fuchs-Robettin (the secret dedicatee of the *Lyric Suite* and several other pieces probably including *Lulu*) between 1925 and 1935, as well as keeping secret the existence of Berg's illegitimate daughter by a servant girl (fathered when Berg was seventeen; he acknowledged paternity).[20] Frau Berg hid information about her husband to protect his reputation, as she saw it. Given this record, it is plausible that she might have suppressed information she would have regarded as even more scandalous. Nevertheless, since I cannot cite any evidence for or against this claim at the present, the theorist's remark can only be counted as rumor, and my reproduction of it in this context might be regarded as irresponsible. Indeed, my repeating the rumor is salacious and sensationalistic—it's gossip, and I don't deny it.

But Berg is one of the few composers of his place and time about whom such a rumor could reasonably be told. I try to imagine someone telling me the same story about Schoenberg or Webern, and it would be impossible to believe, because neither of their personal styles seems to have had the same affinity with the closet as Berg's had. Berg is simply easier to gossip about (sexually, at least) because he kept secrets but busily gave away the fact that he had them; his music and his life always seem to suggest that there was more information to be found (and with little effort) under the surface. He actively collaborated with his wife in creating the illusion of a perfect marriage during his life, as Perle observes (26–27). But, even more important, he had a strong tendency to write himself into his musical works. Wedekind had already inserted references to his own writing of *Earth Spirit* into *Pandora's Box*, and he involved himself further by playing Jack the Ripper in the Vienna production Berg attended. (Wedekind's future wife, incidently, was playing the part of Lulu!) But Berg had the habit independent of Wedekind and autobiographicized even more. Alwa is the locus of many of these elements: Berg turns him from a writer into the composer of a *Schaud-*

eroper, and when Alwa observes that Lulu's life would make an interesting opera, Berg writes the opening chords of *Wozzeck*; several other quotations from *Wozzeck* appear in *Lulu* as well (Perle 59). *Lulu*, along with nearly every other score of Berg's, is filled with complex personal references created through numerological calculation of such things as numbers of bars and tempo markings; in many of the instrumental pieces there are "secret programs," usually dealing with his love for Hanna Fuchs-Robettin, whose initials H-F (in German music notation, B-natural F-natural) are frequently joined with his A-B (A-natural B-flat) to memorialize their relationship. The culmination of Berg's secret record of love, according to Perle, is the final chord of *Lulu*, which contains three of the four initials/notes.[21] Perle, dismissing Berg's claim (made in a letter to Helene) that he lacked interest in the Countess, asks his readers a set of rhetorical questions that reveals the link between Berg's secrets, gossip, and scholarship:

> Can anyone who knows the opera believe for a moment that the composer of this music [the Countess's death song] saw the Countess as merely another of Lulu's "satellites," that he hadn't "much feeling really" for the character whose dying words express the most persistent motive of his secret letters to Hanna and bring the opera to a close in a final cadence that is sealed with her initials and his? Here, too, in this typically affectionate letter to his wife, he is "play-acting": the surface meaning of an assertion that was not required of him in the first place serves a secretly ironic purpose, a verbal camouflage that masks the truth, like the double musical metaphors in *Wozzeck* and *Lulu*. (240)

"Can anyone . . . believe for a moment?" I respond as much to the knowingness behind the question as I do to its tone of high scholarly dudgeon. And to the decided tone of Perle's opinion—he's getting at the truth about Berg, after all, or he wouldn't be able to separate it from its camouflage. These are the accents of gossip, as you can hear if you imagine the words spoken of some other party in a less formal situation. But I think that, to the degree that Perle's tone approaches gossip, his interpretation is true, and a crucial response to the opera's effects.

And isn't it also true, after all, that the gossip I've been describing operates around Berg's devices of concealment/revelation in a way that, if not specifically queer, at least feels very familiar to those of us brought up to keep and reveal the secrets required of protoqueers in a homophobic environment? As Eve Kosofsky Sedgwick notes, "The precious, devalued area of gossip [are] immemorially associated in European thought with servants, with effeminate and gay men, with all women." She quite rightly points out that the affinity between these groups and gossip arises as a self-defensive maneuver, but more broadly represents an informal way of registering human differences (*Epistemology of the Closet* 23).[22] Responding to her arguments, Douglas Crimp further observes that "the most fundamental need gossip has served for queers is that of the construction—and reconstruction—of our identities" (313). When gossip circulates around sexuality, particularly sexual secrets (as it does more often than not when I'm involved, I must admit), what other kind of information is likely to appear? From this standpoint Frau Berg's campaign of disinformation and suppression looks exactly like the construction of a closet around her dead husband, and the process of decoding that is still going on can plausibly take the tint of antihomophobic analysis.

In (semi-) public, Berg identified himself with Alwa through his references to *Wozzeck* in *Lulu*; as I read it, however, his music seems to make the claim that secretly he was the Countess. In this complex weave of desires and kinships, the mechanics of Berg's sexuality begin not to matter, however nice it might be to prove that it was more complicated than we think at present. What I think *does* matter is the relationship between modern gay, lesbian, and queer sexualities and the erotic styles of fin-de-siècle Europe. The vicariousness of Berg's relationship to his own works, in particular, leaves me nearly breathless, because I recognize an affinity between my queer attitude toward the representations of identification and desire in the hetero art of our culture's dominant fiction and Berg's attitude: my identifications occur almost always equally vicariously, or at an angle to the majority's, to the point that desire seems to be allegorical. I express my desires through representations that are self-evidently inadequate to their objects. I feel little difference between Berg's notions of the desire and pursuit of the whole and those of, say, Oscar Wilde. If my sense of self and sexuality, and that of other people, preserves as much of this *symboliste* flavor as I think,[23] then Berg might be claimed as an exemplary retrospective queer regardless of his sexual practice. The Countess, lesbian heroine that she is, stands wrapped in the complex energies of our identifications and desires, making art out of our pain.

5.

I can't really close here; my discussion seems to launch itself heedlessly into the territory of the sentimental without counting its possible costs or making explicit its possible benefits. Leo Treitler, in an important reading of *Lulu*, sees this issue as a problem. "The sentimentality," as he writes, "in [Berg's] treatment of Alwa and Geschwitz in the second and third acts border[s] on the maudlin" (275). Treitler seems to be uncomfortable with the way Berg's musical strategies force sympathy for the characters on the audience; with the composer insisting so unwearyingly on this brew of pain and pleasure, it's hard not to feel as if the response he gets is somehow unearned. In the worst case it seems as if Berg is mostly providing morally dubious opportunities to emote that in the end have less to do with the Countess, say, than with the audience. Maybe Berg feels the way his music suggests about the Countess, but mightn't that be because of Hanna and himself as much as because of the drama? Maybe my feelings agree with Berg's music, but mightn't I have my own extra stakes in this identification?

Of course, and I don't think it could be otherwise. Sedgwick locates the problem when she analyzes the meanings of *sentimental* and its verbal relatives. As she summarizes them,

> they stand for rhetorical—that is to say, for relational—figures, figures of concealment, obliquity, vicariousness, and renaming, and their ethical bearings can thus be discussed only in the multiple contexts of their reading and writing. Though each could be called a form of bad faith, each can also be seen as a figure of irrepressible desire and creativity—if only the sheer, never to be acknowledged zest of finding a way to frame and reproduce the pain or the pleasure of another. (157)

Life and art imitate one another; we imitate what we admire, though we can never become that thing.

Which leads me back to the problem I've been worrying through this essay. Berg builds up a sentimental halo around the Countess. How then can I trust my sympathy not to be self-deluded? Let me offer an exaggerated, lurid, but well-intentioned anecdote illustrating a danger that, given the action of the opera, is not out of place.

During my work on this essay I have been haunted by accounts of a serial murder case dating back to 1945. Edward Joseph Leonski, a U.S. Army private stationed in Australia, was sentenced to die for the murder of three women. He had killed them for sound.

> Under questioning, the stocky Texan made a full confession, telling his interrogators of a twisted fascination with the female voice. "That's why I choked those ladies," he explained. "It was to get their voices." Pauline Thompson had sung for Leonski on their last date, and he recalled that "Her voice was so sweet and soft, and I could feel myself going mad about it."
>
> (Newton 205)

Jack the Ripper, the ultimate representative of all men in *Lulu*, is the paradigmatic heterosexual serial killer; as his patterns of mutilations show, he was concerned with the sexuality of his victims. Thomas Harris's *The Silence of the Lambs* contains the serial killer Jame Gumb, who drifts somewhere near homosexuality, killing women to claim their gender. Leonski somehow seems to be placed somewhere between these histories and fictions. I worry about using the pain of women—the pain of the Countess—for my own relief, all the harder to locate and analyze because it's more attenuated. Then I wonder if my worry isn't itself one of the symptoms of the malady it looks to cure. The question remains unresolved: how can I open myself to honor the Countess's pain without cannibalizing her?

On the other hand, the desirability of my attachment to the Countess might be partially indicated by a venerable joke. One gay man says to another about a certain women, "She's so beautiful she makes me wish I were a lesbian." What's funny about this statement is its defiant transformation of the presumed wish to be straight into the wish to be a woman. To be a gay man identifying with a woman who desires another woman is exactly my position with regard to the Countess. This is seriously queer desire; to want to be the monster (the ghost, the lesbian) because, whatever its real costs in abjection, you find its beauty overwhelming. The Countess teaches such pain, and I respond to her with her own words to Lulu: "Ich bin dir nah! bleibe dir nah, in Ewigkeit!"[24]

Notes

Thanks to Kristie Foell, Jann Pasler, Carol Vernallis, and Christopher Williams for their helpful comments on this essay, and to Renée Coulombe, Martha Mockus, and Katrin Sieg for many wonderful lesbian conversations.

1. The term "female authorial voice" is Carolyn Abbate's. She discusses the possibility of such voices appearing in male-authored works in her luminous essay "Opera, or the Envoicing of Women."

2. Elizabeth Boa offers a reading of Geschwitz's character, however, which, sticking closely to the text of the play, contradicts Wedekind's claims (*The Sexual Circus*, p. 100).

3. The petition eventually grew to over six thousand names, which were published in the 1923 edition of the Jahrbuch. See Lauritsen and Thorstad, *The Early Homosexual Rights Movement (1864–1935)*, and especially Steakley, *The Homosexual Emancipation Movement in Germany*.

4. Translation mine.

5. As Steakley shows, not only was there relative freedom from persecution, especially in Berlin, during the Weimar republic, there were also more than thirty homophile periodicals commonly available during this time. See also Kreische, "Lesbische Liebe im Film bis 1950."

6. See Kramer ("Musicology," pp. 5–18) for a helpful discussion of immediacy-effects in music. Also relevant to Berg's particular tradition are Kierkegaard's comments on music and eroticism ("Immediate Stages," pp. 43–134).

7. These passages are most fully discussed in Jarman, *The Music of Alban Berg*, and Perle, *The Operas of Alban Berg*.

8. The Countess does not appear in act 1, and remains in the background until act 3,

because Berg's libretto is a conflation of Wedekind's two plays. See Perle, *The Operas of Alban Berg,* for an account of the libretto's construction.

9. See Burkholder, "Berg and the Possibility of Popularity," for a discussion of Berg's use of tonal reference.

10. As both Jarman and Perle observe, these passages set forth the tonalities of D-flat and G-flat respectively. See Jarman, *The Music of Alban Berg*, pp. 94–95, and Perle, *The Operas of Alban Berg,* pp. 131–35.

11. I don't mean to suggest that this interpretation exhausts the significance of the tonal passages in Berg's so-called atonal music; on the contrary, the specific cases I have cited include a host of emotional resonances that range much further than melancholy. But I would argue for mourning as their chief purpose nonetheless.

12. See Perle, *The Operas of Alban Berg,* pp. 158–59, for a discussion of this process.

13. The last two notes of the Countess's vocal line—*Sprechstimme*, but without accompanying words—represent her "death sigh" according to Friedrich Cerha, who completed the unfinished third act between 1961 and 1978. Since the Paris premiere of the completed version, however, it has become fashionable (and condemned by scholars) to add the word *verflucht!* (roughly, "Goddammit!"), taken from Wedekind's play, under the notes. I think the added word, besides being unjustified by the composer's score, ruins the poignancy crucial to the last moments of the opera.

14. This link is most often connected with Berg's opinion of marriage as a sanctioned form of prostitution—"Bordel ist Ehe," he is supposed to have remarked, and in one letter to his fiancée he defends prostitutes by equating them with "respectable women who marry for money, selling their bodies and souls for life" (*Letters to His Wife*, p. 101).

15. The Countess shares this odd persistence with a number of other (indicatively female) operatic characters who "go out singing," particularly with Wagner's superhuman Isolde, whose "Transfiguration" at the end of *Tristan Und Isolde* is repeatedly invoked in the Berg literature by calling the Countess's final speech her *Liebestod.* In the terms of the nineteenth-century operatic repertory that is relevant here, this persistence is meant to signify above all the triumph of personality over fate.

16. Translated in Jarman, *Alban Berg: Lulu*, p. 109. For more on Kraus's attitude towards women, see Wagner, *Geist und Geschlecht*.

17. See the discussions in Russo, *The Celluloid Closet*, pp. 19–25, and Kreische, "Lesbische Liebe im Film bis 1950," pp. 187–96.

18. In fact, Smaragda seems to have been rather unstable, though Berg never explains this in any great detail in the letters that have been published. See his account of her attempted suicide in *Letters to His Wife*, p. 110.

19. This is apparent in a number of letters. See *Letters to His Wife*, pp. 250, 266, 279, 299, 331.

20. Recovery of this history is described in Perle, *The Operas of Alban Berg,* chapters 1 and 6.

21. See Perle, ibid., especially chapter 1. I would be more convinced if that last initial were in place, but I'll go along with the interpretation for the sake of its beauty.

Berg's stance may seem to some quite objectionable, a het appropriation of doomed homo love, but its unavailability to general cultural circulation, at least before we musicologists got busy, suggests that a subtle and successfully recuperable form of sentimentality may have been involved. More about that anon.

22. See also Sedgwick's account of gay reading in "A Poem is Being Written."

23. And I touch on this in my "Reading as an Opera Queen."

24. I am near you! will stay near you, in eternity!

Works Cited

Abbate, Carolyn. "Opera, or the Envoicing of Women." In Ruth A. Solie, ed., *Musicology and Difference: Gender and Sexuality in Music Scholarship*, pp. 225–58. Berkeley: University of California Press, 1993.

Adorno, Theodor W. *Alban Berg: Master of the Smallest Link*. Ed. and trans. Juliane Brand and Christopher Hailey. Cambridge: Cambridge University Press, 1991.

Berg, Alban. *Briefe an seinen Frau*. Ed. Albert Langen. Munich: Georg Müller, 1965.

——— *Letters to His Wife*. Ed. and trans. Bernard Grun. London: Faber and Faber, 1971.

Boa, Elizabeth. *The Sexual Circus: Wedekind's Theater of Subversion*. Oxford: Basil Blackwell, 1987.

Burkholder, J. Peter. "Berg and the Possibility of Popularity." In David Gable and Robert P. Morgan, eds., *Alban Berg: Historical and Analytical Perspectives*, pp. 25–53. Oxford: Oxford University Press, 1991.

Crimp, Douglas. "Right On, Girlfriend!" In Michael Warner, ed., *Fear of a Queer Planet: Queer Politics and Social Theory*, pp. 300–20. Minneapolis: University of Minnesota Press, 1993.

Jarman, Douglas. *Alban Berg: Lulu*. Cambridge: Cambridge University Press, 1991.

——— *The Music of Alban Berg*. Berkeley: University of California Press, 1979.

Kierkegaard, Søren. "The Immediate Stages of the Erotic or the Musical Erotic." *Either/Or*, 1:43–134. Trans. David F. Swenson and Lillian Marvin Swenson, rev. Howard A. Johnson. 2 vols. Princeton: Princeton University Press, 1959.

Kramer, Lawrence. "The Musicology of the Future." *repercussions* (Spring 1992), 1(1):5–18.

Kreische, Rosi. "Lesbische Liebe im Film bis 1950." *Eldorado: Homosexuelle Frauen und Männer in Berlin 1850–1950, Geschichte, Alltag und Kultur*, pp. 187–96. Berlin: Frölich und Kaufmann, 1984.

Lauritsen, John, and David Thorstad. *The Early Homosexual Rights Movement (1864–1935)*. New York: Times Change, 1974.

Morris, Mitchell. "Reading as an Opera Queen." In Ruth A. Solie, ed., *Musicology and Difference: Gender and Sexuality in Music Scholarship*, pp. 184–200. Berkeley: University of California Press, 1993.

Newton, Michael. *Hunting Humans: The Encyclopedia of Serial Killers*. Vol. 1. 2 vols. New York: Avon, 1990.

Perle, George. *The Operas of Alban Berg*. Vol. 2: *Lulu*. Berkeley: University of California Press, 1985.

Rode, Susanne. *Alban Berg und Karl Kraus*. Frankfurt am Main: Suhrkamp, 1988.

Russo, Vito. *The Celluloid Closet: Homosexuality in the Movies*. Rev. ed. New York: Perennial Library, 1987.

Schäfer, Margarete. "Theater, Theater." *Eldorado: Homosexuelle Frauen und Männer in Berlin 1850–1950, Geschichte, Alltag und Kultur*, pp. 180–86. Berlin: Frölich und Kaufmann, 1984.

Schopenhauer, Arthur. *The World as Will and Representation*. Vol. 2. Trans. E. F. J. Payne. 2 vols. New York: Dover, 1958.

Sedgwick, Eve Kosofsky. *Epistemology of the Closet*. Berkeley: University of California Press, 1990.

——— "A Poem is Being Written." *Tendencies*. Durham: Duke University Press, 1993.

Steakley, James D. *The Homosexual Emancipation Movement in Germany*. New York: Arno, 1975.

Treitler, Leo. "The Lulu Character and the Character of *Lulu*." In David Gable and Robert P. Morgan, eds., *Alban Berg: Historical and Analytical Perspectives*, pp. 261–86. Oxford: Oxford University Press, 1991.

Wagner, Nike. *Geist und Geschlecht: Karl Kraus und die Erotik der Wiener Moderne*. Frankfurt am Main: Suhrkamp, 1982.

Wedekind, Frank. *German Expressionism: The Lulu Plays and Other Sex Tragedies*. Trans. Stephen Spender. London: John Calder, 1972.

Contributors

Wendy Bashant is Assistant Professor of English at Coe College, where she teaches Victorian and Modern literature and helps coordinate the Women Studies program. She is currently working on a book, "The Double Blossom and a Sterile Kiss: Androgynous Theory and Its Embodiment in the Nineteenth-Century Hermaphrodite," a study of various forms of gender bending in Victorian literature. She has also published articles on Tennyson, the voice of Shahrazad in *The Arabian Nights*, and Pater and Swinburne and the hermaphroditic body.

Corinne E. Blackmer is Assistant Professor of English at Southern Connecticut State University, where she teaches twentieth-century literature and lesbian and gay studies. She has published articles on Gertrude Stein, Nella Larsen, Carl Van Vechten, Ronald Firbank, and Elizabeth Bishop. She is currently working on a book on sexuality and ethnicity in women's literature from Teresa of Ávila to Michelle Cliff.

Terry Castle is Professor of English at Stanford University. Her books include *Civilization and Masquerade: The Carnivalesque in Eighteenth-Century Culture and Fiction* (Stanford University Press, 1986) and *The Apparitional Lesbian: Female Homosexuality and Modern Culture* (Columbia University Press, 1993).

Hélène Cixous is Professor at the University of Paris VIII, and director of the university's Center for Research in Feminine Studies.

Lowell Gallagher is Assistant Professor of English at the University of California, Los Angeles, and author of *Medusa's Gaze: Casuistry and Conscience in the Renaissance* (Stanford University Press, 1991). He is currently working on two books: one on Stoic sign theory and narrative in early modern England and France and one on the cultural semiotics of the Pythian oracle, maenads, and the operatic soprano.

Ralph P. Locke is Professor of Musicology at the University of Rochester's Eastman School of Music. He is editor in chief of the *Journal of Musicological Research* and senior editor of *Eastman Studies in Music*. His publications include *Music, Musicians, and the Saint-Simonians* (University of Chicago Press, 1986), as well as articles on Saint-Saëns's *Samson and Delilah* and the musical life of early-nineteenth-century Paris. His current research interests include operas set in the non-European world and women music patrons in America; on the latter topic he has several chapters in a forthcoming collection that he coedited with Cyrilla Barr, *Cultivating Music in America: Women Patrons and Activists Since 1860* (University of California Press).

Mitchell Morris teaches at the University of California at San Diego. His scholarly work focuses on music of the late nineteenth century, particularly in Russia, and gender and sexuality in opera and American popular music. He is currently completing his UC-Berkeley Ph.D. dissertation "Musical Eroticism and the Transcendent Strain: The Works of Alexander Skryabin, 1898–1908." His essay "Reading as an Opera Queen" has recently appeared in *Musicology and Difference: Gender and Sexuality in Music Scholarship*, Ruth A. Solie, ed. (University of California Press, 1993).

Judith A. Peraino received her Ph.D. in music from the University of California at Berkeley, specializing in the music of the Middle Ages and seventeenth-century England. Her dissertation concerned genre theory and secular music, circa 1300. She has written on musical interpolations in *Tenart le nouvel*, music and homosocial desire in Gottfried von Strassburg's *Tristan und Isolde*, as well as " 'Rip Her to Shreds': Women's Music According to a Butch-Femme Aesthetic," which contrasts women's music of the 1970s and 1980s with that of the New York punk rock group Blondie.

Margaret Reynolds is a lecturer in English at the University of Birmingham and an arts broadcaster for BBC radio. Her critical edition of Elizabeth Barrett Browning's *Aurora Leigh* (Ohio University Press and Norton) won the British Academy Rose Mary Crawshay prize in 1993. She is also the editor of *Erotica: An Anthol-*

ogy of Women's Writing (Pandora and Ballantine) and *The Penguin Book of Lesbian Short Stories* (Viking Penguin).

Mary Ann Smart teaches music at the State University of New York at Stony Brook. She has published articles and reviews in *Cambridge Opera Journal*, the *Journal of the American Musicological Society*, *Opera Quarterly*, and the *Journal of Musicological Research*. She is working on the critical edition of Donizetti's *Dom Sébastien*, forthcoming from Ricordi, and finishing a book on representations of madness in nineteenth-century opera. She recently coauthored for the BBC a radio documentary on the syphilitic decline of Gaetano Donizetti.

Patricia Juliana Smith is Visiting Assistant Professor of English at the University of Connecticut. She specializes in twentieth-century British literature and culture, and is the author of articles on Dusty Springfield, Fay Weldon, Angela Carter, and Virginia Woolf.

Elizabeth Wood, a musicologist and writer of fiction and nonfiction, is on the Committee on Theory and Culture, New York University, and coeditor of *Queering the Pitch: The New Gay and Lesbian Musicology* (Routledge, 1994).

Index